Hartlepool College of FE Library

T00162

D1139357

THE ILLUSTRATED
LONDON NEWS
GREAT
EVENTS
OF THE
20TH
CENTURY

AA

Published by The Automobile Association,
Fanum House, Basingstoke, Hampshire, RG21 2EA
The Automobile Association acknowledges
the assistance given in the preparation of this book
by *The Illustrated London News*

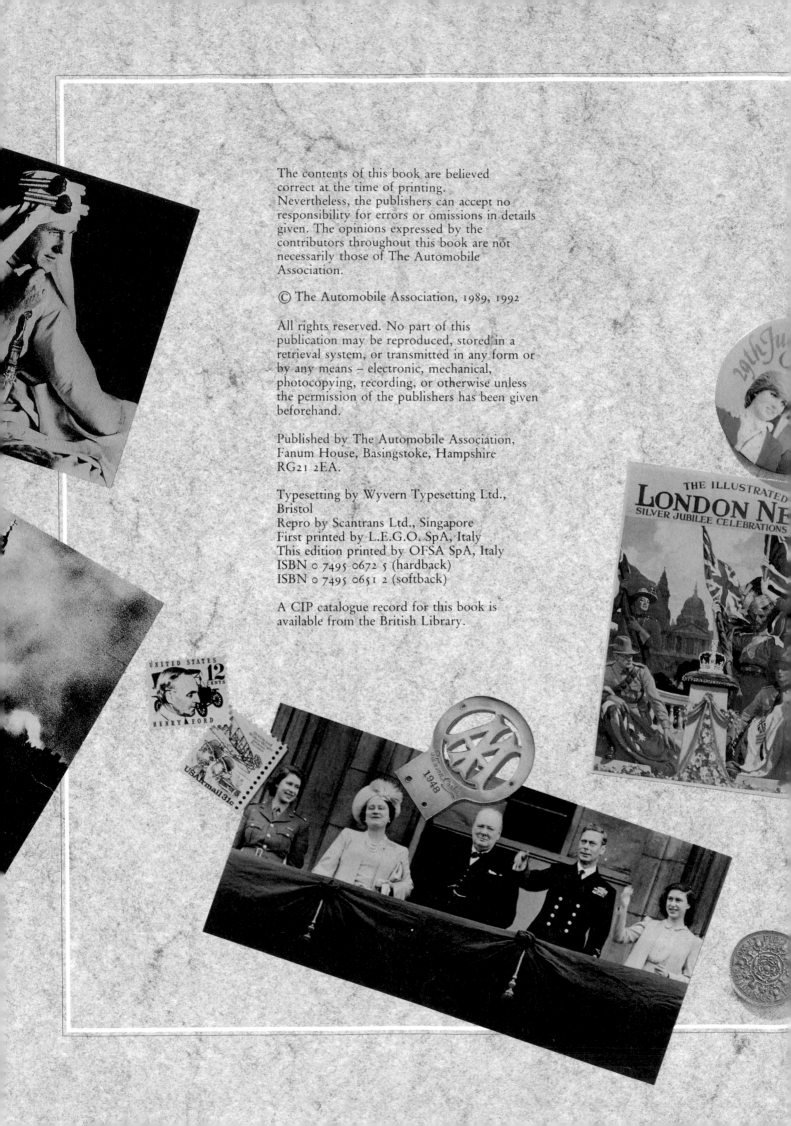

The contents of this book are believed
correct at the time of printing.
Nevertheless, the publishers can accept no
responsibility for errors or omissions in details
given. The opinions expressed by the
contributors throughout this book are not
necessarily those of The Automobile
Association.

© The Automobile Association, 1989, 1992

All rights reserved. No part of this
publication may be reproduced, stored in a
retrieval system, or transmitted in any form or
by any means – electronic, mechanical,
photocopying, recording, or otherwise unless
the permission of the publishers has been given
beforehand.

Published by The Automobile Association,
Fanum House, Basingstoke, Hampshire
RG21 2EA.

Typesetting by Wyvern Typesetting Ltd.,
Bristol
Repro by Scantrans Ltd., Singapore
First printed by L.E.G.O. SpA, Italy
This edition printed by OFSA SpA, Italy
ISBN 0 7495 0672 5 (hardback)
ISBN 0 7495 0651 2 (softback)

A CIP catalogue record for this book is
available from the British Library.

AA

THE ILLUSTRATED
LONDON NEWS.

GREAT
EVENTS
OF THE
20TH
CENTURY

8000/92/1145L

032 ILL ENT/Ref

LIBRARY
HARTLEPOOL C.F.E.
24 MAR 1993

Produced by the Publishing Division of The Automobile Association

Illustration research: Susan Rose-Smith
Design assistance: Neil Roebuck, Tony Truscott, KAG Design
Special features: Richard Cavendish (Crown and Empire, Archaeology, Inventions, Sport, Entertainment, Politics), Nia Williams (Women)
Chronological text: Paul Atterbury, Rosemary Burton, Richard Cavendish, Donald Edgar, Norman Longmate
Events listings: Paul Atterbury, Richard Cavendish
Captions: Paul Atterbury, Richard Cavendish, Enver Carim, Joanne Jones
Archive research: John Canning, David Farr, Georgina Isherwood, Derick Mirfin, James Purnell
Additional research: Linda Ullah
Consultants: Paul Allen, Tom Merriam, Dr Anthony Webster, Martin Young

Contents

•••

SPECIAL FEATURES

•••

About this Book

Great Events of the Twentieth Century *is an account of the last hundred years, seen
primarily through the eyes of* The Illustrated London News *(*ILN *for short),
which—week by week, and later month by month—reported, pictured, dissected and
commented on happenings, great and small, in the world.*

This book can be used in two ways. You can read it as a narrative account of the century since
1890, in order to follow the course of events year by year, or alternatively for reference. To
locate happenings, you can either refer to the brief lists of events included for each year, or to the
index, which will direct you to the appropriate points in the text.

The book is divided into reigns, and then into years. The chapters deal with the reigns of
Queen Victoria (from 1890 onwards), Edward VII, George V (including Edward VIII and the
Abdication in 1936), George VI and Elizabeth II (up to and including 1989). This is not to
suggest that the years of a particular monarch necessarily have a distinctive flavour—though the
Edwardian era certainly has—but because these chapter divisions are a convenient way of
making natural breaks in the otherwise unstoppable flow of history. Please note that at the start
of every chapter the years referring to each monarch span the time covered in the section, and
not, of course, the length of the reign.

Every year since 1890 is represented and in some cases, a year has more space when it has been
particularly eventful or memorable—1982 and the Falklands Crisis, for example, or 1897, the
year of Queen Victoria's Diamond Jubilee.

All quotations are taken from the *ILN*, unless otherwise identified. Longer quotations are
followed by a date, in **round** brackets. This refers to the week (or, after 1971, the month) of
publication in the *ILN*. Where necessary, dates of events have been added within quotations,
and these appear in **square** brackets. Sometimes we have added information to help readers, and
this also appears within quotations in **square** brackets.

The illustrations in this book have been carefully selected from numerous issues of the *ILN*.
The magazine's archive was bombed during the Second World War, and sadly many of the
original photographs there were destroyed. We have therefore chosen contemporary pictures
from other sources where necessary.

At intervals thoughout this book you will also find special features: Crown and Empire,
Women, Archaeology, Inventions, Sport and Entertainment. These pick up some of the
common strands reflected in the *ILN*'s coverage of the passing decades. For example, the
magazine took an active interest in archaeology and was a pioneer in the intelligent
popularisation of the subject. The special features focus on broad developments which have
taken place during a century that has seen more change than any previous period of history.

Introduction

BY JAMES BISHOP,
EDITOR-IN-CHIEF
OF
The Illustrated London News

Pictorial journalism of the kind that forms the core of this book has a precise date of birth—14 May 1842. It was on that day that the first issue of *The Illustrated London News* was published. It is surprising that it took so long for regular pictorial reporting to begin—longer even than to invent the steam engine and the railway. Woodcuts had been used for illustration in this country since the fifteenth century, and the technique of wood-engraving, using the cross-grain of boxwood, was perfected by Thomas Bewick in the eighteenth, but until 1842 illustrations were only occasionally used by newspapers and periodicals, and then usually for coronations or sensational murders. The vision required to change this came from a newsagent, Herbert Ingram, and the money he needed to put his idea into practice came from a best-selling laxative.

Ingram was born in Boston, Lincolnshire, in 1811. He settled in Nottingham as a printer, bookseller and newsagent in partnership with his brother-in-law, Nathaniel Cooke, and their business took off when they bought the recipe of a laxative which they called Old Parr's Pills.

Ingram was also determined to develop his publishing plans. He had observed, standing at his newsagent's counter, that his customers bought more copies of the *Weekly Chronicle* and other papers when they contained illustrations, and that there was always a greater demand for papers carrying news from London. Ingram came to London with the title of a new weekly newspaper already in mind, and on arrival at once set about recruiting staff to produce it. He met Henry Vizetelly, a newspaperman much experienced in illustration, who persuaded him that his proposed weekly newspaper should have wider appeal than reports of sensational crime, and should be aimed at the new middle-class public. As his first editor Ingram appointed Frederick William Naylor Bayley, a minor poet better known as 'Alphabet' or 'Omnibus' Bayley (the first after his string of initials, the second because he formerly edited a periodical called *Omnibus*), with John Timbs, author of *Curiosities of London*, as his assistant.

Ingram's next task was to find good artists and wood-engravers prepared to meet the erratic demands of the news and the relentless discipline of deadlines. It was some time before better artists and engravers were persuaded that an illustrated newspaper was worthy of their professional abilities, as can be seen from the poor quality of some of the illustrations in early issues, but Ingram was able to secure the services of the young John (later Sir John) Gilbert, already one of the leading draughtsmen of the day. His work lent distinction to the first edition and encouraged others to join in the new venture. Those who did included Alfred Crowquill, Birket Foster and Harrison Weir, and later H G Hine, Charles Keene, George Cruikshank, John Leech and Hablot K Browne. Among the *ILN*'s wood-engravers were W J Linton, Orrin Smith and Ebenezer Landells. Premises were taken in Crane Court at the printing works of Palmer and Clayton; a small publishing office was established in the Strand, and work began on the first issue.

It was timed to be launched in the week that the young Queen Victoria was holding a huge entertainment in Buckingham Palace— her first masked ball—to which many of the most eminent in the land had been invited. The *ILN*'s first issue devoted much space to the event, with eight engravings by John Gilbert of some of the costumes, including that worn by the Queen, who went as 'the noble-hearted and tender Philippa, Queen of Edward III', dressed in a velvet skirt with 'a surcoat of brocade, blue and gold, lined with miniver'. She was escorted by Prince Albert as King Edward, in a cloak of the richest scarlet lined throughout in ermine and manufactured— 'like every other external part of the royal attire'—in Spitalfields.

Just as the issue was going to press came news of a great fire in Hamburg. As no instant pictures were available, the editors sent to the British Museum for a print of Hamburg and set their artists to work on the woodblock, adding the necessary smoke, flames and onlookers—a dubious journalistic initiative which may have been accepted in the special circumstances of the time but which, subse-

THE ILLUSTRATED LONDON NEWS.

No. 1.]   FOR THE WEEK ENDING SATURDAY, MAY 14, 1842.   [SIXPENCE.

OUR ADDRESS.

In presenting the first number of the ILLUSTRATED LONDON NEWS to the British Public, we would fain make a graceful entrée into the wide and grand arena, which will henceforth contain so many actors for our benefit, and so many spectators of our career. In plain language, we do not produce this illustrated newspaper without some vanity, much ambition, and a fond belief that we shall be pardoned the presumption of the first quality by realizing the aspirations of the last. For the past ten years we have watched with admiration and enthusiasm the progress of illustrative art, and the vast revolution which it has wrought in the world of publication, through all the length and breadth of this mighty empire. To the wonderful march of periodical literature it has given an impetus and rapidity almost co-equal with the gigantic power of steam. It has converted blocks into wisdom, and given wings and spirit to ponderous and senseless wood. It has in its turn adorned, gilded, reflected, and interpreted nearly every form of thought. It has given to fancy a new dwelling-place—to imagination a more permanent throne. It has set up fresh land-marks of poetry, given sterner pungency to satire, and mapped out the geography of mind with clearer boundaries and more distinct and familiar intelligence than it ever bore alone. Art—as now fostered, and redundant in the peculiar and facile department of wood engraving—has, in fact, become the bride of literature; genius has taken her as its handmaid; and popularity has crowned her with laurels that only seem to grow the greener the longer they are worn.

And there is now no staying the advance of this art into all the departments of our social system. It began in a few isolated volumes—stretched itself next over fields of natural history and science—penetrated the arcana of our own general literature—and made companionship with our household books. At one plunge it was in the depths of the stream of poetry—working with its every current—partaking of the glow, and adding to the sparkles of the glorious waters—and so refreshing the very soul of genius, that even Shakspere came to us clothed with a new beauty, while other kindred poets of our language seemed as it were to have put on festive garments to crown the marriage of their muses to the arts. Then it walked abroad among the people, went into the poorer cottages, and visited the humblest homes in cheap guises, and perhaps, in roughish forms; but still with the illustrative and the instructive principle strongly worked upon, and admirably developed for the general improvement of the human race. Lastly, it took the merry aspect of fun, frolic, satire, and *badinage*; and the school of *Charivari* began to blend itself with the graver pabulum of Penny Cyclopædias and Saturday Magazines.

And now, when we find the art accepted in all its elements, and welcomed by every branch of reading into which it has diverged; now, when we see the spirit of the times everywhere associating with it, and heralding or recording its success; we do hold it as of somewhat triumphant omen, that we are, by the publication of this very newspaper, launching the giant vessel of illustration into a channel the broadest and the widest that it has ever dared to stem. We bound at once over the billows of new ocean - we sail into the very heart and focus of public life—we take the world of newspapers by storm, and flaunt a banner on which the words "ILLUSTRATED NEWS" become symbols of a fresher purpose, and a more enlarged design, than was ever measured in that hemisphere till now.

The public will have henceforth under their glance, and within their grasp, the very form and presence of events as they transpire, in all their substantial reality, and with evidence visible as well as circumstantial. And whatever the broad and palpable delineations of wood engraving can be taught to achieve, will now be brought to bear upon every subject which attracts the attention of mankind, with a spirit in unison with the character of such subject, whether it be serious or satirical, trivial or of purpose grave.

And, reader, let us open something of the detail of this great intention to your view. Begin, *par exemple*, with the highest region of newspaper literature—The Political. Why, what a field! If we are strong in the creed that we adopt if we are honest, as we pledge ourselves to be, in the purpose that we maintain—how may we lend muscle, bone, and sinew to the tone taken and the cause espoused, by bringing to bear upon our opinions, a whole battery of vigorous illustration. What "H. B." does amid the vacillations of

parties, without any prominent opinions of his own, *we* can do with double regularity and consistency, and therefore with more valuable effect. Moreover, regard the homely illustration which nearly every public measure will afford: your Poor-laws—your Corn-laws—your Factory-bills—your Income-taxes! Look at the field of public portraiture presented in your Houses of Legislature alone, and interesting to every constituency in the land. Open your police-offices, your courts of law, your criminal tribunals - all the pith and marrow of the administration of justice—you can have it broadly before you, with points of force, of ridicule, of character, or of crime; and if the pen be ever led into fallacious argument, the pencil must at least be oracular with the spirit of truth.

In the world of diplomacy, in the architecture of foreign policy, we can give you every trick of the great Babel that other empires are seeking to level or to raise. Is there peace? then shall its arts, implements, and manufactures be spread upon our page. The literature—the customs—the dress—nay, the institutions and localities of other lands, shall be brought home to you with spirit, with fidelity, and, we hope, with discretion and taste. Is there war? then shall its seat and actions be laid naked before the eye. No estaffette—no telegraph—no steam-winged vessel—no overland mail, shall bring intelligence to our shores that shall not be sifted with industry, and illustrated with skill in the columns of this journal; and whether the cowardice of China or the treachery of Affghanistan be the theme of your abhorrence or resentment, you shall at least have as much historical detail of both as, while it gratifies general curiosity, shall minister to the natural anxieties at home of those who have friends and relations amid the scenes delineated and the events described.

Take another fruitful branch of illustration, the pleasures of the people !—their theatres, their concerts, their galas, their races, and their fairs ! Again, the pleasures of the aristocracy—their court festivals, their *bals masqués*, their levees, their drawing-rooms—the complection of their grandeur and the circumstance of all their pomp !

In literature, a truly beautiful arena will be entered upon; for we shall not only, in most instances, have the opportunity of illustrating our own reviews, but of borrowing selections from the illustrations of the numerous works which the press is daily pouring forth, so elaborately embellished with woodcuts in the highest style of art.

In the field of fine arts——but let the future speak, and let us clip promise in the wing. We have perhaps said enough, without condescending to the littleness of too much detail, to mark the general outline of our design; and we trust to the kindness and intelligence of our readers to imagine for us a great deal more than we have been able to crowd into the compass of an introductory leader. Moreover, we would strongly premise an expression of gratitude for all suggestions that may hereafter reach us, and assure our subscribers of these, that wherever there seems a possibility of acting upon them creditably, that course shall be taken with promptitude, vigour, and effect.

Here we make our bow, determined to pursue our great experiment with boldness ; to associate its principle with a purity of tone that may secure and hold fast for our journal the fearless patronage of families ; to seek in all things to uphold the great cause of public morality ; to keep continually before the eye of the world a living and moving panorama of all its actions and influences ; and to withhold from society no point that its literature can furnish or its art adorn, so long as the genius of that literature, and the spirit of that art, can be brought within the reach and compass of the Editors of the ILLUSTRATED LONDON NEWS !

DESTRUCTION OF THE CITY OF HAMBURGH BY FIRE.

By the arrival of the General Steam Navigation Company's boat Saledonia, off the Tower, on Tuesday evening, news has been brought of an immense conflagration which took place on Thursday morning, the 5th instant, at one o'clock, in that city. The district in which the fire broke out consists entirely of wood tenements, chiefly of five and six stories high, and covering an area of ground of about thirty to forty acres. The whole of the buildings on this large space have been totally consumed to the number of more than 1000. The fire was by some thought to have originated in the street known by the name of the Stein Twite, in the warehouse of a Jew, named Cohen, a cigar manufacturer, and who, upon good grounds, has been taken up on suspicion as the incendiary. The wind at the time blew a stout north-wester, causing the flames rapidly to spread ; and proceeding in the direction of Roding's-market, and from thence to Deichi-street, entirely consuming the whole of the following streets, among which is the Hoppen-market, and St. Nicholas Church, a fine stone fabric, and the handsomest in Hamburgh. Grutz Twite, Cressnon (back and end), Grosser Burstah, Muhlen Brucké, Alte Borse, Bohnen Strasse, Monke-

View of the Conflagration of the City of Hamburg

The front page of the first issue of *The Illustrated London News*, published on 14 May 1842, carried news rather than the advertisements which were featured on the front pages of other newspapers of that time. The view of St Paul's, with the Lord Mayor's processional barges sailing along the Thames, is still used today.

quent editors have been at pains to emphasise, has not become common practice. Certainly it helped Ingram make his point with the very first issue: the *ILN* was designed to be newsy. Priced sixpence, with 16 pages and 32 engravings, some of them of events that had taken place in the week of publication, and carrying news on the front page at a time when other newspapers carried only advertisements, the magazine was a publishing revolution. The first issue sold 26,000 copies and within weeks the circulation had doubled. By the time of the Great Exhibition of 1851, when the *ILN* obtained and printed Paxton's designs for the Crystal Palace in Hyde Park before Prince Albert had had a chance to see them, sales had risen to more than 130,000 copies a week.

In its second issue the *ILN* reported at length on the findings of the inquiry into the employment of children in the mines, and compared the account of the festivities at court that appeared in its first issue with the sufferings it now recorded:

At this moment of festivity and enjoyment, when the youthful Sovereign of a mighty empire is happy in the possession of her people's love and her courtiers' adulation, we are reluctant to throw the gloom of reality over the bright and laughing influences of the hour. But we have a duty to perform—there is rational enjoyment in the court: but there is irrational suffering in the mine. While the children of the Sovereign (as yet too young to be conscious of their elevated position) are tended with all the affection of parental, and all the servility of mercenary, love, the children of a numerous class of her subjects are, for want of legislative protection, deprived of even the semblance of either. (21 May 1842)

By the summer of 1842 the country seemed on the verge of revolution. Industrial slump brought wage reductions, unemployment and famine to the Midlands and the North. Serious rioting broke out in August, swelling into a torrent, as the *ILN* reported, which 'swept down the barriers of citizenship and order'. Troops and artillery were used to put down the uprising, but the conscience of the middle class, which the *ILN* reflected, was alerted to the fact that 'millions are distressed in a paralysing and most afflicted degree'. The peaceful social revolution that finally took the place of the threatened insurrection can be traced in the pages of the *ILN* during the next hundred years and more, as can be the changes brought about by scientific invention and by war.

In 1848 Omnibus Bayley left the *ILN* and was replaced as editor by Charles Mackay. Revolution in France tested the paper's ability to cover dramatic overseas events. The French artist Constantin Guys was commissioned to record *les événements*, and he can thus fairly be described officially as a war artist, the first of a large and intrepid breed who worked for the *ILN* and other papers, often in extremely hazardous conditions and sometimes at the expense of their lives, to bring pictures of nineteenth-century wars to the Englishman's breakfast table. Demand for the *ILN* greatly increased when its reports from Paris were published: the Distribution Manager was pelted with flour and rotten eggs on one occasion when supplies failed to meet demand.

When the Crimean War broke out in 1853 Guys was one of six war artists sent to the front by the *ILN*. Engravings of photographs taken by Roger Fenton, the first war photographer, were also published, though because of the long exposure times required and because he was sent to represent the government, his pictures from the Crimea were more static and less revealing than the lively drawings sent back by artists. In the field, where speed was imperative, the artist would often make no more than a rough sketch with accompanying notes designed to give the artist back in the office the information needed to produce a finished illustration for publication. Once the sketch had arrived in the office its main outlines were redrawn in reverse on small woodblocks, each measuring only about 3½in by 2in (89mm by 51mm). The smallness was designed for speed, as several artists could work simultaneously on different parts of the picture. Each engraver would work at the subject he was good at: one on landscape, another on sky, another on people. A large drawing, which might, for instance, spread across two pages of the *ILN*, would comprise perhaps 40 blocks, which would have to be bolted together once the drawing was finished. The detailed work that went on to get a drawing ready for publication undoubtedly had a deadening effect on the original, often producing a uniformity that obliterated the style of the original artist, a problem that was later rectified when the *ILN* began to identify its artists and publish their sketches in their original form.

The *ILN*'s detailed coverage of the Crimean War gave the paper another boost in sales, strengthened further in 1855 by the abolition of the penny newspaper stamp duty. Though this stimulated a rapid increase in competition—168 newspapers were launched within 12 months—sales of the *ILN* rose to 200,000 copies a week. Ingram celebrated by publishing a Christmas supplement with colour illustrations, and by buying out one of his

THE MAKING OF THE "ILLUSTRATED LONDON NEWS:" HOW THE PAPER IS PRODUCED EACH WEEK.

The *ILN*'s offices transformed into a studio in 1910 when the special number recording King George V's Coronation was being prepared. Photography gradually transformed the coverage of international events in magazines and newspapers, though the practice of using artists as well as photographers continued for many years.

rivals, the *Pictorial Times*, which had been launched by the Queen's printer, Andrew Spottiswoode, and others at half the price of the *ILN*. In 1860 Ingram visited Canada with his eldest son. Both were drowned with some 300 other passengers on a paddle-steamer which sank after a collision on Lake Michigan. Ingram's body was washed ashore and taken to his home town of Boston, where he was buried and a statue erected in his memory: the body of his son was never found. Control of the *ILN* passed to Ingram's widow for 12 years, until their two younger sons, William and Charles, were old enough to take over as joint managing directors.

The paper continued to flourish in the style set by its founder; the issue covering the marriage of the Prince of Wales in 1863 sold more than 300,000 copies. But it was the reporting of wars that dominated the next few decades. Five artists represented the *ILN* during the Franco-Prussian War of 1870— William Simpson, R T Landells, G H Andrews, C J Staniland, and Jules Pelcoq, who was confined to Paris during the siege and had to send his drawings to London by balloon post. When the Ashanti wars broke out in 1873 a new war artist, Melton Prior, joined the team, and remained to cover 24 campaigns for the paper until his death in 1910. Prior was at Isandhlwana during the Zulu wars, and was one of the party who found the naked body of the Prince Imperial of France, the son of Napoleon III, who had volunteered with the British and was killed leading a reconnaissance party. Prior also covered the Sudan, reaching Khartoum with the Gordon Relief Expedition in 1885. Another *ILN* artist in the Sudan, Frederick Villiers, went on to cover the Boer War and to provide some illustrations from the front during the First World War, during which he served with the French army.

This brings us well into the century covered by this book, which vividly shows how the *ILN* has covered events since 1890. By that year the *ILN* had established a position for itself that attracted distinguished writers as well as artists to its pages, including Walter Besant, Robert Louis Stevenson, George Meredith, Thomas Hardy, J M Barrie, Arthur Conan Doyle, L F Austin, Rudyard Kipling and G K Chesterton (who wrote the *ILN*'s *Our Note Book* for 31 years). In 1901 Bruce (later Sir Bruce) Ingram, grandson of the founder, took over the editorship, a post he held for 63 years—a record in British journalism that seems unlikely to be broken. The young Ingram (he was 22 when he succeeded to the chair) faced a critical time, for the *ILN*'s unique position had already begun to be eroded. Photographs were replacing drawings, and the development of half-tone photo-

engraving had opened the way for the daily picture paper. The first, the *Daily Graphic*, started in 1890, and though the *ILN* and other weeklies could still excel in their coverage of special occasions and big events, they could not compete with the speed and frequency of daily papers in the use of pictures. The two world wars and other dramatic events of the twentieth century provided plenty of material for picture magazines, but the growth of the popular press, the development of colour magazines attached to high-circulation newspapers, and above all the advent of television have since forced many out of business. Magazines like *Picture Post*, *Illustrated*, *Sketch*, *Sphere*, *Graphic* and *Illustrated Sporting and Dramatic News* closed down after the Second World War. The *ILN* survived, but only by the skin of its teeth. Ownership was transferred from the Ingram family to the Thomson Organisation in 1961. When Bruce Ingram died in 1963 the editorship passed to his cousin, Hugh Ingram; but when he relinquished it two years later the last family link was severed.

In 1971 the *ILN* switched from weekly to monthly publication. It was a traumatic change for a publication with such a long tradition, but the need for weekly news picture coverage had been eroded by the communications revolution. Instead, as the *ILN* suggested, a different quality seemed to be needed. The frantic pace of modern life seemed to be demanding a publication that would 'sort out the significant from the vast amount of trivia among the thousands of so-called news events that crowd upon us hour-by-hour and day-by-day'. In 1985 the *ILN* was sold by Thomson to James Sherwood, under whose proprietorship the quality of the editorial coverage and of the paper and printing was improved. A static circulation and declining advertising revenue subsequently dictated a further reduction of frequency to six issues a year, but the *ILN* has retained its essential element, reporting history rather than news. In May 1992 we celebrated the magazine's 150th anniversary by publishing the largest issue in our history. Its contents served both as a reminder of the ILN's distinguished past and as an expression of confidence in our future. We want, while preserving its traditions, to enhance the virtues of the ILN as a pictorial magazine concerned with the quality of life in all its aspects. This is the thread that runs through this record of a tumultuous century.

James Bishop

Victoria
1890-1901

1890

A T THE START OF THE LAST DECADE of the nineteenth century the most familiar, and in some ways, the most important figure in Europe was Queen Victoria. Victoria's great achievement had been the restoration of the monarchy as a popular force both in Britain and throughout Europe. She was in every sense the grandmother of Europe, and her children and grandchildren tied together the royal houses of Britain, Germany, Russia, Norway, Sweden, Spain and Romania. The social life of the monarchy was seen in a continual royal progress through Europe, with regular gatherings for family events and public functions.

The Queen was also inseparable in the mind of the public from the principle of Empire. During her reign the Empire had not only grown but had experienced several decades of relative stability. The management of the Empire provided a way of life for thousands of Britons; its appeal was underlined by the novels and poems of Rudyard Kipling, Robert Louis Stevenson and Joseph Conrad, and it was also a favourite theme of *The Illustrated London News* (*ILN*):

> It has been said that there is no habitable part of the globe where a Scotchman [sic] doing a very good business is not to be found; but the Englishman is not far behind him in that respect. Many of us think it is better to rule in—well, the most unpleasant places— rather than serve in civilised communities. (4 January)

Imperial ambitions were, of course, shared by the other major powers, and international politics was a deadly game, with the world as the playing field. War was the method by which it was played, and the Empire policed. Russia, Germany, Italy, France, Spain, Japan and the USA all took part in the politics of expansion, while the dominant feature of the next two decades was the gradual decline and destruction of the two old empires of Europe, the Turkish and the Austro–Hungarian. Britain's greatest rivals were Russia and Germany, but Japan and the USA were clearly the imperial powers of the future.

On the domestic front, the period from 1885 to 1905 was predominantly one of Tory rule—a time of stability after the Gladstone–Disraeli duels. The great names of the previous decade, Gladstone, Salisbury, Parnell, were now giving way to the rising stars of the new era: Balfour, Asquith, Lloyd George and Churchill. Irish Home Rule was the subject of much debate, but in 1890 the O'Shea divorce case had taken the heat out of the argument. The 1890s also saw the rise of the Labour movement and trade unionism, and the emergence of Socialism as an international force. Industrial unrest was universal as the unions tried out their muscles, with strikes often ending in violence.

At the same time, it was a period of great reform, in education, in factories, in finance and taxation, in the civil service, in local government and in suffrage. In the 1900s female suffrage was to become a burning issue, but in 1890 more traditional views of the woman's role still dominated.

The final achievement of the 1890s was in the arts. It was a decade of revolution, change and great freedom. In fact, the end of Victoria's reign was marked by fashionable bohemianism, reflected in the popular enthusiasm for music hall artists, in the craze for Aubrey Beardsley and other decadent illustrators, and in an independent approach to dress, fashion and interior design.

Bowling them over: the English Cricket and Athletic Association Ltd. organised two teams of women cricketers—'the Original English Lady Cricketers'—to play exhibition matches against each other this year. Although they were specially selected and coached, and were the first female cricketers to play at the Headingley ground in Leeds, the *ILN* was dismissive of them. 'Their Albanian costume enchants us: we are taken captive, as it were, by these semi-scientific brigands. Life, however, is safe: their glances may be dangerous to the susceptible, but certainly not their bowling.' (6 September 1890)

Dropping the pilot: Prince Otto von Bismarck leaving the Imperial Palace in Berlin (above) after resigning the chancellorship of Germany on 20 March 1890. 'The disappearance of so great a figure leaves a blank in the grouping of European political notables that cannot easily be filled.' (22 March 1890). The most formidable German statesman of his time, Bismarck's major achievement had been the unification of Germany under Prussian leadership. Political disagreements with Kaiser Wilhelm II from 1888 onwards forced Bismarck's withdrawal from government.

1890

E · V · E · N · T · S

4 MARCH Opening of the Forth Bridge at Queensferry, near Edinburgh

20 MARCH Bismarck forced to resign after 19 years as Germany's first Chancellor

27 MARCH Universal suffrage was adopted by Spain

1 JULY Britain ceded Heligoland to Germany in exchange for Zanzibar

18 DECEMBER New London underground line opened from Stockwell to the City

LAST RIVET PUT IN BY H.R.H. THE PRINCE OF WALES --- MARCH 4TH 1890---

Hitting the nail on the head: the Prince of Wales (left) drove home the last rivet (above) in the new Forth Bridge on 4 March 1890. 'A temporary wooden staging had been erected . . . and upon it his Royal Highness stepped along with Lord Tweeddale, Lord Rosebery, and Mr. Arrol. The hydraulic riveter was swung from one of the booms, the pressure being supplied from an accumulator . . . Two men were placed on the boom below to manipulate the machine. The gilded rivet having been handed to his Royal Highness by Lord Tweeddale, the Prince . . . finished the work in a few seconds amid cheers.' (8 March 1890)

THE YEAR 1891 STARTED WITH A GREAT FROST, a rare event not greeted with enthusiasm by the *ILN*'s correspondent:

> ... *it is doubtful whether anybody enjoys a Frost Fair. If you are not in perpetual movement, you are reminded by your extremities of the lowness of the thermometer ... we English are not seriously enamoured of the low-born Zero, and only flirt with her occasionally. Her embraces, both to the old and the young, are fatal ...* (17 January)

The Irish question no longer dominated the news. Mr Balfour's fund for Irish relief was well subscribed, and Mr Parnell, while still speaking against the Home Rule Bill, was no longer prepared to play a leading role. His death later in the year was a loss to Parliament as a whole.

An improvement in Anglo–French relations was well received by Russia as an important step in maintaining the 'general peace'. At the same time Russia was involved internationally in a number of events which threatened long-term stability. Although the Bering Sea Dispute with the USA had been resolved, Russia was also active in Afghanistan, and promoting tension along the Sino–Indian border.

In Britain, the position of women in society was under discussion. A judge decided that a woman could not sit as a County Councillor, a decision upheld by the Appeal Court.

AFTER A VIGOROUS CAMPAIGN Gladstone, who had toured the country, was elected to his fourth (but not consecutive) term as Prime Minister in 1892. The Cabinet was largely unchanged, with Mr Asquith the only newcomer.

The *ILN* reported that Europe was gripped by paranoia, following the bombing of a Paris restaurant by anarchists:

> *It is rather difficult for people in this country to realise the state of alarm in which the inhabitants of a few great European capitals have been thrown by the recent Anarchist outrages, the discoveries of bombs and explosives in various towns, and the numerous arrests ... proving the existence on the Continent of a widespread international Anarchist conspiracy.* (30 April)

The royal family was devastated by the death, due to influenza, of the Duke of Clarence, eldest son of the Prince of Wales, and another much-lamented death was that of the Poet Laureate, Lord Tennyson. James Payn, a regular contributor to the *ILN*'s *Our Note Book*, wrote:

> *Tennyson has appealed in turn to every class of his fellow-countrymen, except, perhaps, the sporting fraternity, who are not in the habit of quoting from the poets ... Tennyson was in his lifetime the most popular poet this country has ever possessed.* (29 October)

Earlier in the year, the *ILN* had celebrated its fiftieth anniversary, but at the same time it was disparaging about the general publishing boom that was taking place: 'Of the 896 new works of fiction published within the last twelve months, it is sad to think how much was rubbish.'

In memoriam: Alfred, Lord Tennyson, died on 6 October 1892. 'A light has gone out which stood in ten thousand homes, making gracious even their commonplaces ...' (15 October 1892)

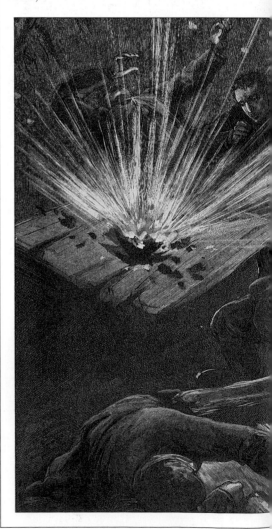

A prince's passing: Albert, Duke of Clarence and the eldest son of the Prince of Wales, died early in 1892. His death, in the midst of preparations for his wedding to Mary of Teck (who later became the consort of George V), was much lamented. 'Never, perhaps, has the death of a Prince exacted a more profound sympathy. The grimmest fantasy could not have invented circumstances more tragic than these.' (23 January 1892)

Life and limb: anarchist bomb outrages on the Continent caused much alarm in 1892. A Paris restaurant was blown up in April and in November a cache of dynamite exploded in a Paris police station (below).

1891-2
E·V·E·N·T·S

20 MARCH (1891) First London to Paris telephone link opened

1 MAY (1891) Mass demonstrations in Hyde Park for an eight-hour working day

6 OCTOBER (1891) Death of distinguished Irish M.P. Charles Stewart Parnell

14 JANUARY (1892) Death of Albert Victor, Duke of Clarence, aged 27

19 NOVEMBER (1892) Ferdinand de Lesseps on trial following Panama canal scandal

25 NOVEMBER (1892) Revival of Olympic Games proposed by Baron de Coubertin

Passage to disgrace: Ferdinand de Lesseps (above) and his associates went on trial in 1892 (below) for embezzlement. Their French company went bankrupt in 1889 building a canal in Panama, although many had invested in the project.

Dspite opposition in both England and Ireland, Gladstone's Home Rule Bill was read in the Commons in September 1893 (although it was subsequently rejected by the Lords). This was the key event of the year in political terms, although it also saw the formation of the Independent Labour Party under James Keir Hardie. Industry was in turmoil, due to long-standing dock and coal strikes; Ben Tillett, the Secretary of the Dockers' Union who was also an Alderman of the London County Council, was cleared at the Central Criminal Court of a charge of inciting a riot in Bristol.

Further afield, the year saw the opening of the Corinth Canal in Greece, a civil war in Argentina, and a cyclone that devasted the south-eastern part of the USA. The International Exhibition at Chicago, celebrating the four hundredth anniversary of Columbus's discovery of the North American continent, was another major event, while back in Britain communications were enhanced when a submarine telephone cable was laid by the Post Office Telegraph ship *Monarch*, placing Glasgow 'in direct communication' with Belfast.

Early in 1894 gladstone resigned, and Lord Rosebery took over as Prime Minister. There was continuing unrest in industry, with the Miners' Union calling for the nationalization of all pits, while mine owners vigorously opposed legislation in support of an eight-hour day. The trade union movement was, by now, having an increasing impact. The *ILN* reported disapprovingly:

> There is, it seems, to be a servants' trade union . . . No fair-minded person would wish that a class to whom we are so much indebted for our comfort should not have the same means of protection as other callings; but an unfortunate feature of trade unions is often to keep the advantage solely on one side without much sense of fairness. (27 January)

The Manchester Ship Canal was opened, the *Evening News* was launched, and George du Maurier caused a sensation with his novel, *Trilby*. The Registrar General estimated that the population of the United Kingdom was an astounding 33,776,134, and the Royal National Lifeboat Institution announced that it had saved 597 lives in the previous year, with its fleet of 303 boats.

In France, Captain Dreyfus, the son of a weathy Jewish manufacturer, was falsely charged with delivering documents connected with the national defence to a foreign government, and was convicted of treason amid vociferous allegations of anti-Semitism in the French army. President Carnot was assassinated by an Italian banker, who claimed to have acted to avenge the deaths of anarchist bomb throwers who had been executed by the French authorities. There were signs of *rapprochement* between the Kaiser and Bismarck in Germany, while the Turks had begun a campaign of massacre against the Armenians. The most important event of the year on an international level was the outbreak of war between Japan and China over disputed territories along the Sino–Korean border. Russia was said to have given its support to Japan 'by almost every means short of making a formal alliance' according to the *ILN*'s correspondents, whereas other nations—Britain, France, Germany and the USA—stood well back from the conflict.

The ministerial crisis: Gladstone (below) bowed out during his fourth term as Prime Minister, 3 March 1894. An advocate of Home Rule for Ireland, he had the previous September seen his Home Rule Bill pass its third reading in the Commons, only to have it rejected by a huge majority of 378 in the Lords a week later. 'No one who heard [Mr Gladstone's] last speech [in Parliament] could imagine that this was his final testament to his followers . . . It declared war on the House of Lords, and committed the Liberal Party to a campaign against the legislative veto of that Assembly . . . So passes out of the stirring life of politics the most tremendous personality Parliament has known since the death of Chatham.' (10 March 1894)

THE ILLUSTRATED LONDON NEWS

1893-4

E·V·E·N·T·S

13 JANUARY (1893) First meeting of Independent
Labour Party
13 JULY (1893) German Army Bill passed
6 AUGUST (1893) Corinth Canal opened
1 SEPTEMBER (1893) Home Rule Bill passed by
Commons (later rejected by Lords)
3 MARCH (1894) Gladstone resigned, Lord
Rosebery took over as Prime Minister
25 JULY (1894) China attacked by Japan
15 OCTOBER (1894) Captain Dreyfus arrested for
treason in France

The burning political issue of 1893—literally: the Rt
Hon A J Balfour acknowledging a demonstration and
procession in Belfast, publicly burning the Home Rule Bill. 'The
series of great demonstration meetings held in Ireland and
attended by the Rt Hon A J Balfour, against Mr Gladstone's
Irish Home Rule Bill, continued to the end of the week. On
Wednesday, April 5, Mr Balfour left Belfast . . . and on
Saturday addressed a meeting of five thousand people in the
Leinster Hall [Dublin].' (15 April 1893)

The salvation of Manchester: the Ship Canal, opened on
1 January 1894, transformed the city into the world's first
inland port. The relocation of industry to the west coast was
now not such a blow, since vessels could use the waterway.
Pictured is the *Norseman*, passing Barton Aqueduct.

**Japanese capture of
Ping-Yang (16
September 1894):**
'The conflict . . . in Corea
[sic] and the Yellow Sea
between the Chinese
and the Japanese is of
much importance. . .
European opinion is
scarcely called upon to
decide the validity of the
Chinese claim to imperial
authority over Corea . . .
They must be left to fight
. . .' (1 September 1894)

1895-6

FOREIGN AFFAIRS DOMINATED 1895. In the Far East, the behaviour of Japanese soldiers caused James Payn to comment in the *ILN*:

> *It seems to have struck most people with a certain shock of surprise that the Japanese should have proved themselves capable of atrocities. Folks [sic] were slow to believe that the civilisation of a nation which in peace were so 'artistic' . . . and in war had shown themselves so scientific and adroit, could, after all, be but skin deep.* (19 January)

In May the war was ended by the signing of the Treaty of Shimonoseki, by which Japan gained Formosa and a free hand in Korea. Japan had declared her intention of becoming a powerful mercantile nation, and most European powers stood to gain by the opening up of Chinese ports.

At the very end of the year the focus switched to South Africa, with the Jameson Raid, an abortive attempt at overthrowing the Boer Republic of Transvaal.

At home, Lord Rosebery resigned, and Lord Salisbury became Prime Minister. Oscar Wilde's plays, *An Ideal Husband* and *The Importance of Being Earnest* opened in London, and Thomas Hardy published *Jude the Obscure*.

Abroad, the Kiel Canal opened, much to the benefit of the German navy; Röntgen discovered X-rays; Freud published his first work on psychoanalysis; an omnibus strike paralysed Paris; and in Vienna a lady of 28 applied for the job of state executioner.

THE CRISIS IN THE TRANSVAAL exposed Britain to widespread criticism, particularly from Germany, during 1896. Dr Jameson and the other leaders of the infamous raid were ultimately released by the Boers and brought back to Britain for trial. Their defence, that they had entered the Transvaal only to help the 'outlanders' to overcome Boer oppression, carried little weight. They were all found guilty of acting without British authorisation and were jailed.

In Britain, plans for a great expansion of London's tramways were made more relevant by a cabmen's strike. James Payn, among others, took this opportunity to voice his concern about the discomforts of rail travel:

> *When we consider how large is the proportion of our time which very many of us spend in railway carriages, it is a matter of real importance . . . Our seaside towns, almost as much as our suburbs, are emptied of their male population every morning, and it returns every evening by the railway. It is monstrous that so huge a portion of their lives should be passed in the mere act of travel, without any of the comforts of existence.* (18 January)

One of the most frequent demands was for separate smoking compartments, and Payn was of the belief that:

> *. . . nothing lubricates the wheels of business so much as tobacco. In old-fashioned establishments, of course, it is still forbidden, being supposed to be somehow disreputable, but the custom is growing in the City.* (18 April)

Wireless telegraphy: Marconi sent a message over a mile by wireless, 1895. 'The recently discovered scientific marvel of the electric telegraph without a wire conductor has earned speedy renown for a young Italian student Guglielimo Marconi . . . A formidable promise, or threat, of increasing the means of naval warfare is supplied by the notion that a gunpowder magazine on board ship might be fired by electrical agency from a long distance.' (31 July 1897)

Trouble in Africa: the Ashanti Expedition of 1895 was mounted to confront Prempeh, King of the Ashanti. The British had asked the Ashanti to accept the stationing of a British Resident; Prempeh sent an envoy to London to secure a guarantee of Ashanti independence and the British took the ensuing delay as a refusal. The capital was occupied in 1896; in 1901 the colony was annexed to the Crown.

THE ILLUSTRATED
LONDON NEWS

1895-6

E · V · E · N · T · S

8 MAY (1895) Japan granted free hand in Korea by Treaty of Shimonoscki

6 OCTOBER (1895) Promenade Concerts founded by Sir Henry Wood

29 DECEMBER (1895) Jameson Raid into Transvaal, South Africa

1 MARCH (1896) Italy defeated by Abyssinia at Battle of Adowa

2 JUNE (1896) Wireless telegraphy patented by Marconi

14 NOVEMBER (1896) First London to Brighton car rally

The Dreyfus case split France in two: Captain Alfred Dreyfus, a Jew, had been accused of spying for Germany. Sentenced to transportation, Dreyfus was stripped of his rank on 5 January 1895. 'For a soldier to betray his country is to stoop to the depths of dishonour.' (19 January 1895). He was pardoned in 1899.

The King Wins the Derby, 1896.

Sport of kings: Derby victory in 1896 for Persimmon, owned by the Prince of Wales (later King Edward VII), ridden to glory by Jack Watts. He was the last horse to win both the Derby and the Ascot Gold Cup. The Prince also owned his brother, who won the 1900 Derby.

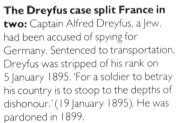

1897

IN APRIL A ROYAL PROCLAMATION ordered that: 'June 22, upon
the occasion of the festive celebration of the sixtieth anniversary of the Queen's reign, shall be kept as a Bank Holiday all
over the United Kingdom.'

For Britain the Diamond Jubilee was the most important
event of the year. It was an opportunity to celebrate not only the
Queen's long reign, but also the ending of a century that had been
notably successful for Britain. The Queen's position as the grand
matriarch of Europe was underlined by the Jubilee procession,
which included not only representatives of every country and
state in the Empire, but also members of the royal families of
Europe. International rivalries and conflicting ambitions were put
aside as the celebrations gripped the nation, and for a time social
harmony and world peace seemed to be within reach.

Although the Jubilee was clearly both an achievement and a
benefit for Britain and her Empire, in practical terms it made little
difference to the pattern of the decade. All over the world little
wars and conflicts continued to create tension. Britain had
resolved her dispute with the USA over Venezuela in January, and
a treaty of arbitration was under way, to be signed in April.

In the Mediterranean a revolt in Crete provoked a war
between Greece and Turkey, with fighting along the Macedonian
frontier. Peace was re-established in August, but the unrest
continued when the Sultan refused to remove the Turkish troops
from Crete for fear that the 70,000 Muslims on the island might be
attacked. The small detachments of European troops there were
thought inadequate for peace-keeping.

Throughout this period the major powers and their nationals had little regard for different attitudes or traditions overseas, or
for foreign religions. James Payn complained in the *ILN* that:

> *The delicacy of religious scruples, though the subject of
> abstract admiration, has been an occasion of much
> inconvenience . . . To kill a cow, even by accident, is to
> risk a rebellion among millions of our fellow-subjects in
> India. Sometimes one cannot help thinking that the
> divinity that hedges a cow is a little artificial. If the
> element of humour could once be introduced into the
> Hindu mind, the whole edifice of superstition, includ-
> ing caste, would probably be swept away.* (30 October)

There was also increasing concern about public welfare in
Britain, with the *ILN* recording factory accidents:

> *In addition to the fatalities we hear of, there is a
> constant loss of arms or fingers, more often through the
> carelessness of the victims than through unfenced
> machinery or other preventable cause . . . About a
> hundred persons lose their right or left arms yearly, and
> two thousand some of their fingers. Females are more
> careful than males in this matter, attaching probably
> considerable importance to the 'engaged finger' which
> is with men a frequent victim.* (10 April)

The widespread interest in working-class attitudes and
behaviour was also reflected in literature, notably in the works of
George Gissing, and in the publication of Somerset Maugham's
Lisa from Lambeth.

Victoria's Diamond Jubilee: 'The occasion
of our Day of Celebration is without
precedent. The period seems like a Grand
Triumphal March,' proclaimed a special
souvenir edition of the *ILN* which reproduced
on its cover a striking portrait of Victoria
commissioned for the Golden Jubilee a decade
earlier. 'To those of us who can remember
English life as it was in the Forties, the changes
that have fallen upon the country are nothing
short of a Transformation. We are
transformed indeed: we no longer think as we
did: our daily manners and customs are
changed: our views of things are changed: from
Peer to Peasant we are, one and all,
transformed. And no one regrets the change:
and younger folk indeed, do not understand it:
they have been born in the later Victorian
period: to their minds things have always been
as they are.' (Record Number, 1897)

1897

E·V·E·N·T·S

31 MARCH Gold discovered in the Klondike, Canada

18 APRIL War declared on Turkey by Greece

15 JUNE Tirpitz appointed German Naval Secretary

22 JUNE Queen Victoria's Diamond Jubilee celebrated

21 JULY The Tate Gallery opened at Millbank, London

13 DECEMBER Russia occupied Port Arthur

Mugs, jugs, plates, tins, boxes: every item that could be decorated was given the Diamond Jubilee treatment by eager manufacturers. The tin pictured is just one example showing how manufacturers capitalised on the demand for lavishly decorated souvenirs. Royal warrants later became stricter, limiting their production.

Milestones for a monarch: 'the Queen's first council', 'opening her first Parliament', and 'the royal procession to the last Parliament she opened in person' featured in the *ILN*'s Diamond Jubilee special issue. The border shows Peel, Russell, Aberdeen, Brougham, Campbell, Melbourne, Dalhousie, Palmerston, Derby, Disraeli, Selborne and Wellington. 'Never has Sovereign been more honoured by the faithful Commons. Yet her sex has not induced them to give new privileges in their House to women . . . There is no longer any party which seriously proposes any change in the Constitution: the whole nation is united in loyalty.' (Her Majesty's Glorious Jubilee, 1897)

The highest homage: a detachment of Volunteers led by Lieutenant John Cameron celebrated the Queen's Diamond Jubilee on the summit of Ben Nevis, the highest point in Britain. They set off from Fort William in heavy rain and made their way up the mountain through dense mist. Once at the peak, they fired volleys, gave rousing cheers and finished with a rendition of *God Save the Queen* on the bagpipes.

The Changing Years

Walk wide o' the Widow at Windsor,
For 'alf o' Creation she owns:
We 'ave bought 'er the same with the sword an' the flame,
An' we've salted it down with our bones.

RUDYARD KIPLING

ON 22 JUNE 1897 Kipling's 'Widow at Windsor' rode in her state landau drawn by eight white horses for six miles through her capital to celebrate 60 glorious years on the British throne. The little dumpy figure sheltering from the bright sun under a black lace parasol was cheered by huge crowds which packed every inch of the way, in perhaps the most tremendous ovation ever accorded by the British people to a public figure. The reception reduced the Queen to tears.

Queen Victoria's Diamond Jubilee was deliberately staged as a celebration of the British Empire. The prime ministers of the colonies were given an important role; the Canadian premier, Wilfred Laurier, was knighted; and the troops who escorted the Queen through London to the thanksgiving service on the steps of St Paul's came from every quarter of the globe—Sikhs from the Punjab, Gurkhas from Nepal, Hausas from West Africa, Chinese from Hong Kong, Dyaks from Borneo, with glittering cohorts of cavalry from India, from Australia, from Rhodesia.

A journalist who watched the procession wrote, with breezy insensitivity, that he began to understand as never before what the Empire amounted to: 'We send out a boy here and a boy there, and the boy takes hold of the savages . . . and teaches them to march and shoot . . . and believe in him, and die for him and the Queen. A plain, stupid, uninspired people they call us, and yet we are doing this with every kind of savage man there is.'

Many others in the crowd certainly swelled with the same pride. Belief in Britain's imperial greatness and imperial mission was a creed which cut across party politics and social divisions. Kipling was its Poet Laureate, and the Empire would soon be hymned by Elgar in music (*God who made thee mighty, make thee mightier yet*) and made monumental by Lutyens in the proconsular architecture of New Delhi.

By 1897, the year of the Diamond Jubilee, the 78-year-old Queen Victoria enjoyed immense popularity and respect.

No sensible person doubted that the Empire had its faults, but it was widely accepted that the British had a mission to bring civilisation, peace and justice to the furthest parts of the earth, and that the mission was being successfully carried out. 'We have to remember,' said the Liberal politician Lord Rosebery in 1893, 'that it is part of our heritage to take care that the world as far as it can be moulded by us, shall receive an English-speaking complexion, and not that of other nations.' And speaking of the Empire in 1900, he said: 'How marvellous it all is. Built not by saints and angels, but the work of men's hands, cemented with men's honest blood and with a world of tears; not without taint and reproach incidental to all human work, but constructed on the whole with pure and splendid purpose.'

The British Empire was the largest and most populous in history, covering one-quarter of the land surface of the globe by 1918. The sun never set on it, and close to 3 million square miles were added to it between 1881 and 1900. It numbered among its inhabitants people of every continent, of every colour of skin, of all the major religions, of innumerable languages, and at every stage of social development from the Stone Age to the Industrial Revolution.

Geographically, the Empire stretched from remote and scattered islets in the Pacific, across Canada and the West Indies, over the Atlantic to Africa, and on by way of India, Burma and Malaya to Australia and New Zealand. The distances involved were gigantic: close to 6,000 nautical miles from London to the Cape of Good Hope, almost as far from Bombay in India to Melbourne in Australia, and further still from Auckland, New Zealand, to Vancouver on Canada's Pacific coast. These immense distances, and the astonishingly varied character and traditions of the Empire's far-flung territories, made it virtually impossible to hold together. Already people were wondering how any British government could be democratic in Australia and despotic in Asia, how a Christian nation could be both the greatest Muslim and the greatest Hindu power on earth, how a country dedicated to freedom could conceivably impose its rule on a quarter of the world's people.

It could not, and within a hundred years of the Diamond Jubilee the empire it celebrated had vanished. In 1899 a serious rift developed in the lute of imperial harmony with the outbreak of the Boer War. The British government used armed force to reduce the recalcitrant Dutch-descended farmers of South Africa to obedience in an operation which proved embarrassingly protracted and costly. It was a bad blow to British prestige. The peace treaty in 1902 promised South Africa self-government.

From the beginnings of the Empire, back in the sixteenth and seventeenth centuries, British-descended colonists abroad gradually gained the same right of self-government which citizens of the mother country enjoyed at home. This was achieved by armed rebellion in the case of the American colonies, which broke away in the eighteenth century to form the United States of America, but thereafter it was achieved more often through peaceful evolution. By the time of the First World War, Canada, Australia, New Zealand and South Africa were all self-governing 'dominions': independent countries allied to Britain by strong ties of blood, heritage, sentiment and commercial tradition, but not governed from London and no longer totally assured markets for British manufactures. Other nations were now moving

After being formally proclaimed Empress of India in 1876, Queen Victoria enjoyed the support of her Indian servants (above left). Her son and heir, the future King Edward VII (above right), was rigorously excluded from affairs of state and the serious business of the monarchy.

Cecil Rhodes, the formidable diamond magnate (right), was a driving force behind British expansion in Southern Africa. The ill-fated Jameson Raid (below) was an episode in the British attempt to take over control of South Africa from the Boers.

ahead industrially, and the British share of exports to her Empire had begun to decline.

The consequence was the growth of nationalism in each of the British dominions. Awareness of an independent Canadian or Australian, New Zealand or South African identity began to grow—and nationalism was a force which inevitably broke the Empire apart, rather than knitting it together.

The Empire reached its apogee in the First World War, when young men from all the dominions and from India fought and died for the mother country in the mud and blood of the Western Front, on the shot-torn beaches of Gallipoli, in the dusty sands of Mesopotamia. The dominions' contribution to the war effort strengthened their own burgeoning nationalism and enabled them to demand a more equal voice in affairs. At the same time, the sacrifice of so many men was bound to raise unease about the extent to which Britain's wars were really the dominions' quarrel. For years after the war, in Australia and New Zealand, the celebration of Anzac Day, which commemorated the Gallipoli landings of 1915, kept alive the memory of heroism and tragic waste. And after 1918 the mother country's declining political, military and industrial clout made it harder to be proud of belonging to the British Empire.

In India, Africa and the West Indies, where colonists of British descent were in a tiny minority among the native populations, the movement towards self-government was slower. British public opinion was far less inclined to think of a Sikh or a Bengali or a Jamaican as a potential Briton than it was to recognise a Canadian or a New Zealander as a fellow citizen. As early as 1917, the British government announced that self-government for India was its eventual aim, but it was believed that it would be a long time before countries which had no native tradition of parliamentary democracy would be able to rule themselves properly.

After the First World War, however, nationalist pressure for independence grew steadily stronger and would eventually not be denied. The lead was taken by Mahatma Gandhi, who had spent 21 years opposing discrimination against Indians in South Africa, and had been decorated for bravery as a British stretcher-bearer in the Boer War. He returned to India after the First World War, where he at first campaigned for Indian Home Rule, and later for total independence.

Small, bespectacled, half-naked, sanctimonious, shrewd, Gandhi had a genius for publicity. He won the hearts and minds of the ordinary Hindus of India, who regarded him almost as a god. Nationalist pressure was given an impetus by the massacre at Amritsar, the Sikh holy city, in 1919, when an unarmed crowd assembled for a political demonstration was fired on at point-blank range by British troops (most of whom were Gurkhas) and about 400 people were killed in less than 10 minutes.

Even Indians would sometimes admit that the British had done much good in India: in keeping peace and order; in uniting under regular administration the many diverse regions of the subcontinent; through advances in medicine and education; by building railways and laying the foundations of a modern industrial society; and in suppressing or ameliorating such features of Indian traditions as suttee, child prostitution and the rigours of the caste system. But the British were all too often arrogant and superior, and they were outsiders, and Indians increasingly wanted to be rid of them.

In Britain, King George V opened a new era in the history of the monarchy by speaking personally to all his subjects at once—the first British ruler ever to do so—in a radio broadcast on Christmas Day, 1932. He spoke to all the teeming millions of the Empire. 'I speak now from my home and from my heart to you all; to men and women so cut off by the snows, the desert, or the sea, that only voices out of the air can reach them.' The words were by Kipling and the broadcast made such an impression that, against the King's initial reluctance, the annual Christmas message became a tradition.

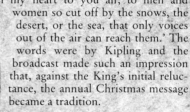

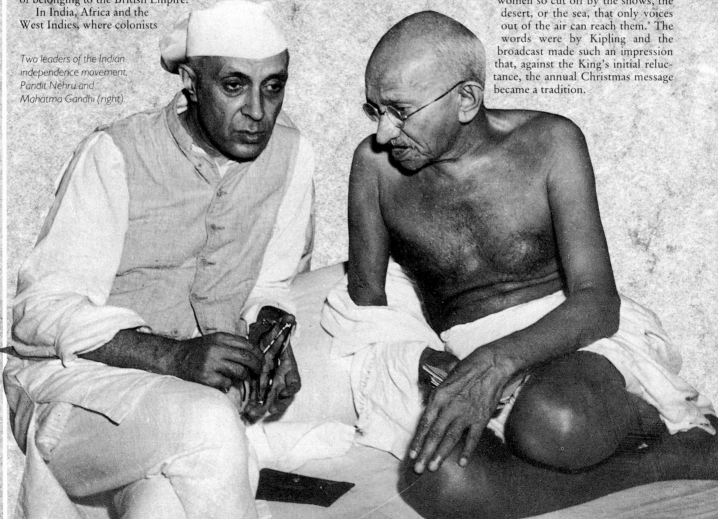

Two leaders of the Indian independence movement, Pandit Nehru and Mahatma Gandhi (right).

Indian nationalism gained an impetus in 1919 when a crowd at the Sikh holy city of Amritsar was fired on by British troops and others (above) were led away to be whipped.

An Edwardian country gentleman at heart, gruff, genial, straightforward, decent, conventional, totally unintellectual, George V had not expected to occupy the throne—he was the younger son of Edward VII—but he was generally admired and liked. When he died in 1936, however, there was a crisis. His successor, Edward VIII, was determined to marry an American, Mrs Simpson, who had already been twice divorced. The new King ran headlong into the British Establishment—led by the Prime Minister, Stanley Baldwin, and Archbishop Lang of Canterbury—at its stoniest and most unyielding. He decided to abdicate, and there was a dramatic royal broadcast to the nation in which he announced his decision to quit the throne rather than give up the woman he loved. As Duke and Duchess of Windsor, he and Mrs Simpson spent the rest of their lives in exile.

Although in retrospect it is clear that the

King George VI and Queen Elizabeth inspecting bomb damage in London in 1940.

Empire could not last, the idea of Empire remained very much alive in the 1920s and 1930s. Baldwin consulted the dominions' prime ministers during the abdication crisis. British Empire Exhibitions, at Wembley in 1924 and Glasgow in 1938, showed the flag for both Empire products and the imperial concept. The Imperial Economic Conference at Ottawa in 1932 set up a system of preferential tariffs to encourage trade within the Empire.

In Britain, George VI and Queen Elizabeth patiently and successfully repaired the damage the Abdication had done to the monarchy's image. They gained special affection for their courage and concern for people in the Second World War, especially during the Blitz, when they refused to leave London and bombs fell on Buckingham Palace (to the relief of the Queen, who said she could now look the East End in the face). British monarchs had long ceased to wield political power, but they still had considerable influence.

In the Second World War the dominions came loyally to the aid of the mother country for the second time in 25 years. Fought against German and Italian fascism and against Japanese imperialism in the Far East, the war was also a last attempt to keep the British Empire together. The attempt

King Edward VIII with Mrs Simpson on holiday on the Adriatic coast in the summer of 1936, before the Abdication.

failed. On 15 February 1942 more than 80,000 British troops surrendered Singapore, one of the bastions of Empire, to the triumphant Japanese. Churchill described it to the House of Commons as 'the worst capitulation in British history'. From then on the Australians and New Zealanders turned to the USA as the dominant power in the Pacific.

The Americans, with their own history of descent from rebellious colonists, disapproved of the British Empire, and Washington pressed London to disband it. After the war the British public, psychologically and financially drained by their efforts, had no appetite for trying to keep hold of former possessions and unwilling populations by force in any case. Britannia ruled the waves no longer, and the land of hope and glory was, at least temporarily, out of ardour.

To Churchill's dismay, the Labour government elected by a landslide in 1945 gave independence to India, Burma and Ceylon (now Sri Lanka). The obstacle in India was the bitter mutual hostility between Hindus and Muslims, Lord Mountbatten was sent out as Viceroy to cut the knot abruptly, by splitting India into two countries with the creation of the new Muslim state of Pakistan (the East Bengal part of which subsequently seceded as Bangladesh). On 15 August 1947 at 8.30 in the morning, the British flag was hauled down across the whole length and breadth of the subcontinent. The immediate consequence was human tragedy on a colossal scale, as millions of Hindus left their homes in the new Pakistan to cross the border into India, while millions of Muslims made the opposite journey, and ancient religious hatreds erupted in massacres in which hundreds of thousands of people were slaughtered. Gandhi himself was assassinated, shot down by a Hindu fanatic in New Delhi on 30 January 1948.

George VI was no longer Emperor of India. The most precious jewel had been wrenched from the imperial crown and the lesser adornments of Empire soon followed. Earlier talk of training the colonies and preparing them for self-government was dropped. In the 1950s and 1960s colony after colony in Africa, the West Indies and the East was given its independence. Britain withdrew from Egypt and the Sudan in 1956. The next year the Gold Coast (now Ghana) became the first black African colony to become an independent nation. The process was repeated in Malaya in 1957, Nigeria and Cyprus in 1960, Sierra Leone in 1961, Jamaica and Uganda in 1962, Kenya in 1963, Malta and Northern Rhodesia in 1964, British Guiana (now Guyana) in 1966. There were many more. By the time Britain was celebrating Queen Elizabeth II's Silver Jubilee in 1977, the greatest empire in history had been reduced to a few miscellaneous territories and military bases, including Hong Kong, Gibraltar, Fiji and the Falkland Islands.

No imperial power in the whole long history of empires has ever so willingly, so swiftly and relatively bloodlessly divested itself of its territories. What has happened in some of them since suggests that in terms of ordinary people's peace and security, the British Empire had a greater value than nationalist sentiment would ever admit, but

in practice nationalism combined with Britain's commitment to democracy could not be resisted.

Dean Acheson, a former US Secretary of State, remarked in 1962 that Britain had lost an empire and had not found a role to replace it. Shrieks of protest went up, but the comment was patently true. The vanished Empire, however, had left a substantial shadow behind it—the Commonwealth, which today consists of some 48 independent countries together covering, as the old Empire did, about a quarter of the land surface of the globe, and containing about a quarter of the world's population, of every race, colour and creed. They are held together by their common history as British dependencies, and by the English language, in an association symbolised by a common loyalty to the Queen. Alphabetically, the Commonwealth countries run the gamut from Antigua to Zimbabwe.

The term British Commonwealth first emerged after the First World War, when it meant the United Kingdom plus the self-governing white dominions. The Statute of Westminster in 1931 formally recognised that the dominions were equal in status with Great Britain and in no way subordinate, while united by a common allegiance to the Crown. After 1946, as non-white territories became members, the adjective 'British' dropped out of use, in official documents at least. India and Pakistan both joined the Commonwealth on becoming independent (though Burma did not), and their example was followed by most of the other former colonies released from the imperial yoke.

A country can leave the Commonwealth whenever it chooses, and some have: South Africa in 1961, because of Commonwealth condemnation of apartheid, Pakistan in 1972 in protest against the recognition of Bangladesh, and Fiji in 1987, when Colonel Rabuka declared a republic which was not recognised by the Queen. The great majority of former colonies, however,

By the time of Queen Elizabeth II's Silver Jubilee in 1977, the British Empire had been replaced by the Commonwealth.

remain members of the Commonwealth. A Commonwealth Secretariat was established in London in 1965 to service the organisation, and the Commonwealth heads of government meet in regular conferences held in various parts of the world, normally every other year, under the presidency of the Queen, who is recognised by all members as Head of the Commonwealth.

Since 1945, under George VI and Queen Elizabeth II, who succeeded her father in 1952, the Sovereign's role as the unifying symbol of the Commonwealth has developed as one of the monarchy's most important functions. The Queen wields no direct political power, but her position and her long experience give her considerable influence.

Between the end of the Napoleonic Wars in 1815 and the mid 1930s some 20 million Britons left the mother country to settle overseas in the dominions and colonies. It was not until after the Second World War that emigration began to flow the other way as well. The inhabitants of the dominions and colonies were British subjects and consequently had the right to move to Britain and work and live there. Few of them did until the 1950s, when, with a shortage of labour in Britain, West Indians and later Indians and Pakistanis were encouraged to move into the country. From 1962 onwards it became increasingly difficult for citizens of Commonwealth countries to emigrate to Britain, however.

Immigration inevitably caused problems, including riots in some British cities: in the Notting Hill area of London in 1978, for example; in St Paul's, Bristol, in 1980; in Toxteth in Liverpool and the Brixton area of London in 1981; and in the Tottenham district of London in 1985. On the whole, however, the newcomers and the British managed to settle down together rather better than pessimists expected.

After the Second World War the old white dominions tended to distance themselves from Britain and the Commonwealth. Australia and New Zealand signed the Anzus pact with the USA, providing for mutual assistance in the Pacific. Canada also moved closer to the USA, and South Africa turned away from Britain when the Nationalist Party took power in 1948.

The countries most interested in the Commonwealth are those in the Third World, which account for nine out of every 10 Commonwealth citizens. In Britain, less interest is taken than in earlier years in the Commonwealth, while closer ties are steadily being forged with Europe. The United Kingdom joined the European Economic Community (EEC) on 22 January 1972 (after being rebuffed nine years earlier by President de Gaulle of France) and a referendum in 1975 confirmed that a majority wanted to stay in it: two-thirds of the votes cast. Frenchmen, Germans and other Common Market nationals now have the unrestricted right to live and work in the United Kingdom, which Commonwealth

Crown and Empire

Jubilant crowds mobbed the Viceroy of India's carriage on the first day of independence.

nationals do not.

Serious difficulties were created for Commonwealth countries which still relied on preferential trade arrangements with Britain: New Zealand over butter and lamb, for example; the West Indies over sugar. Few people in Britain had more affection for the Community than they did for the Commonwealth, but Europe was accepted in the hope of solving Britain's persistent economic problems.

By 1980 no more of the world was ruled from western Europe than it had been 500 years earlier, when Columbus discovered America. The influence of Europe,

An engagement photo of the present Queen and Prince Philip (above right). The 'correct lyrics' of God Save the Queen and Rule Britannia were included in songs to sing for the Coronation in 1953 (right).

The British Empire was succeeded by the Commonwealth, whose leaders are shown with the Queen and Mrs Thatcher in 1986.

however, and in particular of Britain and the English language, has been carried to every corner of the globe by British settlers, soldiers, missionaries, traders and colonial administrators. This is the enduring legacy of the Empire, of that brilliant sunny June day in 1897 when Queen Victoria's loyal troops led her through London's streets in a triumphant demonstration of imperial pride, splendour and power.

1898-9

FTER THE CELEBRATIONS of the Diamond Jubilee and the
British Empire in 1897, 1898 saw British interest focused
on foreign affairs, particularly regarding Britain's
involvement in the campaign against the Dervishes in the Sudan.
The *ILN* reported that a large British force was assembled and sent
out in January:

> *Considerable preparations are being made to strength-*
> *en the British contingent of military . . . under com-*
> *mand of General Sir Herbert Kitchener on the Nile at*
> *and above Berber, in expectation of a renewed conflict*
> *with the Dervishes from Omdurman and Metemmeh*
> *on the route to Khartoum.* (15 January)

Under Kitchener's firm command the situation was brought
under control, and the Dervishes were finally defeated at the
Battle of Omdurman in September.

In the Far East the Russians were ceded Port Arthur, and
there was increasing concern in Britain and elsewhere about
Russian imperial ambitions.

An era ended with the deaths of Gladstone and Bismarck.
Marie Curie discovered radium, and 12 pedigree British Hereford
bulls were shipped to South America to improve the quality of the
beef cattle on the farms there. London society was taken aback by
the founding of the Anti-Scandal League. The *ILN* commented:

> *Heaven forbid that so excellent an enterprise should be*
> *discouraged; but an agitation for the suppression of*
> *tittle-tattle must excite scepticism, like the Czar's pro-*
> *posal for the reduction of armaments.* (22 October)

URING THE SECOND HALF of 1899, storm clouds gathered
quickly over the Transvaal and in October the Boers
issued an ultimatum which gave Britain no alternative but
to go to war. There was enthusiasm in the *ILN* and elsewhere for a
war whose aim was to punish the impudence of the Boers:

> *Firm expression of a determination to maintain the*
> *supremacy of England throughout South Africa cannot*
> *fail to be heartily endorsed by the great majority of the*
> *nation. The Boers court the arbitrament of shot and*
> *shell. They must take the consequences.* (14 October)

A large expeditionary force was assembled and despatched
to join the forces which had been shipped out during the summer,
and by mid October Britain was deeply involved in a colonial war
which initially went badly.

In France there was controversy over the outcome of the
retrial of Captain Dreyfus, who had been accused of spying by the
army in 1894 and imprisoned. The retrial—by civil court—now
ruled his innocence, but the army appeared to reject this verdict.
The *ILN* reported somewhat ironically:

> *France is passing through a struggle between the civil*
> *and military elements, between justice and organised*
> *malignity; but it is also a struggle between a majority of*
> *maniacs and a minority of people in their right minds.*
> (19 August)

An era ended: the deaths in 1898 of
Gladstone, (top), and Bismarck, Germany's
former 'Iron Chancellor'. 'Amid the turmoil of
a world distracted, Mr Gladstone has passed
peacefully to rest . . . In the view of the present
generation, Gladstone stands higher than Peel
or Palmerston . . . we rank him rather with Pitt
and Fox and Walpole . . . The numerous
political changes and social reforms of the last
half-century which he inspired . . . are a
monument to his genius . . . Mr Gladstone's
memory will be kept sweet in the records of
the Victorian Era.' (21 May 1898)

1898-9
E·V·E·N·T·S

14 MAY (1898) Death of Gladstone at the age of 89
30 JULY (1898) Death of Bismarck, Germany's 'Iron Chancellor', aged 83
2 SEPTEMBER (1898) Dervishes defeated by Kitchener at Omdurman
29 DECEMBER (1898) Radium discovered by Marie and Pierre Curie
18 MAY (1899) First International Peace Conference at The Hague opened
10 OCTOBER (1899) Start of the Boer War

Curies honoured: 'Madame Curie, who, with her husband, discovered radium [in 1898], is publishing a thesis on the subject.' (13 June 1903). 'The Royal Society [has awarded] the Davy Medal to M and Mme Curie . . . Madame Curie could not be present owing to the rules of the society . . .' (5 December 1903)

Boer War optimism short-lived: at the outset, the British suffered a succession of defeats, like the Battle of Lombard's Kop (below). These unexpected reverses caused despair in Britain and 'brought home to the government a full sense of the difficulties they have to face in South Africa.' (23 December 1899)

1900-1

THE NEW MILLENNIUM DAWNED with Britain still deeply involved in the South African war. Although Britain had suffered a series of humiliating defeats late in 1899, there was now a general feeling that a turning point had been reached:

> *The arrival of Lord Roberts and Lord Kitchener at Cape Town was heralded by a reassuring despatch from Sir George White as to the severe fighting at Ladysmith last Saturday. It remains to be seen whether New Year's Day was really a turning-point in the history of the campaign, but it is certain that the public mind has since that date experienced on several separate occasions a sense of genuine gratification and renewed hopefulness as to a possible early determination of the war.* (13 January)

Optimism proved to be well placed. Ladysmith was relieved in February and Lord Roberts then took Bloemfontein. But the news that everyone was waiting for came in May, with the relief of Mafeking. Transvaal was annexed and, with the Boer armies broken, many felt that the end of the war was in sight.

The war had caused Britain's dependence on the navy to be questioned, but elsewhere in the world a large navy was still seen as the keystone of foreign policy. The Russians sent their fleet to Korea, and then occupied Manchuria, to the concern of Japan, for whom Britain was in the process of building several new battleships. Germany was also planning a new fleet of 38 battleships.

In China a pattern of unrest culminated in the violent Boxer Rebellion, and more than 1,500 Europeans were massacred before a hastily assembled combined force of British, German, Japanese, Russian and American troops was able to restore order.

ON 22 JANUARY 1901 Queen Victoria died at the age of 81, after a short illness, and the nation mourned the end of the longest reign in Britain's history.

In South Africa the war continued, with the Boers concentrating their efforts increasingly on guerrilla tactics; Lord Kitchener, the British Supreme Commander, was forced to defend main roads and railways with barbed wire and concrete bunkers. Britain was attacked by the press in several countries over the alleged atrocities carried out by British troops and the plight of Boer families held in British concentration camps. The British press, including the *ILN*, attempted to redress the balance:

> *One of the largest refugee camps in South Africa is situated at Volksrust, to the north of Laing's Nek . . . Physically the Boers are a fine race, the men often of tremendous frame, large-boned, broad-shouldered, but entirely lacking that spring and carriage that come to us from long years of athletic training.* (24 August)

In the USA, President McKinley was assassinated, and Vice-President Theodore Roosevelt assumed office. He quickly made his views known by inviting the first Negro to dine at the White House—and race riots followed.

Marconi (who had sent the first message by wireless over a mile in 1895) now sent the first wireless message across the Atlantic. Britain's first submarine, *Holland I*, set off on a trial run, and in Germany the first Mercedes car left the Daimler factory.

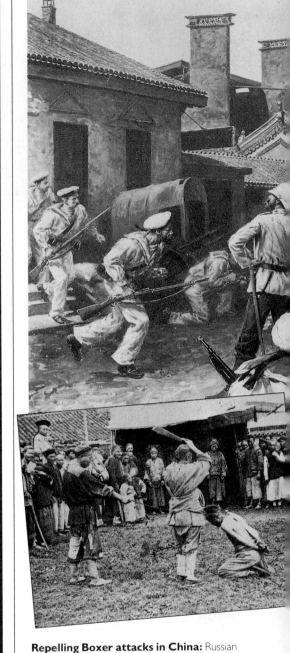

Repelling Boxer attacks in China: Russian troops (main picture) were among those fighting to restore order. 'The relief of the Peking Legations by the Allied forces is a military operation not only of extraordinary interest from the sentimental standpoint, but also of great value as indicating the reality of modern military progress . . . A curiously mixed force, comprising half-a-dozen different nationalities, advancing on a narrow front along a road varying throughout from bad to worse, might well have failed to reach its goal in time, even if no opposition whatever had been encountered . . . The advance . . . is a very striking demonstration of modern military organisation and discipline.' (25 August 1900). Meanwhile, the Chinese enemy meted out punishment both brutally and publicly (above).

1900-1

E·V·E·N·T·S

27 FEBRUARY (1900) British Labour Party
launched, under Ramsay MacDonald
1 JULY (1900) First flight by Count Zeppelin's
airship
14 AUGUST (1900) Peking stormed by Allies to
end Boxer Rebellion
1 JANUARY (1901) Commonwealth of Australia
established
22 JANUARY (1901) Death of Queen Victoria
10 DECEMBER (1901) First Nobel prizes awarded

Death of the monarch: 'The Queen kept at her work
almost to the very last . . . On more than one occasion lately
she showed herself in public to her people in London, and
was received with such a welcome and such enthusiastic
homage as brought tears into her eyes . . . For many months
her heart had been deeply grieved by the losses . . . in South
Africa . . . On the 19th of January the London newspapers
contained some alarming reports about the state of the
Queen's health, and on the 22nd of the month the reign of
Queen Victoria was over.' (Record Number, 1901)

Hurrah for heroes: a
souvenir of the Transvaal
War, featuring portraits of
military leaders with the
slogan *One Flag, One Queen,
One Empire, One Singer.*

Mafeking relieved (17 May 1900): '. . . the streets, the
theatres all places of refreshment and resort, abandoned
themselves to a carnival that embraced all classes . . . Perhaps
these violent delights should be distrusted as indications of a
new spirit . . . When those . . . young patriots in their
perambulators grow up and innocently ask their fathers, "Did
you wave Union Jacks and sing in restaurants when Mafeking
was relieved?", the accused may . . . evade the impeachment
. . . Yes, we shall relapse; but . . . our sombre streets were
lighted up with rapture.' (26 May 1900)

Edward VII
1902–1910

1902

T HE KEY EVENT OF 1902 was the Coronation, delayed by
Edward's sudden appendix operation in June. The royal
progress through London which followed the Coronation
ceremony in August was, according to the *ILN*:

> *. . . celebrated amid much popular rejoicing. Of course
> it was impossible to recall the vanished Colonial con-
> tingents, which would have lent so much interest and
> colour to the scene; but there was a brave show of the
> Home troops, and a splendid pageant, representing all
> arms of the service, was marshalled. Batteries of Horse
> and Field Artillery and squadrons of Household
> Cavalry, Hussars, and Lancers passed in brilliant suc-
> cession, but the brightness of the spectacle was a little
> dimmed by the order from Headquarters which pres-
> cribed that all troops on parade should wear overcoats.
> The procession, though somewhat sombre, was never-
> theless imposing. (1 November)*

The year started well on the international front, with the
signing of the Anglo–Japanese treaty of alliance, and later, in
August, there was a visit to London by the Shah of Persia, who
was, according to the *ILN*, 'greatly impressed by the ease with
which the police controlled the vast traffic of the Metropolis'.
More important was the surrender of the Boer generals in
May, bringing the South African war to an end. Public jubilation
was tempered by the enthusiastic reception the Boer generals
received when they came to Britain. The *ILN* commented:

> *All the fruits of our hard-bought victory were
> destroyed in a few minutes by that dreadful humili-
> ation of the national character. Can nothing be done to
> restrain the people who assemble at railway stations
> from such ill-omened transports? . . . Perhaps the
> Government had better consider the expediency of
> forbidding visits which excite such thoughtless
> enthusiasm. What is the good of living in a sea-girt isle
> if we cannot keep off the insinuating stranger who
> threatens to undermine our authority in the world by
> appealing to our weakness for romantic generosity?
> (30 August)*

One of the direct results of the war was the steady decline in
Anglo–German relations, soured by German support for the
Boers. The *ILN* described the situation in no uncertain terms:

> *It is necessary to make the German people understand
> that we regard their ill opinion of us as compounded
> of arrogant stupidity and organised lying. Count von
> Bülow says 'they are a well-bred people,' and their
> breeding is attested by the popularity of every obscene
> blackguard who defames us in print or picture.
> (18 January)*

Increasing bitterness was little improved by Kaiser
Wilhelm's visit to London in November, but Britain's growing
respect for German technology was underlined by the use of
Krupp armour plating on the new battleship, HMS *London*.

THE ILLUSTRATED LONDON NEWS

1902

E·V·E·N·T·S

25 JANUARY Death penalty abolished in Russia
30 JANUARY Anglo-Japanese Treaty of Alliance signed
19 FEBRUARY Vaccination against smallpox made compulsory in France
26 MARCH Death of Cecil Rhodes in South Africa, aged 48
16 APRIL Protests in Dublin over proposed changes in Irish criminal law
28 MAY Thomas Edison announced the invention of the electric battery

Memories to treasure: Edward's coronation was delayed by an operation—although souvenirs told another story. And 500,000 poor would long remember the free banquet.

Progress of a coronation (9 August 1906): '. . . it was in the gayest of spirits that London went out to do honour to its Sovereign, now happily restored to health and about to set forth on his long-delayed Coronation progress.'
At Westminster Abbey, 'When the King was crowned and enthroned . . . the Prince of Wales paid his homage by making obeisance, kissing hands, and touching the crown. As His Royal Highness was turning away, the King laid a gently detaining hand upon his son, and drawing the Prince towards him, clasped him in an affectionate embrace.'
'At ten minutes past two . . . their Majesties left the Abbey in their State Coach, amidst the booming of guns, the joyful clanging of bells and the cheering of the assembled people.' (16 August 1902)

Africa remained in the news following the death of Cecil Rhodes on 26 March. Opinion in the *ILN* was, however, divided about his qualities: 'Rhodes had imagination . . . a fine quality in a statesman.' However: 'To leave a hundred thousand pounds to one's old college is vulgar. To endow one hundred and sixty scholarships at Oxford is vulgar . . . But how can you expect true nobility of soul from a man like Rhodes?'

This year, Balfour succeeded Lord Salisbury as Prime Minister and faced, among other problems, a rowdy assault in the Commons from the Irish MP O'Donnell over the Irish question. A state of emergency in Dublin, and the increasing efforts of the United Irish League to seek support for the cause of independence, particularly in the USA, formed the background to the noisy scenes.

Social and political unrest was an international phenomenon, with strikes and riots in many countries, including France, Spain, Russia, Switzerland, the USA and Belgium, where there were what the *ILN* regarded as: 'disgraceful scenes in Brussels . . . small sections bent on rowdyism . . . chanting revolutionary songs and fighting the police at every favourable opportunity.'

Overseas, the Royal Navy was in action in Venezuela in a vain attempt to force that country to repay its debts, while the British and Italian armies were planning concerted operations in Italian Somaliland against Mohammed ibn Abdullah (the 'Mad' Mullah), who called himself *Mahdi*, or Messiah, and claimed to possess supernatural powers.

Disasters of the year included earthquakes in Mexico and Turkey, and the destruction of St Pierre, the capital of Martinique, by a volcano. Cholera raged in Egypt, while at Ibrox Park in Glasgow the collapse of a stand during the England–Scotland football match resulted in 20 deaths. On a more positive note, the Aswan Dam was completed, and the world's largest passenger liner, the *Cedric*, was launched by Harland and Wolff. England scored 769 in one innings in Australia, but were defeated by the USA at Headingley in the new game of pushball.

In Nice, Serpollet's steam car achieved a new world record speed of 74.5mph, but at home there was lively debate about the more restricted speeds motorists had to tolerate. The *ILN*'s reporter mused:

> *Prophets tell us that the motor car will supersede the horse. Very likely, but in the meantime the highways are obviously designed for horse traffic . . . does any student of human nature really believe that cars which are built to travel forty miles an hour can be subjected to a law that denies the very reason for their being?* (30 August)

The new increased speeds had not yet penetrated the Royal Mail:

> *. . . the postal service between Shetland and the south is inadequate. The Post Office, with a surplus of about four millions, cannot afford to give the inhabitants of Shetland direct and daily communication with Aberdeen and pleads that there are not enough letters and parcels to justify an increased outlay. So the Shetland hosiery, which is famous, is cramped because it sometimes takes longer to send an order from London to Lerwick than to send to Constantinople.* (19 April)

Friendly foundation: the 1902 Anglo-Japanese Alliance bound the two nations to assist each other in safeguarding their respective interests in China and Korea, and was directed against Russian expansionism. It was a cornerstone of British and Japanese policy in Asia until after the First World War. In the Russo-Japanese War of 1904–5 the French were discouraged by it from entering the war on Russia's side. It was renewed in 1905 and 1911; Japan entered the Great War as an Ally.

Commons commotion: A J Balfour, the new Prime Minister, sparked violent scenes in the Commons when he declared at the reassembling of Parliament (16 October) that debate on the Irish situation was neither wanted nor needed during that sitting. An Irish MP, O'Donnell, dashed across the floor in a frenzy of shouting and shook his fists at the premier. Other ministers rallied to Balfour's aid; O'Donnell calmed down and returned to his seat.

Celebrations in the suburbs: 'When the war with the two Boer Republics broke out . . . even the most pessimistic prophet would scarcely have foretold that it would last over two and a half years . . . The terms of peace may be regarded with sober satisfaction. The Boers levied war against the British Empire, and they have paid the forfeit . . . Nobody can say that the terms are ungenerous. Every burgher who has not misconducted himself will start afresh as a British subject with the help of British credit . . . He will have a voice in the administration of his country . . . But his independence is gone: he must give up his arms, and any remaining stores of ammunition hoarded for another conflict; he must take the oath of allegiance to the King.' (7 June 1902)

1902
E · V · E · N · T · S

31 MAY Terms of surrender signed by Boer generals
24 JUNE Edward VII's coronation delayed by emergency appendix operation
9 AUGUST Coronation of Edward VII
16 OCTOBER Violence in Commons as Balfour refused to discuss Ireland
8 NOVEMBER Kaiser Wilhelm in London to improve Anglo-German relations
10 DECEMBER Aswan Dam completed

Peter Rabbit made his début: destined to become a nursery classic, *The Tale Of Peter Rabbit* appeared after author and illustrator Beatrix Potter had difficulty persuading anyone to publish it.

1903-4

HE KING was proclaimed Emperor of India by the Viceroy, Lord Curzon, on 1 January 1903. In May, Edward VII visited Paris to improve Anglo–French relations, and a few months later he was in Ireland, where the royal visit drew a more mixed response.

Arthur Henderson won the Barnard Castle by-election in July, becoming the third MP in James Keir Hardie's Labour Party, with the Liberals lagging in third place behind the Tories. The *ILN* reported that there was 'a disposition to regard the defeat of official Liberalism as an augury of serious division in the Liberal Party'. Another augury for the future was the October launch of Mrs Pankhurst's militant Women's Social and Political Union (WSPU), with the slogan 'Deeds, not Words'.

Overseas, the British Army brought the rebellion in Nigeria to an end, but the joint campaign with Italian forces against Mohammed ibn Abdullah in Italian Somaliland continued.

On a happier note, London saw its first electric trams, as well as the opening of Kew Bridge and the Gaiety Theatre. Meanwhile, in the USA, the Ford Motor Company was launched, the Pepsi Cola brand name was registered, and the first 'wild west' film, *Kit Carson*, was enjoyed by thousands.

A significant death was that of Pope Leo XIII in July. It was calculated that '350,000 persons paid their last tribute of respect to the dead pontiff' at the lying in state. In August, Pope Pius X was crowned.

Marconi's telegraphy link opened between Britain and the USA, and on 17 December the Wright brothers made the first flight in a heavier-than-air craft—in hindsight one of the landmarks of the twentieth century.

HE MOST SIGNIFICANT international event of 1904 was the outbreak of war in Manchuria between Japan and Russia. The world was taken by surprise by the Japanese successes at first. Their tactical and technical superiority was widely admired by the *ILN*'s reporters:

> It is not to be disputed that hitherto, in celerity of movement, in excellence of tactical disposition, and in strategical forethought and intelligence, the Japanese have demonstrated their advantage over their antagonists. (21 May)

The war had clear global implications and King Edward offered to mediate with the Tsar, even though Britain, along with France and the USA, had declared its neutrality. In this conflicting pattern of imperial ambition the Russians sank a British merchant ship, captured others, and attacked trawlers in the North Sea, events attracting a strong response from the *ILN*: 'This is not law, but travesty . . . they should . . . pay handsome compensation . . .' Russia's expansionist policy in Asia was also blamed for Britain having to send a military mission into Tibet.

In the USA, Theodore Roosevelt was re-elected President in a landslide victory, the New York subway opened, Caruso made his first American record and Henry Ford took the world land speed record. However, the most outstanding event of the year in the USA was the St Louis World Fair, and the city also hosted the third modern Olympic Games. American domination seemed to be a theme for the future: the *ILN*'s correspondent asked: 'In any competition with the United States, where is poor old Europe?'

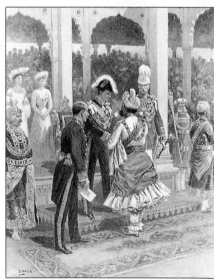

India pledges allegiance to the new Emperor: New Year's Day, 1903, at the Imperial Durbar, Delhi, and the Maharaja of Bundi was among the native princes paying homage to the Viceroy—Lord Curzon—and the Duke of Connaught. 'From every part of our Indian empire came a long array—ninety-eight feudatory chieftains in all, representing nearly one-fifth of the entire human race—to tender their allegiance to the Imperial Sovereignty.' (24 January 1903)

THE ILLUSTRATED LONDON NEWS

1903-4

E·V·E·N·T·S

16 JUNE (1903) Ford Motor Company formed
10 OCTOBER (1903) Mrs Pankhurst formed
Women's Social and Political Union
17 DECEMBER (1903) Wright brothers' first flight
in heavier-than-air craft
10 FEBRUARY (1904) Russian fleet attacked by
Japanese; war declared
30 APRIL (1904) World Fair in St Louis, USA,
opened
3 AUGUST (1904) Dalai Lama forced to flee as
British captured Lhasa

Little short of sublime: Japanese troops removing their dead from wire-entangled heights at Nan-shan in Manchuria (above) after savage fighting in the Russo–Japanese War. 'When the extraordinary difficulties of carrying the Russian positions at Nan-shan are considered, the Japanese valour and recklessness of life appear little short of sublime . . . Within this zone the carnage was tremendous.' (16 July 1904)

Triumph at Kitty Hawk: 'There is much mystery about the doings of the brothers Wilbur and Orville Wright . . . who claim to have solved the problem of flight [on 17 December 1903]. They have maintained so much secrecy, however, that it is impossible to give details of their methods.' (18 April 1907). 'A remarkable speed was obtained with a small motor . . . and the velocity is estimated from 45 to 48 miles an hour.' (13 June 1908)

Highwaymen in blue: the motorist was rapidly becoming a victim of 'hold-ups' by the police force.

1905-6

THE YEAR 1905 STARTED with the capture of Port Arthur by the Japanese, and the surrender of the Russian troops blockaded there. In Russia the disastrous course of the war was pursued against a background of mounting civil strife, and the violent response by the army and the police effectively brought the Tsar's popular support to an end.

The war in Manchuria ended on 5 September, but its effects on the international balance of power continued. A treaty of alliance between Russia and Germany, concluded in July, was seen by many as a response to the Anglo–Japanese treaty of 1902; the Kaiser was beginning to flex his muscles. He threatened to close the Baltic to the British fleet, but this was not taken very seriously in Britain. According to the *ILN*:

> *Great Britain can afford to ignore these manifestations. It was obviously preposterous on the face of it that Germany could persuade the Powers surrounding the Baltic to close that inlet against Great Britain's fleet.* (5 August)

The pressure for change was international. There were strikes and riots in Poland, Crete voted for union with Greece, and Norway gained its independence from Sweden.

Also this year, the Simplon Tunnel through the Alps was completed. Einstein published his Theory of Relativity, and the first exhibition by Matisse and the other Fauvist painters in Paris divided the art world.

THE RISE OF MILITARISM was the dominant feature of the early years of this century. After Japan's victory in Manchuria in 1905, the Japanese government decided to double the size of its navy during 1906, and although Germany's power was also increasing, Britain's dominance of the international scene was still paramount. The Royal Navy launched its new super battleship *Dreadnought* in February 1906. Fred T Jane, writing in the *ILN*, was highly enthusiastic:

> *Neither photograph nor picture, unless artistic licence be taken, can give any very real conception of the* Dreadnought . . . *The details are there, but not the sense of overwhelming size and power . . . You think of John Bull as you look at the* Dreadnought. *She is all John Bull—John Bull afloat.* (6 October)

Yet, by November, Japan had launched an even bigger battleship, the *Satsuma*, and the arms race gathered momentum.

The prevailing pattern of unrest around the world continued. There was a general strike in Spain, and the Spanish King and Queen narrowly escaped an assassin's bomb. A plot was also discovered to blow up the King of Italy. But it was in Russia that social and political turmoil was at its worst. The Duma, Russia's first elected parliament, took office in May. It was granted some powers by the Tsar, but the violence continued and hundreds were killed. In July the Duma was dissolved and martial law was declared.

In Britain, the battle for women's suffrage was gaining strength, and in June a deputation representing half a million women went with a petition to 10 Downing Street to press women's claim to the vote.

The Cossacks' onslaught on Bloody Sunday: strikers marching to the Winter Palace in St Petersburg to petition Tsar Nicholas II for reforms were met by lines of infantry and Cossacks. The troops, ordered to dispel any crowds, fired on the mass and more than 500 men, women and children were killed; hundreds more were wounded. '. . . from a simple labour question has arisen the first serious movement of the long-expected Russian Revolution . . . The strikers, whose intentions were entirely peaceful . . . were treated in a manner that would only have been justified had their mission been murder and rapine . . . Scenes of terrible carnage ensued . . . The shots of January 22 assuredly rang the knell of autocracy. Its burial, however, will not be today or tomorrow.' (28 January 1905). 'The deeds that were done will one day bear a bitter fruit of revolt.' (4 February 1905)

Battleship mutiny: Russia's most powerful battleship, *Potemkin*, was seized on 27 June 1905 by crew members at Odessa in the Black Sea. The mutiny followed the shooting of a sailor by an officer. The commander and several officers were thrown overboard; other officers joined the mutiny. Pictured is a sailor, Mauschenko, who was among the mutineers and who crushed the face of a priest with his gun-butt on board ship. The crew surrendered to the Rumanians 11 days later. Troops had killed many thousands in riots in Odessa following the mutiny.

1905-6

E·V·E·N·T·S

22 JANUARY (1905) 500 strikers shot in St Petersburg on Bloody Sunday

26 JUNE (1905) The Automobile Association formed by early motorists

5 SEPTEMBER (1905) Russo-Japanese War ended by Treaty of Portsmouth

7 FEBRUARY (1906) Liberals won landslide election victory in UK

18 APRIL (1906) San Francisco devastated by earthquake

3 OCTOBER (1906) SOS adopted as international distress signal

First badge of many: the first AA badges were issued in April 1906. Of uniform pattern, they bore AA Secretary Stenson Cooke's signature, but have been redesigned many times since.

Death and destruction: on the morning of 18 April 1906, the most severe earthquake in Californian history flattened the city of San Francisco. More than 2,500 people perished in the quake and the sweeping fires that raged unchecked for three days afterwards, all but destroying the city. The entire business area was destroyed, along with 497 blocks in the centre of the city, at a loss of $350 million. The earthquake was caused by the violent settling of the San Andreas fault on which the city is built and which extends up and down the coast; in some parts the land surface was displaced horizontally by 21ft (7 metres). Rebuilding the city began before the ashes were cool, and was swiftly completed.

WOMEN

New Roles AND Attitudes

*Who knows what women can be
when they are finally free to become
themselves?*

BETTY FRIEDAN

AS THE TWENTIETH CENTURY began, one topic was guaranteed to set newspapers rustling in gentlemen's clubs all over Britain: the women's question. Men and women who raised their eyebrows at the demands of some of 'the fair sex' would have found life in the 1980s quite a shock to the system. In the course of a lifetime, women discarded bustles and bras; and their new freedoms involved far more than fashion. In politics, education, business, health and the home, new laws and new conventions have been a feature of women's lives in the late nineteenth and twentieth centuries. Movements formed by champions of 'women's rights' have made lasting impressions in their determined push for change. In the early years of this century, one such movement heckled, marched and smashed its way into the national memory: the Suffragettes.

The Suffragettes were, in fact, only part of a much wider movement calling for suffrage—or votes—for women. At the turn of the century the franchise was governed by the 1884 Reform Act, which allowed male householders to cast votes in parliamentary elections. This excluded many men from the right to vote, too. By 1914, 7 million could vote under the so-called householder qualification, and another million voters qualified as 40-shilling (£2) freeholders and lodgers. In other words, nearly two-thirds of the adult male population had the vote; and some were able to cast more than one! But women could not vote—at the time of the 1884 Reform Act, William Ewart Gladstone, the Liberal statesman, had feared that women would 'overweight' the bill—and this had

Suffragette election poster against the 'Cat and Mouse' Act.

already become the focus of complaint for a suffrage reform movement in the nineteenth century. The philosopher and politician John Stuart Mill had tried to bring women's suffrage into an earlier Reform Bill of 1867, but with the support of only 73 MPs. In 1869 it looked as though the reformers had made some gains, as the Municipal Franchise Act allowed female householders to vote in local elections. But two years later a

renewed attempt to change the law, led by Jacob Bright, brought about a bill which, though it passed its second reading in the House of Commons, was not allowed to progress further.

By now women's suffrage societies had sprung up all over the country, and towards the end of the nineteenth century these were brought together as the National Union of Women's Suffrage Societies (NUWSS), under the leadership of Millicent Fawcett.

The women involved were mainly people with good social connections, many with successful professional careers, who had been able to take advantage of the new educational opportunities arising in the 19th century: in the 1840s Queen's College and Bedford College in London opened for women, for example, and by 1870 Girton was the first women's college at Cambridge (though not then recognised by the university authorities). Some women were working their way into the higher professions such as medicine and university teaching; but they were still very much exceptions. Distinguished male supporters of women's suffrage included the philosopher Bertrand Russell, whose role in the campaign prompted this anonymous ditty:

*Although we may oppose the plan
Of giving womenfolk a vote,
Still to the ordinary man
Few things are more engaging than
The Russell of the Petticoat.*

The early suffragists' main concern was to win the vote on the same terms as men—without necessarily extending the franchise beyond the property qualification. Even so,

Suffragettes and sympathisers led a procession to Hyde Park (above) in 1908, in protest at the Asquith government's denial of votes to women. Mrs Emmeline Pankhurst, who promoted civil disobedience for the cause, was often arrested (above right). She was greeted by supporters on her release from Bow Street in 1912 (right).

their demands were made in the face of deeply rooted opposition. Women were largely dependent on men; married women's property and income became that of their husbands, and spinsters—from whose ranks the new professional women usually came—were generally expected to aspire to marriage. The very idea that these ladies could take an active part in the political world caused mirth and outrage. In a letter that appeared in the *ILN*, Gladstone insisted that:

> *... men are not disposed to admit that a lady may sit on the Treasury Bench and discharge the duties, for example, of Minister of War, or that a Cabinet may govern the country by virtue of the support of a preponderance of female electors.*
> (30 April 1892)

Nevertheless, the suffragists, under the banner of the NUWSS, used their influence to lobby MPs, produced propaganda, and steadily increased their numbers. Membership soared; from 70 women's suffrage societies in 1909, the movement swelled to 480 societies with 53,000 members in 1914.

But in the mean time a new development had forced one particular faction of the suffrage movement into the public eye. In her frustration at the apparent lack of prog-

ress, Mrs Emmeline Pankhurst, the daughter of a wealthy cotton manufacturer, had set up the Women's Social and Political Union (WSPU) in 1903, with the cry 'Deeds, not Words'. The WSPU's militant tactics at first consisted of heckling and disrupting political meetings. In 1905 Mrs Pankhurst's daughter Christabel and Annie Kenney, a fellow campaigner, were thrown out of a meeting and imprisoned after asking about the new Liberal government's attitude to women's suffrage. This set the pace for nine years of explosive action and reaction. The mainstream movement continued its work, parading in sandwich boards, distributing newspapers and handbills, picketing the House of Commons and organising marches. But at the same time a

campaign of increasing violence marked the policy of the militant Suffragettes. With each political disappointment the violence seemed to grow. In 1910 two bills were drafted including women's suffrage; both passed two readings. But still the government refused to act, and Prime Minister Herbert Asquith was adamantly against giving women the vote, announcing firmly in 1911 that he would bring in a franchise bill 'for male persons only'. Many ministers hardened their attitudes in response to the often indiscriminate violence of the Suffragettes. As well as chaining themselves to railings, the women began a large-scale campaign of civil disobedience, slashing National Gallery paintings, setting fire to buildings and even planting a small bomb in

Westminster Abbey. Windows were smashed at arranged times; policemen were kicked and scratched. Not unexpectedly, the authorities' treatment of the protesters became increasingly brutal. Many of those who were imprisoned went on hunger strike, and suffered the appalling experience of force-feeding. The so-called 'Cat and Mouse' Act (Temporary Discharge for Ill Health) was brought in to allow released prisoners to recover their health before being rearrested and imprisoned; Mrs Pankhurst herself, sentenced to three years in 1913, was imprisoned no less than eight times. Hostility to the Suffragettes, from the public and the press, was often vicious; they were portrayed as wizened old spinsters, and this crude approach was sometimes given a dubious 'scientific' credibility. In 1912, for instance, the bacteriologist Sir Almroth E Wright wrote to *The Times* blaming the Suffragettes' militancy on the bitterness of an excess female population (there were then over a million more women than men), and advising them to seek mates abroad. His argument against allowing women into the political arena centred on what he perceived to be their deficiency in physical force, intellectual stability and appreciation of moral standards; but his opinions prompted a sarcastic reply from Mrs Winston Churchill, who concluded that: 'After reading Sir Almroth Wright's able and weighty exposition of women as he knows them, the question seems no longer to be "Should women have votes?" but "Ought women not to be abolished altogether?"'

A purely male race certainly seemed to be the ideal of some opponents of women's suffrage. But the movement as a whole, and the Suffragettes' tactics particularly, did arouse interest and debate about 'the women's question'. In 1913 this interest was sharply focused on a terrible incident, caught on film at the Epsom Derby. Emily Davison, an Oxford graduate who had previously registered her protest by setting fire to letter boxes, ran out in front of the King's horse as it rounded Tattenham Corner, and was killed. Whether or not her death was a misguided publicity stunt or a deliberate suicide, it provided the Suffragettes with their first martyr; and her funeral procession was attended by vast—if mainly curious—crowds.

How long the Suffragettes would have continued their campaign in a Britain at peace, and how effective it would have been, can never be known. In 1914 the First World War brought shattering and lasting changes to many aspects of British life, and thrust women into a new role which was not easily to be forgotten.

The Great War brought change both in the public response to the Suffragettes and in women's view of their own role. Suffragette prisoners were pardoned, and women in all areas of the suffrage movement threw

Suffragettes provided a guard of honour for the coffin of Emily Davison in 1913.

themselves into the war effort with the same vigour which had characterised their political activities. Suffrage societies brought their organising skills to the fore in setting up voluntary bodies; through the 'Women's Service', the London branch of the NUWSS directed the efforts of thousands of non-professional women seeking useful work. The cry for the right to vote had now become a demand for the 'Right to Serve'. Voluntary Aid Detachments swelled the ranks of the military nursing service; and as the drain on manpower and munitions began to make an impact, the call for women workers became more urgent. In 1915 the Marchioness of Londonderry organised the Women's Legion as a corps of paid women, in khaki uniforms, replacing paid men. The Legion, split into Cookery, Ambulance and Canteen sections, enrolled more than 40,000 women. By spring of the same year women were being brought into munitions factories, working as tram conductors, ambulance drivers and telegraph operators.

The Suffragettes were constantly in the forefront of the effort to bring women to work—while, at the same time, emphasising their abilities and responsibility. On 8 September 1914, at the outset of the First World War, Christabel Pankhurst told supporters in a speech at the London Opera House that: 'If we are needed in the fighting line, we shall be there. If we are needed to attend the economic prosperity of the country, we shall be there. What it is best in

the interests of the State to do, women will do. But it must be clearly understood that if women do not actually take part in the fighting, that argues no inferiority, that argues no diminution of their claim to political equality.' Both Suffragettes and suffragists were suspending any overtly political action in favour of the war effort; but at the same time their war work brought them into a world which was eventually to be associated with the wider issues of industrial conditions and pay. The London Society for Women's Suffrage promoted the introduction of women into occupations once exclusively reserved for men. They set up a munitions and aircraft department, and started the first training classes in oxy-acetylene welding. Their pupils were the first women welders to enter the engineering trade. Some areas of work still saw fierce resistance from the men who had not been called up: tram drivers were determined not to let women into the driving seat, and by the end of the war there was still only a handful of women drivers. Work as conductors was very popular, however, and brought raised hemlines to enable women to tackle the stairs.

Some of the work undertaken by women was risky and unhealthy. Workers

in munitions factories suffered symptoms ranging from coughs to vomiting after dealing with TNT, and earned the nickname 'canaries' because of its effect on their skin colour. Hundreds of deaths resulted from explosions in factories. But women still came in their thousands to find employment of all kinds. The numbers working in banking and finance shot up from nine-and-a-half thousand in 1914 to more than sixty thousand three years later. Women's Services were established—the Women's Army Auxiliary Corps (WAAC), the Women's Royal Naval Service (WRNS), and the

Bus conductresses in London in 1918 (above). The need for women to do men's jobs in the Great War helped to alter the stereotypes of men's and women's roles.

Women putting their case at a 'pilgrimage' to London, a year before the Great War broke out. It was the war which would eventually bring women, or some women, the vote.

Women's Royal Air Force (WRAF). A Land Army was set up.

All over the country women were taking up jobs which would previously have been unthinkable—doing 'men's' work, though at lower rates of pay: a fact which was not lost on many workers.

Before 1914, work for women was strictly defined, in terms of sex and class. Many poorer women took up 'sweated' trades, making hats or boxes, working long hours in terrible conditions for minimal pay. Some exclusion of women from 'men's' jobs was designed to prevent the very worst exploitation of their labour and health. The Coal Mines (Minimum Wages) Act of 1912 included clauses that forbade the employment of women below ground or moving wagons or lifting weights which would cause injury above ground. Domestic service was another means of work for many women, and was often welcomed as a clean, though tough, life with a guarantee of meals and a bed.

But women always earned less than men in equivalent work; their average pre-war industrial wage was 11s 7d (about 58p) a week—a third of the men's. Women of any means or 'status' were expected not to have to work, and there were few ways in which they could earn a living if they wanted to. Despite the new openings in education and in some professions, Edwardian ladies were generally trained in wifely and social duties; any frustrated energies could be dissipated in charity work and voluntary organisations. At the turn of the century only 29 per cent of the working population was female. The First World War gave thousands of women the opportunity to do different jobs without the stigma of class or poverty; they were helping to win the war and proving their worth.

Nevertheless, at the end of the war women were expected—and many were themselves ready—to give up their jobs for the men returning from the Front. In 1921 the figure for women's employment had dropped close to the 1914 level. Women were still seen in the role of home maker, mother and wife. But the changes which came with the war had made a deep impression. Soon after the Armistice, the State Register of Nurses established nursing as a true profession—taken up mainly by women. Social attitudes had been challenged and the particular health problems of women recognised.

In 1918 the National Council for the Unmarried Mother was set up, and in the same year the Maternal and Child Welfare Act allowed the provision of free clinics for pregnant women, as well as day nurseries. In the 1920s Marie Stopes organised a birth control clinic and Dora Russell, wife of Bertrand Russell, started the Workers' Birth Control Group. These developments were made in the face of much opposition, but they signalled a new awareness of the risks, especially for poorer women, of enduring frequent pregnancies and often giving birth in primitive conditions. Contraceptive advice was scarce and giving birth, even in hospital, brought the danger of infection. The mortality rate of women in childbirth was high.

In the inter-war years these were the issues taken up by reformers—along with the role of women in employment. A Sex Disqualification (Removal) Act of 1919 opened the professions of barrister, solicitor, veterinary surgeon and the highest grades of the home civil service to women, and allowed them to serve on juries and enter the police force with the same powers as male constables. However restricted

these changes were, they did lay down the principle that: 'A person shall not be disqualified by sex or marriage from the exercise of any public function or from being appointed to or holding any civil or judicial office.' And now the Suffragettes' call for 'Votes for Women' was finally answered. In 1918 female householders or wives of householders, and women who had been to university, were allowed to vote once they were over 30. By the end of the same year they could stand for Parliament. The first woman to be elected to the House of Commons was Sinn Fein candidate Constance Markievicz, who refused to take her seat at Westminster. In 1919 Nancy Astor won a by-election and took over her husband's seat as he moved into the Lords. Fears of a 'Women's Party' subsided, but the old demands had now widened in scope, and embraced not only a further extension of the franchise but also living conditions, pay and health.

A number of acts of parliament between the two world wars brought further changes to women's lives: giving women the same grounds for divorce as men in 1923; the same rights of guardianship as fathers in 1925; and in the same year giving widows a weekly pension. In 1928, as women were showing their legs, cutting their hair and flattening their chests, the Representation of the People Act extended the vote to all women over 21, without qualification and on the same terms as men. The suffrage campaigners had won their fight; and the struggle for women's rights changed and moved on.

In the 1930s the Depression overshadowed much of the political and social life of Britain. Women who went out to work were often regarded as taking men's jobs, and aggravating unemployment, which was seen primarily as the men's problem. But with the Second World War men were again taken out of the dole queues and out of their jobs and called into the Services. Soon women were also obliged to play their own part: in 1941 every woman aged between 19 and 40—later raised to 50—was required to sign up for war work, and was directed into a specific area by the government. Again women were in a position to prove their capabilities in jobs traditionally associated with the male work-force. According to the government, 'average women' were as capable of welding as they were of knitting, and as the war progressed women took equally readily to the Services, firewatching, ambulance driving and factory work. One of the lasting images of the war is that of young women toiling in the fields for the Land Army. Women who had embarked on higher education were placed briefly at an advantage over their male contemporaries, being able to complete their university degrees while most men had to leave their courses—apart from those taking exempted subjects—to enter the Services. Mothers of young children were initially left outside the reach of compulsory work, but as the need for workers became more

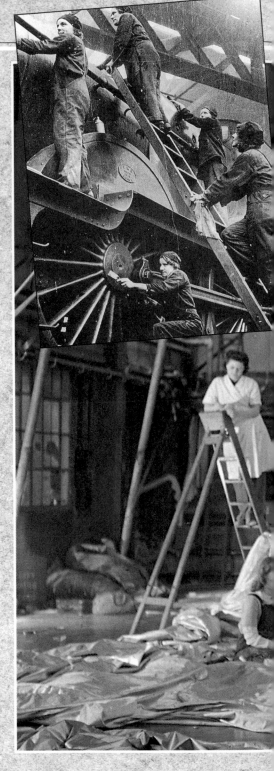

In the Second World War, as in the First, women were needed to do the jobs of men who were away fighting: whether it was cleaning a steam locomotive (top left) or manufacturing giant barrage balloons (above).

urgent they too were brought into employment, and this led to the opening of more than a thousand state nurseries.

Once again, changes were set into motion during the war years, and these gathered pace as votes by members of the Services brought a landslide election victory for the Labour Party in 1945. The rationing system, in force until 1954, provided a fairer distribution of food, and a balanced diet, a

The sight of the Women's Land Army working in jobs that were traditionally the preserve of male farm labourers gave a boost to the cause of female emancipation.

boon to many poorer families. In 1942 Sir William Beveridge produced a report which outlined a plan for free, national health care, and family allowances paid directly to women for the benefit of children. These policies were put into action within a few years of the war coming to an end. The free care provided by the National Health Service (NHS) brought particularly radical changes to women's lives. Although a form of state health care had been introduced by Lloyd George in 1911, this was based on the payment of partial costs by workers, and most women did not come into the 'insured workers' category. Social taboos in the early years of the century often discouraged women from even mentioning their ailments.

The danger of frequent pregnancies and scarcity of contraceptive advice sometimes led to the even greater risk of backstreet abortions. Health care received more public attention in the 1920s and 1930s; organisa-tions such as the League of Health and Beauty set about providing basic fitness classes for women, and changes in the law ensured free information and more help for mothers.

But after the Second World War the establishment of the NHS and, in the 1960s, the development of an effective contraceptive pill, provided a completely new setting for the 'women's question'. By the 'Swinging Sixties', women were living in a world vastly different from that of the Edwardian Suffragettes, and one in which emphasis could shift to a call for economic and social equality.

Equal pay and equal opportunities were now the primary demands of women. With the return to normality after the war, many women had been expected to return to home and family. But home life was vastly different; household gadgets, new or simply more accessible, made many housewives' lives very much easier in the post-war years. The vacuum cleaner and the washing machine were certainly not within everyone's reach, but by the 1960s they were popular and widespread. The greater use of plastics—first developed back in the nineteenth century—in mass-produced household appliances made goods cheaper. At the same time, the proportion of women in employment was increasing. Their numbers rose by nearly 3 million in the post-war years, and in 1951 32 per cent of the labour force were women. This figure rose to more than 40 per cent by 1977. As the economy expanded in the 1960s, more work became available for women as well as men, although the boundaries separating secretarial and retail work from work that was regarded as only fit for men, were still very difficult to cross.

With growing numbers of employed women, however, came louder demands for payment on equal terms with men. In 1955

equal pay was granted to teachers, civil servants and local government officers, but it was not until 15 years later that the Equal Pay Act laid down the principle that women and men in equivalent work deserved equal rates of pay. In the same year, 1970, the Chase Manhattan Bank in the USA calculated that a housewife's work was worth about £100 a week, and some campaigners took up the call for housewives' wages.

During the 1970s and 1980s other developments in the women's movement challenged the established notions of women, both in the home and in every other aspect of life. Modern feminism seeks profound changes in women's roles and attacks the 'sexism' of the social system; and, like the suffrage campaign, the movement has its more militant wing, challenging not just ideas of social roles, but also of sexual relationships and even language. In the 1970s, inspired by writers such as Germaine Greer and her book *The Female Eunuch*, some feminists rallied under the radical banner of 'Women's Liberation', complaining of an oppressive and prejudiced society.

As in the days of Millicent Fawcett and the Pankhursts, the public reaction to feminists and 'Women's Libbers' has been mixed and often hostile. The 'bra burners' of the 1970s certainly had no little publicity, even if most newspapers ridiculed them; and much media coverage has continued to concentrate on the physical appearance and

dress of women's rights campaigners. Fashion has also seemed to reflect some of society's changing views towards women. After the rather masculine look popular in the 1920s, and the economically cut uniform style of the Second World War, the 1950s saw a return to the exaggeratedly 'feminine' form, with the 'New Look' using a great deal of material for flowing skirts and dresses. But in the 1960s, with the heavy influence of the young on marketing trends, women's clothes became lighter, freer and more bizarre; and by the next decade the

Entertainment and the media have helped to fuel feminist protests by perpetuating the image of woman as 'pin-up': in films such as The Seven Year Itch, *starring Marilyn Monroe (right), and in fashion, such as the models (below), sporting pre-war Hollywood beachwear.*

After 1945 individual women came to the forefront of world politics as leaders of governments, East and West. Margaret Thatcher, seen (left) with President Reagan, became one of Britain's longest-serving prime ministers. Elected to that office in 1979, she was re-elected twice in the 1980s.

Golda Meir (left), of Israel, became Foreign Minister there in 1956 and Prime Minister in 1969. She resigned in 1974 and died four years later.

Indira Gandhi with the Queen (below) in 1983. The daughter of the Indian leader Nehru, she became Prime Minister of India in 1966 and was assassinated in 1984.

those of earlier years. Only 6 per cent of MPs are women, and the 300 Group continues to call for more female representation in the political world.

A wide range of demands and attitudes characterises the British women's movement at the end of the twentieth century. Equally, many men and women are still of the firm opinion that men should work and women keep the home. The new freedoms and opportunities of the past century have, nevertheless, made lasting impressions; and in their determination to add to these changes, today's feminists are continuing the lively political tradition which gathered pace with the cries of 'Votes for Women' and 'Deeds, not Words' during the early years of this century.

advent of 'unisex' fashions seemed to mirror the call for equality.

In the later decades of this century, changes in legislation and social policies have continued to alter aspects of women's lives. In 1975 discrimination on the grounds of sex was made unlawful in employment, education and advertising. In the same year legal protection was provided for working women who became pregnant, giving them maternity leave and pay, and the right to take up their jobs again within 29 weeks of giving birth. Social issues have continued to be tackled: Erin Pizzey's refuge for battered women, for instance, brought the problem of domestic violence to public attention. Today, 'women's issues' and the supporters of change are still a feature of British life. Women with careers are no longer a curiosity, but many still complain that they rarely reach the senior levels of most professions. Men's roles, too, have been challenged, with calls for paternity leave and shared domestic duties. There are still fewer women than men active in politics: Margaret Thatcher became Britain's first woman Prime Minister in 1979, but in 1987 there were still only 41 women in Parliament. Many present-day protests echo

1907-8

HE YEAR 1907 STARTED with an earthquake in Jamaica in January. Famines in Russia and China also threatened thousands with starvation, disasters made worse by social unrest. There were riots in India; Bulgaria was in a state of ferment following the assassination in March of the premier, Petkov; and in South Africa Gandhi started a campaign of civil disobedience over restrictions imposed on Asians by the Transvaal government.

On the positive side, a peace conference at The Hague, attended by representatives of 44 nations, proposed the setting up of an international court of justice. Britain, France and Spain formed the Triple Alliance, and, in response, the Triple Alliance between Germany, Austria and Italy was renewed. However, Britain and Germany were now more friendly, and the Kaiser was well received by cheering crowds on his State visit to London.

In Britain, a bill proposed a reduction in the power of the House of Lords, but this was not taken too seriously, least of all by the *ILN*:

> ... the English political aristocracy will probably continue to reign ... The death scene will probably continue for centuries yet ... The House of Lords will die like Sarah Bernhardt on the stage. It will die so well and so slowly that it will be called upon with thundering encores to die all over again. (26 January)

Major-General Sir Robert Baden-Powell formed the Boy Scout movement, and the first Scouts to be enrolled went camping in July on Brownsea Island. The King and Queen opened the new Central Criminal Courts at the Old Bailey, and Kipling became the first Briton to win the Nobel Prize for Literature. In France, Picasso shocked the art world with his painting *Demoiselles d'Avignon*. The Cunard liner *Lusitania* captured the Blue Riband in October, after crossing the Atlantic in four days 19 hours and 52 minutes.

HE ARMS RACE gathered momentum in 1908 as Germany launched its first Dreadnought-class battleship, the *Nassau*, and the Reichstag passed a bill to boost the German navy. However, Britain was still winning the race, with seven Dreadnoughts scheduled to be in service by the end of the year.

On the international front, a crisis in the Balkans once again threatened the stability of Europe, and in Portugal unrest came to a head in February with the assassination of the King and the Crown Prince.

In Britain, the Suffragette movement was gaining momentum. In June the largest demonstration to date attracted 200,000 to Hyde Park, and there was increasing, if grudging, support for the campaign, echoed in the pages of the *ILN*: 'The defendants' (Mrs Emmeline Pankhurst and Mrs Flora Drummond) 'conducted their case with qualities of sagacity, courage and eloquence ...' But there was less support for the methods used by the ladies: 'If, instead of a few women boxing and wrestling for the suffrage, all the women nagged for it, it would unquestionably be granted in a week.'

Also in Britain, Herbert Asquith became Liberal Prime Minister, and Old-Age pensions were introduced for the first time. The major event of the year in London was the Franco-British Exhibition, housed in the new White City, which was also the setting for the summer Olympic Games.

War hero's enduring campaign: Major-General Sir Robert Baden-Powell, hero of the defence of Mafeking, had organised a boys' camp on Brownsea Island near Poole on 25 July 1907. The 20 youngsters—a mixed bunch with varied backgrounds—were taught woodcraft, tracking, firemaking, first aid and lifesaving. Baden-Powell's aim—to encourage self-discipline, a sense of duty and good citizenship—was inspired by the army scouts he encountered while serving in Africa, India and Afghanistan. This first camp heralded the founding of the Boy Scout movement for which Baden-Powell is remembered.

THE ILLUSTRATED LONDON NEWS

1907-8

E·V·E·N·T·S

22 MARCH (1907) Gandhi began civil disobedience campaign in South Africa

3 APRIL (1907) Worst famine on record reported in Russia

11 OCTOBER (1907) Fastest-ever Atlantic crossing made by Cunard's *Lusitania*

7 MARCH (1908) The *Nassau*, Germany's first Dreadnought, launched

12 APRIL (1908) Winston Churchill included in Asquith's Cabinet

24 SEPTEMBER (1908) Old Age pensions introduced in Britain

THE FRANCO-BRITISH EXHIBITION 1908 MAY to OCTOBER

SHEPHERD'S BUSH, LONDON

A great white city: 'At Shepherd's Bush . . . the Franco-British exhibition promises to be the most splendid that London has seen. [Most] interesting is the huge Stadium . . . for the Olympic Games.' (28 March 1908)

New era in the Kaiser's navy: Germany's first Dreadnought-class battleship. 'The German Government is not disposed to listen to any proposals for the limitation of naval armaments . . . the British position will be much strengthened when Rosyth has been made a great naval base, for it is clear the German warships are not being constructed to move far from their home waters.' (12 September 1908)

A rose between two thorns: Mr Asquith ambushed: 'As the Prime Minister left Toynbee Hall . . . two suffragettes approached him, took him by the arms, and asked him whether he was going to give votes for women. Mr Asquith . . . answered laughingly that he could not discuss the matter. Eventually, the ladies were induced to release their hold.' (28 November 1908)

1909-10

POLITICALLY, 1909 WAS A YEAR OF CRISIS. War threatened again in the Balkans, with Serbia demanding the independence of Bosnia and Herzegovina from an unyielding Austria. Turkey accepted Bulgarian independence, but in Turkey itself thousands of Armenians were murdered by Muslim fanatics, and then, in April, the Sultan was finally toppled by the Young Turks.

In Europe the arms race continued; Lord Northcliffe, the proprietor of *The Times*, claimed that Germany was preparing for war with Britain. The French government fell, and Clemenceau, the French premier, resigned. In Britain, the budget introduced a supertax on anyone earning more than £5,000 a year and increased taxes on alcohol, tobacco and a range of other domestic products, partly to pay for newly-introduced Old Age pensions. This 'People's Budget' divided the country, and in the autumn the Lords rejected it. A constitutional crisis resulted, and in December the government resigned.

There were great advances in the air; in July, Blériot flew his monoplane across the Channel in 43 minutes, and the Comte de Lambert flew over the Eiffel Tower in a Wright bi-plane. According to a report in the *ILN*:

> *... no one knew he was about to undertake his magnificent flight to Paris and back ... he suddenly left the field and, heading away over the hills, disappeared into the distance, leaving an amazed and somewhat anxious crowd behind him.* (23 October)

ON 6 MAY 1910 King Edward VII died from pneumonia, and he was buried at Windsor two weeks later, with full pomp and circumstance. His son took oath as King George V on 7 May.

The January election resulted in an equal number of seats for both the Liberals and the Tories, but Asquith's Liberal government remained in power, with support from the 42 Labour and 82 Irish Nationalist MPs. However, the debate over the 1909 Budget and the Lords' veto was unresolved. Uncertainty continued throughout the year, but a second election in December again produced no clear result.

Against this background there was increasing industrial unrest, and the Suffragette debate grew more intense. It was observed in the *ILN* that:

> *The female opponents of Female Suffrage do maintain, rightly or wrongly, that there is something unwomanly about mixing in politics ... Millions of ordinary women do associate voting with a cold, coarse, arrogant kind of woman, with a necktie and a new morality. This impression may be unfair, but it is positive.* (23 April)

This was also a year of disasters. The Brussels World Exhibition was badly damaged by fire, the Hon C S Rolls was killed in the first fatal air crash in Britain, 350 miners died in a pit in Lancashire, there were floods in Paris and other parts of Europe, Mount Etna erupted, and a cholera epidemic in Russia continued unabated. Many misfortunes were blamed on Halley's Comet, which swept past the earth in May.

On top of the world: Commander Robert E Peary of the American navy reached the North Pole on his sixth attempt (on 6 April 1909) after a gruelling trek from Greenland. Peary reached the Pole accompanied by his assistant, Matthew Hensen, and four Eskimos. 'Commander Peary tells: "We arrived at 90° North at ten o'clock in the evening of April 6 and we left there about four o'clock in the afternoon of April 7 ... The silent guardian of the earth's remotest place will accept no man as a guest until he has been tried and tested by the severest ordeals".' (29 January 1910)

1909-10

E·V·E·N·T·S

6 APRIL (1909) North Pole conquered by
Commander Peary
25 JULY (1909) Blériot first to cross the Channel
in an aeroplane
7 DECEMBER (1909) Union of South Africa
proclaimed in London
10 MARCH (1910) First Hollywood film released;
Griffith's *In Old California*
6 MAY (1910) Death of Edward VII
31 JULY (1910) Dr Crippen arrested at sea for
murder

France's Louis Blériot flagged down at Dover: the first cross-Channel flight took 43 minutes—without the benefit of a compass. Blériot's bumpy landing was aided by a French journalist waving the tricolour flag. 'M Blériot is the most unlucky of flying-men, for he has had more accidents, minor and major, in his career as an aviator than all the other flying-men put together. Yet luck was with him when he flew the Channel [on 25 July].' (31 July 1909)

The guest who remained as mourner: ex-president Theodore Roosevelt of the USA attended the funeral of King Edward VII, who died on 6 May 1910. Roosevelt was '. . . a conspicuous figure, the black of his evening dress standing out in contrast to the resplendent uniforms worn by the other mourners.' (28 May 1910). Of the dead monarch: 'He found England isolated; to his supreme tact and genius for friendship it is due that he leaves her secure in the goodwill of the nations . . . Men of all shades of political opinion united to reverence him as the Peacemaker . . . Supreme in statecraft, a pioneer in all deserving works of philanthropy, he was truly, and in the noblest sense of the term, The First Gentleman in Europe.' (14 May 1910)

Killer collared: mild-mannered murderer Hawley Harvey Crippen was arrested after fleeing London with his mistress Ethel le Neve. American-born Dr Crippen had poisoned his wife Belle and buried parts of her in the cellar at their home in Hilldrop Crescent. Crippen and le Neve—disguised as a boy and posing as Crippen's son—set off for Canada aboard SS *Montrose*. The Captain, suspicious of the pair's affectionate behaviour and le Neve's disguise, radioed London. Chief Inspector Dew of Scotland Yard, who had by now found remains of Mrs Crippen, confronted the runaways on 31 July 1910. It was the first time wireless was used in a murder hunt. Crippen was hanged.

George V
1911-1936

1911

ON 23 JUNE King George V was crowned in Westminster Abbey and proclaimed 'King of the United Kingdom of Great Britain and Ireland and of the British Dominions beyond the seas, Defender of the Faith, Emperor of India'. Throughout the country there were celebrations and bonfires, and at the Crystal Palace there was a party for 100,000 children.

Royal events turned the spotlight away from the political arena, where there were changes and upheavals. Ramsay Mac-Donald took over from Keir Hardie as leader of the Labour Party, and Andrew Bonar Law replaced Balfour as leader of the Tories, but the man of the moment was Winston Churchill, who left the Home Office to become First Sea Lord. He had made his mark, and many enemies, for his forthright handling of civil unrest as Home Secretary. In January he had taken personal control of the siege of Sidney Street, leading troops and armed police in their gun battle with anarchists. Less popular was his use of troops to try to break the wave of strikes that brought the docks and the railways to a virtual standstill. In July troops opened fire in Llanelli, killing rioting strikers, and three weeks later in Liverpool riots were quelled by the police, supported by 50,000 soldiers, and with warships anchored in the Mersey.

In Parliament the House of Lords surrendered its power of veto, knowing that the King was prepared to swing the balance of power by creating new peers. A scheme for National Insurance, to cover sickness and unemployment, was introduced by the Chancellor, Lloyd George, but there were objectors—some 20,000 maids and mistresses gathered at the Albert Hall to protest at the government's plan to make householders pay contributions for their servants. MPs voted themselves a then considerable salary of £400 per annum, and in September Ulster Unionist MPs, led by Sir Edward Carson, rejected any possibility of Home Rule for Ireland.

London suffered from a summer heatwave, with temperatures reaching 97 degrees F (36 degrees C); 2,500 children were reported to have died as a result. Meanwhile, there was fierce debate in the press about the spread of the Mormon religion, which was regarded as a threat to British society, and British women in particular. G K Chesterton was gently mocking:

> There is inevitably something comic . . . about the panic aroused by the presence of the Mormons and their supposed polygamous campaign in this country. It calls up the absurd image of an enormous omnibus, packed inside with captive English ladies, with an Elder on the seat, controlling his horses with the same patriarchal gravity as his wives . . . (29 April)

Change and upheaval were also the order of the day overseas. A revolt in Morocco threatened European residents, and so the French government sent in troops to restore order. The Germans, concerned about the increasing French influence in the country, sent a gunboat to Agadir. In November a new Franco–German treaty established Morocco as a French protectorate. A rebellion in Mexico brought US troops into action in support of the government there, but the rebel army under Madero swept through the country and Díaz was deposed after 45 years as a virtual dictator. Madero became President of the new republic, but the popular heroes of the revolution were Zapata and Villa.

Duties first: 'The King acted at the outset of his reign with a simple fidelity to his plain duty that accomplished all that the highest statesmanship could have achieved.' (Silver Jubilee Record Number, 1935). George V opened his first parliament in February 1911, four months before coronation and nine months after ascending the throne.

Air mail takes off: to mark the Coronation, a Blériot monoplane set off from Hendon bound for Windsor on 9 September 1911, carrying cards and envelopes specially designed for the occasion. Unfavourable weather delayed pilot Gustave Hamel's historic flight; the Post Office's view was that 'an aeroplane is at present so dependent on the weather that it is practically useless as a means of ordinary and regular transport'. (28 October 1911)

THE ILLUSTRATED LONDON NEWS

1911

E·V·E·N·T·S

3 JANUARY Siege of Sidney Street ended as anarchists burn to death

21 JANUARY Publication of the discovery that cancer is spread by a virus

21 FEBRUARY Ramsay MacDonald elected Labour Party leader

23 JUNE George V crowned at Westminster Abbey

1 JULY Union of South Africa became a British dominion

8 AUGUST Troops called in to control rioting strikers in Liverpool

The Coronation of George V: '... the crowning jewel of the most brilliant season that London could remember ... the streets were full of decorations, the sun seemed to shine almost continuously, and trade returns soared.' (Silver Jubilee Record Number, 1935). 'A beautiful object though covered in improprieties' was how 18th-century author Horace Walpole had described the state coach, designed by Sir William Chambers and with panels (below) painted by Italian artist Cipriani

Of Britain in 1911, the *ILN* later wrote: 'It was ... a realm curiously contrasted. To a foreign traveller, viewing its more fortunate aspects, it must have seemed an almost unbelievable sanctuary of peace and hallowed tradition. Yet across that mellow sunlight, long and sinister shadows were stealing.' (Silver Jubilee Record Number 1935)

A new republic was also declared in China, when a brief civil war ended there, once the five-year-old boy-emperor had surrendered power to Dr Sun Yat-Sen. At the same time, floods in China killed thousands. Italy declared war on the Turkish troops in North Africa and attacked Tripoli and Benghazi in a rapid campaign that led to the annexation of Libya and Tripolitania. This war was notable for the first military use of aeroplanes, both for observation and bombing. In Russia the premier, Stolypin, was assassinated at the Kiev opera.

There was also unrest in the Holy Land, reported by the *ILN* in *Portraits and World's Events*:

> *If there is any spot on this earth where one would expect to find worshippers dwelling in peace and in harmony it would be at the Church of the Nativity in Bethlehem, which marks the place where Christ was born. Yet at this time of year, after Christmas, it is invariably the scene of rivalry and strife. In it worship various religious sects—Latins, Greeks, and Armenians. On account of the hatred that exists between these religious bodies the Turkish government has been forced to issue special decrees . . .* (28 January)

In Britain, the King unveiled the Victoria Memorial outside Buckingham Palace, the liner *Titanic* was launched in Belfast (with her sister ship, *Olympic*, the largest vessel afloat), and writers and musicians celebrated the new copyright law which protected their work for 50 years. In December the Norwegian explorer, Amundsen, beat Captain Scott to the South Pole—a journey of nearly 2,000 miles. Marie Curie received an unprecedented second Nobel Prize for her work on radioactivity. The Crystal Palace was bought for the nation, and thus saved from destruction. In Paris, the art world was shaken first by the theft of the *Mona Lisa* from the Louvre, and then by the display of Cubist paintings at the Salon d'Automne, while Stravinsky's *Petrushka* was the highlight of the Russian Ballet's Paris season, with Nijinsky dancing the title role. In Dresden the first performance of Strauss's *Der Rosenkavalier* was rapturously received. Gustav Mahler died in Vienna aged only 50, leaving behind nine symphonies and his famous song-symphony, *Das Lied von der Erde*. The first Indianapolis 500 motor race took place in the USA, and on Broadway the Ziegfeld Follies launched the Irving Berlin hit song, *Everybody's Doing It*.

One of the more unusual events of the year was the first meeting of the Universal Races Congress, which tried to promote the philosophy of world harmony by racial integration. G K Chesterton was more than a little scathing:

> *. . . so long as you tell everybody, red, white, black, and yellow, that they are all pretty much alike, and will soon be even more so, the effect at a congress and soirée will be soothing . . . But the more one sees of enterprises, philanthropic and other, in all parts of the earth, the more one sees that (under whatever specious names) contact is more often collision than reconciliation. The schemes for rescuing niggers are, as a rule, rather more rapacious and inhuman than the old open schemes for enslaving them . . . whenever I hear that Nicaragua must be stopped from oppressing Indians, I always have an unpleasant feeling that someone is trying to oppress Nicaragua.* (5 August)

Anarchists perished in siege of Sidney Street: more than 1,000 troops and armed police battled with anarchists holed up in an East End house after the killing of three policemen. 'Without parallel in the history of London was the scene enacted . . . last Tuesday [3 January] when two armed men, believed to have been concerned in the Houndsditch murders, were besieged for seven hours in a house in Sidney Street . . . by a large force of police and detachments of the Scots Guards, with a continuous fusillade on both sides, and, when the house at length took fire, finally perished in the ruins and the flames . . . Mr Winston Churchill, the Home Secretary, came on the scene . . . The men inside continued firing until about 1.40 when the end soon came.' (7 January 1911). Once the house ignited, Churchill forbade the fire brigade to act and two bodies were found in the ruins. A third anarchist, Peter the Painter, allegedly escaped.

THE ILLUSTRATED
LONDON NEWS

1911

E·V·E·N·T·S

22 AUGUST *Mona Lisa* stolen from the Louvre
23 OCTOBER Winston Churchill appointed
First Lord of the Admiralty
23 OCTOBER First Ford Model T produced
outside USA, in Manchester
10 DECEMBER Madame Curie awarded her
second Nobel Prize
14 DECEMBER Amundsen won the race to the
South Pole
29 DECEMBER Centuries of imperial control
ended by first Chinese republic

Race for the South Pole won: 'Captain
Amundsen said: "On December 14 (1911)
. . . we camped. There was a brilliant sun . . .
we observed the position of the Pole as
close as it is in the human power to do".'
(16 March 1912). Norway's Roald
Amundsen had beaten Scott's British
expedition by four weeks.

**Widespread riots in wake of dock and transport
strikes:** 'Affairs took a most serious turn at Liverpool on
Sunday last [8 August] when a series of ugly fights
occurred between a mob flinging bricks, bottles, pieces of
granite, and stones, and police armed with truncheons.
There were some two hundred casualties amongst
constables and civilians . . . On Tuesday night, a violent
attempt was made to rescue prisoners . . . on their way to
Walton jail in five police vans . . . Six men [of the escort]
were unhorsed. Then the order was given to fire. One
civilian was killed on the spot, and four were wounded.
One of those died later.' (19 August 1911)

1912

I N FEBRUARY King George and Queen Mary returned from India, where the King had been crowned Emperor in December 1911. They returned to a Britain in the grip of a big freeze, with temperatures as low as −35 degrees F (−37 degrees C) and many dying from cold in London. Things were made worse by widespread coal strikes, which ended after the government passed the Coal Mines Act. This established, for the first time, the principle of a minimum wage, but shortly afterwards the country was paralysed by a series of dock and transport strikes.

Meanwhile, Asquith continued his programme of political reform. The Franchise Bill introduced votes for all men at 21, and abolished all the earlier regulations concerning ownership of property. However, the Cabinet was still split on the issue of female suffrage, and the Suffragettes were becoming more violent at the lack of progress. Many demonstrations turned into window-smashing rampages and 96 were arrested during a raid on the House of Commons.

Asquith also managed to force the Irish Home Rule Bill through its second reading in the Commons, but in Ireland the Protestant response was becoming more militant. There were massive demonstrations in Ulster against the Home Rule proposals, but the climax came in September when nearly half a million Loyalists signed a pledge to fight Home Rule.

Reform was a powerful force in other countries. In Germany the Socialists won the general election, but the Kaiser refused to meet Socialist leaders; while in the USA, Roosevelt broke away from the Republicans to form a new Progressive Party. The subsequent US presidential election was won by Woodrow Wilson for the Democrats.

Stability in Europe was threatened by the situation in the Balkans once again, as Turkey came under pressure from many directions. During the war between Turkey and Bulgaria, the Turks lost 40,000 soldiers at the Battle of Lule Burgas, and, with the end of Turkish power in Europe in sight, peace talks opened. An armistice was signed in December.

Against this background of unrest, the western powers continued their arms race. The German fleet was expanding; British naval power was shifted from the Mediterranean to the North Sea; and the *Iron Duke*, the largest and most powerful battleship in the world, was launched.

On 15 April the *Titanic* was lost on her maiden voyage and more than 1,500 passengers and crew drowned. Captain Scott reached the South Pole, only to discover that Amundsen had been there before him; the Piltdown Man, the so-called 'missing link' between man and ape, was discovered in Sussex; the first issue of *Pravda* was published by the Bolsheviks in Russia; and the greatest hit in London was Irving Berlin's song *Alexander's Ragtime Band*, from the show at the Hippodrome, *Hullo Ragtime*. The *ILN* also reported good news from the Far East:

> Some months ago it was reported that Mr Staniforth Smith, the Administrator of Papua [New Guinea] had been killed and eaten by cannibals in the interior, and circumstantial details were not wanting. Fortunately, the report was not true; but it is true that the Administrator and his party had numerous arduous experiences. He is to address the Royal Geographical Society. (20 January)

Action for Home Rule: Ulster Unionist leaders 'hanged'. 'Outside the Ulster Club, Belfast, the crowd called for Sir Edward Carson and for Lord Londonderry, and both [received] warm welcome. In the district hostile to their policy and friendly to that of the Government they had, in effigy, a different fate. In one part of the Nationalist quarter, indeed, they figured as . . . dummies . . . dangling from a rope across the street. Elsewhere, the Leader of the Irish Unionist Parliamentary party was seen in effigy, marked "The King of Bluffers" . . . Many of the demonstrators . . . were mill-hands, a large proportion of whom were women.' (17 February 1912). 'Sir Edward Carson was the first to sign the Covenant in . . . Belfast on Ulster Day [28 September] . . . "to defeat the present conspiracy to set up a Home Rule Parliament in Ireland . . .".' (5 October 1912)

South Pole anguish: Captain Robert Scott reached the Pole on 12 January 1912, only to find Amundsen had beaten him. None of Scott's party survived the return journey; a search party found three bodies—including Scott—and Scott's diaries eight months later. 'The last of the greater adventures of exploration has ended in a disaster such as may always overtake those who tempt the perils of the Polar waste . . . It has proved . . . the inherent heroism of British men of action.' (15 February 1913)

Reflections on the *Titanic* tragedy: '. . . the analogy which springs to the mind [is] between the great modern ship and our great modern society that sent it forth . . . Our whole civilisation is indeed very like the *Titanic*; alike in its power and its impotence, its security and its insecurity . . . the fact remains: that there was no sort of sane proportion between the extent for the provision of luxury and levity, and the extent of the provision for need and desperation.' (27 April 1912)

1912

E · V · E · N · T · S

12 JANUARY Captain Scott reached South Pole, in wake of Amundsen

1 MARCH Window-smashing rampage in London's West End by Suffragettes

15 APRIL *Titanic* sunk on maiden voyage

28 SEPTEMBER Ulster Loyalists determined to fight Home Rule by force

1 OCTOBER Turkey invaded by Bulgaria, Serbia, Greece and Montenegro

5 NOVEMBER Democrat Woodrow Wilson elected to US Presidency

1913

I
N BRITAIN, the year was dominated by events in Ireland. The Home Rule Bill, after its stormy passage through the Commons, was rejected twice by the Lords, while in Ulster, Loyalist resistance was increasing. The Ulster Unionist MPs planned a provisional government to come into operation in the event of the Home Rule Bill becoming law, with the aim of making any Dublin-based government unworkable. The Loyalists' militant arm, the Ulster Volunteer Force, paraded 15,000 armed men near Belfast, but the Irish National Volunteers came into being in November to oppose them. At one stage British troops were landed to quell an outbreak of unrest after the shooting of a Loyalist.

The Suffragette campaign was also becoming more vociferous and militant, and gained much publicity when Emily Davison died after throwing herself under the King's horse in the Derby. Emmeline Pankhurst was sentenced to three years in prison for planting a bomb that destroyed Lloyd George's new golfing villa in Surrey. Lloyd George was also implicated in a business scandal this year, along with other senior ministers, all except one of whom were subsequently exonerated. According to G K Chesterton, writing in the *ILN*:

> *It is not the virtues of the democrat that restrain a man from . . . wrong-doing: it is not the vices of the demagogue that urge him to it . . . The plain, natural history of all political institutions is that you want a policeman to keep his eye on the traffic; but you also want somebody to keep his eye on the policeman.* (18 January)

On the international stage, Turkey's dispute with the Balkans remained in the spotlight. A coup by the Young Turks deposed the Turkish government and the Grand Vizier, and threatened to sabotage peace talks that were being held in London. The Turks attacked the Bulgarians and were then heavily defeated, Serbian troops slaughtered Muslims, and the Montenegrins captured Scutari after a six-month siege. The Turks fought back, but the final blow was the Balkan armies' capture of Adrianople. Despite these battles, a treaty was finally agreed and signed by all parties in London in May. However, the peace did not last long, for the removal of Ottoman control exposed national jealousies that quickly tore apart the Balkan League; Balkan affairs continued to overshadow events in the rest of the world.

Technological progress was made when President Wilson opened the Panama Canal, connecting the Atlantic and Pacific, by remote control, detonating the final charge by pressing a button on his desk in the White House. In New York the Grand Central station was opened, and a couple were arrested for kissing in the street; in Germany the Kaiser banned soldiers and sailors from dancing the tango; and in Paris the première of Stravinsky's *The Rite of Spring* caused a riot.

An Anglo–Turkish treaty gave Britain the sole right to oil exploration in Arabia, Mesopotamia and Syria—guaranteeing British supplies of crude oil for the foreseeable future—but on the whole it was not a good year for Britain. Captain Scott was found dead in Antarctica, with the other members of his party. More than 400 miners died in a pit fire in the Aber Valley, and a report stated that half a million children in Britain were ill-fed and diseased.

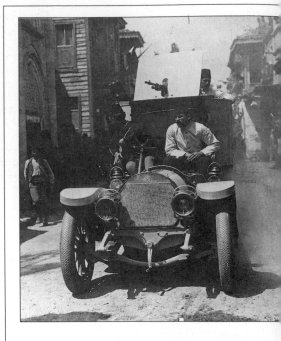

So much for a penny: launched on 3 May 1913, *Woman's Own* was a weekly paper that survived five years, offering hints, recipes and dress tips. It had its foundations in two series of publications—the *Jeannie Maitland Stories* and *Horner's Pansy Stories* which were incorporated in 1907 and underwent various name changes until *Woman's Own* was created. The modern-day publication of the same name was started in 1932 and has no connection.

Turmoil in Turkey: negotiations to end the war in the Balkans were threatened in January 1913 when the reformist and strongly nationalist Young Turks revolted and deposed the government in a *coup d'état* and put their leader, Enver Pasha, in power. They had refused to accept the terms set by the London peace talks, whereby Turkey would hand over the fortress of Adrianople to Bulgaria. The Young Turks movement had been growing and strengthening since the turn of the century, gaining many adherents in the army. In 1908 they forced the restoration of the 1876 Constitution, which had been dismissed by the despotic Sultan. Pictured (left) are Young Turks patrolling in an armoured car in 1909.

THE ILLUSTRATED
London News

1913

Death at the Derby: 'The Derby of Wednesday, June 4, will be remembered for a long time for two sensations—for the disqualification of Craigenour and, much more, for the unprecedented accident at Tattenham Corner . . . when a woman rushed onto the course and caused . . . the King's horse . . . to fall.' (7 June 1913). 'Even those of us who most denounce militancy can hardly deny that (unlike most of the Suffragette outrages) the act committed by the late Miss Emily Davison . . . required courage and self-sacrifice, though accompanied by a lack of consideration for the jockey.' (14 June 1913)

The parting of the shores: 'Although the Panama Canal will not be open for navigation by large vessels for some months, as the channel is not yet deep enough throughout . . . yet the blowing up of the Gamboa Dyke [10 October] removed the last obstruction to the navigation of most of the Canal by small vessels. The dynamite was exploded by an electric current set in motion by President Wilson at Washington, 4000 miles away.' (1 November 1913). The Canal, connecting the Atlantic and Pacific Oceans, was made available for commercial shipping from 3 August 1914. In 1903 the USA had signed a treaty with Panama which gave the US rights in perpetuity over a strip of the isthmus in order to build and run the Canal. Seventy-five years later agreement was reached to turn over the waterway to Panama by the year 2000.

E · V · E · N · T · S

31 JANUARY Irish Home Rule Bill rejected by Lords
17 FEBRUARY Modern and abstract art introduced in the USA at Armory Show
14 APRIL Typhus vaccine discovered
30 MAY Peace declared between Turkey and the Balkan League, in London
1 JULY War declared on Bulgaria by Greece and Serbia
10 OCTOBER Panama Canal effectively opened by blowing up of Gamboa Dyke

1914

FOR THE FIRST HALF OF THE YEAR events in Ireland dominated the news. With the government still committed to its Home Rule Bill, there were increasing fears of civil war breaking out in Ulster. The Bill passed its third reading in the Commons in May, after the rejection of a Scottish Home Rule Bill earlier in the month. Meanwhile, the Ulster Volunteer Force had been gaining strength and claimed to have 110,000 armed men ready to fight. Stocks of ammunition were being imported. Things came to a head in the summer when the Third Battle Squadron was anchored off Belfast; however, many army officers preferred to resign than be posted to Ulster. Faced by the threat of bloodshed, the government prepared to concede that Ulster could be excluded from the Home Rule Bill, and the King summoned all parties to a conference at Buckingham Palace and outraged liberal opinion by appearing to side with the Loyalists. In the event, developments elsewhere in Europe took the heat out of the situation, and the Bill was abandoned on 30 July.

Suffragette outrages became more frequent. Mary Richardson slashed the *Rokeby Venus* at the National Gallery, and was sentenced to six months' imprisonment. Attacks on the British Museum and the Royal Academy followed, and a bomb destroyed Yarmouth pier. Wargrave Church was burnt down; and 57 protesters were arrested during a raid on Buckingham Palace on 22 May, when an attempt was made at presenting a petition to the King. Mrs Pankhurst was arrested for the eighth time. There was also widespread industrial unrest, with miners, builders and electricians on strike. Even cricket-ball makers in Kent struck for better conditions. In South Africa, a general strike met with a severe response when General Botha ordered that union leaders should be arrested and secretly deported, following the declaration of martial law.

Prompt action defused a tense situation in Mexico, when American marines landed and seized the port of Veracruz to stop German arms reaching General Huerta in his fight against rebels. Despite their dislike of Huerta, the Americans supported a treaty signed in July that left him as President.

On the positive side, George V's visit to Paris in April was a popular success. The British government agreed to buy a large share in the Anglo-Persian Oil Company, laying the foundations for what was to become British Petroleum; and Ford introduced profit-sharing and the eight-hour day. George Bernard Shaw's new play *Pygmalion*, first performed in April, was a great hit, with Mrs Patrick Campbell as Eliza and Sir Herbert Tree as Professor Higgins.

In the second half of the year, everything was overshadowed by the events leading up to the outbreak of the First World War. The stage was set in the Balkans, where the continual pattern of unrest was maintained by a civil war in Albania; but it was the assassination on 28 June of the Archduke Franz Ferdinand, the heir to the Hapsburg Empire, and his wife by Gavrilo Princip in Sarajevo, the capital city of Bosnia, that lit the fuse. The Serbians seemed to be implicated in the plot, and in Austria feelings ran high, resulting in the severance of diplomatic relations between the two countries. Germany affirmed its alliance with Austria, Serbia mobilised, and then Austria invaded Serbia. Russia also mobilised; and on 1 August the Kaiser declared war on his cousin, the Tsar. From this point events moved so fast that international diplomacy was left powerless.

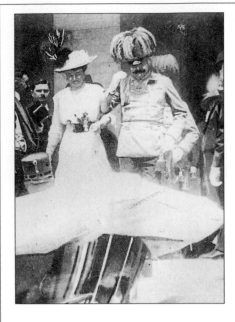

Unguarded moments spell disaster: Archduke Franz Ferdinand of Austria and his wife, the Duchess of Hohenberg, (pictured above) leaving the town hall at Sarajevo in Bosnia, after a reception. On the way, they had survived an assassination attempt, and the Archduke interrupted speeches at the town hall to say: 'You have received me with bombs! It is shocking.' Certain that another assassination bid would not be made the same day, the authorities provided no extra guards for the royal couple. Shortly after they left, two fatal shots were fired by Gavrilo Princip, sparking war in Europe.

Looking for a fight: early in 1914 the threat of civil war loomed large in Ulster. 'Nearly two thousand men of . . . the Tyrone Regiment of the Ulster Volunteer Force, with one hundred transport waggons, took part in field manoeuvres on a large scale held recently in Dungannon Park [in Dungannon, Co. Tyrone] . . . the total strength of the Ulster Volunteer Force is near 110,000 . . .' (7 March 1914). War in Europe was to overtake these events.

Palace protest: 'A woman must be very tired to think of tying herself to a man's railings: but the man must be even more tired if he is really irritated at her doing so. Why should she do it, and why should he forbid it? If the Suffragette wants to be thus physically attached to the household of the politician, why not indulge the harmless tenderness? . . . Nine times out of ten the Suffragists have forgotten why they wanted the Vote . . . and the Anti-Suffragists have forgotten why they didn't want it.' (13 June 1914)

THE ILLUSTRATED LONDON NEWS

1914

E·V·E·N·T·S

12 APRIL Bernard Shaw's *Pygmalion* had a triumphant opening

15 JANUARY Warnings of threatened civil war in Ulster over Home Rule

21 APRIL US marines seized the Mexican port of Veracruz

22 MAY 57 arrested after 'Votes for Women' protest at Buckingham Palace

28 JUNE Heir to Austro-Hungarian Empire assassinated in Sarajevo

1 AUGUST German declaration of war on Russia

Join the brave throng that goes marching along

"YOUR COUNTRY NEEDS YOU"

Taking the King's Shilling: recruits, (pictured left), receiving their pay at HQ in Trafalgar Square. 'It is the new German complaint that they are "hirelings". It was the old English boast that they were volunteers. It would be easy to frame taunts either way—against the English adventurers who are free to serve for pay, or against the German slaves who would be forced to serve without pay. Still, it would be equally false to describe the professional army as fighting merely for money, as to describe the conscript army as fighting merely from fear . . . nobody can understand how we feel about our "hirelings" who does not know . . . about the stages of our development . . .' (7 November 1914)

The German declaration of war on France was followed by the German invasion of Belgium, and on 4 August Britain declared war on Germany to protect Belgian neutrality under the terms of the 1839 Treaty of London. By 17 August the British Expeditionary Force had been landed in France, fully supported by an enthusiastic public, who believed that the Germans would be quickly 'put in their place'. The *ILN* reported patriotically:

> *None of us has any doubt that, wherever this expeditionary force of ours has to fight it will, as usual, give a very good account of itself, to say the least: but on the other hand, it is by no means so clear to what extent the Kaiser himself will prove of corresponding value to his own army ... with the withdrawal of the German Army to the right bank of the Rhine ... the Kaiser will doubtless return to his watch-tower, or lofty platform of observation at Berlin, to moralise, among other things, on the infernal predicament of the man who, through his own suicidal madness, at last finds himself between the Devil and the Deep Blue Sea.* (22 August)

Events proved this spirit of optimism to be woefully misplaced. The German armies swept through Belgium and into France, drove the British and French into retreat from Mons, stopped the Russian advance and defeated them thoroughly at the Battle of Tannenburg, and captured Brussels, Ghent, Lille and Rheims. Their advance in the West took them to the Marne, where, in September, the French armies finally stopped them and saved Paris. At this point the German armies dug in, and, after the British had secured Ypres, a line of trenches and barbed wire reached from the Swiss border to the Channel. It was stalemate and, although no one knew it at the time, the pattern was set for the next four years. At sea, the Royal Navy was more successful, despite losing ships to both mines and submarines. The German navy was defeated at Heligoland and at the Falklands; the promised British domination of the seas was becoming a reality.

The global nature of the conflict was now becoming clear. Turkey mobilised and attacked Russia, and the British and French shelled the Dardanelles. The Italians were beginning to rethink their neutrality, and the Japanese joined the Allied cause. In Africa, the colonial war was running strongly in Britain's favour, and Australia showed her potential by sinking the German cruiser *Emden*. At home, it was now accepted that the war was going to be long and expensive in terms of both lives and money. British casualties at Ypres totalled 100,000, and the war was costing £1,000,000 a day. The government decided to double income tax, and Lord Kitchener redoubled his efforts to encourage men to enlist, using both pay and patriotism as inducements. Yet a general mood of optimism still prevailed; the collapse of Germany was expected daily, by the *ILN*'s correspondents and the British public:

> *That these designs, based on diabolic intrigue, are begotten of downright desperation can scarcely be doubted when we consider the general course of the war, which has so far been so shattering to German aims and hopes, as well on the Vistula as on the Yser. In the east the Germans have been retreating, in the west they have not been progressing, while the rebellion of their fomenting in South Africa has fizzled out. Altogether, their affairs are decidedly unprosperous ...* (7 November)

THE ILLUSTRATED LONDON NEWS

1914

E · V · E · N · T · S

4 AUGUST British declaration of war after
German invasion of Belgium
23 AUGUST British retreat from Mons
14 SEPTEMBER German armies stopped by the
French at the Marne
17 NOVEMBER Announcement that income tax
was to be doubled in UK to finance war
29 NOVEMBER Former President Roosevelt
criticised US neutrality policy
16 DECEMBER North-east coastal towns shelled
by German warships

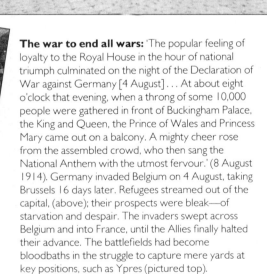

The war to end all wars: 'The popular feeling of loyalty to the Royal House in the hour of national triumph culminated on the night of the Declaration of War against Germany [4 August] . . . At about eight o'clock that evening, when a throng of some 10,000 people were gathered in front of Buckingham Palace, the King and Queen, the Prince of Wales and Princess Mary came out on a balcony. A mighty cheer rose from the assembled crowd, who then sang the National Anthem with the utmost fervour.' (8 August 1914). Germany invaded Belgium on 4 August, taking Brussels 16 days later. Refugees streamed out of the capital, (above); their prospects were bleak—of starvation and despair. The invaders swept across Belgium and into France, until the Allies finally halted their advance. The battlefields had become bloodbaths in the struggle to capture mere yards at key positions, such as Ypres (pictured top).

'It is just about three months since the war began, and Germany, the prime mover of that war, is no nearer her object than ever . . . How long the present war is likely to last can only be a matter of conjecture, but the best judges—including . . . Lord Kitchener—are inclined to think that its duration [will] not be less, at least, than that of the South African War, which went on for two and a half years.' (1 November 1914). Destruction wrought by German bombardments was immense; guns mounted on barges, like the one pictured (above, left) were used in the Belgian campaign by the Germans. In France, the town of Arras was dubbed 'a Pompeii made by German shells . . . Nothing could save it from fierce bombardments: not the historic Hôtel de Ville . . . not its handsome cathedral . . . not its museum with its rare paintings . . .' (14 November 1914). Left, the ruined Rue St. Géry, in Arras.

1915

I N ITS SECOND YEAR, the war in Europe was both consolidated and expanded, and all hopes of a speedy return to peace perished in the stalemate of the trenches. The British capture of Neuve-Chapelle aroused great enthusiasm in the *ILN*:

> *Neuve Chapelle has conclusively proved that our British soldiers are not a whit worse, but rather better, than they were at Badajoz and Albuera, Seringapatam, Sebastopol and Delhi, though the proof cost us a casualty-list of some 13,000 officers and men, or considerably more than a half of Wellington's purely British force at Waterloo.* (24 April)

However, the main offensives of the year, launched in the spring by the British at Ypres and Loos, and by the French from the Meuse to the Moselle and at Champagne, gained little ground at enormous cost. On the Eastern Front the war was more mobile, with the Russians at first gaining ground against both Germany and Turkey, and then being driven back. As the Russians retreated, Warsaw and then Brest-Litovsk fell, and the Tsar took personal command of his armies. In order to relieve pressure on the Russians, the Allies tried to open a second front against the Turks at Gallipoli and a large force of British, Anzac and French troops was landed as the Royal Navy tried to force the passage of the Dardanelles. Turkish resistance and disease combined to doom the campaign. The Allies withdrew, moving many of their forces to Salonika to try to defend Serbia from attack by Bulgarian, German and Austrian forces. At the end of the year Joffre took over command of the French forces, and Haig replaced French as the British Commander-in-Chief.

The war at sea was more in Britain's favour, despite the sinking of HMS *Formidable* by a submarine in January. At an engagement off the Dogger Bank in the same month, the Royal Navy sank the *Blucher*, Germany's most powerful battle-cruiser, and brought to an end German naval raids on east coast ports. More significant was the German announcement of a submarine blockade of Britain, with merchant vessels now the target. The first ships were sunk in February, and from then on the number of victims increased steadily.

In May, the *Lusitania* was sunk without warning off the Irish coast by a German submarine, with 128 American citizens among the 1,400 who died. Civilians were also drawn into the war by the start of the Zeppelin bombing campaign. The threat posed by this new style of warfare was quickly understood by the *ILN*'s correspondent:

> *The moral to be drawn . . . is that, if a Zeppelin can reach Lowestoft, it can also reach London, and that consequently we must be prepared to give a warm reception to these aerial visitants.* (24 April)

The first Zeppelin raid on Britain took place in January, but it was not until June that the first Zeppelin was destroyed in the air by a British aeroplane. Another new style of warfare was tear gas, first used by the Germans against Russia, and then on the Western Front in April. The global scale of the conflict widened when Italy abandoned its pre-war alliance with Germany and Austria and joined the Allies. The Austrians promptly bombed Venice.

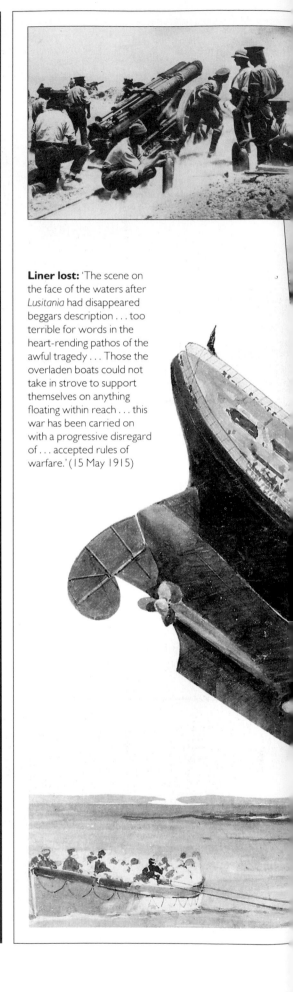

Liner lost: 'The scene on the face of the waters after *Lusitania* had disappeared beggars description . . . too terrible for words in the heart-rending pathos of the awful tragedy . . . Those the overladen boats could not take in strove to support themselves on anything floating within reach . . . this war has been carried on with a progressive disregard of . . . accepted rules of warfare.' (15 May 1915)

Balkan battles: 'Better news from the Dardanelles . . . "the general attack . . . was resumed [26 April] . . . disembarkation began before sunrise at various points on the Gallipoli peninsula and . . . was completely successful".' (1 May 1915). The British offensive was aided in no small way by heavy guns like *Annie*, left. Below, Allied landings at Anzac Cove. 'Our oversea [sic] "sons of the Empire" from the Southern Cross continue to fight with superb bravery and enthusiasm . . .' (5 June 1915)

1915

E·V·E·N·T·S

Labour's loss: James Keir Hardie (below), died on 26 September 1915. Founder of the Independent Labour Party in 1893 (which eventually jointly formed the British Labour Party in 1900 with the trade unions and the Fabian Society), Hardie was known as a champion of the unemployed.

19 JANUARY First Zeppelin bombing raids on Britain
2 FEBRUARY Submarine blockade of Britain launched by Germany
18 MARCH British government appealed to women to sign on for war work
22 APRIL First British offensive at Ypres, and first German gas attacks
26 APRIL Allied landings at Gallipoli
7 MAY *Lusitania* sunk by German submarine; 1,400 drowned, including 128 Americans

Early in the year a combined German and Turkish force attacked the Suez Canal from the Syrian side, and was roundly defeated by the defending British and Indian soldiers:

> . . . the baffled remnant of the Ottoman rabble-force of 12,000 which is said to have reached the Canal . . . turned tail and went rolling back to Syria as fast as ever it could. It was one of the maddest of military enterprises ever attempted, and will probably never be renewed . . . It also furnished welcome food for merriment to our invincible men in Flanders, who are likewise weltering about in a world of ditch-water and canals which the Germans find equally impossible to cross . . . (13 February)

At home, Churchill was dropped from the War Cabinet following the Gallipoli disaster, and resigned from the government in November. Income tax was increased by 40 per cent. Duty on tea and tobacco was also raised to help pay for the war, which was now costing more than £3,000,000 per day. The government launched an anti-drinking campaign, to improve industrial output, and the King took a lead by giving up alcohol for the duration of the war. At the same time, an army of women workers was taking over many factories, and proving to be more successful than men in terms of production.

The Stock Exchange reopened in January, but Wimbledon was cancelled, along with the Football League programme and the Olympic Games, planned to take place in Berlin. Race meetings continued, however; the Derby was held at Newmarket in June, as the Epsom course had been requisitioned by the Army.

Considerable interest was shown in the behaviour of birds on the Western Front, with reports from soldiers of thrushes building nests and hatching their eggs right beside 18-pounder guns. Another report, published in the *ILN*, commented:

> Birds at night serve as the guardians of our soldiers in the trenches when threatened by the approach of poison-gas fumes, for before the fumes can be perceived in the trenches the sleeping men are awakened to their danger by the rustle of the wings and low cries of the birds which have gone to roost in the zone between our lines and those of our unscrupulous foes. (16 October)

Rupert Brooke died on his way to the Dardanelles, and in Belgium, Edith Cavell was shot as a spy. Britain's worst ever rail disaster took place in May at Quintinshill, near Gretna Green, with 227 fatalities. In the USA the scenes in D W Griffith's epic film *Birth of a Nation*, portraying the Ku Klux Klan, caused an outrage when it opened in New York, but at the same time the Klan was officially recognised in Georgia.

An anti-German campaign was being waged in the British press, and the *ILN*'s correspondents readily took part:

> In all Germany's public actions we see the fatal inability to weigh facts which is the dominant attribute of the German mind. (24 April)

> The legend of the natural military mastery belonging to the Teuton has already received its death-blow . . . It is of less importance at this moment than the theory that the earth is flat. (7 August)

FLIGHT SUB-LIEUT. R. A. J. WARNEFORD, V. C.

Daring deed: naval pilot Reginald Warneford was awarded the VC after he destroyed a Zeppelin over Ghent, on 7 June 1915. 'It was the gasbag [of the Zeppelin] and not the car which should have been armour-plated, for its contents were a good deal more explosive than the cartridges, shells and bombs stored in the gondolas, and the . . . English were not long in finding this out.' (16 October 1915)

THE ILLUSTRATED LONDON NEWS

1915

E · V · E · N · T · S

26 SEPTEMBER Allied offensives in Flanders and Champagne started

12 OCTOBER Edith Cavell executed by German firing squad

23 OCTOBER Death of the legendary cricketer W G Grace

11 NOVEMBER Churchill left government after exclusion from War Cabinet

20 DECEMBER Gallipoli campaign abandoned by Allies in face of Turkish resistance

If I should die, think only this of me:
That there's some corner
of a foreign field
That is forever England.
Rupert Brooke

War poet's passion: the carnage of the Great War, 'the war to end all wars', was to prove beyond all expectation, largely due to out-of-date techniques of trench warfare combined with new, even deadlier, means of mass extermination, such as poison gas and aerial bombardment. The result was the slaughter of a whole generation of young men, with 10 million lives lost world-wide. In Britain, three-quarters of a million soldiers were to die in the mud of the Western Front, together with more than 200,000 soldiers from the Empire. Casualties on the French and German sides were equally appalling, as the picture (above) of a German trench after it was captured by the French testifies. The horrors of trench warfare were inspiration for Wilfred Owen, killed in action a week before the Armistice, and for Rupert Brooke (above), whose tragic death on 23 April 1915 made him the romantic hero of a generation.

1916

NO LONGER ABLE TO RELY ON BRITISH CIVILIANS to volunteer for military service in sufficient numbers, the government introduced conscription at the beginning of the year. There was much debate about the new law:

The difference between Conscription and Voluntaryism is comparatively a matter of form for us, who are unquestionably . . . fighting because we want to. The difference is a matter of vivid and vital fact to the Irish, who have so often been made to do things when they did not want to. The Irishman must be a volunteer, not in order to show he is not a mutineer, but in order to show that he is not merely a pressed man. Unless the Irish come in freely, we shall not be able to say they came in at all. (22 January)

The exclusion of Ireland from conscription was seen by the government as a sop to the supporters of Home Rule, but it was not enough. Over Easter an armed uprising in Dublin led to the proclamation of an Irish republic. The British acted quickly and firmly with the Royal Navy shelling rebel-held buildings and the Army moving in to restore order. The rebel leaders were executed, but a more unexpected feature of the rebellion was the involvement of the British diplomat, Sir Roger Casement, later hanged for treason.

On the Western Front the stalemate continued. In February the Germans launched their offensive against Verdun, but the French held firm and in the autumn roles were reversed, with a French offensive forcing the Germans to retreat. In July the British launched their offensive on the Somme, but the grand plan to destroy the German lines soon became bogged down in mud and barbed wire. Even the introduction of the first tanks in September had little impact. The carnage was fearful, with the battles of Verdun and the Somme costing nearly 2 million lives.

Apart from the normal horrors of trench life, French and British soldiers now had to cope with a new threat:

Rats infest the trenches to such an extent that the military authorities have had to adopt special measures to deal with them. The French army has appointed rat-catchers, who pursue the ubiquitous rodent with dogs . . . In the British trenches too, ratting has become quite a popular and very necessary sport . . . (8 April)

Elsewhere there was greater mobility. In the East the Russian offensives swept through the Turkish lines and then broke the Austrian lines at Sokal, where 200,000 prisoners were taken. There was a Turkish rout at Erzinjan in July, and then the German lines in Galicia were broken. The Romanians joined in, and attacked the Germans and Austrians. Austria struck back against Italy in the Tyrol. The conflict grew; Germany declared war on Portugal and the Allies occupied Athens. In the Balkans the British and French forced the Bulgarians to retreat. In Africa, Cameroon fell to a combined French and Belgian force, while in Kenya the Germans were driven back by General Smuts, the newly appointed commander of British and South African troops in East Africa. By the end of the year the Allies controlled 75 per cent of German East Africa.

Count me out: a conscientious objector makes his feelings plain. 'There was a significant absence of excitement in the House of Commons when the Bill involving . . . the compulsory principle of military service came on for reading . . . The calm atmosphere . . . reflected the resolute spirit of the nation to carry the war to a successful conclusion.' (29 January 1916)

6 JANUARY House of Commons voted in
favour of conscription in Britain
21 FEBRUARY German offensive launched at
Verdun, checked by French
25 APRIL Easter Rising in Dublin
21 MAY British Summer Time introduced
27 MAY Call for a 'League of Nations' by
President Wilson of the USA
31 MAY Battle of Jutland; heavy losses by
British and German navies

Somme campaign opens: gas helmets (above) were only a small part of the British Tommy's 70lb kit borne in the battlefield. 'The news that the long-looked-for offensive by the Allies in the West had begun [3 July] was received with enthusiasm both in this country and in France, although both nations realise that the time has not yet come for flag-flying and celebrations of victory . . . The forward movement was rather hailed as an auspicious beginning of what is likely to prove a long and costly operation, but at the same time as an event which might be regarded as the turning-point of the war.' (8 July 1916). The offensive saw the biggest-ever British Army in battle.

An epic of self-sacrifice: 'It is no exaggeration to say that the official films of the great Battle of the Somme, which the War Office . . . caused to be taken are the most wonderful that have ever been thrown upon a screen . . . Particularly thrilling is the sight of our men leaping over the trench-parapet . . . and moving forward to attack the German trenches.' (26 August 1916). 'The . . . illustrations [above] show British shells of a kind we are using in big guns of much the same class as the French Titans . . . We see an artillery dump in rear of the battery lines . . . A shell is shown quite close, its size being suggested by the size of the NCO lying down beside it. The message chalked on [it] is scored by way of jest, after a time-honoured usage among gunners.' (26 August 1916)

In the Middle East the Arabs, encouraged by the British, rose against the Turks and started a campaign that launched the reputation of T E Lawrence—Lawrence of Arabia. The British and the Russians formed an alliance with the Shah of Persia. German imperialist ambitions were, in effect, in tatters, a point not missed by *ILN* correspondents at the time:

> *. . . what she coveted was the rest of the earth, that she might satisfy, not the material needs of her people, but their inordinate vanity . . . Germany, in the near future, may advance arguments . . . to show her need of 'territory' beyond the boundaries of Europe. But she must be treated as the 'rogue elephant' among the nations . . . Germany will either rule us or we must rule her.* (12 August)

At sea, the greatest naval confrontation of all time took place near Jutland in May. There was no outright winner, but the German Hochseeflotte never ventured forth again from the security of its bases. There were changes at the top with von Hindenburg taking over as the German Chief of General Staff in August, while at home Lloyd George had become Secretary for War in July after Lord Kitchener's death in the sinking of HMS *Hampshire*. At the end of the year Lloyd George became Prime Minister, having conspired with the Tory leader Andrew Bonar Law to oust Asquith. In November, Emperor Franz Josef died in Austria, and in the USA Woodrow Wilson just held on to power in the presidential election.

The impact of the war was becoming more apparent daily. In Britain there were government appeals for economy in staff, in private transport and in women's dress. Income tax was raised again and the war loan now totalled £2,382,000,000. Daylight Saving Time (British Summer Time) was introduced, with the clocks going forward one hour on 21 May. More than 3 million women were now employed outside the home. The British Museum and the Natural History Museum were closed for the duration of the war. In France taxes on milk, sugar and coffee were introduced, while in Germany there was food rationing and the shortages provoked riots in Berlin. The other side of the coin was seen in the USA in September, when John D Rockefeller became the first billionaire, thanks to the stock market boom directly encouraged by the war in Europe. At the same time, the USA was increasingly supporting the Allied cause, with President Wilson demanding that Germany should scale down submarine warfare and saying that the USA was prepared to fight for a 'just cause'. There was certainly American sympathy for the widespread European revulsion against German militarism which, in its most extreme Prussian form, was described in damning terms by the *ILN*:

> *Destruction is their only originality. Their notion of progress and invention is to kill something that nobody else has killed, or to burn something that nobody has ever burned before. To fight outside the ropes, to hit below the belt, to disregard a boundary or break an understanding—this is the spiritual essence of that elusive yet real element which their philosophers call German Freedom . . . The Prussian is forced to keep up an incessant excitement of these destructive novelties. He is obliged to do wilder and wilder things to prove that he is a devil of a fellow, lest the world should find out what a poor devil he is.* (12 August)

German version: scenes published in the *ILN* on 11 June 1927, taken from a German film of the events of 1915, *Der Weltkrieg*. Naval scenes of the Battle of Jutland (above), show a battleship gradually overturning and the survivors swimming away. The interior of a German U-Boat is pictured (right), described as 'The Menace' to Allied shipping of the time. 'The losses [of the Battle of Jutland, which took place on 31 May 1916] were severe on both sides, but . . . the Grand Fleet pursued the fleeing enemy until light had wholly failed . . . It need not be pointed out, in connection with Germany's claim to victory, that a victorious fleet does not leave the sea in possession of the enemy, which is precisely what the Hochseeflotte did when it retreated in face of the Grand Fleet . . . What can compare with the triumph of sea power?' (10 June 1916)

1916

E·V·E·N·T·S

6 JUNE Lord Kitchener, Britain's War Secretary, drowned on HMS *Hampshire*

21 JUNE Arab rising against the Turks started

3 JULY Somme offensive launched

6 JULY David Lloyd George appointed War Secretary, in succession to Kitchener

3 AUGUST Sir Roger Casement executed for high treason

15 SEPTEMBER Tanks first used in battle, on the Somme

28 SEPTEMBER John D Rockefeller became the world's first billionaire

7 DECEMBER David Lloyd George took over as British Prime Minister

Flocking to a spectacle: the first Zeppelin to crash on Britain, at Potters Bar, 23 September 1916. 'As a military weapon she is useless, unless she takes the enemy so entirely by surprise he cannot get up guns to compel her to keep at a respectful distance above the earth. She will always be at the mercy of the daring aviator . . . anything which pierces her very sensitive envelope can be trusted to release enough hydrogen to catch fire from the next flame with which it comes in contact; and thus to bring her to grief with terrible speed and no chance of rescue.' (14 October 1916)

Nobles' revenge: Grigori Rasputin, the notorious 'holy man' of the court of Tsar Nicholas II, was murdered by a group of Russian noblemen on 30 December 1916. Rasputin (above, centre), a semi-literate peasant whose doctrine combined religious fervour and sexual indulgence, held the Tsar and Tsaritsa in his thrall. His harmful influence in affairs of state grew until the nobles acted; they poisoned him, shot him and threw him in the freezing Neva river.

1917

URING THIS YEAR it was the world rather than the European stage that began to determine the course of the war. In Russia, against a background of mounting civil and military unrest, the Tsar finally yielded to pressure and abdicated. A provisional government under Kerensky was established, pledged to continue the war. The Tsar's assets were seized and the royal family was sent in exile to Siberia. Lenin returned from exile to meet Stalin and Trotsky, and in July a Bolshevik uprising was crushed by Kerensky's government. Lenin fled again and the war in the East continued, much to the relief of the Allies. The final straw came in September when the demoralised Russian army was heavily defeated at Riga, opening the way for the Germans to the Russian capital, Petrograd. Early in November a second Bolshevik uprising was more successful. Petrograd fell with the storming of the Winter Palace and Kerensky was ousted. A republic was declared and a truce was agreed with Germany and Austria, followed by the opening of peace talks.

Reaction in the West was mixed, with the British government taking a firm line and refusing to have any communication with the Bolshevik government. The impact on the war in western Europe was bound to be considerable, because all the German troops in the East could now be moved westwards. However, no one doubted that the war had to go on, not least the *ILN*:

> *It may be a good thing that Russia has achieved liberty, or a bad thing that she has achieved anarchy: but neither can have any conceivable effect on the plain fact that Prussia has never achieved anything but tyranny, that we set out with the avowed object of breaking that tyranny, and that it remains unbroken.* (1 September)

The balance of power had, in any case, been restored in the Allies' favour by the USA's declaration of war on Germany in April, an event provoked largely by German submarines continuing to sink American ships. President Wilson had broken diplomatic relations with Germany after the sinking of the *Housatonic* off Sicily, and Germany had responded by intensifying her submarine campaign. The Germans also began to attack hospital ships, and took as hostages all US citizens in Germany. The final act of provocation came in February with the Zimmerman telegram, in which the Germans asked Mexico to declare war on the USA. The USA seized the 91 German ships in New York harbour and began to arm its merchant fleet, and the first shots were fired on 19 April when an American ship, the *Mongolia*, sank a German submarine. In May, Congress passed the Selective Service Act, which drafted all men aged between 21 and 30, and 10 million were soon enrolled. The first troop ships arrived in France in June, and in October American soldiers went into action, with a background of broad public support:

> *Nobody expected England to have a conscript army or America to wage a European war. But the moral ground on which America came in at the end was of exactly the same sort as the moral ground on which England came in at the beginning. It was that Germany does intolerably treacherous and cruel things: and the things have become more treacherous and more cruel.* (1 September)

Change by the sword: a band of Cossacks taking part in a demonstration in Petrograd in 1917, holding placards bearing the words *Down with the Monarchy*. Inset, Tsar Nicholas II who abdicated on 16 March 1917; a provisional government was set up by the revolutionaries to replace him. 'In his dignified manifesto announcing his abdication, the Emperor Nicholas said: "The destinies of Russia . . . demand that the war should be conducted at all costs to a victorious end . . . It is for the good of the country that we shall abdicate the Crown . . . and lay down the Supreme Power . . .".' (24 March 1917). 'A message was sent . . . by the King [George V], who said: "I recognise all that Russia is now called upon to bear, but I have faith in her . . .".' (18 August 1917)

Sentry duty here is far from unpleasant.

Hi there: greeting the troops.

1917

E · V · E · N · T · S

1 FEBRUARY German submarine war
intensified, US ships armed
16 MARCH Tsar of Russia abdicated
6 APRIL War declared on Germany by the USA
16 APRIL Lenin returned to Russia from exile in
Zürich
1 JUNE Convoy system introduced as defence
against U-Boats
13 JUNE First bombing raid on London by
German aircraft

Primed for revolution:
Bolshevik soldiers and students
pictured (above) firing in the Nevski
Prospekt, Petrograd, in a battle
between Lenin's Bolsheviks and
Kerensky's followers. The sudden
coup known as the November
Uprising overthrew the provisional
government and led to the rise to
power of Lenin and Trotsky. 'Lenin
and his party have . . . succeeded in
getting the upper hand, though
perhaps only for a time. It was
reported recently that emissaries
from Lenin had opened negotiations
for an armistice with the Germans.'
(8 December 1917).
Joseph Stalin (right), became a
member of the Politburo under
Lenin.

Ready response:
'Preparedness for
war has been a
watchword in the
United States for a
considerable time
past . . . President
Wilson said that a
declaration that the
United States was in a
state of war with
Germany would
involve . . . "the
immediate addition
to the armed forces
. . . of at least 500,000
men who should . . .
be chosen upon the
principle of universal
liability to service; and
also the authorisation
of . . . increments of
equal force, so soon
as they might be
needed and could be
handled in training".'
(14 April 1917)

There was limited movement on the Western Front during the year. The Allies mounted the Arras offensive in April and this was followed by a much larger attack against the Hindenburg line in Flanders. The third battle of Ypres, in August, is remembered more for the mud than the bullets but despite the appalling conditions the Allied line advanced, with Passchendaele falling to the Canadians in November, an achievement that matched their successful assault on Vimy Ridge earlier in the year.

The war broadened further, with Brazil, Cuba and Panama declaring war on Germany. In the Middle East the Allies continued to force the Turks to retreat. Baghdad fell in March and a heavy Turkish defeat at Gaza in the same month opened the road to Palestine. Beersheba and Jaffa fell as the British advanced in October and November, and at the end of the year Jerusalem surrendered to Allenby's forces. The news from the Italian front was not so good, with a massive defeat at Caporetto in October, and 293,000 Italian soldiers captured.

At home, with the war now costing £5,700,000 a day, a new British War Loan was launched at the beginning of the year, and was well subscribed. Loans were also negotiated with the USA. The first bombing raid on London by aeroplanes took place in June, with more than 100 fatalities, and these became a regular occurrence. The King asked the country to eat less bread, and ordered his family to drop their German names and adopt those of Windsor and Mountbatten.

The War Office introduced the convoy system to try to reduce shipping losses, and promised to supply the troops with Christmas puddings. A form of non-military national service for women was introduced, and women were allowed to drive taxis. Chequers was given to the government as a country residence for the Prime Minister, and Churchill was back in the Cabinet; he was appointed Minister for Munitions in July. At the end of the year the Balfour Declaration gave British support to the Jewish desire for a permanent national homeland in Palestine.

Overseas, there were race riots in June in Illinois and Texas, and in December the US Senate voted for the prohibition of alcohol. Buffalo Bill died, and in New York at Reisenweber's Restaurant the Original Dixieland Jass (later Jazz) Band introduced a wild new music to the world; a few weeks later the world's first jazz record, *The Original Dixieland One-Step*, was selling in thousands. Puerto Rico became part of the USA, and its people American citizens. In France, Mata Hari was executed for spying, Degas and Rodin died, and restaurants were compelled by government decree to have menus with only two courses, just one of them including meat.

However, it was in Britain that the true impact of the war was being felt—but the changes wrought by it were often taken for granted. The *ILN* wrote that:

> ... it may be well for a moment to picture England sprinkled with scarlet instead of khaki. If every soldier were as red as a pillar-box, we might begin to realise what a miracle the making of the new English Army has really been. It would astonish us as much as an interminable fence or railing made entirely of pillar-boxes. As it is, curiously enough, the change of colour has actually concealed the change of fact ... We have hardly realised that all this light brown, littered everywhere unlimitedly like autumn leaves, is really our old friend the red sentry at Whitehall multiplied a hundred times. (20 January)

THE ILLUSTRATED
LONDON NEWS

1917
E·V·E·N·T·S

20 AUGUST Third Ypres offensive launched by
Allies
17 SEPTEMBER Russian army defeated by
Germans at Riga
27 OCTOBER American troops had their
first engagement on the Western Front
31 OCTOBER Italians defeated at Caporetto
7 NOVEMBER Kerensky's government ousted
by Bolshevik coup in Russia
9 NOVEMBER Jewish homeland in Palestine
promised by Balfour Declaration
29 NOVEMBER Peace talks announced
between Russia and Germany
9 DECEMBER Jerusalem captured by British

Sappers' shining hour: 'In the great Battle of
Flanders the British troops had to work under the
worst conditions . . . Mr Philip Gibbs says: "The fields
are quagmires, and in the shell-crater land, which is
miles deep around Ypres, the pits have filled with
water. The woods loom vaguely through a wet mist,
and road traffic labours through rivers of slime." [He]
made particular mention of the splendid work of the
Engineers: ". . . the bridging work . . . is beyond any
praise. One division . . . in a single day and under fire,
succeeded in throwing 17 bridges over the river".'
(18 August 1917)

Bread sliced: the King himself took the lead in the
national campaign to curb bread consumption to
conserve resources. *Save the Wheat, Help the Fleet—
Eat Less Bread* exhorted posters aimed at families up
and down the land. In May 1917, when the King made
the call to cut bread consumption by a quarter, it
emerged that Buckingham Palace had been on strict
rations for three months already. The King was not
prepared to ask his people to make sacrifices he was
not prepared to make himself.

The spy they all loved: Mata Hari, the notorious
Dutch exotic dancer and adventuress, was executed
for spying in Paris on 15 October 1917. Born
Margaretha Geertruida Zelle in Leeuwarden, she
married a Dutch army officer—oddly enough named
McLeod—an alcoholic. She left him in the Dutch East
Indies and made her way to Paris, where she took the
Malay name Mata Hari (meaning 'eye of the morning')
and became a dancer. She joined the German secret
service in 1907 and passed on military secrets to them
that had been given her by lovers—usually prominent
Allied officers. She was tried by the French at court
martial, found guilty of spying and was executed,
protesting innocence.

1918

AT THE START OF THE YEAR, events in Russia still dominated the headlines. The shaky armistice agreed between the Bolshevik government and Germany soon failed, and German armies swept into Russia and threatened Petrograd in order to force the Bolsheviks to accept the treaty conditions. This they finally did, and the punitive Treaty of Brest–Litovsk was signed in March. Moscow was declared the new capital of Russia, but peace was not so easily won. Soon civil war threatened, as the new 'red' armies of Lenin and Trotsky were increasingly challenged by the 'white' armies of former Tsarist officers. The white armies had considerable overseas support. A combined British, American and Japanese force landed in Vladivostok in April, and in June British Marines seized Murmansk to stop the port falling into German hands. A similar motive lay behind the landing of a much larger British, French and American force at Archangel in August. In July the Tsar and his family were murdered, and anarchy reigned throughout Russia.

In the USA the year began with President Wilson's publication of a 14-point peace plan, which aimed to turn the German people against their government—a hope based in part on the wave of strikes and unrest in both Austria and Germany. In Berlin, martial law was declared.

However, in France the German armies, greatly strengthened by the troops released from the Eastern Front, were on the offensive. A massive assault all along the Front in March broke the Allied lines in many places and the Germans quickly advanced, taking thousands of prisoners. Soissons fell in May, Rheims was threatened and Haig issued his famous 'Backs to the Wall' orders. With the Allied defences crumbling and the Germans only 45 miles from Paris, Marshal Foch took over as Commander-in-Chief of all Allied Forces. In the end the German advance was stopped, but not before Paris had been shelled by the 'Big Bertha' guns, positioned on railway trucks 65 miles from the city. The Allied counter-attacks now started and advances were soon made, with the support of large numbers of tanks and aeroplanes, which had, in effect, brought the trench warfare to an end. Indeed, by this time the Allies had gained air superiority over the Western Front and were destroying three German aircraft for every Allied machine lost. The new Allied power in the air was underlined by the formation in April of the Royal Air Force, combining the Royal Flying Corps with the Royal Naval Air Service. The German lines were broken all along the Western Front and soon the German armies were in full retreat.

Other theatres of war could tell a similar story. The Italians pushed the Austrians across the Piave and out of Italy, and in the Middle East the Allied advances continued. Jericho fell to Australian cavalry and the Turks were steadily forced to retreat, their lines of communication constantly harried and broken by the Arab forces of Feisal and Colonel Lawrence. Ultimately Damascus, the major Arab city, fell. It was reported in the *ILN* that:

> *Sherif Feisal, whose Army has taken so notable a part in the Palestine victories, entered Damascus on October 3 on horseback, attended by some 1500 of his kinsfolk and adherents, and rode through the city at full gallop ... An Arab administration has been established in Damascus.* (2 November)

Awaiting fate: 'On the roof of their prison at Tobolsk, for a breath of air . . . Nicholas II suffered . . . a more dreadful fate than . . . Louis XVI of France. He was not tried: he was not even ceremonially executed. He was shot like a dog, and he died knowing that in a moment the whole of his family—his wife, four daughters and little son would be similarly butchered [16 July 1918].' (1 January 1921)

THE ILLUSTRATED
LONDON NEWS

1918

E · V · E · N · T · S

8 JANUARY 'Fourteen Points' for peace
announced by President Wilson
25 JANUARY Food rationing introduced in
Britain
3 MARCH Treaty of Brest-Litovsk signed by
Russia and Germany
31 MARCH German offensive launched,
breaking all Allied lines
1 APRIL Royal Air Force formed in Britain
16 JULY Tsar and his family murdered in Russia

'Red Baron's' last dogfight: Germany's most feared and famous pilot, Manfred von Richthofen, was shot down in flames and killed during the second battle of the Somme (21 April 1918). The 25-year-old flying ace's nickname came from the colour of his Fokker triplane. 'The pilot of one of the hostile machines, which was brought down in combat . . . was the well-known German airman and fighter . . . von Richthofen, who claimed to have brought down 80 machines. His body to-day [29 April] will be buried with full military honours.' (25 May 1918)

Irresistible force: 'The . . . illustration shows the almost perpendicular steepness of the places the Tanks crossed in passing over German trenches in the Cambrai battle. The way Tanks can crash through a wood forcing a path among the trees, and through the undergrowth, like primaeval mastodons in chase, is shown . . . One can understand . . . how the Tanks ploughed up, tore gaps through, and flattened out the most formidable German barbed-wire entanglements.' (9 February 1918)

Charlie's call-up: the world's favourite funny man, Charlie Chaplin, starred in *Shoulder Arms* (1918) as the most unmilitary of soldiers imaginable—complete with mousetrap, razor and gas mask. Chaplin was born in Kennington, London, in 1889 of theatrical parents; his father's early death left the family in poverty. Charlie appeared in music halls from an early age, and in 1910 joined Fred Karno's company, where he developed his comedy skills. The troupe visited the USA in 1914, where young Charlie caught the eye of film-maker Mack Sennett, of the Keystone Company. It was for the short film *Kid Auto Races in Venice* that Chaplin created his enduring character, the tramp, with turned-out feet, bowler hat, moustache and cane. Chaplin's career as actor, director, and producer spanned decades. He died at his Swiss home on Christmas Day, 1977.

At home Britain was still on a war footing. Rationing was introduced, at first for meat, butter and margarine, but the restrictions quickly became general. Coal was in short supply and theatres and restaurants had to close early. Rationing had one unexpected side-effect:

> *The health of the nation was never better, which lends much colour to the statement frequently made before the war that three-fourths of the maladies of well-to-do people were caused by over-eating. By the rationing of the nation, whether voluntary or compulsory, this cause of ailment is now done away with ...* (19 January)

The conscription age limit was raised to 50 in March, and Ireland was included for the first time. This provoked a wave of protests and strikes led by Sinn Fein, and 500 Sinn Fein supporters were arrested, including Eamon de Valera, the Sinn Fein MP for East Clare. Faced by this opposition, the government abandoned the Irish conscription plans, and postponed any discussion of the Home Rule Bill. Women aged 30 or over were now to be given the vote for the first time, and the school leaving age was raised to 14. The Labour Party, with its eye to the future, published its plans for state control of industry. Stonehenge was presented to the nation, and Dr Marie Stopes published *Married Love*, the first handbook on sex.

In the USA, Daylight Saving Time was introduced and the House of Representatives voted for female suffrage. George Gershwin had his first hit with the song *Swanee*. As the war in Europe drew to a close, its last weeks were marked by an epidemic of Spanish influenza, which had already killed millions in China and India. It swept through France and reached Britain in September, and by October more than 2,000 people a week were dying in London alone. The Allied armies were also devastated, and more American soldiers died from 'flu than were killed in battle.

The end of the war came quickly and took the Allies by surprise. Bulgaria surrendered at the end of September. A month later the Turkish armies, in a state of collapse, also surrendered. On 31 October Germany appealed for an armistice and peace talks began. Three days later Austria signed the Armistice and on 9 November the Kaiser abdicated and a republic was declared in Germany. On 11 November, Marshal Foch accepted the German surrender in a railway carriage at Compiègne, and at 11am the guns fell silent all over Europe. Jubilation greeted the end of the Great War, then people started to count the cost. Ten million had died, including nearly a million from Britain and her Empire, and 'the lost generation' was soon a familiar phrase. The war had redrawn the map of Europe, with the Hapsburg Empire now broken up into four new countries: Austria, Czechoslovakia, Hungary and a Pan-Slavic group led by Serbia. Poland, Finland, the Ukraine, Latvia and Estonia were established as independent countries, and Alsace-Lorraine once more became part of France.

Thoughts were also turning towards the future. There was much debate about a League of Nations as a means of maintaining international peace. In the opinion of the *ILN*:

> *A League of Nations ... will be an admirable idea if it means a league to defend the nationality of nations ... But a League of Nations in the sense of something to internationalise nations is not an ideal at all. It is a mere stop-gap.* (10 August)

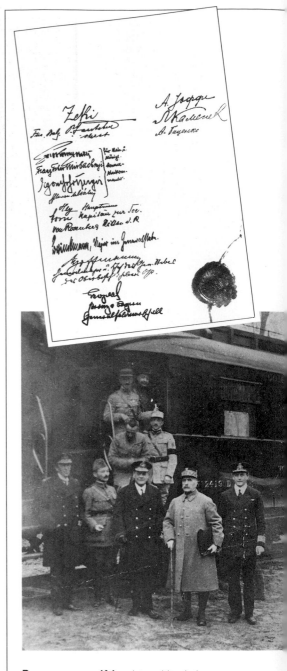

Peace came swiftly: pictured (top), the 'scrap of paper' signed by Russia and Germany in January 1918, agreeing to an armistice between the two countries, which soon collapsed.
Above: 11 November 1918. Marshal Foch, Admiral Sir Rosslyn Wenyss and General Weygand leaving the railway saloon at Compiègne after signing the Armistice that ended the First World War. 'The end ... has come as suddenly as an explosion', wrote G K Chesterton. 'It is at least due to all those who have died, and all those who have suffered in their dying, to vindicate their work ... and to say plainly that very little of the pacific politics of our time ... has been half so ... fruitful for God and man as these four years of destruction.' (16 November 1918)

Just like Daddy: women over 30 voted for the first time in a general election (on 28 December 1918). Of the 1,600 candidates, 17 were women. One was successful—Sinn Fein candidate Countess Markievicz. She would not take the oath of allegiance and thus could not attend Parliament. The coalition government won 478 seats; the opposition parties 229.

1918
E·V·E·N·T·S

2 AUGUST Allied troops landed in Archangel to support white Russians

8 AUGUST Allied counter-offensive launched on Western Front

3 OCTOBER Damascus taken by Arab forces under Lawrence

31 OCTOBER Germany appealed for an armistice

11 NOVEMBER Germany signed Armistice with Allies at Compiègne; end of war

28 DECEMBER First women voted in UK; Lloyd George's government re-elected

All over: 'London broke into a spontaneous outburst of joy when it learned "the greatest piece of news that England has ever heard" . . . a crowd gathered outside Buckingham Palace . . . and sang *God Save the King* and *Rule Britannia*.' (16 November 1918)

1919

B Y THE BEGINNING OF THIS YEAR the natural jubilation felt by the nations of Europe at the end of the Great War had mostly evaporated. There remained heartfelt relief that the terrible bloodletting was over, and that the men were coming home. But to what? 'A land fit for heroes' had been Lloyd George's election promise in December 1918; yet Britain was torn by industrial unrest.

The *ILN*, while not wholly unsympathetic to strikers, was inclined to celebrate strike-breakers. In August, during a series of coal strikes, Royal Navy 'bluejackets' worked to keep the coal mines from flooding 'without a word of complaint'; two months later, 'in Birmingham . . . an appeal for volunteers was made from the pulpit' to feed and water railway workhorses left neglected by the rail strike. Strikes raised the spectre of Bolshevism, although the *ILN* reassured its readers that, in Britain at least, 'the Red Flag barred with black has not yet been hoisted'.

The outcome of the Bolshevik revolution in Russia which gave rise to these fears was still uncertain, and Sir Ernest Shackleton called for recruits: 'A three months' campaign by a volunteer army would break the Bolshevik monster.' In Ireland, police barracks were being fortified against possible Sinn Fein attacks.

On a broader scale, the world was readjusting to the collapse of the old European empires, and Britain, while less physically scarred than other countries, had to adapt painfully to its new status. Before the war, it had been the world's banker, financing governments and enterprises, reaping in return power, prestige and wealth. Much of that wealth had been spent on the war effort, and Britain now owed vast sums to the USA, which had emerged as the leading world power. President Wilson of the USA went to Versailles this year for the peacemaking which was 'to make the world safe for democracy'. Wilson was an an idealist who did his best to create a more just and democratic Europe, and to ensure future peace by developing the idea of a League of Nations. 'You can abolish war, and still not abolish fighting,' fulminated G K Chesterton in the *ILN*, at an early stage in the proceedings. 'It is intolerable that they should waste so much time over a League of Nations that they have no time left for the nations.' The Treaty of Versailles, signed on 28 June, humiliated Germany and led to massive reparations.

The Atlantic was flown for the first time this year by two RAF pilots, Alcock and Brown, who landed their Vickers-Vimy bi-plane in an Irish bog on 15 June. It had taken them 16 hours to fly the 1,890-mile route. Nancy Astor also made history this year when she became the first woman MP to take her seat in the Commons, where, it was reported, 'her entrance was greeted with hearty cheers'.

Optimistic speculation greeted the work of Rutherford and others on the atom. The *ILN* hoped that as a result:

> *Such an immense source of energy would be placed at the disposal of man that manual labour would well-nigh be unnecessary, . . . all social questions . . . disappear . . . and the distinction between rich and poor . . . vanish.* (18 October)

But in the mean time 'this source of energy must remain to us like a child's locked money box—a potential source of wealth indeed, but one entirely beyond his power to use'.

Long, long trail a-winding: a national rail strike in September left Britain's commuters without trains or tubes. 'Hundreds of thousands of Londoners living in the suburbs had to "foot-slog" . . . but by many thousands more all sorts of auxiliary transport was utilised. The trams were at first besieged by crowds far in excess of the carrying capacity, and other means of locomotion had to be devised.' (4 October 1919). These included horse and cart, bicycle and motor lorry, but the strike ended almost as suddenly as it had started.

Making the world safe? 'All eyes were centred on the six chief German delegates at the historic conference in the Trianon Palace Hotel at Versailles on May 7, when the Treaty containing the Allies' terms of peace was presented to them.' (17 May 1919). The Germans refused to sign terms widely regarded as excessively harsh until, threatened with occupation by Allied troops, they gave way in June. British Prime Minister Lloyd George gloomily predicted another war.

THE ILLUSTRATED LONDON NEWS

1919

E·V·E·N·T·S

3 JANUARY Atom split by Rutherford
3 MARCH Comintern launched by Lenin to promote world revolution
23 MARCH Fascist party launched by Mussolini in Italy
15 JUNE Alcock and Brown first to cross the Atlantic non-stop by air
28 JUNE Treaty of Versailles finally signed by Germany
28 NOVEMBER Nancy Astor elected as Britain's first woman MP

Brilliance on court: young Suzanne Lenglen was 20 when she won the women's singles at Wimbledon for the first time in 1919, taking the last of three sets 9–7 against the reigning champion, Mrs Lambert Chambers. She would win the title five more times, along with many doubles triumphs, before she turned professional in 1926. Brilliantly skilful and highly temperamental, she pioneered new fashions in tennis dress for women.

Feminine brilliance at the polls: 'There was tremendous enthusiasm in the Guildhall Square at Plymouth on November 28 when it was announced that Lady Astor, the Coalition Unionist candidate, had been returned at the head of the poll with a majority of 5,203 over the Labour candidate . . . and that she would thus enter the House of Commons as the first woman Member to take her seat in Parliament.' (6 December 1919). Lively and sharp-tongued, Lady Astor remained a prominent Member of Parliament until 1945.

The Atlantic conquered by bi-plane: a new landmark in the history of aviation was established in June 1919 when a Vickers-Vimy bi-plane piloted by an Englishman and an American, Captain John Alcock and Lieutenant Arthur Whitten Brown, took off from Newfoundland and arrived safely in Ireland 16 hours later, completing the first non-stop flight across the Atlantic at an average speed of 120mph. The dangers of the new means of transport were tragically highlighted when John Alcock died before the year was out, from injuries which he sustained in an aeroplane accident.

1920

F OR HILAIRE BELLOC, writing in the *ILN*, the general renewal of pleasure-seeking immediately after the Great War had a poignant side:

At 'The Gondoliers' the other night, how many faces I saw that were the faces of my contemporaries in the eighties, when we were boys and when the world was still firm and all things seemed immortal . . . Do you remember that world? . . . We have come to the end of one time and are not yet at the beginning of another. (17 January)

The Prince of Wales, 'our very popular prince', travelled overseas. In 1919 he had made a triumphant progress through North America; and this year he visited Australia and New Zealand, stopping at Honolulu, Fiji and the West Indies. He was 26 and had endeared himself to millions by his presence in France during the war. Some argue that his popularity was useful for the Establishment at what was a difficult time in Britain socially and politically. There was a national coal strike in October; the *ILN* pointed out to its readers that:

The present unrest may have causes undreamed of by those who consider only the enormous wages which the underground worker now receives, the recklessness and extravagance with which he spends them, and his rooted objection to staying underground an hour longer than he can help. (9 October)

Mrs Lloyd George became one of the first women JPs in Britain this year, and was pictured in the *ILN* in January, hearing her first case. Four months later her husband was featured in a grimmer context: 'We return a verdict of wilful murder against David Lloyd George, Prime Minister of England', the jury reported at the inquest on Thomas MacCurtain, the late Lord Mayor of Cork. The 'astounding finding' was that the British government and the Royal Irish Constabulary had organised the shooting of the Sinn Fein Lord Mayor.

Eight hundred unemployed ex-servicemen were formed into a new force of special constables, and sent to Ireland to quell the troubles. They were nicknamed the Black and Tans. In December, martial law was imposed in Ireland.

On paper, the British Empire had reached its greatest extent, acquiring a large share of former German colonies following the war. Britain acquired lesser possessions too: 'The *Imperator*, once German, now sails under the Cunard flag', reported the *ILN*. In the dismantling of the Ottoman Empire, Britain had gained a dominant position in the Middle East, shared only to a small degree by France. Arab risings were reported from Mesopotamia (present-day Iraq); and in Russia, the Bolsheviks defeated the white armies in November.

There were two sombre ceremonies at the end of the year. On 11 November, Armistice Day, the King unveiled the Cenotaph in Whitehall, and a two minutes' silence was observed nationally. Designed by Lutyens, the simple Cenotaph memorial became the centre of national mourning thereafter. The other ceremony held on the same day was the burial of the Unknown Warrior in Westminster Abbey.

Searched at the bayonet's point: 'Remembering the events of Easter Monday, 1916 [an armed uprising against British rule], the military authorities in Dublin took stringent precautions against the occurrence of a similar rebellion this Easter. All vehicles entering Dublin were stopped and searched by soldiers, including even tram-cars . . . The fears of another "Easter Rebellion", however, proved unfounded. The Sinn Feiners have found their new "guerrilla warfare" more effective and more difficult to deal with. This has so far taken the form of sporadic incendiarism.' (10 April 1920). About 144 Irish police stations were burned down.

THE ILLUSTRATED LONDON NEWS

1920

E · V · E · N · T · S

16 JANUARY Prohibition introduced in the USA

16 JANUARY Inauguration of the League of Nations, without US representation

19 MARCH US Senate voted against ratification of Treaty of Versailles

26 MARCH Black and Tans arrived in Ireland

31 MARCH House of Commons passed the Irish Home Rule Bill

Prayers and sympathy: a woman leading prayers for Sinn Feiners on hunger strike in a prison in Dublin. Some of them were released in April. 'Dublin was in a state of ferment for several days during the agitation for the release of the hunger-strikers in Mountjoy Prison. On April 14 (the day their release began), the tanks, armoured cars and barbed-wire entanglements outside the prison were removed . . .' (24 April 1920)

PRICES *from* **£165** *ex Works*

Lying in state: Alderman McSwiney, the Lord Mayor of Cork, died on hunger strike in October (his predecessor, Alderman MacCurtain, had been assassinated in March). The body was taken to Cork and lay in state in the City Hall. '. . . the lid of the coffin was removed, and his body was in full view, dressed in the uniform of his rank as Commandant in the Irish Republican Army. At the head was a Commandant's hat, and at the foot a gold crucifix, while the lower part of the coffin was draped with the Sinn Fein tricolour (yellow, white and green) on either side of the bier.' (6 November 1920). The coffin's inscription stated that he had been 'murdered by the foreigner'.

Off the production line: the founder of Morris Motors, William Morris, started as the owner of a bicycle shop and went on to manufacture motor cycles and cars before the First World War. He built up one of the country's biggest business firms and in the 1930s was created Viscount Nuffield. A notable benefactor to Oxford University, and the founder of Nuffield College, he gave away millions of pounds to good causes.

On an international level, this year saw the inauguration of the League of Nations in the Clock Room at the French Foreign Office in Paris in January. Delegates from the USA were absent, however, despite the fact that President Wilson had been one of the League's most ardent supporters during the Paris peace talks. The reason for this was the fact that the US Congress had objected to Article 10 of the Treaty of Versailles, whereby the USA would be obliged to declare war if another member was attacked. While a compromise was being worked out for presentation to the US government, the Council of the new League of Nations met at St James's Palace in London, and agreed to establish an international court of justice. Delegates from Britain, France, Japan, Belgium, Spain, Greece, Italy and Brazil attended the Council of the League. The *ILN* reported:

> *Mr Baker opened the proceedings. Alluding to the fact that the United States were not represented, he said: 'There is one blot on the assembly . . . which is that we are eight instead of nine . . . I am sure that none of my friends in America will think that I am doing wrong in expressing my personal regret that . . . we have not reached our complete number.'* (21 February)

In March, the US Senate refused to ratify the Treaty of Versailles, despite the compromise solution that had been presented to it by some US Senators. This meant that the USA would not become a member of the League of Nations after all. Although President Wilson had been one of the architects of the Treaty, he, too, refused to vote for the compromise solution, thereby ensuring its defeat.

In the US presidential election in November, the Republican candidate, Warren Harding, was elected President with a comfortable majority, defeating James Cox, the Democratic candidate and Governor of Ohio, who had lost popularity due to his support for the (now disliked) Treaty of Versailles and League of Nations. This was a blow to former President Wilson, who had also suffered a stroke earlier in the year, but in December he was awarded the Nobel Peace Prize for his work at the Paris peace talks.

This year also saw the introduction of national prohibition in the USA, when the Eighteenth Amendment to the US Constitution, passed in January, prohibited the manufacture and sale of alcohol in all states. Legislation had already been passed to this effect in many US states, beginning in Maine in 1851, and following in many states thereafter. The prohibition introduced in 1920 was the outcome of sustained agitation by churches (who perceived drinking as a sin), and women (who saw liquor saloons as a threat to the home).

In Europe, confusion was the artistic order of the day with the growing popularity of a revolutionary new style—Dada—at festivals of art, poetry and music held in Paris and Berlin. The Dadaists' slogan was *Destruction is also Creation* and they set about proving their theory by challenging all conventional ideas of art, scandalising the Establishment.

In Antwerp, the first Olympic Games since the Great War took place, and were generally regarded at the time as an outstanding achievement; world sport appeared to have undergone a remarkable revival, despite the sufferings that Belgium and other competing countries had recently endured. Albert Hill, a British railway guard, distinguished himself by winning gold medals in both the 800 metres and the 1,500 metres.

The quiet before the storm: men of the Civic Guard pausing for a snack by the Bismarck Monument in Berlin, in January. Blood was soon shed when Communist agitators incited a mob to attack the parliament building and the Guards opened fire with rifles and machine guns: 22 of the crowd and two guardsmen were killed. Ironically, the figure on the monument in the background is busy beating a sword into a ploughshare.

1920

E·V·E·N·T·S

25 APRIL Britain given mandate over
Mesopotamia and Palestine
1 SEPTEMBER State of Lebanon established by
France
18 OCTOBER Start of national coal strike in
Britain
11 NOVEMBER King George V unveiled the
Cenotaph in Whitehall
15 NOVEMBER Bolsheviks defeated white forces
in Crimea; civil war ended
10 DECEMBER Martial law declared in Ireland
after wave of IRA killings

**At the going down of the sun and
in the morning, we will
remember them:** George V unveiled
the Cenotaph in Whitehall, the
monument to the war dead, on
Armistice Day, 1920. On the same day
the body of the Unknown Warrior was
interred in Westminster Abbey.

After the storm: 35 people died
when a bomb exploded in Wall Street,
New York, in September. '. . . it is
agreed on all hands that it was the work
of "Reds" of some kind, foreign or
domestic', but 'no definite clue has been
found leading to the authors of the
outrage.' (2 October 1920)

Down with drink: Prohibition
made less headway in Britain than in
the USA. G K Chesterton sounded
off: 'I think Prohibition a piece of
low, provincial persecution of the
dirtiest and most dismal sort. I defy
anybody to say what are the rights
of a citizen if they do not include the
control of his own diet in relation to
his health.' (26 November 1921)

LIBRARY
2 4 MAR 1993
HARTLEPOOL C.F.E.

1921

NINETEEN TWENTY-ONE saw the start of a long-lasting slump in Britain. There were more than 2 million unemployed by June, and with an inadequate 'dole', they and their families endured great hardship.

Those in work found that employers cut wages, often savagely, in their effort to survive in a harsh economic climate. Great industries such as cotton manufacturing in Lancashire had lost markets during the war, and although the greatest burden was borne by the working class, many factory owners were forced out of business. Death duties and cheap food imports encouraged landowners to sell their estates, which were often bought by those who had made money in the war. Titles were available, too. Lloyd George sold honours in an unprecedentedly business-like way for his so-called 'political treasure chest'; £10,000 for a knighthood; £50,000 or more for a peerage. Beaverbrook, the newspaper proprietor who had helped Lloyd George to power, became a baron despite the rage of the King, who regarded him as a 'cheap little Canadian adventurer'.

Not all was gloom. Younger 'society' enjoyed dances, which, according to the *ILN*, were 'small quiet affairs on the simple and more intimate lines that the Prince of Wales has made so well-beloved of the really right sort of people'. Meanwhile, in the world of fashion, it was reported that:

> *... smart hats still have feathers, ospreys and furs*
> *sticking out at all sorts of unexpected angles. They are*
> *rather embarrassing when close quarters ... are*
> *required for confidences, or for other reasons ...*
> (12 November)

Cinemas were springing up all over the country and drawing huge audiences. Rudolf Valentino was becoming a cult figure with his roles in *The Four Horsemen of the Apocalypse* (1919) and *The Sheikh* (1921). Hollywood was already the centre of the industry, but Cricklewood had its own Stolls studio, where a screen-struck *ILN* correspondent described the process:

> *Each scene or incident is played up to a title which is*
> *shown on the screen first, and the actors actually speak*
> *the lines to get the necessary action and effect.*
> (6 August)

Shooting on location was easy to arrange: 'everyone seems interested in and anxious to help the "movies",' the *ILN* remarked, although that caused problems too. 'Mr and Mrs British Public are very anxious to be seen on the screen, and if it is possible to slip into the picture, their ambitions have been achieved.'

A new phenomenon, 'a sort of social flutter, which is produced by the mere word "relativity",' was noticed when Albert Einstein won the Nobel Prize for Physics.

In Ireland, escalating violence caused widespread public protests in Britain, led by the Archbishop of Canterbury. Public opinion forced Lloyd George to invite the Irish leaders to a peace conference. In December a treaty was signed giving the southern part of Ireland, the 'Irish Free State', dominion status, while six counties in the North remained a province of the United Kingdom.

A test of relative values: 'In connection with the International Congress of Astronomical Societies, whose proceedings opened recently in Potsdam, a special tower telescope [left] has been constructed to test the Einstein theory of Relativity.' (3 September 1921). This was the year when the great theoretical physicist was awarded the Nobel Prize.

The unemployed on the march: with thousands out of work, there was pressure to increase the amount of dole paid by local authorities, and unemployed men marched through Shoreditch in London. A strike by the 'triple alliance' of miners, railwaymen and transport workers had been threatened earlier in the year, but was called off at the last moment when the miners' allies backed out.

Boycotting the European: M K Gandhi, (above), had started a campaign in India to boycott all things European. 'In India he has come to be regarded by thousands of ignorant natives as a "Mahatma" possessed of miraculous powers.' (17 September 1921)

THE ILLUSTRATED LONDON NEWS

1921

E·V·E·N·T·S

16 FEBRUARY Unemployment in Britain exceeded one million
18 FEBRUARY Etienne Oehmichen made first flight by helicopter
17 MARCH First birth control clinic opened in London by Marie Stopes
4 AUGUST Lenin asked for world help to overcome Russian famine
5 NOVEMBER Prince Hirohito appointed Regent of Japan
7 DECEMBER Agreement signed to set up the Irish Free State

Boycotting the English: hoping to make peace in Ireland, the British premier, Mr. Lloyd George, invited Sinn Fein leader Eamon de Valera (left) and his Irish colleagues to a conference. 'While there is a general desire that the Irish question should be settled in accordance with the more moderate aspirations of Southern Ireland, it cannot be forgotten that the violent methods of Sinn Fein extremists have not been disowned by Mr. de Valera . . .' (2 July 1921). The body of a Sinn Fein terrorist lies in a Dublin street (below), as people pass by. He had been shot in an attack on the Custom House, which had been seized by the rebels.

1922

'THE QUEEN has pleased everyone by coming ashore frequently', beamed a reporter from the *ILN* at 'breezy, cheery, and sunny' Cowes in August. Admittedly, 'the days of the great yachts, steamers on which there were nightly dinners and frequent dances . . . and of seventy-ton sailing craft on which women went racing' were almost over, but the annual round of high society festivities, interrupted by the war, was back in full swing. In dress, there was 'a distinct return to the waist line of nature', and the Duchess of Sutherland 'enjoyed a cigarette, and showed herself one of the women who can smoke prettily'.

Later that month, Queen Mary was to accompany George V to Moy, the Highland seat of the Clan Mackintosh, for the shooting. Afterwards there was fishing and deer-stalking at Balmoral, then Christmas and the shooting of thousands of pheasants at Sandringham. Preparations began around Easter for the London season, with its dances, garden parties and presentation of débutantes (soon to include Americans) at Buckingham Palace; later in the summer came racing at Ascot and Goodwood, and the return to Cowes.

The *ILN* perceived the increase in car ownership as 'a hopeful sign of better days for the automobile, engineering, and allied industries'. With close on 160,000 members in August, the AA was growing 94 per cent faster than in 1914.

The middle class still had staffs of servants (often living 'a subterranean life without sufficient light and air'); coal fires heated the rooms, and among the better-off, gas lighting and gas cookers were replacing paraffin lamps and cooking by coal. Gramophones were becoming widely owned, and the choice of records ranged from classical to the latest American jazz. Last-ditch objections to the craze for all things American were raised in the pages of the *ILN*:

> *. . . it is not American virtues that are being imitated. It is rather American vices, and especially American vulgarities. We are not imitating their democracy, but rather their plutocracy.* (21 January)

It was an import from materially richer America that most expressively cast doubt on material progress. T S Eliot, American by birth, British by adoption, published *The Waste Land* in the *Criterion* magazine, suggesting that western civilisation was on the wrong path. A year later, it was published by the Hogarth Press of Leonard and Virginia Woolf, prominent figures in the 'Bloomsbury Group'. The year's other literary landmark was James Joyce's *Ulysses* (banned in Britain and the USA), which took the reader through Dublin and into the minds of its main protagonists.

In the real Dublin, a truce was declared in July to end the bitter fighting over whether or not to accept the proposals for the Irish Free State. Three months later, in Britain, the Conservative and Liberal coalition broke up and Lloyd George resigned. Canadian-born Andrew Bonar Law, a close friend of Lord Beaverbrook, became Conservative Prime Minister; Labour, the largest opposition party, was led by Ramsay MacDonald. He was called 'a prince among men' by Emmanuel Shinwell, but others of the party, like the intellectual Beatrice Webb, wondered if he knew which way the party should go. At the end of October, Benito Mussolini, leader of the Fascists, took power in Italy.

A new era in Ireland: 'The Irish Free State was called into existence on January 15, in the Mansion House, Dublin [top], at a meeting of 65 elected members of the Southern Parliament . . .' (21 January 1922). The new President, Arthur Griffith, said: 'We are starting on a new era, and we want all the old differences that existed between sections of Irishmen to be banished for ever.' It was not to be. Sinn Fein boycotted the Parliament and a bitter civil war broke out between the factions in the South. In June the Irish Republican Army was forcibly evicted from the law courts in Dublin by Free State troops: the building was bombarded and caught fire (above). In August the moderate leader Michael Collins was assassinated and Griffith himself died of an illness.

The march of advertising: techniques pioneered in the 19th century gained strength in the 20th, as manufacturers sought to reach a mass market for their products.

THE ILLUSTRATED LONDON NEWS

1922

E·V·E·N·T·S

22 AUGUST Irish Nationalist leader Michael Collins shot dead in Cork
7 OCTOBER First woman senator sworn in in the USA
18 OCTOBER British Broadcasting Company (later Corporation) formed
19 OCTOBER Coalition government ended in UK; Bonar Law new Prime Minister
30 OCTOBER Benito Mussolini took over as dictator of Italy
26 NOVEMBER Treasures of Tutankhamun's tomb first revealed by Howard Carter

The march on Rome: blackshirt leaders, with Benito Mussolini (below, centre), the veteran General de Bono on his right. Mussolini took no part in the triumphant march from Naples to Rome of thousands of his Fascist supporters, which encountered practically no opposition. Summoned by the King, he followed them to the city and formed a new government, as virtual dictator of Italy. 'The Fascist movement was a patriotic reaction of the youth of Italy against the Bolshevism which became rampant two years ago and, by the seizure of factories, threatened to ruin the country. Mussolini himself is still young—only thirty-nine. He was born in 1883, near Forli, in Romagna, the son of a blacksmith, and became, like his father, an ardent Socialist . . . The war completely changed his views . . . he served at the front in 1915 as a sergeant of Bersaglieri [riflemen], and was wounded. In personal appearance he has been described as "a Napoleon turned pugilist".' (11 November 1922)

Glittering treasures of antiquity: the archaeologist Howard Carter and his aristocratic backer, the Earl of Carnarvon, discovered the tomb of Pharaoh Tutankhamun of the 18th Dynasty of Ancient Egypt, in the Valley of the Kings, in November 1922. Sixteen steps led down to the door of the tomb, which had lain undisturbed for 3,000 years and was so packed with treasures that it would take years to clear it.

1923

'FROM THE OSTRICH-FARMERS OF SOUTH AFRICA: A WEDDING GIFT TO THE DUKE OF YORK'S BRIDE—A SPLENDID MANTELET OF OSTRICH FEATHERS, IN "TUTANKHAMEN" STYLE.'
A caption in the *ILN* on 28 April neatly encapsulated the twin preoccupations of the year. The fabulous treasures of Tutankhamun's tomb had been revealed in February and a craze for 'Egyptian' styles had begun. The other topic of the year was a wedding:

> *The engagement of the Duke of York to Lady Elizabeth Bowes-Lyon intrigues everyone. She is such a dainty, pretty, picturesque and bright little lady that she is a general favourite. The Duke of York has been her constant admirer for a long time.* (27 January)

'You'll be a lucky fellow if she accepts you', King George V is reputed to have said to his son. The bride, according to the *ILN*, had been 'intimidated at first by the thought of all the responsibilities she would have as his wife'. At that time, no one suspected that her husband would one day become King in place of his socially brilliant brother, Edward. The wedding ceremony on 26 April in Westminster Abbey was covered by the British Broadcasting Company (later Corporation), which had started public service programmes in late 1922.
Egyptian treasures, royal pageantry and innovations such as flappers and the *thé dansant*, filled a need in 1923. Politics had become dull: Stanley Baldwin had replaced Andrew Bonar Law as Conservative Prime Minister, but the *ILN* observed that:

> *People have grown cold towards Parliament, not because it is a tyranny, but because it is a bore. They do not attack Parliament: it would be truer to say that they flee in terror from its daily attack.* (4 August)

The election that year produced an indecisive result.
'These days, money is so hard to come by', the women's section of the *ILN* said plaintively in January, and the economy puzzled others too. Guest contributor Signor Guglielmo Ferrero suggested that:

> *Former wars mobilised the work of the past accumulated in idle treasures; we have mobilised the riches of the future, especially by multiplying paper money.* (20 October)

Inflation was worst in Germany, where the mark depreciated billion-fold during the year, a crisis caused in part by the war reparations demanded by the Allies. In January, when Germany had refused to pay, France had begun to occupy the industrial Ruhr area to seize payment in kind.
A report in the *ILN* welcomed Dr F G Banting's discovery of insulin as a treatment for diabetics:

> *The results of its administration have, with very few exceptions, been extraordinarily good; and with it patients who have wasted tremendously have regained their weight and their energy to such an extent that they can resume a more or less normal life.* (4 August)

For better, for worse: engagement photograph of the Duke of York and Lady Elizabeth Bowes-Lyon in January 1923, when neither had the slightest idea that they were future King and Queen. 'The Duke of York is deservedly popular. Like his brother the Prince of Wales, he regards his great position as a public stewardship, for the responsibilities of which he has fitted himself with conscientious toil . . . it is no flattery, but simple truth, to say that Great Britain may count herself fortunate in her Princes.' (28 April 1923)

A face that would haunt the future: Adolf Hitler, leader of the fledgling National Socialist (Nazi) party in Germany. He was in his middle thirties in November 1923, when he attempted to seize power in a coup in Munich, known as 'the beer hall putsch', because it began in a beer cellar. Hitler had the support of Field Marshal von Ludendorff, the brilliant First World War commander, and relied on the fierce hostility aroused in Germany by the French seizure of the Ruhr. Even so, the attempt failed. Hitler was arrested and sentenced to five years in prison. It was these events which first brought him out of obscurity and into the limelight. He used his time in prison to write *Mein Kampf* ('My Struggle').

THE ILLUSTRATED LONDON NEWS

1923

E · V · E · N · T · S

11 JANUARY Ruhr occupied by French
27 JANUARY First Nazi party rally held in Munich, addressed by Hitler
1 SEPTEMBER Tokyo and Yokohama destroyed by earthquake
29 OCTOBER Turkish republic proclaimed by military leader Mustafa Kemal
11 NOVEMBER Hitler arrested after failed coup in Munich
15 NOVEMBER German currency worthless; cost of loaf now 200 billion marks

Inflation run wild: in Germany low value paper notes were now so utterly worthless that they were given to children (right) to use as building blocks. Mark notes were sold to rag-and-bone men as waste paper, barter replaced money transactions and people took a suitcase to work to collect their pay. French troops (below) occupied the Ruhr industrial area to commandeer coal due from Germany as war compensation under the Treaty of Versailles.

From hustings to hoardings: a sample (right) of advertising from the election campaign in Britain, in 1923. 'A good poster is a very effective form of political propaganda, as its pictorial argument leaps to the eye and is easily retained by the memory, whereas long and elaborate orations often pass in at one ear and out at the other. The wording of a poster also tends to brevity and affords scope for pithy utterances that stick in the mind of the passer-by. From an artistic point of view, the modern poster is a great improvement on the old style, and this in itself tends to arrest attention.' (1 December 1923). In the event Labour and the Liberals had substantial gains but the Conservatives lost their overall majority. In January the following year, Labour took office for the first time in British history.

1924

Tʜᴇ ᴋɪɴɢ had invited Ramsay MacDonald to form Britain's first Labour government, which included several working-class men in its Cabinet, on 22 January, saying: 'The immediate future of my people, and their happiness, is in your hands, gentlemen. They depend on your prudence and sagacity.' There was much trepidation, but Labour was cautious because it depended on Liberal support to retain power. Its only significant achievements were in housing, and in early October another general election was called when the Tories and Liberals united against it. G K Chesterton took a convoluted swipe at Mac-Donald's Labour government when he wrote in the *ILN*'s *Our Note Book*:

> *I do not think even Prohibition likely to lead to all Americans drinking themselves to death; I do not think even Mr Ramsay MacDonald conservative enough to conserve all England against all possible revolutions.* (24 October)

Only days before the general election, a letter was published in the national press purporting to be from Zinoviev, the President of the Communist International, urging British Communists to prepare for armed revolution. Although it is now generally considered to have been a forgery, it did the trick for the Conservatives at the time. Labour retained its support, but the Conservatives gained votes from the Liberals, and the Tories were swept back to power. Baldwin became Prime Minister once again.

The *ILN* devoted many pages this year to pictures of the treasures of Tutankhamun's tomb, and bought sole colour reproduction rights of everything appertaining to it. Another source of excitement in August was a series of pictures of Venus obtained from the Mount Wilson Observatory in California. 'In high latitudes the climate is probably productive of abundant vegetation and teeming animal life. The poles are covered by a white deposit resembling our polar snows.'

Less enthralling, but more practical progress was being made elsewhere. The British Post Office decided to convert some 70 telephone exchanges 'within a 10-mile radius of Oxford Circus from manual to automatic working . . . language, dialect, accent and eccentricities of pronunciation will no longer matter', rejoiced the *ILN*. 'The phrase: "You gave me the wrong number" will, in fact, disappear from the language.'

The *ILN*'s reporter wrote that a different system of voice projection was tested in Westminster Abbey, when: '. . .the preacher's voice was amplified by "loud speakers", and the sermon was distinctly audible in the remotest parts of the building . . . The Abbey experiment . . . is known as the Public Address system.' A similar system had been used to distribute the King's speech throughout Wembley Stadium when he opened the British Empire Exhibition in April; and the speech was also broadcast to millions of wireless listeners. So successful was the exhibition that it was extended into 1925.

Also this year, George Bernard Shaw's *Saint Joan* was produced on the London stage, establishing the witty iconoclast and social critic as a man of profound understanding. The Derby was won by Sansovino, owned by the Earl of Derby, and the Olympic Games were held in Paris.

Desperately seeking success: a defiant placard over the East Ham headquarters in London of Labour candidate Susan Lawrence in the ballot of October 1924. As it proved, the Tories won the election handsomely—with the aid of the Zinoviev letter, which ostensibly gave orders for Red revolution in Britain—and ousted the Labour government led by Ramsay MacDonald. Stanley Baldwin returned to No. 10 Downing Street and Winston Churchill was a surprise choice as Chancellor of the Exchequer. The worst casualties were suffered by the Liberals. They were reduced to 40 MPs and their leader, the former Prime Minister H H Asquith, lost his seat.

Tutankhamun to the life: one of the two life-size statues of Pharaoh Tutankhamun, found in his tomb by the British archaeologist Howard Carter. 'Here we get a full-face view of the right-hand statue, showing very clearly the wonderful detail of the face and costume. Both the statues are . . . magnificently carved in wood covered with a black pitch-like substance. The head-dress, armlets and wrist-bands, mace and staff, are heavily gilt, and over the left arm hangs a fabric of fine linen. On the forehead is the uraeus, or cobra, the emblem of royalty, of inlaid gold and bronze. The eye-sockets and eyebrows are of gold, and the eyeballs of arragonite, with pupils of obsidian. On the right is part of the funeral bouquet . . .' (3 February 1923). The burial place of Tutankhamun, the youthful ruler of the Egyptian 18th Dynasty, continued to reveal an astonishing wealth of treasures in 1924.

1924

E·V·E·N·T·S

21 JANUARY Death of Lenin, founder of the
Soviet state, at 54
22 JANUARY Britain's first Labour government
appointed under MacDonald
31 MARCH Imperial Airways formed as
Britain's national airline
4 APRIL The BBC broadcasted the first radio
programmes for schools
23 APRIL British Empire Exhibition opened at
Wembley
31 OCTOBER Labour routed by Tories after a
'red scare', provoked by Zinoviev letter

Buried to a salute of factory sirens: the body of the Russian leader Lenin lying in state (above). 'The funeral of Lenin took place in Moscow on January 27, and the ceremonies, which began at 9 am, lasted over seven hours . . . In digging the grave dynamite had to be used, as the ground was frozen so hard. A temporary mausoleum had been erected, and the coffin was placed outside it until four o'clock in the afternoon, when it was taken within and lowered into the grave. At that moment all traffic was stopped throughout the country for five minutes, and all factory sirens were sounded . . .' (9 February 1924)

Breaking the tape: Harold Abrahams of Cambridge University won the 100 yards at the Amateur Athletic Association's championships (below). 'The meeting was memorable not only for some very fast times and a general high standard of quality, but for the fact that it constituted the final trials for the choice of a team to represent Great Britain at the Olympic Games in Paris next month.' (28 June 1924). Harold Abrahams won the Olympic 100 metres, and Eric Liddell the 400 metres (as recorded long afterwards in the film *Chariots of Fire*).

ARCHAEOLOGY

Revealing Man's Past

I met a traveller from an antique land
Who said: Two vast and trunkless legs of stone
Stand in the desert. Near them, in the sand,
Half sunk, a shattered visage lies . . .
And on the pedestal these words appear:
'My name is Ozymandias, king of kings;
Look on my works, ye Mighty, and despair!'
Nothing beside remains. Round the decay
Of that colossal wreck, boundless and bare
The lone and level sands stretch far away.

PERCY BYSSHE SHELLEY

The magnificent gold mask of Tutankhamun.

'THE CURSE OF THE PHARAOHS', screamed the headlines in the popular press in April 1923, when the Earl of Carnarvon died of pneumonia in Cairo. Only a few weeks before, he and Howard Carter, an experienced English Egyptologist, had entered the sealed tomb of Pharaoh Tutankhamun of the eighteenth dynasty. The tomb had been undisturbed for 3,000 years and contained an astounding wealth of treasure, protected by curses on anyone who dared disturb the Pharaoh's rest. Fuel was added to the media's blaze by the fact that a mysterious power failure put all the lights in Cairo out as Lord Carnarvon was dying. It was soon reported that at his family seat in England his dog had begun to howl and had actually dropped dead at the moment when its master expired.

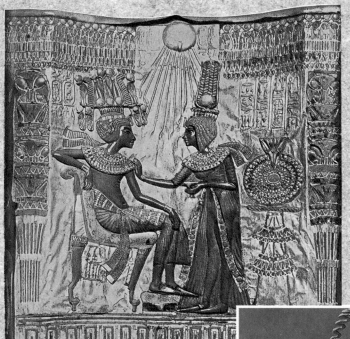

Tutankhamun and his wife (left), depicted on the back panel of the Pharaoh's throne. This was covered in sheet gold and inlaid with coloured stone, faience and glass.

Head of the cow goddess Hathor (right), from a couch in the tomb. Between the huge gilt horns is a gilt solar disc.

The gold diadem (left), surmounted by the royal emblems of the vulture and the serpent, was bound around the brow of Tutankhamun's mummy as the Pharaoh lay in his tomb.

Carter and Lord Carnarvon had discovered Tutankhamun's tomb in the Valley of the Kings in November 1922. They dug down through stone and rubble to the entrance and entered the antechamber. On 17 February 1923, watched by a small group of government officials and archaeologists, and with a feeling of profound awe, they broke into the inner burial chamber. Here they were confronted by a massive shrine of gilded wood. Inside were three more shrines, one inside the other. Inside the innermost lay a stone sarcophagus, on which were carved four guardian goddesses in high relief.

The lid of the sarcophagus was raised in February 1924. Inside was a coffin of wood and beaten gold, 7ft 4in (2.24m) long, with a golden effigy of the Pharaoh forming its lid. Inside this was another similar coffin, slightly smaller, and inside this again was a coffin of solid gold, over 6ft (1.8m) long and ⅛in (3mm) thick. It weighed more than a ton and it took eight strong men to lift it. Inside this innermost coffin, at last, was the mummified body of Tutankhamun himself. He was about 18 when he died in 1352BC. Over his face was a superb portrait mask in gold, and on his head a diadem of gold and carnelian. Little golden sheaths had been fitted over his toes. Found in other rooms were statues, ornaments, jewels, chariots, pieces of furniture and weapons, in such quantities that clearing the tomb took three years. The *ILN* was the only British magazine to show the finds in colour at the time.

The discovery aroused intense excite-

ment, and for a time there was a craze for all things Ancient Egyptian, which affected women's clothes and hats as well as fashions in cinema décor, and also objects ranging from cocktail shakers and ashtrays to statuettes and furniture. There was also a rash of 'mummy's curse' horror films.

The Tutankhamun furore showed what a tremendous popular interest there was in the mystery and romance of ancient civilisations. For all the press hysteria, the episode helped to bring archaeology out of its nineteenth-century obscurity and into the light of public interest and approval. It was also a landmark in the transformation of archaeology from an amateur pursuit—compounded of vague antiquarianism and treasure-hunting—into a respected professional discipline.

Some of the essential spadework, as it were, had been done before 1890. A key date in the early history of serious modern archaeology is 1822, when the young French scholar Jean François Champollion deciphered Egyptian hieroglyphics. When he realised that he had unlocked the secret, he fainted, and the feat led on to the

Howard Carter, the Egyptologist who discovered the tomb in 1922, is seen here looking into the shrine.

development of modern Egyptology.

The familiar chronological division of prehistory into Stone Age, Bronze Age and Iron Age, after the materials used for tools and weapons, had by now been worked out in Denmark. Serious investigation of the ancient Assyrian and Babylonian civilisations of Mesopotamia began in the 1840s, and cuneiform writing was deciphered in 1846. The discovery in 1872 of the Babylonian story of the Great Flood, with its striking similarities to the story in the Bible, aroused intense interest. In the 1870s a German-American business magnate named Heinrich Schliemann sent a thrill of excitement through the learned world by digging into a mound in Asia Minor and finding Homer's Troy, which many classical scholars had written off as a myth. In 1879 in a cave at Altamira in northern Spain, wonderfully vivid and vigorous Stone Age paintings of wild bulls, deer and boar were found, some of the earliest known human art.

A significant moment came in Britain in 1882, with the passing of the Ancient Monuments Protection Act, for the first time giving some measure of protection to the country's major antiquities. The period from the 1880s to the 1930s was dominated by a succession of brilliant British archaeologists who combined high standards of scholarship with a flair for publicity and popularisation. Busily digging up an estate he had inherited in Cranborne Chase in Dorset, General Augustus Pitt-Rivers laid the foundations of modern archaeological field technique. He was the first Inspector of Ancient Monuments appointed under the 1882 act. In Egypt, Flinders Petrie applied similar principles to the first detailed survey of the pyramids and the excavation of the tombs of the earliest

The throne room at Knossos in Crete, in the palace discovered by Arthur Evans.

Egyptian kings. Like Pitt-Rivers, he believed in the potential importance of the most minimal details and he insisted on rigorously accurate and systematic recording of finds.

In 1899 Arthur Evans set his hand to one of the most exciting and fruitful excavations in the history of archaeology when he started to dig at Knossos in Crete and swiftly uncovered not only the royal palace of the Cretan kings, but a previously unknown Bronze Age civilisation which he called Minoan, after Minos, the King of Crete in Greek legend. He discovered features of the palace which he believed had inspired the romantic legend of the Cretan labyrinth and

the Minotaur, the half-man, half-bull which lived at its heart. Evans did not succeed in deciphering the three Minoan systems of writing he discovered, but one of them, Linear B, which was eventually decoded in 1952 by Michael Ventris, turned out to be an early form of Greek.

What Evans did uncover, however, was the advanced character of Minoan civilisation, with its efficient plumbing and its symbols of the double axe and the horns, its stunning works of art, wall paintings, pottery, bronze and gold work, its figurines of a bare-breasted snake goddess and its astonishing pictures of the sport or cult of bull leaping, with boy and girl athletes somersaulting over the backs of ferociously horned bulls.

In one of the designs, described by

Evans: 'The girl acrobat seizes the horns of a coursing bull at full gallop, one of which seems to run under her left armpit. The object of her grip . . . seems to be to gain a purchase for a backward somersault over the animal's back, such as is being performed by the boy. The second female performer behind stretches out both her hands as if about to catch the flying figure or at least to steady him when he comes to earth the right way up.'

With the coming of the twentieth century, archaeology's horizons widened to areas of the earth beyond the Near East, the Mediterranean and western Europe. Interest in archaeology was developing across the Atlantic, and in 1911 Hiram Bingham discovered the Inca city of Machu Picchu in Peru, perched dizzyingly in the Andes Mountains. The Incas, 'the sons of the sun', were worshipped as gods and ruled a South American empire until the arrival of the Spanish conquistadors in the sixteenth century.

On the other side of the globe, the first prehistoric site recognised in China was identified in 1921. In the same year a previously unknown civilisation was discovered in India, in the valley of the Indus. Its twin capital cities were Harappa and Mohenjo-Daro, which were laid out on a grid system and are the earliest examples of town planning yet known. They had substantial public buildings and elaborate drainage systems, and were possibly ruled by priest-kings. Seals discovered among the

The grand staircase at Knossos, where Minoan civilisation was revealed.

Horns of consecration, Knossos (below). Bulls were important in Minoan religion.

ruins show a horned figure who is perhaps an ancestor of the great Hindu god Siva.

The Indus civilisation may have been overwhelmed, somewhere about 2000BC, by the invasion of India from the north-west by the all-conquering Aryans. That the Aryans spoke a language closely related not only to Sanskrit but to Greek and Latin, and almost all modern European languages, had been demonstrated back in 1786. Scholarly interest in them had disagreeable side-effects in the 1920s and 1930s in Germany, where it fuelled the Nazi mythology of the superiority of the German master race: an obsession which was zealously propagated by the archaeologist Gustav Kossinna, who was Professor of German Prehistory at Berlin University from 1902 until his death in 1931.

In Britain in the 1920s and 1930s, interesting and less ominous developments included the discovery that the 'bluestones' which had formed two of the circles at Stonehenge had come from the Preseli Hills of Pembrokeshire, far away in the remote south-west corner of Wales. This was demonstrated beyond all cavil—a rare phenomenon in the interpretation of Stonehenge—by H H Thomas of the Geological Survey of Great Britain. It meant that these great stones, weighing 4 tons apiece, must have been transported 200 miles to be put in position at Stonehenge. Probably they were carried on rafts as far as possible by sea and river, and were then dragged the last part of the way overland on rollers. The implication was not only that Stonehenge had deep religio-magical significance for its builders—otherwise, why bring stones from such a distance?—but also that an authority of some kind existed in southern England (at a date now reckoned as about 2000BC) which was capable of a substantial feat of planning, organisation and logistics. It was another demonstration of something which archaeology was making increasingly clear—that our distant ancestors were nothing like as backward as Victorian opinion had assumed.

From the 1920s onwards, two important developments took place in archaeology; the introduction of ever more effective technology, and a growing sense of the importance of effective popularisation. Both were combined in the career of O G S Crawford. He was the leading pioneer of the new art of aerial photography, which was used to help make better sense of sites and also to discover prehistoric sites which were not detectable at ground level but which showed up from the air by way of crop marks and soil marks. Crawford served in the Flying Corps in the First World War. Afterwards he was the Ordnance Survey's first archaeology officer and it is due to him that the Survey's maps are so archaeologically comprehensive. In 1927 Crawford founded *Antiquity*, the leading archaeology magazine for specialists and intelligent non-specialists alike, which he edited for 30 years until his death in the 1950s.

Another leading British archaeologist with a gift for popularisation was Leonard Woolley, who from 1922 to 1934 carried out an excavation with wildly spectacular results at Ur in Mesopotamia, the Ur of the Chaldees which is famous as the original home of Abraham in the Bible. The discovery of the royal graves, with their riches of gold and lapis lazuli, caused almost as great a sensation as the opening of Tutankhamun's tomb. The rulers of Ur went to their last home in tombs of stone or brick, buried deep in vast pits. Inside the tomb the dead King or Queen rested in royal finery with two or three attendants, who were killed and whose bodies were placed close by. Then the tomb was walled up and a great procession of the dead ruler's ministers and officials, dancing girls and musicians, soldiers and servants, oxen and asses, descended into the pit. After a religious ceremony each of them drank a draught of a narcotic and lay down to sleep, all in their places in orderly rows, and then the earth was shovelled in on top of them to fill up the pit.

In the USA meanwhile, A E Douglass had developed dendrochronology, or dating by the growth rings of trees, as a scientific archaeological technique. He used it to date the prehistoric communities of the Pueblo Indians in south-western states.

In England in the 1930s the spiritual successor of Pitt-Rivers and Petrie, Evans and Woolley, was Mortimer Wheeler, who devised the grid square method of excavation for the meticulous recording of finds. Digging at Maiden Castle, the great earthwork fortress outside Dorchester, in the 1930s, he welcomed visiting members of the public to the site and made sure that they were shown round by well-informed guides. He understood the thrill of the macabre and skeletons were left in place in uncovered graves for visitors to see. Skeletons were in plentiful supply because Maiden Castle had been stormed after the Romans invaded Britain in AD43. Wheeler found thousands of pebbles gathered from Chesil Beach which had been placed ready as ammunition for the defenders' slings, but the Roman legionaries under a future Emperor, Vespasian, took the fortress, killing many of the defenders, who were buried in graves dug near the east gate.

Wheeler was Director of the London Museum and founded the Institute of Archaeology in London University.

Sir Mortimer Wheeler (left), a leading figure in British archaeology. Maiden Castle in Dorset (below), a formidable earthwork fortress which had been stormed by the Roman legions, was excavated by Wheeler in the 1930s.

Archaeology had become a recognised academic subject and university archaeology departments and learned journals multiplied. After the Second World War, Wheeler and Glyn Daniel (editor of *Antiquity* after Crawford and later Professor of Archaeology at Cambridge) brought archaeology enjoyably to a mass audience for the first time, on television in *Animal, Vegetable, Mineral* and *Buried Treasure*. Both programmes ran for years and the formidable Wheeler, who has been described as 'God's gift to television', was certainly a gift to archaeology's public relations.

Just before the outbreak of war in 1939 came another sensational discovery, when a mound was excavated at Sutton Hoo, near Woodbridge in Suffolk. It proved to contain what was left of a 38-oared Saxon ship and a rich treasure of gold and silver coins and jewellery, a fine helmet and shield, bowls and dishes and many other objects. It is thought to have been a memorial to King Raedwald, who ruled the East Anglians in the seventh century. The treasure can now be seen in the British Museum.

At Lascaux in the Dordogne in France, on a September day in 1940, four schoolboys lightheartedly pushed their way down into a hole revealed by a fallen tree. They found themselves inside a fantastic gallery of Stone Age cave art, with vivid pictures of bulls and cows, bison and horses, unseen by human eyes since the last Ice Age. Four years later, something altogether grimmer was found in a bog at Tollund in Denmark. It was the blackened but well-preserved body of a man who had been strangled or hanged, some 2,000 years before, probably as a sacrifice to the goddess of fertility. He was naked except for a leather cap and belt, and the leather rope was still tight around his neck.

During the Second World War, in a reverse contribution of archaeology to technology, the photographic intelligence departments of the warring nations relied heavily on archaeologists for their staff. After 1945 the pace of technological innovation in archaeology quickened dramatically. Among major new methods were electrical

This grimly impressive helmet was one of the finds from the Sutton Hoo ship burial in Suffolk.

and magnetic prospecting. Electrical prospecting was adopted from the oil industry in the late 1940s and applied to prehistoric sites. Magnetic prospecting, which involves locating buried features such as ditches, pits and hearths through the magnetic disturbances they cause, started 10 years later.

A fundamental innovation was radiocarbon dating (or C-14 dating), developed from 1946 by the American chemist Willard F Libby, who subsequently won the Nobel Prize. It depends on the fact that the radioactivity of carbon-14 in bones, wood and other animal and vegetable material declines at a known rate. Measuring the amount of radioactivity still present consequently gives an indication of how old a sample is, within a certain margin of error. Although it had protracted teething troubles, radiocarbon dating gave archaeology a desperately needed method of absolute dating. Other methods developed from it later, including potassium argon dating, which depends on the rate of decay of the isotope K-40 in potassium, and thermoluminescence, which dates pottery by measuring the emission of alpha particles.

Suitably enough, while all this exciting technology was coming into play, one of British archaeology's elderly bogies was at long last laid to rest, with the demonstration in 1953 that Piltdown Man was a hoax. In 1912 an archaeologist named Charles Dawson discovered, or said he had discovered, pieces of a human skull of great antiquity on Piltdown Common, near Lewes in Sussex. With them were bones of long-extinct animals, so that it appeared that Dawson had found the remains of the oldest human being ever discovered in Britain. It was

The Lascaux caves, discovered in 1940, held a rich treasure of prehistoric art.

thought that he might even have discovered the 'missing link', the creature which bridged the gap between the apes and the first human beings.

Distinguished authorities flocked to exclaim over this remarkable phenomenon, but unfortunately Piltdown Man never fitted into the pattern of evolution which later discoveries of very early human beings suggested, and 40 years later it was shown that this alleged ancestor of mankind was actually made of fragments of a modern human cranium plus the jawbone of a modern orang-utan, while the supposedly associated animal bones had been brought from elsewhere. The finger of suspicion was pointed at Charles Dawson, who was by then safely dead. Piltdown Man's Latin name, *Eanthropus dawsoni*, was evidently appropriate in a different sense from the one intended.

The buzz over Piltdown Man was swallowed up in excitement over a startling discovery which had been made a few years earlier in Palestine. At the north-west end of the Dead Sea, an Arab boy was searching for a strayed goat one day in 1947 when he entered a cave in which a row of jars stood on the floor. These jars, it turned out, had been standing there unnoticed and undisturbed since AD68 or thereabouts. In them were manuscripts, including a Hebrew text of the prophet Isaiah a thousand years older than the oldest version then known. Over the next 10 years or so, many more scrolls were found in caves in this area. They had been hidden to keep them safe from the conquering Romans and had originally formed the library of a Jewish monastic community at Khirbet Qumran. The monastery, which was the headquarters of a small ascetic sect, the Essenes, was excavated in the 1950s.

In 1947, in a cave near the Dead Sea (background) an Arab boy stumbled across a row of jars (top) which were found to contain ancient manuscripts of books of the Old Testament, including Isaiah (right).

The scrolls yielded a complete copy of the Hebrew Old Testament (except for the Book of Esther) far older than anything known before. Other documents threw light on the previously obscure history of Palestine and Judaism in the last centuries BC and the first AD, and so on the historical and ideological background of Christianity. There were even suggestions that John the Baptist might have been trained at Qumran in his youth and that Jesus himself might have spent some time there.

The Jewish war against Rome broke out in AD66 and two years later the monastery at Qumran was destroyed by fire, probably as a result of a Roman attack (curiously enough, by troops under the command of the same Vespasian who stormed Maiden Castle). Detailed study of the Dead Sea Scrolls has been going on for years, and no doubt will take years more, but the tremendous public interest in them was shown when exhibitions were mounted in Britain and the USA, and people queued patiently for hours to get in.

In the 1950s and 1960s interest revived in Stonehenge and Britain's other stone circles. They had long been recognised as temples, but evidence was developing that they had also been skilfully laid out as astronomical observatories for measuring and predicting the movements of the moon and the sun, probably in connection with both religion and the calendar. Archaeologists at first resisted what seemed a lunatic fringe idea, but methodical, unsensational surveying work of previously unmatched accuracy by Alexander Thom, a retired Oxford Professor of Engineering, eventually persuaded even the most conservative authorities on the Stone Age. Again, prehistoric culture was shown to be more complex and more advanced than had been assumed.

It was also being realised that man and his ancestors had appeared on the world's stage far longer ago than earlier theories had supposed. In the Olduvai Gorge in Tanzania in the late 1950s, two British archaeologists, Louis and Mary Leakey, found bones of very early man-like beings that were nearly 2 million years old. The one which most took the media's fancy was nicknamed 'Nutcracker Man' (correctly *Zinjanthropus boisei*) for his enormous jaws and teeth. He had lived in East Africa one-and-three-quarter million years ago.

A dramatic piece of rescue archaeology hit the headlines in the 1960s. At Abu Simbel in Egypt the temple erected by Pharaoh Ramses II in about 1250BC, with four gigantic statues of himself, 60ft (18.3m) high, was in danger of submerging under water. An international rescue operation under the auspices of UNESCO saved the temple and the figures and moved them to higher ground.

In the late 1960s the magic name of King Arthur drew visitors in unexpectedly large numbers to the top of Cadbury Castle, a prehistoric hillfort in Somerset, where archaeologists were revealing a powerful stronghold of about AD500 which could well have been the headquarters of the British war-leader against the invading Saxons around whom romantic legends have gathered.

The 1970s saw the discovery of two particularly exciting tombs. The first, found in 1974, was the last resting place of the builder of the Great Wall of China, the Emperor Chi'in Shih Huang Ti, who was buried in about 210BC with thousands of life-size pottery warriors to guard him. Three years later, at Vergina in northern Greece, excavation revealed the tomb of one-eyed Philip of Macedon, assassinated in 336BC, the formidable father of Alexander the Great, buried with a treasure of gold and silver, bronze and ivory.

Underwater archaeology was an important development after the Second World War, powered by the invention of the aqualung in the 1940s, which made work on the seabed a practical possibility for the first time. An American team working off the coast of Turkey in 1960 discovered the oldest shipwreck then known, the remains of a freighter of the thirteenth century BC which had been carrying a cargo of copper from Cyprus. In 1961 a seventeenth-century Swedish warship, the *Wasa*, was raised from her watery bed in Stockholm harbour.

The star archaeological event of the 1980s, however, was the raising of the Tudor battleship *Mary Rose*, the pride of Henry VIII's fleet, which had heeled over and sunk in 1545 when sallying out to repel an attack by the French. Manoeuvred on to a great wooden cradle, the ship's hull was heaved up from the murky waters of the Solent by a crane and moved safely to a dock in Portsmouth, where she and the mass of equipment recovered from the seabed are on display to the public.

In 1988 it was announced that the oldest human footprints ever discovered in Britain

An international rescue operation saved the temple of Abu Simbel in Egypt, erected in the thirteenth century BC, with its gigantic figures of Pharaoh Ramses II of the nineteenth dynasty (above) and its hall of colossal statues (right). The temple had been threatened by the building of a lake in connection with the Aswan Dam. Ramses II, a formidable builder of monuments, is thought to have been Pharaoh when Moses led the Israelites out of Egypt.

had been found two years before, in mud on the bank of the River Severn. They had been made by someone about 5ft 6in (1.7m) tall, and radiocarbon dating of the mud put them at about 5200BC. The announcement serves as a pleasing footnote to an era of discovery and development which has made archaeology not only a professional discipline, but a subject of intense media and popular interest.

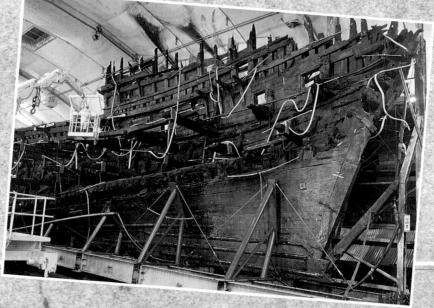

The hull of the Mary Rose, in the special dock which was provided for the Tudor warship in Portsmouth.

1925

IN 1925 P G WODEHOUSE PUBLISHED HIS SECOND BOOK about Bertie Wooster, the rich young idler living in Mayfair, tended with a blend of obsequiousness and firmness by his man Jeeves. *Carry On Jeeves* epitomises with brilliant wit the lifestyle of a certain type of rich young man in 1920s Britain, too young to have fought in the war, though his father might well have died in it.

Among the less privileged classes there was widespread disillusion. Many felt there was little future in Britain and emigrated to Canada, Australia, New Zealand or South Africa, or (if they had capital), to Rhodesia (Zimbabwe) to grow tobacco. For millions of workers who could not escape, there were low wages, bad housing, poor education and scant health care.

Harder times were promised: Baldwin declared that: 'All the workers of this country have got to take reductions in wages to help put industry on its feet.' An understandable support for left-wing ideas among the working classes was matched by suspicion from the Establishment. The *ILN* told its readers that on 14 October, officers of the Special Branch of Scotland Yard had visited the headquarters of the Communist Party of Great Britain in King Street, Covent Garden, and that six leading Communists had been arrested. Eight Communists were taken in total, and charged under the Incitement to Mutiny Act of 1797. They were remanded for eight days: the intention was evidently to show the hand of the government, which had also begun preparing for a general strike.

This year, Hitler published his political ideology, *Mein Kampf* ('My Struggle'), and *The Life of Benito Mussolini* appeared in Britain. A revealing extract from the latter was published in the *ILN*:

> *'I must get this people into some kind of order. Then I shall have fulfilled my task. I shall then feel that I am someone . . . And yet!—and yet! Yes; I am obsessed by this wild desire—it consumes my whole being. I want to make a mark on my era with my will, like a lion with its claws! A mark like this!' And as with a claw, he scratched the covering of a chair-back from end to end!* (24 October)

Not everyone was a politician or a Bertie Wooster. In the wake of the excavation of Tutankhamun's tomb, which had been illustrated in colour by the *ILN*, there was a good deal of public interest in unearthing the past. Pictures were also published of a Roman mosaic unearthed at Colchester and of the Roman ruins at Jemila, Algeria, 'an African "Pompei"'. Mr L S B Leakey's account of the British Museum Expedition in Tanganyika (Tanzania) provided much interest. The *ILN* reported that the main object of the expedition was to obtain bones of *Gigantosaurus*, a huge dinosaurian reptile.

Back in Britain, ever-increasing numbers of cars prompted suggestions for a three-tier system for cities: pedestrians above, cars at ground level and railways below. The dazzle of car headlights was a continuing problem:

> *The motoring organisations have now definitely decided that dimming or blacking-out is dangerous . . . For the average country cyclist does not carry a rear light, and trusts to the skill of the motorist to get out of his way.* (18 April)

Action against Communists: In October 'a few hundred people collected and sang "The Red Flag" outside Bow Street court as leading Communists were charged'. (24 October 1925). The accused included Thomas Bell (below), Ernest Cant (centre) and Willie Gallacher (far right).

A great American disaster: a view of devastated Murphysboro, Illinois, which took the full force of the April tornado that 'tore a track 150 miles long through five states, killed over 800 people, and injured 3000 . . . The damage to property was immense and was said to constitute the greatest disaster in the United States' since the floods of 1913. (4 April 1925)

THE ILLUSTRATED
LONDON NEWS
1925

E·V·E·N·T·S

16 JANUARY Trotsky removed from Soviet War
Council by Stalin
13 MARCH Daylight Saving Summer Time
made permanent by Parliament
30 APRIL Art Deco style launched by Paris
Exposition des Arts Décoratifs
25 MAY John Scopes brought to trial in
Tennessee for teaching about evolution
29 JUNE Colour bar made legal in South Africa
with work ban for blacks
18 JUNE Hitler's personal testament, *Mein
Kampf* ('My Struggle') published

"You needn't be shy with me Felix!"

Cartoon cat: by the 1920s the Americans
dominated the world of animated cartoon films
with characters like Felix (above) and Mickey
Mouse, though the first animated cartoons had
been made in France before the First World War.

Buried in golden splendour: inside the
sarcophagus of Pharaoh Tutankhamun was a coffin
whose lid was formed by a magnificent golden
effigy of the King, his arms crossed on his breast,
holding the royal emblems, the crook and the flail.
The fifth Earl of Carnarvon, whose enthusiasm and
support made the whole sensational discovery
possible, had taken up Egyptology while he was
recovering from a serious motor accident.

1926

STEP BY STEP, in the early months of this year, Britain moved closer to a General Strike. The miners became convinced that the government was determined to beat them down, and the Trades Union Congress (TUC), which, like the Labour Party, was not eager for a fight, had its hand forced. Some members of the Cabinet, including Winston Churchill, the Chancellor of the Exchequer, wanted a showdown. Last-minute attempts to compromise failed. The TUC called out the key unions—railwaymen, dockers, road transport workers, printers, iron and steel workers, builders, electricity and gas workers—and the strike began at midnight on 3 May.

The government's well-organised measures to combat the strike went into action. The Army and the Royal Navy were at the ready, and London, it was said, seemed as if it was at war, with troops in battle order and armoured cars driving up and down the streets. The *ILN* reported that:

> *Large stocks of flour were lying at the London Docks, and could not be moved owing to the obstruction of the strikers. On Saturday (May 8) a great train of lorries, escorted by a battalion of Grenadier Guards, with armoured cars, marched from Hyde Park to the docks, where the flour was loaded and taken away, the watching crowds offering no opposition.* (15 May)

For the middle classes, the strike was a chance to realise long-cherished fantasies:

> *Young men in tweeds or sports coats, and wearing school or college ties, were to be seen driving trains or acting as guards or porters, and very well they did it . . . The Headmaster of Eton (Dr. Alington) and about fifty of his assistant masters, have enrolled as special constables . . .* (15 May)

By 12 May it was over. On the face of it, this was a massive defeat for the working-class movement, but the TUC had shown considerable power and Baldwin did not seek to exploit the government's victory.

An Imperial Conference defined the new position of the dominions, dissolving much of the Empire into a free association of equal states. John Logie Baird gave the first demonstration of pictures transmitted by wireless. The Duchess of York gave birth in April to her first child, Elizabeth, and Britain enjoyed overwhelming superiority in the athletics field:

> *In spite of a massed attack by German athletes, competing for the first time since the war, the Amateur Athletic Association's championships at Stamford Bridge resulted in ten out of the eighteen championships remaining in British keeping.* (10 July)

Also in this year, Leonard Woolley unearthed the royal graves and the temple of Nin-Gal, the moon goddess of Ur, in Mesopotamia, and T E Lawrence, 'Lawrence of Arabia', published *The Seven Pillars of Wisdom* for private circulation. Lawrence had caught the imagination of the public when he fought with the Arabs against the Turks during the First World War.

Woman against the strike: with the General Strike looming up, 20,000 women marched through London on 17 April in 'a great demonstration for industrial peace' (24 April 1926). Led by a horsewoman bearing a Union Jack, they marched to the Albert Hall, where they held a meeting and passed an anti-strike resolution.

The return of the wage packet: at Clipston Colliery in Nottinghamshire, miners drew their first wages since the strike began. The dispute followed a Royal Commission's recommendation that pay must be cut. The miners stayed out after the General Strike ended in May, and not until August did they admit defeat.

Pioneer of television: John Logie Baird (above), a Scots electrical engineer, showed the first television images in January 1926 in London. The BBC adopted his system initially, but dropped it in 1937.

The first woman to swim the Channel: an 18-year-old American, Gertrude Ederle, in grease and goggles, swam the Channel from France to England in 14 hours 39 minutes on 6 August, 'thus beating the previous fastest time by nearly two hours'. (14 August 1926)

THE ILLUSTRATED LONDON NEWS

1926

E·V·E·N·T·S

27 JANUARY Television first demonstrated by its inventor, John Logie Baird

3 MAY Britain's first General Strike started, in support of miners

3 AUGUST London's first traffic lights installed at Piccadilly Circus

8 SEPTEMBER Germany admitted to League of Nations after unanimous vote

25 DECEMBER Hirohito became Emperor of Japan on death of his father

The Daily Mirror: General Strike, Day 1.

1927

IT WAS A TIME WHEN CHURCHES were losing their congregations in Britain. The trend affected not only the Church of England, but also the main nonconformist sects—Methodists, Presbyterians, Baptists, Congregationalists. People still used the churches for baptisms, marriages and deaths, and at the great Christian events of Christmas and Easter. But the heart was going out of it all. The decline had started long before the war, and now the pace quickened.

There were now more divorces, but legal procedures were still long, expensive, and often humiliating. As for birth control, it was obviously being practised on an increasing scale, especially by the middle and upper classes; the size of families proved this. As far as abortions were concerned, doctors feared the danger of being struck off the medical register if they helped to terminate a pregnancy. For those women who could afford it, a stay at a Swiss clinic was the safest method. For the less fortunate, back-street abortions were also common, and often resulted in serious illness or death.

On a lighter note, this year the BBC had sponsored the Promenade Concerts for the first time, and the result was judged by the *ILN* to have been 'an unqualified success'. The audiences had been consistently large, contrary to fears that broadcasting would cause a decrease in attendances. For the conductor and creator of the 'Proms', Sir Henry Wood, the financial aid of the BBC opened up new horizons. The *ILN* correspondent discussing the 'Proms' suggested that the BBC should finance a permanent symphony orchestra in London, for in general:

> *Our orchestras at present muddle through as best they can. We only become aware of how painfully they are muddling through when we take a distinguished for- eigner to hear one of our symphony concerts. Then the imperfections in the actual playing, and in the inter- pretation become glaring. We realise suddenly how accustomed we are to overlook faults and defects which we should not overlook; in short, we are conscious of the bad habits we have got into.* (1 October)

The suggestion that the BBC should establish its own permanent orchestra was realised in January 1929.

This year, the world watched closely as the frontiers of science and technology continued to be pushed back. In May, the young American, Charles Lindbergh, touched down at Le Bourget airport, Paris, watched by a crowd of thousands. He had become the first person to fly solo, non-stop across the Atlantic in his monoplane, *The Spirit of St Louis*, and he became an inter- national hero.

In Germany, Adolf Hitler held his first National Socialist German Workers' (Nazi) Party meeting in Berlin, and the chant, *Heil Hitler*, was increasing in strength and magnitude. Revolu- tionary riots in Vienna prompted renewed German demands for the annexation of Austria. In China, the civil war raging between the Nationalist army under General Chiang Kai-shek and the government in Peking took a decisive turn when the Nationalists entered Shanghai, the richest port in the country, despite efforts by British, French and Italian troops to defend foreign nationals living there. Meanwhile, in Russia, Stalin routed his political opponents by expelling Leon Trotsky and Grigori Zinoviev from the Soviet Communist Party.

Robot-woman, a man-made Eve: the German silent film *Metropolis*, set in the world of a hundred years ahead, featured an artificial woman.

Everything but the kitchen sink: the Red Chinese soldier, equipped with modern arms, and also his tea-kettle and towels, could look deceptively slovenly. 'This one's array of utensils . . . rather suggests the White Knight in "Alice".' (22 February 1927)

A triumph of the silent screen: thousands of extras did duty as Bonaparte's army of Italy in Abel Gance's *Napoleon*, (left), shown on a 16-yard triple screen. Pains were taken to cast actors who looked like the characters they played. 'The likeness of M. Albert Dieudonné to Bonaparte, as portrayed by David, is really astonishing'. (22 October 1927)

A new ruler for the land of the Rising Sun: Japan began the year with a new Emperor, the 25-year-old Hirohito, who had toured Europe in 1921, the first prince of his line to visit the West. His 62-year reign would see a period of aggressive Japanese militarism and imperialism in the Far East, leading to the attack on the Americans at Pearl Harbor.

THE ILLUSTRATED LONDON NEWS

1927

E · V · E · N · T · S

8 JANUARY First scheduled London–Delhi air service started

25 FEBRUARY British troops in action defending foreign nationals in Shanghai

21 MAY First solo transatlantic flight by Lindbergh ended at Le Bourget, Paris

6 OCTOBER First talking picture, *The Jazz Singer*, with Al Jolson, shown

18 NOVEMBER World Cup soccer competition proposed by FIFA head Jules Rimet

The Atlantic crossed in less than two days: Charles Lindbergh touched down in *The Spirit of St Louis* at Le Bourget airport in Paris on 21 May to cheers from a huge crowd, at the end of the first solo non-stop flight from the New World to the Old.

The **FOREMOST CLEANING DEVELOPMENT** *of our Day*

Household word: the vacuum cleaner, invented in 1907, had already become indispensable.

IN MAY, women in Britain were permitted to vote at the age of 21 on equal terms with men; in 1918 the first enfranchisement had been restricted to women aged 30 or over. The popular press called it 'the flapper vote', as if a tide of girlish silliness would wash over the country. Baldwin, however, believed that, on balance, giving votes to women would help the Conservatives, especially in a time of crisis.

Also in Britain this year, the new *R100* and *R101* airships were being built. The *ILN* was effusive: 'This year will see take the air the most wonderful flying machine ever constructed—the new rigid airship . . .' On a sadder note, the year saw the passing of Thomas Hardy, Emmeline Pankhurst and Herbert Asquith; the nation grew anxious when the King became ill in November with a lung ailment, and Queen Mary temporarily took over his duties. He grew worse in December and bulletins were posted on railings outside Buckingham Palace with the latest news. The *ILN* noted that: 'From the time the first bulletin regarding King George's illness was posted . . . there has been a constant stream of people gathering there to read the latest announcement.'

Abroad, Amsterdam hosted the Olympic Games, and in August delegates from Britain and representatives from other countries met in Paris to sign the Kellogg-Briand Pact, an idealistic document eventually signed by 65 countries who agreed to outlaw war as an instrument of international policy. Herbert Hoover won the presidential election for the Republicans in the USA. In China the Peking government surrendered peacefully to the Nationalist forces of General Chiang Kai-shek, ending the civil war there; and in October, General Chiang Kai-shek became President of the Chinese republic.

In Turkey, premier Mustafa Kemal introduced the Roman alphabet to replace Arabic in a series of measures to westernise the country. G K Chesterton of the *ILN* expressed his approval; although 'there was no such thing as a European nation of Turkey', he thought that:

> *The great Moslem religion . . . has one great and glorious superiority to many of the fads of Western Europe. It has no Chosen Race; it has no nonsense about lesser breeds without the law; it has no rant of merely racial superiority; there is a brotherhood of men, if it be a brotherhood of Moslems. That was the whole difference between the Turks and the Prussians, and that is why any civilised Christian would infinitely prefer the Turks.* (11 August)

Books of the year included the *Oxford English Dictionary* – finally complete after decades of work, and more controversially, Marguerite Radclyffe Hall's *The Well of Loneliness*, which dealt with lesbianism. D H Lawrence's *Lady Chatterley's Lover* was published in Florence, in order to avoid censorship at home.

Paul Robeson's role in *Show Boat* at Drury Lane in London, drew comment from Michael Orme, writing in the *ILN*:

> *There is, of course, the regulation chorus of musical comedy to be seen and heard in 'Show Boat'; but there is a 'Chorus' in the older manner in the person of Joe, who links the passing years with the refrain 'Old Man River'.* (26 May)

A beauty from 5,000 years ago: the golden head-dress from the Queen's tomb at Ur in Mesopotamia. As archaeologist Leonard Woolley explained, the head-dress was 'found on the Queen's skull inside the stone-built chamber. Though crushed by stones and earth, every one of its component parts kept its position in the soil', which made reconstruction easy. (30 June 1928)

Beauty in the fashion of the 1920s: seven Beauty Queens, from Italy, Belgium and France, England (centre), Germany, Spain and Luxemburg, were off to Texas in May to vie for the title of the most beautiful woman in the world. Beauty changes with time, like all fashions.

THE ILLUSTRATED
LONDON NEWS

1928

E·V·E·N·T·S

6 JANUARY Central London flooded by
Thames after thaw and high tide

7 MAY Equal Franchise Act gave all British
women the vote at 21

15 MAY Start of flying doctor service in
Australia, to cover 250,000 miles

27 AUGUST Kellogg–Briand 'no war' Pact
signed by 15 nations, including Germany

30 SEPTEMBER Announcement of discovery of
penicillin by Alexander Fleming

22 NOVEMBER First £1 and 10 shilling notes in
circulation in Britain

Beauty and the machine:
beauty parlour equipment,
including this 'fireman's helmet'
drier, went on display at the
Hairdressers' Exhibition.

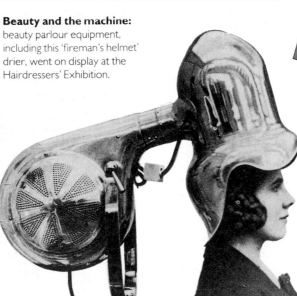

Under her bell-like hat: a smart
young lady looks out from the cover
of *Feminine Life* in August 1928. The
fashion of the time was for a boyish
look, simple lines, short skirts and
freedom from the elaborate
constricting women's clothes of the
Victorian and Edwardian eras
before the First World War. This
was to fit the image of the 'new
woman' as a free spirit, on equal
terms with men.

In this year Baldwin called a general election. During the campaign one of the main topics of debate was how the 5 million new women voters would respond. The economy was ailing; unemployment remained high, and there was a growing feeling that new ideas were needed to give politics fresh impetus. The Conservatives, however, decided on an electoral campaign employing the slogan 'Safety First', and a picture of Baldwin. Labour under Ramsay MacDonald offered gradual, rather than rapid improvements. Lloyd George and the Liberals wanted to introduce radical measures, such as a loan to boost industry, but the country had lost confidence in them.

In the *ILN*'s *Our Note Book*, G K Chesterton commented dryly:

> To hear the average Liberal and Parliamentarian talk, you would think that nothing had ever needed to be reformed since the Reform Bill. You would think that the modern Parliament, which professes to be based on a popular theory, was really a popular thing.
> (2 February)

The result was historic, for Labour was returned to the House of Commons with the largest number of MPs—although it had actually polled fewer votes overall than the Conservatives. It was an indecisive result, leaving Labour dependent on Liberal support. One of the Labour government's priorities was to set about reducing unemployment. A woman, Margaret Bondfield, became Minister for Labour (the first woman to sit in the Cabinet), and an able man, J H Thomas, was appointed Lord Privy Seal. He was given special responsibility for tackling unemployment.

A commission had been set up two years earlier to consider the future constitutional position of India, where civil disobedience, led by Gandhi, was creating a situation which could not, in the long run, be put down by force. In October this year, the high-minded Viceroy, Lord Irwin, stated that granting India dominion status would be the natural consequence.

Baldwin's position in the Conservative Party was inevitably insecure after the election, and was to become more so, largely due to a campaign for Empire Free Trade supported by Lord Beaverbrook and Lord Rothermere, who controlled the *Daily Express* and *Daily Mail* newspaper groups. Baldwin was sure that the idea behind the campaign was useless, for the dominions would never be in favour of sacrificing their new industries to the 'mother country'. Stung by venomous attacks on him, Baldwin denounced the two press barons as men seeking power without responsibility, which he described in no uncertain terms as 'the prerogative of the harlot throughout the ages'.

Some memorable books and a remarkable play appeared this year, describing with realism the degradation of the men who had fought and died in the trenches. Robert Graves' *Goodbye to All That* was an account, based on personal experiences, of how the million volunteers Kitchener had asked for ('the flower of the nation') were butchered on the Somme and in other battles, mainly as a result of the obstinate stupidity of the generals. Erich Maria Remarque's *All Quiet on the Western Front* told the story from the German side of the almost unspeakable horrors of trench warfare.

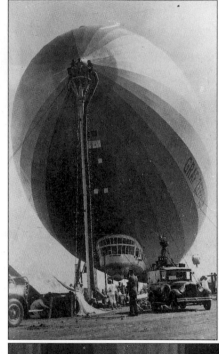

A dinosaur of the skies: the majestic German airship *Graf Zeppelin* arrived in Los Angeles after crossing the Pacific from Tokyo on the second leg of a flight which took the mighty dirigible round the world in 21 days, with only three stops. Her actual flying time was 12 days. The airship was named after Count Ferdinand von Zeppelin, who built the first rigid airship in 1900.

Titans of the motion picture screen: in May Douglas Fairbanks, seen here with Mary Pickford, presented the first 'Oscars' for outstanding cinema achievement.

THE ILLUSTRATED LONDON NEWS

1929

E·V·E·N·T·S

11 FEBRUARY Mussolini and the Pope agreed to create Vatican state
17 FEBRUARY First in-flight movie shown on an internal flight in the USA
7 JUNE First British woman cabinet minister, Margaret Bondfield, appointed
27 JUNE First colour television image demonstrated in New York
19 AUGUST Death of Sergei Diaghilev, impresario of the Russian Ballet

Crash and despair on Wall Street: the bottom fell out of the New York Stock Exchange at the end of October, as share prices plummeted and investors sold at virtually any price. There were tales of bankrupt business men, pictured outside the New York Stock Exchange, jumping from high windows in despair. The Crash, which followed a period of wild speculation on Wall Street, was widely blamed on greedy financiers. The tidal wave of selling hit the stock exchanges in London and the rest of the world, to set off the Great Depression of the 1930s. At its worst in the USA, roughly one person in three available to work was unemployed, and production statistics fell like stones. 'The fever of speculation succeeded by a long depression is a kind of incurable malady of our civilisation.' (21 December 1929)

The Academy of Motion Picture Arts and Sciences made its first awards (Oscars) for outstanding cinema achievements in May, and the *ILN* was catering for cinema-goers in its regular page entitled *The World of the Kinema*, written by Michael Orme. He examined with skill the world of 'all-talking pictures'. Orme wrote of Al Jolson, the supreme sob-song maestro in *The Singing Fool*: 'When it comes to the talking-films, the personality of Al Jolson sweeps the board.' He wrote of Mary Pickford, Charlie Chaplin, Dolores del Rio, and Vilma Banky (how beautiful they seemed!) of Ramon Novarro, the great romantic hero, and of Clive Brook and Herbert Marshall (the English gentlemen-types). In his article, Orme also wrote: 'It is an interesting study, this exploitation of screen personalities by the American producer. Sex-appeal, male magnetism, temperament, innocence, mystery, intensity . . .'

The 'talkies' were also used in other contexts, as the *ILN* reported in a feature article *From the World's Scrap-Book: Curiosities and Innovations*:

> *The American Police . . . have lately adopted the method of making sound-films of prisoners under interrogation. If necessary, it is said, these films are shown in court, and are regarded by the Police, furthermore, as valuable evidence for the purpose of refuting any charges that may be made by defending counsel as to the use of 'third degree' methods.* (23 November)

In the USA, a general sense of optimism since the First World War, and policies of non-interference by the state in the economy under three successive governments, had led Americans to believe that they had entered 'The Golden Age of Capitalism', and that they had discovered 'the springs of inexhaustible prosperity'. As a result, more and more people were being led into an orgy of speculation, drawing out savings, mortgaging homes and farms. Prices on Wall Street went up and up and up, encouraging British and other European speculators to borrow more than they could prudently afford to get on the band-wagon in New York.

Then, as prices finally climbed to absurd heights, the professionals coldly decided it was time to make sure of their immense profits and sell. The word went round, rumours spread and then, following four disastrous days in October, 5 billion dollars (worth more than 70 billion dollars in today's prices) were wiped off stock and share values.

No one could believe it. For many working in and around Wall Street, the Crash spelt immediate ruin. After the immediate impact of the Crash, there was a slight recovery when dealers bought shares at low prices, believing the market must recover. However, in November there was a second terrible crash, which just about wiped out the survivors. The American banks called in their loans, but there was often nothing left to collect. Then American loans to Europe and other countries were called in, often with great difficulty. The financial world was in ruins.

Meanwhile, in the world of aviation, there was an increasing number of successful pioneering aeroplane flights. The airship was also believed to have a future. The British government was investing considerable funds in constructing a new class of 'super airships'. Count Zeppelin, a brilliant designer, had built airships for the Germans during the First World War. The Germans had returned to building airships after the First World War, and this year the *Graf Zeppelin* flew round the world in 21 days and seven hours (the actual flying time was 12 days).

Nation speaking unto nation: the new British premier Ramsay MacDonald rode in procession through New York City. 'I think I can say that this morning nation speaks to nation,' he told the Mayor of New York, '. . . we must be inspired by a new faith in fraternity, with a new courage to follow large inspiring moral aims . . .' (19 October 1929)

The first British woman cabinet minister: Margaret Bondfield (below), a minister in the new Labour government

THE ILLUSTRATED LONDON NEWS

1929

E · V · E · N · T · S

28 AUGUST The airship, *Graf Zeppelin*, flew
round the world in only 21 days
5 SEPTEMBER United States of Europe
suggested by French premier, Briand
24 OCTOBER Wall Street Crash began, with
13 million shares changing hands
18 NOVEMBER The Japanese began to invade
Manchuria
2 DECEMBER Britain's first 22 public telephone
boxes came into service
8 DECEMBER Nazi Party victorious in Bavarian
municipal elections

Berlin's protest: 'The May Day
demonstrations of Communists in Berlin led to
riots and street fighting that lasted for three
days, during which the casualties were 23
people killed and about 150 injured . . .'
(11 May 1929)

A triumph for *Il Duce*: a
treaty signed by Cardinal
Gaspari, the Pope's
Secretary of State, and
Benito Mussolini recognised
the sovereignty of the
Vatican as an independent
city state. 'The event is hailed
as a personal triumph for
Signor Mussolini, who made
the first moves in
negotiations two years ago.'
(16 February 1929)

1930

HAVING ENDED 1929 by recounting the triumphant round-the-world journey of the *Graf Zeppelin*, it seems best to record straight away the disaster that destroyed the British *R101*, 'the world's largest airship', in the early hours of 5 October 1930, on its experimental flight to India by way of Egypt. Among those who died were Lord Thomson, Secretary of State for Air, Sir Sefton Brancker, Director of Civil Aviation and several high officials of the air ministry. The airship was carrying considerably fewer people than if it had been on a normal flight. As it happened, 48 died when the airship came down in flames at Beauvais in northern France. The King called it 'a national disaster' in his message of sympathy.

The *R101* had been created to embody all that was most advanced in British technology. After the accident the government, accepting expert advice, decided to abandon the airship programme. Germany and the USA carried on building airships for some years, but the future belonged to the aeroplane.

Meanwhile, the world-wide economic situation had deteriorated further following the Wall Street Crash. Unemployment rose in Britain from 1,520,000 in January to 2,011,467 in August, and to 2,500,000 by the end of the year. Employers said once more that wages would have to be cut, and there was growing opposition to this negative policy. The Labour Party's election programme stated that: 'To attempt to cheapen production by attacking the standard of life of the workers of the nation is not only socially disastrous, but highly injurious to the economic prosperity of the whole community.'

The economic crisis, however, was now affecting many countries, and the foundations of society, never very secure since the war, were beginning to shift. In Germany, where 4,500,000 people were unemployed by the end of the year, the struggle between the Communists and Adolf Hitler's Nazis was intensifying.

Mussolini, Italy's Fascist dictator, addressed his supporters on 17 May, saying: 'Words are a very fine thing; but rifles, machine-guns, warships, aeroplanes, and cannon are still finer things. They are finer because right unaccompanied by might is an empty word ... Fascist Italy, powerfully armed, will offer two simple alternatives: a precious friendship or an adamantine hostility.'

Meanwhile, in India, civil unrest was spreading, as the *ILN* noted:

Mahatma Gandhi was arrested at Surat early on the morning of May 5, and was conveyed to Poona, where he is being detained. This move was a sequel to the Bombay Government's decision that it was no longer possible to allow him to remain at large without grave danger to India's tranquillity. (10 May)

It was an age when speed records, amazing at the time, were made and then soon broken again. Here Britain was well to the fore. Major Henry Segrave, who had broken land-speed records in both 1927 (203.79mph), and 1929 (231.36mph), also won the world motorboat water-speed record on 13 June this year. He achieved a record speed of 98.76mph in his boat *Miss England*, but during the attempt on Lake Windermere, *Miss England* overturned and he was killed.

Indian rebel honoured:
Gandhi about to be decorated by a supporter for his campaign of civil disobedience to British rule. His subsequent arrest and imprisonment were followed by strikes and riots. The Viceroy said that the campaign was rapidly developing into 'violent resistance to constituted authority'. (3 May 1930)

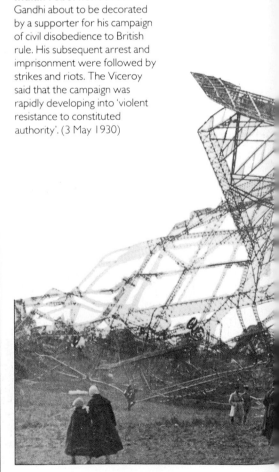

The coming storm: Nazis saluting at a demonstration as Hitler's Fascist movement gathered strength. 'The Nazis originated . . . at Munich in 1919, when Herr Hitler, their leader, joined the German Workers' Party, then consisting of "a group of six people". Their numbers have since increased to about six and a half millions. The Nazi's slogan is "Germany, awake!" and they carry red flags adorned with the swastika emblem. Their general idea is to make Germany strong.' (27 September 1930)

THE ILLUSTRATED LONDON NEWS

1930

E·V·E·N·T·S

5 JANUARY Collectivisation of all Soviet farms announced by Stalin

18 FEBRUARY Planet Pluto discovered by US astronomer Clyde Tombaugh

24 APRIL Amy Johnson completed her solo flight from Britain to Australia

5 MAY Gandhi arrested as civil disobedience campaign spread in India

30 JUNE French troops left Rhineland, as agreed after First World War

Empire of the air: as airships crashed, the early passenger services by aeroplane and flying boat were making headway and gaining customers.

G-EBLF

IMPERIAL AIRWAYS

R101 tragedy: the British airship 'struck the ground near Beauvais, in the north of France, at about 2 a.m. . . . and was totally destroyed by fire'. (11 October 1930)

On 15 February, the *ILN* published a page with descriptions by Professor W Scheffer of the 'zip' fastener, which was about to become widely used. The article was entitled *A new puzzle of modern mechanism: mysteries of the 'Zip' fastener*, and *How the 'Zip' fastener works: details and explanatory diagram*. It was also the year when nylon was first invented in the USA.

In the world of the cinema, Marlene Dietrich became famous through her appearance in a German film, *The Blue Angel*. She was a new type of 'vamp'—her allure was provocative and dangerous. Her German accent added mystery and increased her sex-appeal, and she made American film-stars suddenly seem very suburban. At the theatre this was the year in which Noël Coward staged *Private Lives*, one of his most brilliant works portraying the life of the rich and privileged.

On the pitch, Donald Bradman, the Australian cricketer, continued to astound crowds with his brilliance as a batsman. This year he had an aggregate of 974 runs in the England v Australia Test series. In the world of racing, the Aga Khan won the Derby with his horse, Blenheim, at odds of 18–1. He was to dominate the English racing scene in the 1930s.

A serious proposal to build a Channel tunnel was examined and rejected this year (mainly for defence reasons). It was the second time a proposal had been turned down. In the 1880s, preliminary work had begun in Kent to show that the idea was feasible.

London's airport in the 1920s was at Croydon. It was a modest, rather cosy place, efficient, but agreeably informal. By this year, however, with the growth of air transport and the prospect of even greater development, there was discussion about building a new airport. One imaginative plan, featured in the *ILN*, was for an airport in Central London behind King's Cross. It was designed as a circular structure on two levels, with aircraft landing and taking-off on the higher level, and with all the necessary facilities, including warehouses, on the lower. Although the plan never progressed, due to safety and noise considerations, it showed that men were thinking ahead and trying to adapt the environment to the new world which was fast emerging.

In his article featured in the *ILN* entitled *The England of 1893-1910 and 1930: A Study in Contrasts*, Signor Guglielmo Ferrero, the distinguished Italian historian, observed that:

> In 1893 Great Britain was still, for a Continental European, a lost island in an immense lonely ocean, lying at an incalculable distance from all inhabited countries ... And on that lonely island, work, riches, political liberty, were wrapped in a strong religious spirit ... which afforded the stranger a wonderful spectacle of rigid hierarchism ... at the same time original and solid.
>
> The England which I [have] found again in 1930 seems to me much gayer, more supple, living, profane and continental. The religiosity of the Victorian era seems, to a great extent, to have evaporated. Social rank is no longer so sharply divided; everywhere one finds traces of the dumb but continuous working of a process of levelling and fusion. A breath of gaiety, a ray of elegance and grace, a new spirit of liberty and equality have given greater suppleness and softened, at least in external life, that je ne sais quoi of rigidity and almost sombreness, which thirty years ago struck a Frenchman or Italian so forcibly. (16 August)

Struggle for work: marchers confronted by police during an unemployment demonstration on Tower Hill in London, held on 6 March 1930. The Great Depression was beginning to bite, and there was much anxiety that left-wing political groups were making capital out of the misery of those who were out of work.

The world's longest bridge span: the new Sydney Harbour Bridge in Australia, under construction in June 1930, with a 1,650ft single span at 170ft above the water level, was the biggest built up to that time. The cost was £8 million.

1930

E·V·E·N·T·S

7 JULY Death of Sir Arthur Conan Doyle, creator of Sherlock Holmes
30 JULY First World Cup won by Uruguay in Montevideo
7 AUGUST British unemployment exceeded 2 million as the Depression deepened
14 AUGUST The Church of England gave cautious backing to birth control
15 SEPTEMBER Over 100 Reichstag seats gained by Nazis in German election
5 OCTOBER The world's biggest airship, the *R101*, crashed in France

The world's tallest building: another symbol of the times was the Empire State Building in New York, at 1,222ft high. The photographer risked his life to get this shot (above) of 'a man . . . nonchalantly waving to his mates from the top of a vertical section of steel framework'. (11 October 1930)

Anyone for tennis? A London Transport poster for the Wimbledon Championships of 1930, in a style typical of the period. Bill Tilden and Helen Moody were the champions, in a year when the men still played in long trousers.

Architectural styles as the 1920s gave way to the 1930s: a new building in Berlin, characterised by rectangular lines and unsupported balconies, made possible by reinforced concrete. 'The structure of modern buildings is largely governed by considerations of utility and hygiene, especially the need for the fullest provision of light and air, while many novelties of design are due to the new possibilities opened up by the use of modern materials.' (18 January 1930)

1931

THIS YEAR was dominated by the deepening world-wide economic crisis. MacDonald's government set up a Committee on National Expenditure, headed by Sir George May, the former Secretary of the Prudential Assurance Company, which reported on 31 July that to deal with a probable budget deficit of £120,000,000, £96,578,000 should be met through drastic reductions in spending on unemployment benefits and wages of state employees.

Rumours were rife in New York and Paris that Britain, which was on the Gold Standard, was verging on bankruptcy. This led, inevitably, to a run on the pound, draining reserves.

Paris, which had built up vast gold reserves since the war, at first refused to help Britain. Then the New York banks were approached by the British government. On Sunday 23 August, the deeply divided Cabinet learned that the American financier, John Pierpont Morgan, representing the New York banks, had advised that they would not agree to help Britain unless the proposed budget cuts were made.

MacDonald now faced a revolt by his colleagues and went to Buckingham Palace to offer his resignation, suggesting the formation of a national coalition with the Conservatives and Liberals, to which the King agreed. On Monday, MacDonald said he would lead a national government to deal with the financial crisis, headed by a smaller Cabinet with four Labour, four Conservative and two Liberal members. Viscount Snowden, the Chancellor of the Exchequer in MacDonald's Labour government, and J H Thomas, the Lord Privy Seal, supported MacDonald. For most of the Labour Party, however, it was 'the great betrayal'.

Savage measures were taken by the newly formed coalition. Income tax was increased; higher duties were imposed on beer, tobacco and petrol. All-round cuts were made on government salaries. Unemployment allowances were also cut by 10 per cent, and a means test was imposed.

There were widespread public demonstrations, and even a mutiny by some of the Atlantic Fleet at Invergordon. There was, naturally, a renewed run on the pound, which lost a fifth of its value. Britain came off the Gold Standard, thus deepening the financial crisis in other countries.

A rush general election was held in October. The result was the biggest landslide in British parliamentary history. The government was now largely dominated by Conservatives. Labour now had only 52 seats. The pattern of British politics was set for the 1930s. It was to last until the general election of 1945.

The *ILN* carried a dramatic picture of a demonstration by the unemployed at the City Hall, Philadelphia, on 14 February. The headline ran: THE UNEMPLOYMENT PROBLEM IN AMERICA: CONDITIONS THAT MAY LEAD TO A 'DOLE'. In the USA there was no government insurance scheme at all—only the charity of soup kitchens. The *ILN* tried to cheer its readers up:

> *It is a fact ever to be remembered, and remembered gratefully, that the British Empire ... offers the resources of a quarter of the world ... As long as the British commonwealth of nations holds together, and our ocean-borne trade is kept secure, there is no reason why this country, or any other part of the King's dominions, should ever suffer any shortage in either necessities or luxuries.* (12 December)

Restless tides in India: the police dispersed demonstrators (top) in a procession. Mahatma Gandhi 'claimed that the "Civil Resisters" had only resisted interference with "common rights", such as the right to persuade persons to give up drink or drugs, or not to buy or sell any foreign cloth, or the "natural right" of manufacturing salt. "I am hungering for peace," he said, "if it can be had with honour ..." ' (21 February 1931)

Swan song: the great Russian ballerina Anna Pavlova (below) died in January 1931. She was in her forties. She danced with Nijinsky in Diaghilev's *Ballets Russes* in Paris in 1909 and later formed her own company. She was especially famous in the role of *The Dying Swan*, and for her *Giselle* and *Autumn Leaves*.

1931

E·V·E·N·T·S

28 FEBRUARY Fascist 'New Party' launched by Sir Oswald Mosley in UK
14 APRIL Spain declared a republic after abdication of King Alfonso
24 AUGUST National coalition government formed in UK to fight financial crisis
15 SEPTEMBER Royal Navy mutiny at Invergordon over servicemen's pay cuts
20 SEPTEMBER Pound devalued as Britain leaves Gold Standard
4 NOVEMBER Gandhi received by King George V on a visit to Britain

Fascism raising its head in Britain: Sir Oswald Mosley hoisting the Fascist flag over his party headquarters in London. The New Party was founded in 1931 and its public meetings were extremely rowdy, such as one in Glasgow, for instance. 'The meeting was rendered tumultuous by Communists and other interruptions; stones were thrown and free fights took place.' (26 September 1931)

Soup of the evening, beautiful soup: soup mixes were among the new 'instant' foods which would transform the life of the housewife as the century wore on.

Holiday traffic in England: a Whitsun holiday scene (above) near the popular beauty spot of Box Hill in Surrey, on a Tuesday late in May 1931, during a spell of fine, sunny weather which drew people out on to the roads. Cars, motor cycles with sidecars, motor buses, advertising signs, roadside ice-cream vendors, clôche hats and trilbys were all familiar sights by now.

1932

NOW THAT THE POUND HAD LOST VALUE abroad, many British men and women who had enjoyed a pleasant life on a modest income from inherited investments in the more agreeable areas of Europe found they had to return home. Hotels and pensions abroad were deserted.

For many people in Britain it was a bitter winter, as they tried to make do on reduced unemployment benefits and suffered the humiliation of the means test, while prying officials examined household effects. There were 2,700,000 unemployed and, taking into account their families, at least 7,000,000 were existing on the 'dole'. The National Unemployed Workers' Movement (NUWM) campaigned for them, but because its leaders were often Communists, the Labour Party and the trade unions did not want to be involved. It had, however, much unofficial support, shown in the national hunger march of this year. The way led to London, and when people in the comparatively prosperous South saw marching columns of their fellow countrymen from the North, where so much of the real wealth of Britain had been created, there were feelings of sympathy and shame.

On 14 March the Swedish match manufacturer, Ivar Kreuger, committed suicide in his Paris flat. His financial collapse caused further panic on international stock exchanges. His liabilities as an international financier amounted to £50,000,000 (worth around £750,000,000 today). To try to save himself, Kreuger had forged 42 Italian Treasury Bonds for £500,000 (worth about £7,500,000 today). For weeks the press uncovered details of his life-style: luxurious houses and flats in all the main capitals of Europe, and mistresses galore.

The kidnapping in the USA of the 20-month-old son of Colonel Lindbergh, the American revered in Britain since he flew across the Atlantic solo five years earlier, led to intense press coverage that quickly turned a personal tragedy into an international event. The *ILN* carried a full page of photographs on 12 March—the father, the mother, the Scottish nurse, the secluded house near Hopewell in New Jersey. Lindbergh deposited the ransom of $50,000, and promised to take no further steps if the baby was returned unhurt. He even enlisted the aid of the New York underworld, including such men as Salvi Spitale and Irving G Blitz, but it was all to no avail. Finally the remains of the child were found, and the Lindberghs left the USA to escape further publicity.

Miss Amelia Earhart, already a famous American airwoman, became the first woman to fly the Atlantic solo this year. Setting off from Newfoundland, she landed at Culmore, near Londonderry, on 21 May. On 28 May the *ILN* devoted its front page to her triumphant arrival.

In Germany this year, general elections in July and November left Hitler's National Socialist Party the largest in the Reichstag, and the elections for the provincial Prussian Diet also brought gains for the Nazis, although not complete control. On 4 June the *ILN* published some alarming pictures of damage caused by Nazi members of the Prussian parliament, following a taunt by a Communist representative, Herr Pieck: 'In your ranks are many murderers.'

Aldous Huxley, a brilliant, often satirical writer, published *Brave New World* this year, and that great man of British music, Sir Thomas Beecham, founded the London Philharmonic Orchestra.

Murder by a madman: President Doumer of France was shot by a Russian *émigré*, Paul Gorguloff, claiming to be 'chief of the Russian Fascists'. (14 May 1932)

Spirit of the New Deal: Governor Franklin Delano Roosevelt of New York, in Los Angeles during the American presidential contest. 'In his speeches he said little about foreign policy, but regarding home trade undertook to look after "the little man" and prevent exploitation by "corporations" . . .' (12 November 1932)

1932

E · V · E · N · T · S

28 JANUARY Shanghai captured by advancing Japanese forces

18 MARCH Sydney Harbour Bridge opened— the world's largest single-arch span

24 APRIL Mass trespass by hikers to gain public access to Peak District

30 OCTOBER Riots in many cities in Britain provoked by hunger marchers

8 NOVEMBER Landslide for Franklin D Roosevelt, after promise of New Deal

25 DECEMBER First royal Christmas radio broadcast to the Empire by George V

Welcome in the valleys: the Prince of Wales touring the Rhondda Valley coal-mining area of South Wales The future Edward VIII was now in his thirties. An extremely popular figure, of great charm, he seemed to be genuinely concerned for ordinary people's lives and problems in the depths of the Depression.

Star struck: the first number of a new cinema magazine. Films were now the western world's most popular entertainment.

Star athlete: Mildred 'Babe' Didrikson, the formidable all-round American track and field star (extreme right), winning her first heat in the 80–metres hurdles in a record time, at the Los Angeles Olympic Games. She won the gold medal in this event and in the javelin, plus a silver in the high jump.

1933

THIS YEAR TWO MEN ASSUMED POWER who were to change world history—one for bad, one for good. The first was Adolf Hitler, the second Franklin D Roosevelt. One became Chancellor of Germany at the end of January, the other took oath as President of the USA at the beginning of March. These two men were given extensive coverage by the *ILN*, as they took their places on the world stage.

The *ILN* carried a full-page picture on its cover of a great crowd giving Hitler 'a tumultuous ovation in Berlin, on January 30, when the news of his appointment as Chancellor was announced'. Hitler is in the background leaning out of the window of the new palace built for German chancellors, giving the upraised arm salute. The *ILN* reported that afterwards, there was a torchlit procession of Nazis, estimated at 100,000. In vivid language, the magazine's correspondent described how:

> *Herr Hitler stood at a window, his figure sharply silhouetted by a flood-light in the room behind him, while President von Hindenburg watched the march-past from a window of the old Palace on the other side of the Wilhelmstrasse.* (4 February)

Von Hindenburg, who had narrowly beaten Hitler the previous year for the presidency, had now appointed him Chancellor in the face of the Communist threat. The *ILN* gave full details of Hitler's rise to power in its 4 February issue, giving a biographical summary of this unattractive little man, who held the proud Germans enthralled.

On 4 March the *ILN* carried more pictures from Germany, this time showing the burning of the Reichstag in Berlin, which had occurred on the evening of 27 February. One showed Hitler in the burning ruins with Dr Goebbels and the Nazi Commissioner for the Prussian Ministry of the Interior, Captain Goering. Another election was being staged, and Goering later used the burning of the Reichstag as evidence of a Communist plot.

A campaign of terror and violence was instigated by the Nazis in subsequent months. In the election which followed in March, the Nazis managed to achieve 44 per cent of votes cast, and this was just enough to secure a majority in the Reichstag. An Enabling Act was passed giving Hitler dictatorial powers for four years. German democracy, a delicate post-war plant, had been trampled underfoot by Nazi Storm Troopers.

Meanwhile, across the Atlantic, the USA was also facing a time of great change. When Franklin D Roosevelt took his oath of office as President of the USA on 4 March, millions of once prosperous, even rich Americans, had been reduced to begging; the entire banking system had collapsed and 13 million wage-earners were unemployed. In his Inauguration Address, reported in the *ILN*, the President said:

> *'I am prepared to recommend measures that a stricken nation may require. . .In the event of a critical national emergency, I shall not evade the clear course of duty. I shall ask Congress for the one remaining instrument to meet such a crisis—namely, a broad executive power to wage war against the emergency as great as the power that would be given to me if we were, in fact, invaded by a foreign foe.'* (11 March)

Blood and iron: the 85-year-old President of Germany, Field-Marshal von Hindenburg, victor of First World War battles, riding through Berlin (below), Adolf Hitler beside him. Hindenburg defeated Hitler for the presidency in 1932, but on 30 January 1933 appointed him Chancellor. Hindenburg was afraid of civil war if Hitler could not somehow be appeased. By March, Hitler's Nazis had gained a majority in the Reichstag.

THE ILLUSTRATED LONDON NEWS

1933

E·V·E·N·T·S

10 JANUARY Martial law declared in Spain after attempted revolution

30 JANUARY President von Hindenburg appointed Hitler Chancellor of Germany

16 FEBRUARY England won the Ashes at end of controversial 'bodyline' tour

25 FEBRUARY Japan left the League of Nations after censure over Manchuria

27 FEBRUARY Reichstag fire used by Hitler to crush political opposition

15 MARCH Third Reich proclaimed by Hitler against background of terror

Do not buy from Jews! 'The persecution of Jews in Germany entered upon a new phase on March 28, when Nazi Headquarters issued an order for the whole of the machinery of their organisation to be set in motion against the Jews. Personal violence was forbidden: but it was decreed that a national boycott of Jewish goods and of Jews in professions should begin . . . the instructions against personal violence were not obeyed in their entirety . . . uniformed Nazis were stationed outside the Jewish shops and other undertakings, and every effort was made, with success, to hold up the work of Jewish traders and professional men.' (8 April 1933)

Fun for children everywhere: Bobby Bear first appeared in the *Daily Herald* in 1910, but by the 1930s his adventures were recorded in annuals and there was even a Bobby Bear club.

Unemployment: a diagram taken by the *ILN* from the *Berliner Illustrierte Zeitung*, showing the cost of unemployment in various countries. 'Those who are employed get smaller salaries than they did. From these shrunken incomes must also be deducted the money spent on the unemployed . . .' (15 April 1933)

The panic-stricken Americans were only too willing to grant power to a man who was taking control with calm confidence, and Roosevelt's concept of the 'New Deal' was born. Vast schemes of government-aided projects were created; labour laws were passed; help was given to the poor and sick. But above all, there was the birth of a new confidence and a new social awareness. To curb the excesses of speculation which had triggered the crisis, the President gave considerable power to one of the most astute and daring operators on Wall Street, Mr Joseph Kennedy (the father of John F Kennedy, the now legendary post-war President who was to be assassinated in Dallas in 1963). Just before he took office Roosevelt miraculously escaped an assassination attempt. The *ILN* gave the 'dastardly' event extensive coverage on 4 March, and was also busy reporting on the activities of the Hitler regime in Germany, including the increasingly violent attacks on the Jewish community there by Nazi Storm Troopers. On 8 April, the magazine carried a page of pictures and captions about: *The Nazi Boycott of the Jews: Shops and Offices put under Taboo.* One picture showed two Nazis in uniform outside a women's dress shop bearing the notice: *Germans! Warning! Do not buy from Jews!*

The policy of Hitler's Germany was already becoming apparent. On Saturday 14 October, Germany announced her withdrawal from the League of Nations and the Geneva Disarmament Conference. Hitler announced this in a special broadcast on all German radio stations, and the *ILN* published a full-page picture of Hitler making the statement.

Whatever might be happening elsewhere, England and Australia were locked in conflict this year over a matter that caused heated discussion in pubs, bars and clubs up and down the country. Harold Larwood, a member of the English team captained by Douglas Jardine, was accused of very fast, short-pitched 'bodyline' bowling by the Australians, when the Australian wicket-keeper was struck on the head while batting in the third Test at Adelaide in January. In reporting the incident, the *ILN* delicately concluded:

> *The match was unfortunately marred by a certain atmosphere of friction inimical to the best interests of cricket: and, while it was in progress, the Australian Board of Control sent a cable to the M.C.C. protesting against the 'unsportsmanlike' methods of the English bowlers.* (18 February)

The view of the *ILN*'s correspondent was, however, bland:

> *Although our photographs might seem to indicate somewhat sensational play, it should be emphasised that nothing really exceptional occurred.* (18 February)

The controversy did not end there, however. Opinion in Australia grew so heated that some said unless this type of bowling strategy was banned, Australia might stop playing cricket with England, or even withdraw from the Commonwealth.

Prohibition came to an end in the USA on 5 December. The well-meaning policy had been a disaster, leading to crime and corruption on a scale previously unknown, even in America's world of gangsterism. The *ILN* reported on 23 December that: 'Its passing was celebrated in New York with restraint and decorum . . . while hotels and restaurants made elaborate preparations for special dinners.'

The machine with a mind: Helen Wills Moody won the Wimbledon women's singles for the sixth time in seven years, defeating Dorothy Round over three sets.

THE ILLUSTRATED
LONDON NEWS

1933

E·V·E·N·T·S

23 MARCH Powers of dictator adopted by
Hitler through Enabling Act
8 MAY The first execution by gas chamber took
place in Nevada, USA
10 MAY Nazis burn books judged to be
'un-German' in Berlin
21 MAY Non-aggression pact agreed by Britain,
Italy, Germany and France
14 OCTOBER Germany left League of Nations
5 DECEMBER Prohibition ended in USA

SUPER 1933 HOMES

BARNEHURST PARK ESTATE
BARNEHURST. KENT
Estate Office: Station Approach, Barnehurst, Kent.
Telephone: Bexleyheath 408.
NEW IDEAL HOMESTEADS LTD
BRITAIN'S BIGGEST BUILDERS
9/6 WEEKLY
£395 FREEHOLD

Summons to action:
taking his oath of office,
President Roosevelt
declared himself ready to
recommend the
measures that a nation in
crisis might require. 'I
shall ask Congress for the
one remaining
instrument to meet such
a crisis—namely, a broad
executive power to
wage war against the
emergency as great as
the power that would be
given me if we were, in
fact, invaded by a foreign
foe.' (11 March 1933)

**The Englishman's new
home is his suburb:** while America had
the New Deal, England had its 'new ideal'
homes. The rash of suburban estates, with
comfortable family houses and gardens set
among greenery came in for many sneers,
but people liked living in them.

The glamour of speed: snarling through the
streets of Monaco in May 1933, a Bugatti, the
eventual winner, leads an Alfa-Romeo driven by
the Italian ace Nuvolari. The development of cars
and racing moved rapidly after 1900 and Grand
Prix racing resumed after the First World War.
The motoring pioneer Sir Frederick Royce, of
Rolls-Royce fame, died this year, while Sir
Malcolm Campbell put the land speed record up
to 272mph in Florida in March.

1934

IN THE CATALOGUE OF BAD NEWS, seemingly endless, in the world, there were some attempts at economic improvement in Britain in 1934. New industries were being created, making motor cars, wireless sets, chemicals, synthetic fibres and electrical goods, such as vacuum cleaners. Most of these factories were set up in the South and East, for the national electrical grid meant that industry no longer had to be near the coal fields. Men and women from Wales and the North were only too willing to come south to fill vacant jobs. Large estates of small, modern houses were being built in the South by private developers, to be bought on mortgages by those with regular employment.

A royal marriage generally tends to cheer up the British, even the underprivileged, and this year, Prince George, later Duke of Kent, the youngest son of George V and Queen Mary, became engaged to Princess Marina, the daughter of Prince Nicholas of Greece. The *ILN* carried pictures of the happy couple shortly after the announcement of their engagement on 29 August.

In the autumn, Mrs Wallis Simpson, an American divorcée, was presented at court to the King and Queen. According to Lady Diana Cooper, a prominent member of high society at the time, Mrs Simpson often appeared 'dripping with jewels given her at enormous cost by the Prince of Wales'. The King and Queen knew of their son's infatuation with Mrs Simpson, but apparently they never broached the subject with him. The King did say to Baldwin, however: 'After I am dead the boy will ruin himself in twelve months.'

On an even darker note, there was tragic news of a major mining disaster on 22 September at Gresford Colliery, near Wrexham, in which more than 200 men lost their lives. The *ILN* published harrowing pictures, showing women at the pithead waiting for news of their entombed men.

The many ominous events of this year in Europe were covered by the *ILN*'s correspondents in graphically illustrated reports. The story of Dr Dollfuss, the Austrian Chancellor ('youngest and smallest of Europe's "strong men"') was told on 4 August, following his assassination by a squad of Nazis in the Chancellery in Vienna on 25 July. Dollfuss had previously been described by the *ILN* in favourable terms: 'He makes up for small stature (he is only 4ft 11in) by an immense energy, and has great charm of manner.'

In Germany meanwhile, much was taking place that found its way into the pages of the magazine. The *ILN* described the Führer's meeting with Mussolini in Venice in June ('the two dictators were on excellent terms with each other'), and the death of Field-Marshal von Hindenburg, the President of Germany, in August. This was an occasion seized upon by Hitler to assume the dual role of President and Chancellor of Germany by means of a national referendum:

> *A most intensive campaign began almost at once to reach its height at Hamburg on the 17th, when Herr Hitler broadcast an appeal to the people to support him. . .The result was overwhelmingly in favour of the Leader-Chancellor. The provisional figures . . . were: votes for Hitler 38,362,760; votes against Hitler, 4,294,654; spoiled papers 872,296. Every effort was made to persuade all to poll, and 95% of the electorate voted: 2,034,846 did not vote. (25 August)*

A great player in full spate: Fred Perry, who came from Stockport in Cheshire, was the last Englishman to dominate the Wimbledon tennis championships. He won the men's singles there for three years running in 1934, 1935 and 1936, and captained Britain's team to four consecutive victories in the Davis Cup. He turned professional in 1936.

1934

E · V · E · N · T · S

30 APRIL Chancellor Dollfuss made dictator of Austria

19 AUGUST Hitler became President and Chancellor of Germany by referendum

26 SEPTEMBER The *Queen Mary* launched at Clydebank

7 OCTOBER Fierce fighting in Spain crushed Catalonian bid for independence

9 OCTOBER King of Yugoslavia assassinated in Marseilles

1 DECEMBER Purges in Russia after murder of Stalin's associate, Sergei Kirov

Requiem for an old master: 'After a long illness, Sir Edward Elgar died at his Worcestershire home on February 23. He was, by common consent, the greatest of modern English composers and one of the master musicians of the world. The son of a Worcester organist . . . he never underwent any academic training of any kind.' (1 March 1934). He was most famous for the tune of *Land of Hope and Glory*.

Putting on the Ritz: Fred Astaire and his partner Ginger Rogers, the great Hollywood dancing stars of the 1930s, at the centre of a typically lavish spectacle in *The Gay Divorcee*. Astaire was originally a performer in Broadway musicals with his sister Adèle, and started in films in 1933. In the dark, gloomy days of the Depression, Hollywood brought romance, glamour and escape into people's lives; the cinema had the advantage of being warm, comfortable and cheap.

Partners in crime: Bonnie Parker playfully holding a gun on Clyde Barrow. The two bank robbers died riddled with bullets in an ambush in Louisiana in May 1934, after a career of crime in which they killed at least a dozen people. They became folk heroes as 'Bonnie and Clyde'.

1935

THIS WAS THE YEAR OF THE SILVER JUBILEE of King George V and Queen Mary, which became a quite extraordinary event. The colour pages of the Silver Jubilee issue of the *ILN* have left a memorable record of the festivities.

Long before the day of national celebration, flags and decorations appeared in streets throughout the country. Jubilee tea-parties for children were held; everywhere the King and Queen were met by cheering, flag-waving crowds. The King was deeply moved by his reception and after visiting London's East End he wrote in his diary: 'I'd no idea they felt like that about me. I am beginning to think they must like me for myself.'

The climax was Jubilee Day itself, celebrated on 6 May, a few weeks before the King's seventieth birthday, when he and the Queen drove to St Paul's Cathedral for a Thanksgiving Service. The *ILN*'s correspondents were effusive:

> *The sunlight gleaming down from the clerestory windows, through the tranquil spaces of the great Cathedral, touched the splendid uniforms of the assembled congregation and evoked patches of brilliant colour. Against the majestic background of Wren's architecture was displayed the vivid splendour of gold and scarlet and blue: while the elegance of the ladies' gowns mingled with garbs from far distant lands, many-coloured turbans and bright* saris, *plumed helmets and jewelled headdresses.* (11 May)

Another notable event was the reception given by Stalin, the Soviet leader, to Anthony Eden (then Lord Privy Seal) on 29 March. This was, as the *ILN* stated on 6 April, the first visit of a British minister to Soviet Russia. There was a full-page picture on the front cover showing Stalin and Eden, Molotov (the President of the Council of People's Commisars), and Maisky, (the Soviet Ambassador to London), gathered together in Moscow.

This was the year of the great Peace Ballot in Britain, when 11 million people declared themselves in favour of the League of Nations, of an international agreement for the reduction of armaments, and of the prohibition of the private manufacture and sale of arms in Great Britain.

Stanley Baldwin, who took over once again this year from Ramsay MacDonald as Prime Minister, was obliged to take account of the Peace Ballot, and declared: 'I give you my word that there will be no great armaments.' He also promised to uphold the League of Nations, especially over Abyssinia, which was being threatened by Mussolini.

In the June general election in Britain, the Conservatives won an easy victory with 432 seats, but Labour regained some strength with 154 seats. Clement Attlee, a middle-class man who had fought in the trenches, succeeded George Lansbury as leader of the Labour Party.

Labour was now firmly committed to the League of Nations, and resolutely against rearmament. Winston Churchill was one of the few MPs in Parliament who spoke out in favour of rearmament in the face of the Nazi threat at this time, whereas Baldwin was bitterly criticised during the Second World War for his lack of foresight during this period. The tragedy was that the British people wanted peace, but peace was in increasing peril. They would eventually have to pay the price of their folly.

Happy and glorious: King George V and Queen Mary (right) celebrated their Silver Jubilee in 1935. 'The reign of King George the Fifth is a study in survival and continuity, aptly symbolised by a King who has stood firmly for social sanity and the normal.' (4 May 1935). The King had only months to live.
In May 1935 T E Lawrence, 'Lawrence of Arabia' (above), died after an accident on his motorcycle in Dorset: he was only 46 years old.

SATURDAY   THE ILLUSTRATED   MAY 4, 1935
LONDON NEWS
SILVER JUBILEE NUMBER

THE ILLUSTRATED
LONDON NEWS

1935
E·V·E·N·T·S

29 MARCH Stalin and Eden met in Moscow to discuss German rearmament

11 APRIL Agricultural heart of USA paralysed by dust storms

6 MAY Silver Jubilee of George V celebrated throughout Britain

3 SEPTEMBER Sir Malcolm Campbell set land speed record of 301mph in *Bluebird*

2 OCTOBER Abyssinia invaded by Italy with ground and air forces

20 OCTOBER End of Communist army's 'Long March' under Mao Tse-tung

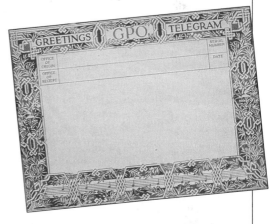

Cause for congratulation: it was in 1935 that the Post Office introduced the first greetings telegram form, as an addition to the rapidly expanding telephone service.

Wild blue yonder: Sir Malcolm Campbell at the helm of his 5-ton monster of a racing car, *Bluebird*, on the beach at Daytona in Florida. Powered by a 12-cylinder Rolls-Royce engine, he smashed the world land speed record in March with a new figure of 277mph. Only six months later, in September, at the Bonneville Salt Flats in Utah, Sir Malcolm drove the record up to 301mph. After this he turned to breaking water speed records and in 1939 he set a new water-speed record of 141mph. His son, Donald, was to raise this water-speed record to 260mph in 1959.

1936

THE WORLD WAS NOT STANDING STILL. In fact, it seemed hell-bent on another world war; there was not long to wait.

In March, the German army marched into the demilitarised zone of the Rhineland, a breach of the Treaty of Versailles and a provocative move against France. Hitler's gambles always seemed to come off. The German army was not yet in a state to challenge the French, and the German commanders carried sealed orders to withdraw if the French moved in. But the French did not do so, for they were in confusion.

On 16 May, the *ILN* carried a dramatic front-page picture of Mussolini with King Victor Emmanuel of Italy, who had been proclaimed Emperor of Abyssinia on 9 May. Mussolini said to a vast crowd: 'Italy has finally her empire . . . an empire of civilisation and of humanity for all the populations of Abyssinia.' Yet the Italian armed forces had used poison gas and bombed defenceless villages in their advance to Addis Ababa, the capital.

In Spain, a republic since April 1931, the Liberal and left-wing parties had formed a Popular Front to combat the threat of a right-wing revolt by officers, landowners and banks. Soon afterwards General Franco, who had been exiled, returned to lead the revolt. It became a savage, international war. Germany and Italy intervened, and within nine months, about 25,000 Germans and 75,000 Italians were fighting in Spain. The Popular Front was aided by International Brigades, and many British fought and died in their ranks. Russia helped by sending some supplies, but not much more. For Germany, the Spanish Civil War proved a valuable testing-ground for new equipment and techniques.

Meanwhile, in Austria, Kurt von Schuschnigg had succeeded the assassinated Dr Dollfuss as Chancellor and dictator. He was more or less a German nominee. On 18 July the *ILN* reported him saying: 'As Fate binds both the German peoples together, Austria recognises herself to be a Germanic State.' The news of an Austro–German Pact in July 'aroused deep interest in Europe' according to the *ILN*.

Even in the realm of sport, Nazi influence was apparent. Hitler's regime intended to use the Berlin Olympic Games as a massive political event, a gigantic spectacle glorifying Nordic men and women. It did not quite turn out that way. The hero of the Games was a black American athlete named Jesse Owens, who triumphed in the 100 metres, 200 metres and the long jump. Owens also received a gold medal (his fourth) as a member of the US team winning the 400 metres relay, which also set a new record for the event. On 15 August the *ILN* published a happy picture of Owens with his medals, describing his achievements as 'the most wonderful of many memorable performances' at the games.

There was good news too, from the USA, when Roosevelt was elected President for a second term. The *ILN* described this as 'one of the most decisive triumphs in the history of American elections'; the New Deal was evidently proving a success.

Economic recovery was not the case in Britain. On 31 October the *ILN* pictured the 200-strong 'Jarrow Crusade' setting off to present a petition with 11,572 signatures to Parliament. The marchers aimed to draw attention to the plight of the Tyne area, where 80 per cent of the working population was unemployed, and to demonstrate the community's 'deep sense of despair'. Although the marchers received much public sympathy, it took the Second World War to give Jarrow's economy the boost it needed.

Crusade in the rain: 'A party of men from the distressed area of Jarrow-on-Tyne set out to march to London to present a petition at the Bar of the House of Commons. The object of the march was stated to be the expression of the community's deep sense of despair and a demonstration to the country of the plight of the distressed areas.' (31 October 1936). Completing their long tramp on 31 October (below), the men 'proceeded along Edgware Road in heavy rain, displaying a banner with "Jarrow Crusade" on it. Everywhere they were met with evidences of friendly feeling [and were] cheered by the music of their own mouth-organ band. They held a demonstration in Hyde Park.' (7 November 1936)

THE ILLUSTRATED LONDON NEWS

1936

E·V·E·N·T·S

20 JANUARY Death of King George V at
Sandringham, aged 70
20 FEBRUARY Left-wing government took
power in Spain under Manuel Azana
7 MARCH Rhineland occupied by Germany in
defiance of Treaty of Versailles
27 MAY The *Queen Mary* left Southampton on
her maiden voyage to New York
3 JUNE Emperor Haile Selassie of Ethiopia
arrived in London in exile
6 JUNE Gatwick Airport came into operation

Civil war in Spain: after holding out for
10 weeks against a determined siege by
government forces, the Alcazar, the
famous Moorish citadel in Toledo, was
relieved by General Franco. He is seen
(centre) congratulating Colonel Moscardo,
the leader of the Alcazar garrison. The way
was now open for Franco to advance on
Madrid, but there was still much bitter
fighting to come before his final victory.

Going out in a blaze of glory:
observers watched as the Crystal Palace
was gutted in November. Flames shot up
300ft into the sky; the glow was visible as
far away as Brighton and the Chilterns. 'As
one account put it, "Brock, in his wildest
dreams, had never conceived such a
firework display".' (5 December 1936)

A peaceful close: 'The first act of [the new] King
Edward VIII was to send a telegram to the Lord
Mayor of London, Sir Percy Vincent, informing him
of the death of his father . . . The telegram was
received at the Mansion House at 12.35 [am] . . .
and a reply expressing the deep sympathy and
condolences of the citizens of London was at once
despatched.' G K Chesterton said of the late King
George V: '. . . his personality most immediately
recalled a certain sort of lively though experienced
naval officer; animated, anecdotal, fond of talking
about important things in a casual way . . . He was
quite unusually considerate; not only in the loose
sense of being kind, but in the literal sense of
considering how to be kind'. (25 January 1936)

On 15 January, King George V, who had been in failing health for some time, became seriously ill at Sandringham, and on the evening of 20 January a bulletin was issued, to the effect that the King's life was 'moving peacefully towards its close'. Just before midnight he died, surrounded by his family.

The *ILN* gave full coverage to these events, and on 1 February it published a drawing by Stephen Spurrier showing Queen Mary with her family attending a service in Westminster Hall, where the King was lying in state.

As far as the public was concerned, the new King, Edward VIII, was a charming man. His frequent appearances in public and his visits to underprivileged areas of the country had ensured his popularity as Prince of Wales. It was, however, a situation that would not continue for long.

At the request of the government, the British press had kept silent about Edward's romance with Mrs Wallis Simpson, the American divorcée whom he had first met in 1931. Abroad it was different. However, on 1 December, Bishop Blunt of Bradford alluded publicly to the King's 'need for grace', and two days later *The Times* spoke openly about 'a marriage incompatible with the Throne'. The abdication crisis had broken.

The new King and Mrs Simpson had been frequently in each other's company since Edward's accession, and they had enjoyed a holiday cruise together in the summer. The royal romance had become common knowledge throughout the world. However, Mrs Simpson, now twice-divorced, was considered an unsuitable candidate for the hand of the King of England by the standards of the day, and since the Church of England refused to bless the marriages of divorced persons at this time, Edward could neither marry Mrs Simpson in a religious ceremony, nor have her crowned Queen. As King, he was also the Supreme Governor of the Church of England, so his dilemma was more than a personal one. Baldwin, the Prime Minister, informed the King that his marriage to Mrs Simpson would not receive the approbation of the country, to which Edward replied: 'I have made up my mind and nothing will alter it—I have looked at it from all sides—and I mean to abdicate to marry Mrs Simpson.'

There really was no more to say. Parliament, the Church of England, the dominions and the Establishment were implacably against the marriage. Mrs Simpson left England for Cannes.

On 10 December Edward signed the Instrument of Abdication, which was witnessed by his three brothers; the eldest, Albert, Duke of York, would succeed him as George VI. Two days later, the *ILN* commented:

> *None can deny that Mr Baldwin has handled the constitutional crisis not only with firmness, but with tact and understanding—to the satisfaction of those who have heard him in the House, and to that of the country as a whole.* (12 December)

The *ILN*, like other magazines, continued to devote pages to the Abdication. The historian Arthur Bryant, who took over the *ILN*'s regular page, *Our Note Book*, from G K Chesterton this year, concluded that:

> *The Crown, though sometimes it may divide, in the end unites . . . What the soil of France is to a Frenchman, the Crown is to a Briton. There is scarcely one of us who would not sooner die than see it fail.* (19 December)

And all for the sake of a lady: placards reflected the air of uncertainty when news of the King's involvement with Mrs Simpson broke. There were demonstrations in his favour and 'some 300 young men and girls marched in procession to the Palace gates, bearing a banner inscribed, "Let the King know you are with him".' (12 December 1936)

The woman he loved: Mrs Simpson and the King. Determined to marry her, he hoped a morganatic marriage might allow him to keep his throne as well, but political and church leaders, with the support of the dominions, refused to permit any compromise.

THE ILLUSTRATED
LONDON NEWS.

1936

E · V · E · N · T · S

17 JULY Civil war began in Spain between Republicans and Nationalists
25 AUGUST 16 of Stalin's opponents executed after show trial
5 OCTOBER Start of Jarrow march to publicise the plight of the jobless
23 OCTOBER German 'Condor' Legion sent to Spain to help Franco's forces
29 NOVEMBER Crystal Palace destroyed in huge fire watched by thousands
10 DECEMBER Abdication of Edward VIII ended constitutional crisis

The lost leader: the Instrument of Abdication (left) was signed on 10 December. The King (right), who had broadcast to the nation on his accession, now spoke on the radio to tell the country of his decision to go. Arthur Bryant commented: 'The Empire has lost the service of one on whom it had pinned its hopes for the future, one who was known to possess gifts of leadership and inspiration possessed by very few. Yet the price was paid with such consummate dignity and with such frankness that all criticism and all rumour, so menacing a week ago, has been disarmed. In an age when vulgarity has become standardised, the world was suddenly made aware that it was witnessing a tragic drama . . . With touching simplicity, he [the King] made his renunciation, and nothing in his whole brilliant and generous career of service became him like the leaving it . . . It is the inescapable and overwhelming price that we have to pay for the irrevocable past that we have lost one who might well have been one of the greatest of British Kings.' (12 December 1936)

George VI
1937-1952

1937

THE YEAR BEGAN IN GLOOM. The nation was still stunned by the sudden and, for most people, totally unexpected departure of its formerly much loved, almost idolised, King less than three weeks before. The Abdication seemed to have struck at the very foundations of British society. If the Sovereign himself could put the attractions of an obviously unsuitable foreign fortune-hunter, as she was universally regarded, above the call of duty, why should humbler citizens respond to it? And if divorce, hitherto considered a disgrace, was accepted in royal circles, what marriage would remain safe?

The success of those in authority in concealing the royal romance from the British public for so long now rebounded against the government and the press. The public had discovered that politicians, newspapers, the BBC and the upper ranks of society had conspired for years to keep the majority of the population in the dark over a matter that deeply concerned them. If the ordinary citizen could be so easily deceived on so great a matter, it was asked, what other important facts were being concealed?

With the Coronation of the Duke and Duchess of York as King George VI and Queen Elizabeth on Wednesday 12 May the nation put behind it a chill and dismal spring. The 41-year-old King George VI was a rather shy figure with a strong sense of duty. On Coronation Day all went well; the ceremony was, for the first time, broadcast on the wireless and eagerly listened to in the 8 million homes which possessed receiving sets. The procession on the way to Westminster Abbey was also televised; its audience was estimated at a few thousands, although television cameras were not allowed to enter the building. That night the King gave a radio broadcast, which was reviewed by the *ILN*:

> *King George VI had the whole world as audience when, on Coronation night, he broadcast his message to the Empire from Buckingham Palace. It was a historic occasion, since he spoke to his people for the first time as King-Emperor and delivered the first broadcast by a monarch within a few hours of his crowning. The total number of his hearers has been conjectured at 500,000,000.* (12 May)

The King stressed the affection of which he had been conscious since his accession: 'If,' he summed up, 'in the coming years, I can show my gratitude to you, that is the way above all others that I would choose . . . for the highest of distinctions is the service of others.'

The patriotic euphoria generated by the Coronation encouraged the British public's natural tendency to turn its back on Europe. The King-Emperor ruled over about a quarter of the world's surface and rather more than a quarter of its population. To Arthur Bryant, writing in the coronation issue of the *ILN*, there seemed no reason why this situation should ever change:

> *If mankind as a whole can be brought to believe that the British Empire is a power that makes for just dealing and concord between men, then the British Empire, if its own people are strong in the same faith and ready to live and die in its service, may endure as long as the earth.* (15 May)

Long to reign over us: the new King, George VI, with Queen Elizabeth and the two young princesses, in their coronation robes. The King is wearing the Imperial State Crown. The Queen's crown and the circlets worn by the princesses were specially made. '. . . the Coronation symbolises all the long history that has gone to make our race what it is and to make our British culture and institutions. In one sense the Coronation is a purely religious service, reminding the King and through him the nation that there is a Power above kings and earthly powers. In another it is a re-dedication of the nation to the purposes for which it was first created. It is the outward and visible form of the inward and spiritual grace of a racial and historical commonwealth.' (8 May 1937)

The ride to the crowning: the scene in packed Trafalgar Square as the glittering state coach bore the new King and Queen to the Coronation in Westminster Abbey. 'Once again the famous "gingerbread coach" has served as the climax of a gorgeous royal pageant; a function it fulfils as well in the service of the sixth George in 1937 as it did in the days of George III, for whom it was built. It constitutes what is probably the most magnificent conveyance for monarchy in the world, and it is so constructed that their Majesties may see and be seen plainly in all directions.' By two o'clock in the morning Trafalgar Square 'seemed absolutely full, with men, women and children jammed twenty deep behind the barriers. Here they waited beneath the outline of Nelson's column, for a cold, foggy dawn. The spirits of the crowd were, however, entirely undamped, and later the weather cleared.' (15 May 1937)

THE ILLUSTRATED LONDON NEWS

1937

E·V·E·N·T·S

30 JANUARY Neutrality of Belgium and
Netherlands guaranteed by Hitler
1 APRIL London County Council proposed
formation of 'green belt' around London
27 APRIL Bombing of Spanish town of
Guernica by German air force
6 MAY Giant German airship, *Hindenburg*,
exploded over New Jersey, USA
12 MAY Coronation of King George VI and
Queen Elizabeth

Thanks for the memory: there was a
thriving trade in coronation souvenirs (above),
tins, plates and mugs. The official invitation to
the ceremony (below) was bordered by coats
of arms and floral emblems. As Earl Marshal,
the Duke of Norfolk presided over all the
details of the ceremony.

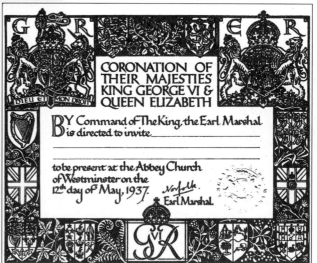

CORONATION OF
THEIR MAJESTIES
KING GEORGE VI &
QUEEN ELIZABETH

BY Command of The King, the Earl Marshal
is directed to invite _____
_____
to be present at the Abbey Church
of Westminster on the
12ᵗʰ day of May, 1937. *Norfolk*
✠ Earl Marshal.

The Prime Minister, Baldwin, the archetypal Englishman, was proud of his lack of interest in foreign affairs. 'Wake me up when you are finished with that,' he would remark, ostentatiously closing his eyes, when such matters were raised in Cabinet. He had, in January, signed a 'Gentleman's Agreement' with Italy, under which both sides agreed not to upset the *status quo* in the Mediterranean or to give help to either side in the Spanish Civil War. In fact German and Italian 'volunteers' continued to pour in to reinforce General Franco's forces.

On 28 May Baldwin was succeeded as Prime Minister by Neville Chamberlain, whose personality was reflected in his already out-of-date 'uniform' of dark suit, wing collar and immaculately rolled umbrella. Arrogant and obstinate, he ignored unwelcome advice in his pursuit of peace at almost any price, the doctrine soon named 'appeasement'. The immediate aim of his diplomacy was to detach Italy from 'the Axis', the term coined by Mussolini to describe the 'iron link' between Rome and Berlin. Chamberlain dismissed the economic sanctions imposed on Italy by the League of Nations for her attack two years before on Abyssinia as 'midsummer madness'.

A new war had begun in the Far East. Japan invaded China: on 9 November Shanghai was captured and on 13 December Nanking also fell to the Japanese, when the city was sacked and at least 20,000 civilians butchered. These events the British public regarded as too distant to concern them.

What interested everyone and seemed likely to provide, if anything did, the flashpoint for a European crisis, was the civil war in Spain. Although several popular papers, and many Roman Catholics, were pro-Franco, British opinion as a whole was sympathetic to the Spanish government: most of those who slipped abroad to fight in Spain joined the International Brigade, on the Spanish government's side.

One Welsh captain, henceforward nicknamed 'Potato Jones' after his cargo, became a minor national hero after running the blockade imposed by 'unknown' (Italian) submarines. In June a German 'pocket battleship' bombarded the little port of Almeria, which they claimed to have been in self-defence. The *ILN* reported that:

> *Announcing these events in Parliament, Mr. Eden said that some twenty badly wounded seamen from the* Deutschland *were being cared for in the military hospital at Gibraltar ... The Valencia Government gave a different version of the affair, stating that their aeroplanes were first fired on by a German warship ... Thirty-five buildings have been entirely destroyed. Up to the present 19 dead have been found among the ruins.* (5 June)

But the most influential event was the bombing of the little market town of Guernica, 12 miles from Bilbāo, a place of no military importance, by 40 German aircraft on Tuesday 27 April. The town was undefended and the streets crowded. Graphic accounts of the resulting slaughter appeared in the world's press and profoundly influenced public opinion. Ninety per cent of the houses in Guernica were said to have been destroyed and up to 1,000 people killed. Guernica, immortalised in Picasso's painting exhibited that year, came to symbolise the horrors of indiscriminate aerial bombing. It also generated an exaggerated fear of its likely effectiveness, encouraging the appeasers already in the ascendant in the western democracies.

Gentlemen prefer blondes: the Hollywood blonde bombshell Jean Harlow died in June, aged only 26. First seen in *Hell's Angels* in 1930, she went on to play tough, sexy roles in such films as *Platinum Blonde* and *Public Enemy*.

1937

E·V·E·N·T·S

28 MAY Neville Chamberlain became Prime Minister after Baldwin resigned

3 JUNE The Duke of Windsor married Mrs Wallis Simpson in France

11 JULY Death of US popular composer George Gershwin, aged 38

14 AUGUST The Japanese bombed Shanghai in a new offensive against China

22 OCTOBER Duke and Duchess of Windsor met Hitler in Berlin

13 DECEMBER Nanking occupied by Japanese forces amid much bloodshed

Ship of flames: yet another airship disaster occurred in May when the German *Hindenburg* caught fire on coming in to land at her mooring mast in Lakenhurst, New Jersey. More than 30 perished.

A Nazi welcome: the former King Edward VIII and Mrs Simpson, now the Duke and Duchess of Windsor, were entertained by Herr Hitler in Berlin in October, 'when investigating social conditions in Germany. (30 October 1937). The Duke's apparent sympathy with Nazi aims and attitudes caused the royal family and the British government some unease.

Read all about it: In its heyday, *Woman's* circulation reached nearly 4 million.

On a bicycle made for two: bicycling became a craze in the 1880s and 1890s, when flocks of riders swooped along the roads on club outings. The coming of the car put a spoke in bicycling's wheel, but this French advertisement shows there was life in the cycle yet.

1938

NINETEEN THIRTY-EIGHT was undoubtedly Hitler's year. Germany dominated politics and in Britain, the government somewhat reluctantly put its rearmament programme into action.

On 20 February Mussolini scored a great success when Anthony Eden, who had seemed a model Foreign Secretary—he had even had a style of hat named after him—resigned. The Italian press openly hailed Eden's departure as a victory for *Il Duce*. Two months later Britain formally recognised Italian sovereignty over Abyssinia. Aggression, it was clear, *did* pay.

Hitler, now emerging as the leading partner in 'the Axis', had already demonstrated the same truth. In February he forced the Austrian Chancellor, Dr Kurt von Schuschnigg, to release all the Nazis imprisoned in Austria for earlier attempts to overthrow his government, and to appoint a notorious Nazi lawyer, Dr Artur von Seyss-Inquart, Minister of the Interior. 'Don't believe that anyone in the world will hinder my decisions!' Hitler told him. '. . . England will not lift a finger for Austria.' A month later, after von Schuschnigg had called a plebiscite to let the Austrian people decide their own future, the Germans marched in.

'The Rape of Austria', as the British press described it, left the public uneasy, but rearmament was equated with 'warmongering'. Those who volunteered to join the new Air Raid Precautions Services, following broadcast appeals, found themselves told by friends: 'It's people like you who cause wars.'

Then, in September, came Hitler's threat to invade the independent state of Czechoslovakia, supposedly to protect the 3 million people of German origin it contained. Most of them were in the frontier province of the Sudetenland, the loss of which would leave the country defenceless. On Wednesday 8 September, as Chamberlain was telling the House of Commons of the failure of his recent visits to Hitler at Berchtesgaden and Godesberg, some papers were thrust into his hand: a dramatic scene followed, recorded by the *ILN*:

> *Mr Chamberlain, pausing in his speech, studied them silently. Then he continued. . .'I have now been informed by Herr Hitler that he invites me to meet him at Munich tomorrow morning. He has also invited Signor Mussolini and M. Daladier [the Prime Minister of France] . . . I need not say what my answer will be.' At these words the House rose and broke into a storm of cheers.* (8 October)

There were more cheers when Chamberlain landed back in England and waved before the newsreel cameras the Munich Agreement, signed early on 30 September, which gave the Germans all they had demanded; the Czechs had not been consulted. From 10 Downing Street the Prime Minister later told the wildly applauding crowd: 'I believe it is peace for our time.'

The news of Munich was greeted with hysterical relief by most of the British public. Later the realisation spread that, as the Labour leader Clement Attlee put it, a small democracy which had looked to Britain for protection had been 'betrayed and handed over to a ruthless despotism'. The chief Conservative opponent of appeasement, Winston Churchill, declared shortly afterwards to a hostile House of Commons: 'We have passed an awful milestone in our history.'

A deep dream of peace: 'I believe it is peace for our time,' Neville Chamberlain announced on his return to London after his September meeting with Hitler in Munich. 'But for Mr. Chamberlain's persistence, indeed, Europe might by this time have been plunged into the most terrible war in history. His single-minded resolve to do all in his power to save the world from a great catastrophe and untold suffering, regardless of his own political career, immensely enhanced his prestige . . .' Crowds outside Buckingham Palace cheered him to the echo and sang 'For he's a jolly good fellow', when he appeared on the balcony with the King and Queen. 'Then the King motioned Mr. Chamberlain forward, and he stood alone, acknowledging the acclamations'. (8 October 1938)

1938
E·V·E·N·T·S

3 JANUARY Announcement that all British schoolchildren to be given gas masks

11 MARCH German *Anschluss* of Austria at von Seyss-Inquart's invitation

30 SEPTEMBER 'Peace in our time' claim by Chamberlain after Munich Agreement

1 OCTOBER German invasion of Sudetenland (Czechoslovakia) began

31 OCTOBER *War of the Worlds* broadcast on radio, causing panic in USA

8 NOVEMBER *Kristallnacht* pogrom against Jews in Germany

Find the lady: flamboyant film producer David O Selznick mounted a highly publicised search for the right actress to play Scarlett O'Hara, tempestuous heroine of *Gone with the Wind*, adapted from the block-busting novel of the Deep South in the Civil War by Margaret Mitchell. To the dismay of several reigning screen queens, he finally cast an obscure English stage actress named Vivien Leigh to star opposite Clark Gable in the coveted role. The film was made early in 1939 and Vivien Leigh won the Oscar for best actress in the following year.

The tramp of the jack boot: sympathisers in Salzburg cheered and saluted as German troops marched into Austria. 'The Nazification of Austria has had the unfortunate effect of giving extensive powers to the Austrian Storm-troopers . . . and lorry-loads of these young men scoured Vienna looking for Jewish shops, on the windows of which they daubed the word "Jude", and a swastika in red and black paint. The official measures against non-Aryans are also being prosecuted with great vigour; many who held public office have been dismissed . . .' (26 March 1938)

The lion in his pride: in May the King and Queen opened the Empire Exhibition in Glasgow, with its red lion emblem.

SCOTLAND CALLING

EMPIRE EXHIBITION SCOTLAND 1938

BELLAHOUSTON PARK, GLASGOW. MAY—OCTOBER

1939

IN NOVEMBER THIS YEAR, the Nobel Peace Prize Committee decided that the annual Peace Prize should not be awarded. It had been a year in which might had triumphed. The Spanish Civil War had ended when Franco captured Madrid:

> *On March 29, the Nationalist wireless station at Burgos broadcast the announcement: 'The war has ended.' On the previous day General Franco's forces had entered Madrid without a shot being fired, and so brought to a close the battle for the city which had lasted for thirty-three months.* (8 April)

By then Spain seemed a mere side-show, for on 15 March German troops had occupied the whole of Czechoslovakia. Chamberlain explained that the promise given by Britain at Munich to guarantee Czechoslovakia's new boundaries could not be kept, as there was now no state left to protect, but two days later he told the audience of a public meeting in Birmingham that he shared 'their disgust, their indignation' at Hitler's perfidy. On 31 March he wrote in his own hand an undertaking to Poland that if its independence was threatened: 'His Majesty's government and the French government would at once lend them all the support in their power.'

During the summer the rearmament drive was speeded up, and priority was given to air defence. Going back on an earlier promise, the government announced in April the peacetime call-up for military training of men aged 20.

On 21 August the Germans announced that they had made a Non-Aggression Pact with the Soviet Union. On 1 September Germany invaded Poland, and in Britain evacuation began, which in the next three days moved 1½ million schoolchildren and other vulnerable groups, such as hospital patients, into safer areas. That night the black-out descended. The official announcement of the declaration of war on Sunday 3 September came almost as a relief. The *ILN* did its best to boost morale:

> *In face of a massed German onslaught on the Polish capital, Warsaw at the time we go to press is still valiantly holding out and the defence is declared to be unshaken under the continuous bombing attacks...* (16 September)

For Britain it was 'the phoney war'. A British Expeditionary Force was sent to France but waited for the enemy to attack it. RAF bombers flew over Germany but only to scatter leaflets. On 19 September a U-boat torpedoed the aircraft carrier *Courageous*; a month later another submarine slipped into Scapa Flow to sink the battleship *Royal Oak*. The scuttling of the 'pocket battleship' *Graf Spee* off Montevideo on 17 December provided a rare ray of hope in a dismal winter.

By Christmas a new war had started. On 30 November Russia attacked Finland, which the British public, in their new-found role of protector of small nations, seemed eager to help. Meanwhile the existing war with Germany was bad enough. A mass observation poll revealed that 19 per cent of the population thought that it would go on for at least three years and one per cent that it would last for ever or until, as one pessimist put it, 'Hitler dies of old age'.

The will to win: in September Winston Churchill returned as First Lord of the Admiralty—the one really pugnacious member of the War Cabinet. 'On September 26 he pointed out that the British attack upon the U-boats was only just beginning. "Our hunting forces are getting stronger every day," he said. "By the end of October we expect to have three times the hunting force operating ... We have only to persevere to conquer".' (7 October 1939)

See, the conquering hero comes! Hitler made his triumphal entry into Brno in Czechoslovakia in March. By this time he believed that Europe's political leaders would tolerate practically any act of aggression.

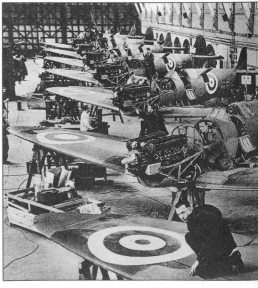

Unleashing the dogs of war:
bystanders in London with the grim newspaper headlines. 'It is to force the German
Leader has now appealed . . . That he
should have done so is an act of the most
tragic and criminal significance. It unlooses
forces of evil which no man can measure
. . . It imposes upon mankind suffering
which no human being has a right to impose
upon his fellow-creatures. The lust for
power is a very terrible thing. And in the
last resort it can only be met by force.'
(16 September 1939)

THE ILLUSTRATED LONDON NEWS

1939

E · V · E · N · T · S

15 MARCH German forces marched into
Czechoslovakia; Prague taken
28 MARCH Spanish Civil War ended as Franco
took Madrid
21 AUGUST Non-Aggression Pact signed by
Germany and Russia
1 SEPTEMBER Germany invaded Poland with a
force of 1.25 million men
3 SEPTEMBER War declared on Germany by
Britain and France
4 SEPTEMBER Churchill appointed First Lord of
the Admiralty by Chamberlain

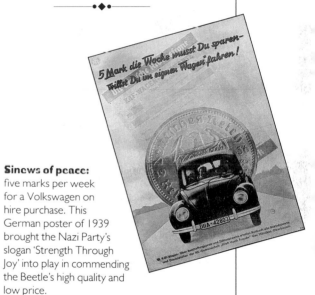

Sinews of peace:
five marks per week
for a Volkswagen on
hire purchase. This
German poster of 1939
brought the Nazi Party's
slogan 'Strength Through
Joy' into play in commending
the Beetle's high quality and
low price.

Sinews of war:
Spitfire fighter planes
(left) on the
production line in
Southampton. With
the Hurricane, the
Spitfire would prove
crucial to the defeat
of the German air
force over Britain.
Trapped by British
cruisers, the German
pocket battleship
Graf Spee (right) was
driven to take refuge
in Montevideo
harbour, where she
was scuttled.

1940

IT WAS THE COLDEST JANUARY for half a century. The Thames froze over and the nightmare of frozen pipes, snow-blocked roads and paralysed railways seemed all the worse because all weather news was censored. The start of food rationing on 8 January, at first covering bacon, ham, sugar and butter, but extended to tea in July, was reassuring rather than alarming, but the Minister of Information noted privately a general lack of enthusiasm for the war. Only Winston Churchill, with his inspiring calls to action—'Come then, let us to the task, to the battle, to the toil'—seemed to have his heart in the war. It was Churchill's Admiralty which raised spirits during a bleak February with the rescue of 300 British seamen from the German prison ship *Altmark* in a Norwegian fjord. Finland's fall in March rounded off a miserable winter, but Chamberlain was complacent on 4 April: 'After seven months of war I feel ten times as confident of victory as I did at the beginning . . . Hitler missed the bus.'

Four days later, the Germans occupied Denmark and began, against determined resistance, to occupy Norway. British forces sent to Norway's aid suffered heavy losses and the land operations were a shambles. On 10 May the Germans burst into Holland, Belgium and France, and Chamberlain was swept away along with 'the phoney war'. That evening Winston Churchill became head of a national (all-party) government. He promised nothing but 'blood, toil, tears and sweat'.

This date marks a revolution in national attitudes to the war. A dejected, apprehensive people was transformed—just in time. A glorious spring was followed by a golden summer, when every day brought blue skies, and bad news. On 14 May Holland fell, followed on 28 May by Belgium, exposing the British Expeditionary Force to the apparent certainty of being killed or captured, leaving Britain without a trained army. Then, in the 'miracle of Dunkirk', thousands of British soldiers and French troops were rescued from the beaches in a brilliantly improvised operation involving not only the RAF and the Royal Navy but also amateur yachtsmen and even pleasure boats. Churchill spoke to the Commons on 4 June; his words appeared in the *ILN*:

> *The enemy sowed magnetic mines in the Channel and on the seas. They sent repeated waves of aircraft . . . Their U-boats . . . were attacking the vast traffic which was taking place . . . It was in conditions such as these that our men carried on with little or no rest for days and nights on end, making trip after trip across the dangerous waters. At least 335,000 men were brought out of the jaws of death.* (8 June)

On 10 June Italy declared war on Britain and France, marking the collapse of Chamberlain's policy of 'dividing the Axis', and on 'Black Monday', 17 June, France asked for an armistice. 'Let us so brace ourselves to our duty and so bear ourselves', said Churchill to the Commons on the next day, 'that if the British Commonwealth and Empire last for a thousand years, men will still say, "This was their finest hour"'.

On 3 July the Royal Navy attacked the French fleet at Oran in Algeria, killing 1,000 French sailors, because their ships seemed open to seizure by the Germans under the peace terms—a 'hateful decision', as Churchill said, that demonstrated that Britain was in earnest.

To the victors the spoils: German artillerymen (above) in action during the invasion of France. In June the German army entered Paris (top). 'After dark there was a graveyard hush, broken only by the tramp of German boots. Swastika flags flew over the Eiffel Tower and the Arc de Triomphe. German troops were everywhere . . . Only two cafés were open on the Champs Elysées, and most of the hotels, restaurants, theatres and cinemas were closed.' (22 June 1940)

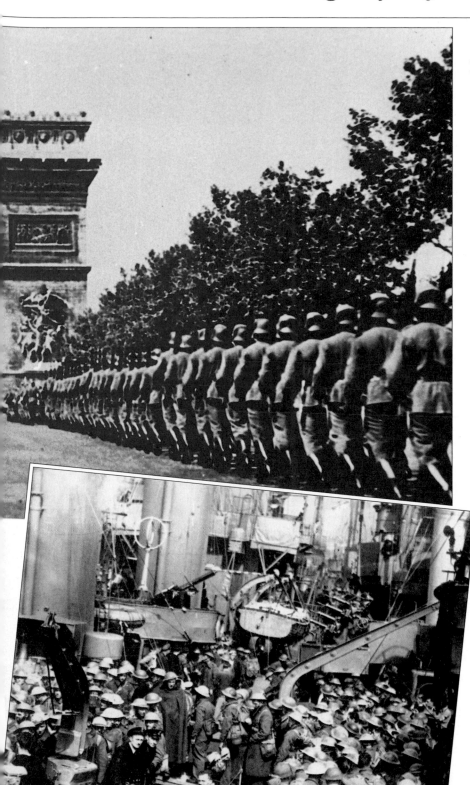

THE ILLUSTRATED LONDON NEWS

1940

E·V·E·N·T·S

8 APRIL German forces overran Denmark and invaded Norway
10 MAY Winston Churchill became Prime Minister, succeeding Chamberlain
30 MAY Evacuation began of Allied troops from Dunkirk beaches
10 JUNE Italy declared war on Britain and France
14 JUNE German troops marched through the city of Paris in triumph
22 JUNE French delegates signed armistice with Hitler at Compiègne

Beware of the spy: at home in Britain there was anxiety about German secret agents. A cartoon by Fougasse warned against letting slip information which might find its way to the enemy.

Out of the jaws of death or captivity: boatloads of British and French soldiers, stranded at Dunkirk under heavy attack from the air, were evacuated from the beaches and taken safely back to Britain—to fight again another day. Royal Navy ships brought many of the men out, and yachts and pleasure boats swarmed across the Channel to give a hand. 'Destroyers, for obvious reasons, have had to do a large part of the work, and magnificently they have done it, aided by as motley an armada of small vessels as has ever been seen. The air battles, the shelling, and the bombing under which all these small craft have worked, bringing away the troops, have been terrific, and their success in doing so has aroused the admiration of the world.' (8 June 1940)

Another painful decision had been to leave the Channel Islands undefended. They were occupied by the Germans on 1 July, and in that month the Germans began detailed preparations for the invasion of southern England. Behind the British Army stood the Local Defence Volunteers, men aged from 17 to 65 who had come forward to train, unpaid, in their spare time, following an appeal by the new Secretary of State for War, Anthony Eden, on 14 May. A million recruits had been enrolled by August when the new force was renamed the Home Guard.

There was a similarly enthusiastic reaction when the newly appointed Minister for Aircraft Production, the dynamic Lord Beaverbrook, issued an appeal to 'the women of Great Britain for everything made of aluminium that they can possibly give to be made into aeroplanes'. Patriotic housewives instantly stripped their kitchens of saucepans for conversion into Hurricanes. A public opinion poll in July showed that 88 per cent of the population had complete confidence in the new Prime Minister. According to the *ILN*, danger seemed to suit the nation:

> *With France overthrown, the shores of Britain have become a front line of defence, and the men of the anti-aircraft defences are finding a thorough contrast to the winter's inactivity. Night raids by as many as a hundred planes are not conducive to boredom . . .* (29 June)

The Germans, outclassed at sea, knew that a successful invasion depended on air superiority. The Luftwaffe outnumbered the RAF by three to one, and its flamboyant commander, Reichsmarschall Goering, was confident of success. His British opponent was Air Chief Marshal Dowding, head of Fighter Command.

What Churchill named the Battle of Britain began on 10 July with attacks on British shipping in the Channel and the coastal ports, followed, from 8 August onwards, by an all-out attempt to destroy Fighter Command in the air, and, far more successfully, on the ground. Then, on 25 August, after bombs had been dropped on London by mistake, Bomber Command was ordered to attack Berlin. The move, which was totally ineffective in military terms, infuriated Hitler; and Goering, much to Dowding's relief, changed his tactics. The massive daylight raids dwindled away after a major attack on 15 September, and ended in late October. Instead, on 7 September, the large-scale night bombing of London and other cities began, and lasted to the end of the year and beyond. The *ILN* told how:

> *Immediately after the heavy raids of September 7 and 8 the King went to the areas where poor people had suffered so much . . . Near the docks a number of people were removing their belongings from a damaged block of flats, and one woman called out, 'Are we downhearted?' All responded with a hearty 'No!'*
> (14 September)

The casualties, though bad enough—430 killed on the first night, with 1,600 seriously injured—were nothing like grim pre-war predictions, even when, as on 14 November, a compact target like Coventry was raided.

The destruction of property was, however, enormous, and on the night of 29 to 30 December the Germans succeeded in laying waste most of the 'square mile' of the City of London in a second great fire. This year of disgrace, heroism and above all endurance, thus ended spectacularly, in flame and destruction.

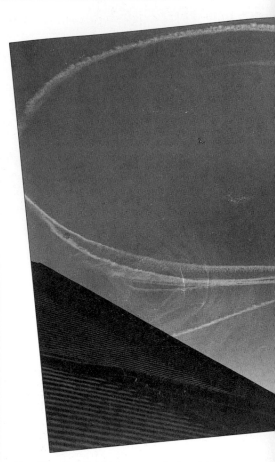

Death out of the blue: vapour trails swirled in the sky (above) as British fighter planes set out to do battle with the enemy bombers. On the ground some of the Oxford Street stores in London took a pounding (right): the picture was taken on 19 September. 'They are bombing London,' Cyril Falls wrote, 'because London is the capital and by far the greatest city in the British Isles, and their main object seems to be that of scaring and wearying out Londoners until they put pressure upon the Government to come to terms with Nazi Germany. They have not achieved their object, but neither have they accomplished anything else.' (29 September 1940)

The magnificent few: Battle of Britain pilots raced for their Hurricanes when an enemy raid was reported. The battle occupied the summer skies from July to October. In the end the Luftwaffe lost over 2,000 planes, the RAF less than 1,000. 'An American eyewitness of the air battle over Southern England on August 12, when another sixty-one raiders were brought down, wrote: ". . . I saw four German 'planes apparently bagged by British fighters and anti-aircraft shells. Gunfire rolled like thunder. The battle raged so furiously that it was impossible to keep accurate count of the 'planes which fell. Throughout the firing balloon-barrage crews worked calmly preparing new balloons to replace those shot down".' (17 August 1940)

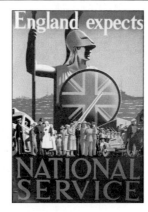

Clarion call to duty: Nelson's battle signal at Trafalgar—'England expects that every man will do his duty'—now summoned men and women to Britannia's service.

1940

E · V · E · N · T · S

10 JULY Battle of Britain began with raids on shipping in Channel
21 AUGUST Leon Trotsky died in Mexico, murdered with an ice-pick
7 SEPTEMBER The London Blitz began with a raid by more than 300 bombers
5 NOVEMBER Franklin D Roosevelt re-elected President of the USA
9 NOVEMBER Former premier Neville Chamberlain died of cancer, aged 71
14 NOVEMBER Coventry Cathedral destroyed in an air raid

Taking it on the chin: civil defence parties came to the aid of those injured in the Blitz, here rescuing a man who had been buried in the debris of a bombed building for 14 hours. 'The cheerful endurance of London's teeming population, which in the week ending October 20, underwent its 200th air raid, and had suffered almost continuous non-stop air attacks by day and night . . . called forth the warmest praise from the United States' and other neutral countries. (26 October 1940)

IT WAS THE MOST DISMAL YEAR OF THE WAR, but 'Britain can take it' was a popular phrase as cities such as Birmingham, Manchester and Sheffield, and the principal ports—Liverpool, Glasgow, Bristol, Portsmouth, Southampton, Hull, Belfast, Newcastle, Cardiff—suffered major raids along with London. Some, notably Plymouth, were bombed long after the main offensive had ceased elsewhere. Normal life continued to a remarkable degree, despite spells in 'Anderson' garden shelters, the new indoor 'Morrisons', introduced in March, or public shelters. On 'The Saturday', 10 May, London faced its heaviest and last major raid: 1,400 civilians were killed and 1,800 seriously injured. After that the German Luftwaffe was mostly elsewhere.

The *ILN* reported the arrival, in Scotland on 10 May, of a most unexpected visitor:

> A Scottish ploughman named David McLean saw [Rudolf] Hess [Hitler's Stellvertreter, or deputy] land with his parachute and found him lying injured in a field. 'He smiled,' McLean later told a reporter, 'and as I assisted him to his feet he thanked me in perfect English.' . . . Hess sat beside Hitler at the recent session of the Reichstag . . . He has been medically reported to be quite sane and healthy, apart from a leg injury. (17 May)

Conscription was extended. Eventually all men aged from 18 to 51 were liable to be called up. An appeal for women volunteers, 'War Workers Wanted', went out in March, and was followed in December by the first ever call up for women aged from 20 to 30. Within two years all women aged from 19 to 51 were obliged to register for some form of national service.

Clothes rationing was introduced on 1 June to save increasingly precious labour. Sixteen of his annual 66 coupons bought a man an overcoat; while 11 bought a woman a dress.

Food shortages were at their worst as the Battle of the Atlantic raged and the benefits of the 'Dig for Victory' campaign had yet to be felt. Bananas, lemons and tinned fruit disappeared from the shops. A single onion raffled in a newspaper office in February fetched over £4, more than a working man's wage for a week. In March jam, marmalade, and golden syrup were rationed; in May cheese was reduced to its lowest level at 1oz (about 25g) a week. 'Points rationing' was soon extended to most groceries. Thanks to the Minister for Food, Lord Woolton, the 'Kitchen Front' was one on which the country could feel victorious, with far-reaching effects. Centralised planning was seen as the best protection against private greed, and the potent 'Fair Shares' slogan inspired a desire for social change.

On other battle fronts, hopes were alternately raised and dashed. In September 1940 the Italian army had invaded Egypt, the start of the 'Desert War'. By December it had been driven back with enormous losses. An Italian army which had invaded Greece in October 1940 suffered a similar rebuff. In January 1941 the British captured the Libyan port of Tobruk, in February Benghazi: although 400 British died, 113,000 Italian prisoners were taken. In May, five years after the first act of aggression which had led up to the war, the Italian forces in Abyssinia surrendered and the exiled Emperor Haile Selassie returned in triumph.

Sweet are the uses of utility: women's utility wear, designed by the Society of London Fashion Designers to meet the requirements of the Board of Trade. Austerity on the home front in Britain, with the paramount need to concentrate all possible resources on winning the war, inevitably imposed severe restrictions on styles and materials for clothes.

THE ILLUSTRATED
LONDON NEWS

1941

E · V · E · N · T · S

22 JANUARY Australian and British forces captured part of Tobruk from Italians

28 MARCH The novelist Virginia Woolf committed suicide, aged 58

10 MAY Rudolf Hess, Hitler's deputy, arrived in Scotland by parachute

11 MAY House of Commons destroyed in a night air raid

27 MAY The German battleship, *Bismarck*, was sunk in the North Atlantic

22 JUNE German armoured forces began the invasion of Soviet Russia

Unyielding in the inferno: 'St Paul's still stands, saved by the heroic work of the wardens . . . who risked their lives in grappling with the incendiary bombs which fell on the roof . . . , (4 January 1941)

The tide of war in the desert: a stretcher party near Tobruk. As 1941 began, British and Anzac troops were driving the Italians across the North African desert, and took the port of Tobruk in January. The German Afrika Korps, under General Rommel, drove the British back to the Egyptian border and eventually recaptured Tobruk in June 1942.

Women's work: women played an important role in the war, in a far wider range of jobs than had been available to most of them in peacetime.

Unexpected visitor: Hitler's deputy, Rudolf Hess, arrived in Scotland to general astonishment in May, apparently in the hope of arranging a peace settlement between Britain and Germany. He was promptly put in the Tower of London and at the end of the war, at Nuremberg, was sentenced to life imprisonment as a war criminal. How far Hess was sane and what exactly lay behind his dramatic flight are matters which have remained the subject of speculation ever since.

The Germans still seemed invincible. In January the Luft-waffe joined the Italian air force in the bombardment of Malta, which became almost a daily event. In February the advance guard of the Afrika Korps under the 'Desert Fox', General Rommel, landed in Tripoli. 'A resourceful commander', remarked the *ILN*, but found some crumbs of consolation:

> *The opinion is that relations between Germans and Italians are steadily deteriorating. Mr. Richard Capell, the 'Daily Telegraph' correspondent...said...'There is nothing less than hate between these allies...'*
> (4 October)

The Germans also occupied most of Yugoslavia (whose partisans became a thorn in the German side), and on 6 April invaded Greece. A force of 62,000 British troops was sent to its aid in a disastrous move which fatally weakened the Desert Army.

Evacuation followed; more than 12,000 men were lost, along with most of the equipment of the 50,000 who got away. Then it was Crete's turn. The first German parachutist landed on 20 May, and the last British soldier scrambled on board ship seven days later, after a campaign in which nine major warships were lost and 12,000 soldiers captured. Two weeks later a new British offensive in the desert was a total failure. Its commander, the once-victorious General Wavell, was sent off to the military backwater of India.

The *ILN* gave full coverage to the events that followed:

> *At 2.45 a.m. on Sunday, June 22, the German Army suddenly attacked the Russians along an 1800-mile front without the slightest warning, and within a few minutes, the* Luftwaffe *passed over, bombing indiscriminately, followed by the* Panzer *divisions and troops.* (12 July)

By December, having carried all before them, the German armies were held outside Moscow as the grim Russian winter descended. Then, on Sunday 7 December, Japan bombed the American naval and air base at Pearl Harbor, Hawaii, leaving more than 2,000 Americans dead and almost every major unit of the US Pacific Fleet sunk or crippled:

> *The reputation of Japan for treachery under an outward veneer of bows and politeness has long been apparent...Yet it was certainly unexpected that at the moment when Kurusu, Japan's Special Envoy, and Admiral Nomura, her Ambassador to Washington, were actually calling upon Mr Cordell Hull [the US Secretary of State] with pretended plans for preserving the peace, her fleets were attacking Hawaii and Manila.* (13 December)

Simultaneously the Japanese began an invasion of Malaya and on 10 December shocked Britain by sinking two great warships, the *Prince of Wales* and the *Repulse*. The following day, Germany and Italy declared war on the USA, lifting the danger that she might fight a Pacific-only war. Churchill spent Christmas in Washington, cementing the new military alliance with his powerful ally. On Christmas Day the 6,000-man garrison of the British colony of Hong Kong surrendered. 'So ends a great fight against overwhelming odds', declared the Governor. Was this to be, some wondered, Britain's epitaph for the whole war?

Stab in the back: rescue operations at Pearl Harbor as the American battleship *Virginia* and other ships lay crippled by the sudden Japanese air attack, which was launched without warning at the moment when the Japanese ambassador in Washington was discussing plans for keeping the peace in the Pacific with the American Secretary of State. '... both the United States and Great Britain have steadily prepared for the day when the Japanese should show themselves in their true colours.' (13 December 1941)

Dance of death: Nazi atrocities in Poland (below) as doomed men were made to dig their own graves before being executed. 'Following the death of a German soldier, one hundred Polish men were rounded up—many of them Jews—and were marched through the streets with their hands tied behind their heads. They were then ordered to dig their own graves and, to gratify the barbaric sadism of the soldiers, forced at the point of the bayonet to perform for the Germans' amusement a "Dance of Death". Methods of execution varied, some of the men being shot, some hanged and others tied to posts and stoned to death.' (22 March 1941)

THE ILLUSTRATED LONDON NEWS

1941

E·V·E·N·T·S

19 SEPTEMBER German troops captured the Ukrainian city of Kiev

3 OCTOBER *The Maltese Falcon*, with Humphrey Bogart, had its première

7 DECEMBER Japanese attacked US fleet at Pearl Harbor; war declared

10 DECEMBER Sinking of the *Prince of Wales* and the *Repulse* off Singapore

11 DECEMBER Germany and Italy declared war on USA

25 DECEMBER Hong Kong surrendered unconditionally to the Japanese

Hitler will send no warning—
so always carry your gas mask

ISSUED BY THE MINISTRY OF HOME SECURITY

Flight from the invader: Russian refugees fled their homes as the German armoured divisions drove towards Moscow. Hitler's forces had invaded on a front extending for 1,800 miles , from Finland to the Crimea. '. . . this is not a materialist war. It is a war essentially of ideals. And for the peoples of the British Empire it is primarily a war to put a term to the belief that anything can justify the destruction of the national liberty of one nation by another. The protagonist of that belief—so fatal and horrible in our overcrowded modern industrial world—is Nazi Germany. Russia has through Germany's ruthless and perjured action to-day become our partner in the crusade against that belief.' (5 July 1941)

Masked and ready: while the armies battled abroad and German bombing raids reduced areas of London and some of the provincial cities to rubble, people in Britain kept their heads up and their morale high. There were fears that the enemy might use gas, and gas masks had been issued to the entire population in 1939. The mask came in a cardboard box on a string, but people seldom carried them.

1942

THIS WAS THE YEAR when everything changed; described later by Churchill as 'the hinge of fate'. At the start of the year, the Japanese seemed as invincible in the Far East as the Germans in Europe. Malaya seemed already lost as the Japanese advanced, almost unchecked. At the end of the Malay peninsula lay the island of Singapore and its vast naval base, the heart of Britain's defence network in the Pacific. On Sunday 15 February, out-fought, out-generalled and demoralised, its defenders surrendered and 60,000 British soldiers went into captivity. British prestige abroad was severely damaged by this massive humiliation, but the loss of Singapore had an almost equal impact in Britain. Criticism of the public-school educated élite, hitherto assuming top places in British society as if by right, increased, and 'Colonel Blimp' became a cartoon character almost as much pilloried as Hitler.

After Malaya, Burma, too, was soon abandoned. Thereafter the British public took little interest in the Far East. Whatever happened there, the public felt that the Channel would surely remain safe, but on 12 February this faith was rudely shaken, along with confidence in both the Royal Navy and the RAF. Everyone had been accustomed to hearing of raids on the German battle-cruisers *Scharnhorst* and *Gneisenau*, moored at Brest. Now, with the *Prinz Eugen*, the ships, still obviously undamaged, made a sudden escape up-Channel into German waters, defying a whole series of air and sea attacks on the way. The *ILN*, describing the 'spectacular dash' of the warships, commended the 'remarkable self-sacrifice' of the men in the Royal Navy and RAF 'in the face of tremendous danger' for their 'dauntless part in the fray'. However, Arthur Bryant, was quick to point out that:

> *Popular reaction to events is always an uncertain quality . . . the other day . . . the public was presented with two similar items of news: the Japanese landing in Sumatra and the sailing of a German squadron through the Straits of Dover. The former, though constituting a strategic threat . . . of the first magnitude, passed without comment: the latter aroused a storm.* (28 February)

A new Commander-in-Chief, Air Marshal (later Air Chief Marshal Sir Arthur) Harris now took over at Bomber Command. 'The Bomber', as Churchill called him, believed that, given sufficient resources and determination, the war could be won by air power alone. A broadcast in his name made to Germany soon afterwards threatened: 'We are going to scourge the *Reich* from end to end', and the scourging began in earnest a month later, on the night of 28 March. The target was chosen because of its vulnerable medieval wooden houses. 'Lübeck,' commented Harris, 'was built more like a fire-lighter than a human habitation', and it was successfully set ablaze. Similar attacks, designed to wipe out whole cities, henceforward became Bomber Command's hallmark. The nation finally appreciated that in the air at least, times had changed when *Operation Millennium*, the first raid by a force of more than 1,000 bombers, was directed against Cologne on 30 May. Later, some began to question the morality of Harris's strategy, but in the defeat-ridden first half of the year, the nation as a whole was delighted to see Britain at last hitting back against the enemy.

The Baedeker reprisal raids: a scene of destruction in Canterbury after the raid of 31 May. 'Following the R.A.F.'s greatest raid of the war, when over 1000 'planes attacked Cologne, Canterbury suffered a sharp attack, during which damage was done to shopping and residential areas. About 25 German bombers attacked the beautiful old Cathedral City, and among those killed was the Town Clerk'. (6 June 1942)

The production arsenal of the West: 'America is manufacturing millions of steel helmets for civil defence workers. A girl working in a West Coast factory inspecting the output.' (15 August 1942). It was in 1942 that the first US troops reached Europe, but the war effort of America was crucial in terms of materials as well as men, as the vast energy and production capacity of the US was turned to winning the conflict.

The Red Army on the offensive: a battalion commander leading an attack. In the summer of 1942 the Germans were still advancing on the Eastern Front, but later in the year they were halted and the Soviet armies took the offensive to drive them back.

1942
E·V·E·N·T·S

29 JANUARY The first *Desert Island Discs* broadcast by the BBC
15 FEBRUARY The island base of Singapore surrendered to the Japanese
27 MAY German armoured forces under General Rommel advanced in Libya
30 MAY Over a thousand RAF bombers took part in a raid on Cologne
10 JUNE Czech village of Lidice wiped out by German units

Scourge in the air: under Air Marshal Harris (left) a new bombing offensive was mounted. His weapon was the formidable Lancaster bomber (below). With a load of bombs weighing more than seven tons, it was 'capable of making a bombing trip to the farthest point of German territory'. (10 October 1942)

Bully beef: business used wartime themes to sell its products as in this advertisement from 1942.

For most places in Britain, this was a raid-free year, but between April and June came the 'Baedeker raids', in which a series of historic cities was attacked as a reprisal for those recently damaged in Germany. Bath, Canterbury, Exeter, Norwich and York suffered to no purpose, except to harden British hearts. Rationing was extended, with soap rationed to one small tablet a month in February, and sweets and chocolate to around 2oz (57g) a week in July. That month the basic petrol ration was abolished; henceforward anyone running a car had to prove it was essential for war purposes. Coal became increasingly scarce, due to the demands of war industry and an exodus of miners from the pits earlier in the war. A scheme of voluntary restraint based on a 'fuel target' for each home, introduced in June, was not a great success, its chief legacy being a 'Plimsoll line' painted on baths to mark the recommended 5in (about 13cm) limit for hot water.

The Lend-Lease Act, passed by the US Congress the year before, meant that America's allies could, in effect, be given goods they could no longer afford to buy, and the British now received their first dried eggs; Spam, initially regarded with suspicion, was eagerly welcomed. The greatest novelty, however, was provided by 'the Yanks' themselves, who landed in Northern Ireland on 26 January, and soon began to appear in increasing numbers throughout the mainland. The *ILN* wrote in glowing terms: 'The populace of Northern Ireland have had plenty of opportunity to admire the splendid physique and fine discipline of these overseas men who have come afar to fight for democracy.'

In the Pacific, Japan's tide of conquest seemed to have reached high-water mark. Halted on land on the approaches to India, she had been defeated by the US fleet at the Battle of Midway, fought by naval aircraft in June. Russia, after a year's hard fighting, was still very much in the war and keeping 180 German divisions occupied. It was Egypt which was to transform the military situation, however. In June Tobruk, the coastal outpost 80 miles beyond the Egyptian frontier long held by the British, was lost when 30,000 men surrendered to half that number of Germans. By late July, after constant withdrawals and frequent changes of commander, the Eighth Army had been forced back to a defensive position at El Alamein, a mere 65 miles from Alexandria, beyond which lay Cairo and the Suez Canal. Now a new British commander, General (later Field Marshal Lord) Montgomery, managed to inspire his troops with his own boundless self-confidence and at last brought about the victory for which the British hungered. On 23 October 'Monty' attacked at El Alamein. By midnight on 4 November the BBC was able to broadcast a jubilant bulletin: 'The Germans are in full retreat.'

The Grand Alliance, as Churchill called it, now began to display its strength. On 7 November 140,000 American troops under the supreme command of General Eisenhower landed in French North Africa in *Operation Torch*, and began the long drive east, into Tunisia and Libya, just as Montgomery's forces were advancing to 'hit the Germans for six'.

Commenting on the victory of El Alamein, Cyril Falls wrote in the *ILN*:

> *For perhaps the first time in this war, a considerable British army went into action equipped on a full scale, with really good material...There has been throughout no frittering away of strength. Everything has been concentrated upon suitable and vital purposes, remorselessly and unsparingly, but at the same time prudently and economically.* (14 November)

Hit for six: General Bernard Law Montgomery (above) in a characteristic pose. Masterful, shrewd, cocksure and trusted by his troops, Montgomery was a veteran of the First World War, who believed in meticulous planning and was careful with the lives of his men. 'The son of a bishop, short and stocky, with lean features and a long nose, he is as hard as nails. He is a great believer in physical exercise and knows desert fighting...' (14 November 1942). At El Alamein, after a typically careful build-up and with a very substantial advantage in numbers, he launched a formidable assault on the Axis forces with infantry (right) and tanks (below), preceded by a tremendous air and artillery bombardment. After days of hard fighting, Rommel and the Afrika Korps were forced into swift, though methodical retreat. The news of the victory was received with great acclaim in Britain.

Award for gallantry: bomb damage in the dockyard, Malta. The highest civilian decoration for gallantry, the George Cross, was bestowed on Britain's vital island base in the Mediterranean. The award was announced in April, after Malta had heroically withstood months of intensive enemy bombing.

1942

E · V · E · N · T · S

7 AUGUST American Marines landed on Guadalcanal in the Solomon Islands

19 AUGUST Canadian, British, US and Free French force raided Dieppe

24 AUGUST The Duke of Kent lost his life in an air crash, aged 39

5 SEPTEMBER The first German troops entered the city of Stalingrad

23 OCTOBER The Battle of El Alamein began in the Egyptian desert

Green fingers for victory: one way to help the war effort was to produce as much food as possible, and the ordinary citizen was urged to grow his own.

On the offensive: '. . . amid the roar of British bombers overhead, General Bernard Montgomery . . . received the Press . . . in a tent near El Alamein. "Gentlemen," said the General, "the battle starts to-night . . . It will be terrific—quite terrific . . . For three years we have been trying to plug holes all over the world. Now, thank God, that period is over." ' (31 October 1942)

THIS WAS A YEAR of preparation and anticipation, of solid achievement but also of hopes deferred. With ultimate victory now seeming assured, the nation, civilians and servicemen alike, began to look to the long-term future and to consider what type of world would follow the war.

The massive victories of the Russian armies, the most important military development of the year, encouraged this new mood. Few people in Britain really understood what was happening in Russia, with its vast territories. Everyone could grasp, however, the significance of the Russian victory at Stalingrad, which was located on the River Volga nearly 900 miles deep inside Russia, and which dominated the news at the start of the year. The masterly tactics by which the Germans had been lured on in their drive towards the Caspian Sea, only to be encircled and forced to capitulate at Stalingrad, were plain to every newspaper reader. The *ILN*'s account did not exaggerate:

> *Although the resistance of isolated German groups at Stalingrad was not finally over until February 2, the surrender of Marshal Paulus with his Chief of Staff and fifteen other generals on January 31, put the seal of completeness on the most catastrophic defeat inflicted on the German Army since 1918 . . . the tide was finally turned on January 10, when the relieving forces turned a defensive action into a superb counter-offensive, gradually squeezing the enemy into an ever smaller bag, and eventually cutting his army in two. . .This destroyed or captured army originally numbered no fewer than 330,000 men. . .Germany went into mourning for three days for Stalingrad, but it will take more than that for the people to forget this . . . and it will do nothing to reassure them as news of fresh Soviet victories comes in daily.* (13 February)

This was undoubtedly the Russians' year. In June 1941, 164 German divisions had, in Churchill's phrase, 'rolled eastwards'. Their ultimate objective had been a line nearly 1,400 miles long, stretching from Archangel on the White Sea to the Caspian Sea beyond Astrakhan, about 250 miles south-east of Stalingrad. Nowhere had they reached it, despite advancing 300 miles in the first month and, by the end of 1941, encircling Leningrad (which suffered appalling privations during the subsequent siege), and getting within 20 miles of Moscow. Leningrad was at last relieved, the German army at Moscow was forced back 250 miles, and in the South, after Stalingrad, the German army in the Caucasus was forced back 300 miles, beyond Rostov.

The Russians were difficult allies. For two years the western Allies' Arctic convoys had sent supplies by the dangerous 'Northern Route' from Iceland to Archangel, the prey of German surface vessels, U-boats and aircraft, as well as rough weather and icy seas. The only response, Churchill resignedly recorded, was 'a cataract of abuse and insult from the Soviet government'. When, in January this year, Churchill and President Roosevelt met at Casablanca, Stalin did not attend, professing himself too busy with 'front business'. His would-be hosts proceeded to declare their intention to accept from Germany, Italy and Japan nothing less than unconditional surrender—an aim which no longer seemed unattainable.

Image of devastation: the historic city of Kiev, capital of the Ukraine. The Red Army drove irresistibly forward this year. The Germans surrendered Stalingrad in February, in July the German tanks were smashed in a titanic conflict at Kursk and in November Soviet troops re-took Kiev.

'Berlin robber band': a grim cartoon of Hitler and his henchmen from a leaflet inviting German soldiers on the Eastern Front to desert and find safety in the Soviet lines. They were promised repatriation to Germany when the war was over, among other things.

DIE BE

Hitler   Göring

Downcast in Africa: German soldiers seen surrendering to a British tank. 'The crumbling morale of the German troops . . . began to show itself some time before the final collapse . . . A German told a war correspondent that the British had beaten them down by incessant gunfire. "It has been nothing but tanks, tanks, tanks, guns, guns, guns," he said. "We just couldn't stand up against it . . ."' (22 May 1943)

1943

E · V · E · N · T · S

2 FEBRUARY The last German troops in
Stalingrad laid down their arms
28 MARCH The composer Sergei Rachmaninov
died, aged 69, in Los Angeles
26 APRIL Discovery of mass grave of 4,000
Polish officers at Katyn
17 MAY The RAF dropped bouncing bombs on
the Ruhr dams and breached them
1 JUNE British actor Leslie Howard died when
his plane was shot down

Return journey: German soldiers streaming westwards
over the snowy Russian steppes in winter, 1943. 'At every
point along the vast Russian front—where there is any
movement—our allies are forging ahead, and the invaders
are beginning to behave like a tired army—tired by the
exertions which they have had to put forth against an
unbreakable adversary. The Russians . . . have rallied their
undying spirit'. (16 January 1943)

We go and fly against England: morale-
raising German war game, in which the players,
heartened by the swastika flag, attacked the
United Kingdom by air and sea. The Irish Free
State was carefully marked as neutral and,
indeed, when Southern Ireland had been
bombed by German aircraft in 1941, the
Dublin authorities would not officially condemn
the attack. When American troops arrived in
Northern Ireland a year later, Dublin
complained that Eire's neutrality had been
compromised.

In declining the invitation to participate in the Casablanca conference Stalin had pointedly expressed his 'confidence that . . . the promises about the opening of a Second Front in Europe . . . in regard to 1942, and in any case in regard to the spring of 1943, will be fulfilled'.

Public opinion in Britain shared Stalin's hopes; there was now a universal desire to help Russia and a feeling that she was being left to bear the main burden of fighting alone.

The Americans feared with reason that Churchill did not really have his heart in the Second Front. He was haunted by the ghastly slaughter on the Western Front in the First World War, and the failure of the Dieppe Raid in 1942 confirmed his arguments. The lack of troops and landing-craft also posed difficulties. At the White House in May the Americans accepted Churchill's strategy that the first objective was in the Mediterranean, and that 'the great prize there' was to get Italy out of the war.

Italy was removed from the war more easily than anyone had dared hope. The Allies had entered Tunis on 7 May. The North Africa campaign had ended in total victory, and the army of what Churchill had privately called the 'Third Front' was now free to invade Europe. A joint Anglo-American assault on Sicily, on 10 July, was followed by the capture of Palermo on 23 July. Two days later came the sensational news of Mussolini's fall from power. The new Italian government's unconditional surrender was formally announced on 8 September.

Although Italy soon declared war on Germany, Hitler's troops proved well able to hold out. The Allies' slow progress towards Rome proved a poor substitute for a Second Front on the Channel coast.

However, another turning point in the war had been reached that May, in the Battle of the Atlantic. That month, thanks largely to the new airborne radar devices which could detect U-boats on the surface, 40 were destroyed. In the following month another 19 were sunk. Thereafter the transatlantic supply line was secure.

Victory over the U-boat was achieved despite 'Bomber' Harris's refusal to divert any of his bombers fighting against German industry. On 17 May, in *Operation Chastise*, he achieved his most spectacular success so far, when 19 Lancasters breached the two largest dams in the great manufacturing district of the Ruhr. The *ILN* vividly described the results:

> *134,000,000 tons of water [from the Möhne dam] roared down the Ruhr Valley sweeping away power stations, factories, whole villages and built-up areas that lay in its path . . . Meanwhile the 202,000,000 tons of water that lay behind the Eder Dam. . .were sweeping down in a 30ft-high tidal wave towards Kassel, a town of 177,000 people . . . Up to Tuesday it was reported that 4,000 Germans had lost their lives in the flooding and 120,000 lost their homes.* (22 May)

In the long term the devastating series of raids, code-named *Gomorrah*, delivered against Hamburg around the end of July, had more effect, but there was to be no short cut to victory via the skies over Germany. General Eisenhower left for England to become Supreme Commander of the Allied Expeditionary Force now being assembled for the cross-Channel assault, taking Montgomery with him. In late November Churchill, Roosevelt and Stalin, meeting at Tehran, jointly 'took note', the conference minutes recorded, 'that *Operation Overlord* would be launched during May 1944'.

Miracle man: Alexander Fleming was elected a Fellow of the Royal Society in 1943, having discovered the 'miracle' antibiotic penicillin in the 1920s. Once its value in the treatment of war casualties was realised, work on improved production methods was encouraged. Fleming was now a professor at London University. He was knighted in 1944 and shared the Nobel Prize for Medicine the following year.

Wild scenes of welcome: women held up babies to greet American troops (right) in a small town on the route to Palermo. 'One of the features of the Sicilian campaign has been the tumultuous welcome given to Allied troops by the islanders . . . Many of the women had obviously put on their best dresses to welcome the advancing Allied troops, and no sooner did the vanguard appear than flowers and fruit began to shower into the vehicles, which, whenever they slowed down or stopped, were besieged by excited civilians seeking to kiss and shake hands with the men in them. The Allied advance, in fact, in many parts could scarcely be distinguished from a victory parade.' (31 July 1943)

The Big Three meet: in November a conference in Tehran, the capital of Iran, brought Stalin, Roosevelt and Churchill together in the first occasion of the kind that the Soviet leader attended. The aims were to plan strategy, improve Allied co-operation in the war effort, reassure Stalin that the Second Front in Europe would be opened next year and discuss post-war policy, including the treatment of a defeated Germany. Stalin undertook to move Soviet forces into the war against Japan.

1943

E·V·E·N·T·S

10 JULY Allied invasion forces began landing on the Sicilian coast

25 JULY Benito Mussolini, Fascist dictator of Italy, deposed

3 SEPTEMBER Allied troops invaded Italy across the Straits of Messina

6 NOVEMBER Soviet forces driving back the Germans re-took Kiev

28 NOVEMBER Churchill, Roosevelt and Stalin meet at Tehran

Raising morale: the pocket magazine *Lilliput* (right) was considered saucy at the time. It was published for 23 years and was incorporated into *Men Only* in 1960.

Blazing the trail into Sicily: the Allied invasion army going ashore on Sicily (centre). While advanced troops held the beach-head, working parties 'were wielding picks and shovels to construct beach roads for the passage of the following wave of invasion armour. Troops standing in the surf up to their waists formed a human chain to unload supplies from the invasion vessels to the beach, while Bren carriers, having been driven down the ramps of their landing craft, ploughed their way through water to dry ground.' (24 July 1943)

1944

EVERYONE KNEW that this would be the year of D-Day, the start of the liberation of occupied Europe, and, it was hoped, the year of victory. The first few months of the year were a time of expectation in which the nation took what interest it could in campaigns which seemed mere side-shows to the grand assault on Fortress Europe. The successful landing, in late January, of 50,000 British and American troops in a major amphibious operation at Anzio in southern Italy, seemed an encouraging dress-rehearsal, until they were pinned down at the beach-head. It was not until May, after a fiercely contested advance via Monte Cassino, that the US Fifth Army linked up with the troops from Anzio. The *ILN* reported that on 4 June the Allies entered Rome after a highly successful campaign:

> *The series of brilliant moves which has led to the capture of Rome reflects the greatest credit on Allied commanders in Italy. The enemy has been outwitted and outmanoeuvred from the start, and although he has fought bitterly to hang on to various key points . . . he has more than met his match.* (10 June)

In the Far East there was also progress. By the end of 1943 the Japanese had already been dislodged from part of New Guinea by General MacArthur and by June the Americans and Australians had, in the words of the American Chief of Staff, General Marshall, 'pushed 1,300 miles closer to the heart of the Japanese Empire'. This 'island-hopping' progress continued throughout the year, with one Japanese conquest after another being regained. A new land supply route, 500 miles long, to replace the original Burma Road to Chungking, was begun in January. In February a British counter-offensive was launched in Burma to disrupt the supply lines of the enemy forces. Its great novelty was that one brigade of Major-General Wingate's Long-Range Penetration Force, (the Chindits), while marching through 450 miles of mountain and jungle, was supplied by air; while the other brigade, 7,500-men strong, landed on air-strips 100 miles behind the enemy lines by glider and transport plane. In April the main Japanese attack was held at Kohima, on the frontier of India.

At home in Britain in April, a 10-mile deep strip of the coast from the Wash to Land's End was closed to visitors, although preparations for D-Day had become impossible to conceal. Everywhere there were tanks and army vehicles, with heaps of shells piled up along the roadsides of the southern and south-western counties. As April gave way to May, tented camps sprouted like mushrooms near the coast. The ports and rivers seemed so crammed with vessels that not one rowing boat more could be squeezed in. There were US GIs (Government or 'General' Issue soldiers) everywhere, but especially in Dorset and Devon, since they were to occupy the right flank of the invading force; Kent, Sussex and Hampshire were the preserve of British and Commonwealth units, who were to attack on the left. By early June tension ran high among civilians as well as soldiers. And then, after a restless night in which an endless stream of aircraft seemed to be passing overhead, the long-awaited moment arrived. At 9.32am, on Tuesday 6 June, the authoritative voice of John Snagge told the nation over the radio that: 'D-Day has come. Early this morning the Allies began the assault on the north-western face of Hitler's European fortress.'

Chuffed to meet Churchill: troops could not conceal their joy when they welcomed the British Prime Minister to France after the D-Day landing in Normandy. 'Many dangers and difficulties which appeared extremely formidable are now behind us,' he said. The eventual liberation of France was under way, but behind the smiles lay grim statistics.

Planning attack: US infantrymen (above) practised disembarking from the ships that would take them from England (below) in the invasion of Fortress Europe. More than 4,000 ships were involved in the landings.

1944

E · V · E · N · T · S

1 JANUARY The discovery of DNA, the basic chemical of life, announced

2 APRIL Soviet armies crossed the borders of Poland and Romania

4 JUNE The city of Rome fell to Allied forces, virtually unopposed

6 JUNE D-Day: Allied troops crossed the Channel to land in Normandy

1 JULY The Bretton Woods Economic Conference began in the USA

Safe in shelters: many Londoners slept secure from flying bombs in deep shelters, dug below the tube lines. The shelters had canteens staffed by volunteers (below), and medical posts. Humour (right) was important in the face of V2s, which hit the ground without any warning of their approach.

Unlike General Eisenhower, who had prepared a communiqué in advance for use if the operation failed, the ordinary British citizen never doubted that *Operation Overlord* would be a success. By nightfall on 6 June, 156,000 men had been put ashore at the cost of perhaps—the precise total is still uncertain—10,000 casualties. The heaviest losses were among the airborne forces and on the American assault area known as *Omaha*, just to the west of Port-en-Bessin, the only beach where determined resistance was encountered.

By 17 June, when the *ILN* published a panorama of the whole battlefield, the nation had grasped the main features of the basic strategy, and very heartening the *ILN*'s report seemed:

> *When they battled their way ashore on the coast of Normandy and stormed up the beaches in the early hours of D-Day . . . the first wave of Allied seaborne assault troops wrote history with their blood.* (17 June)

The choice of Normandy as the objective instead of the obvious target—the Pas de Calais—and the masterly use of paratroopers and glider-borne infantry, were points which every armchair Napoleon could grasp. The news a little later of the creation of the two great artificial harbours, code-named *Mulberries*, off the beaches at Arromanches and 10 miles further west, in the American sector, also evoked popular admiration.

The start of the German flying-bomb offensive, from 13 June onwards, saw the launch of up to 100 missiles a day. It bred a despairing suspicion that whatever the Allies did, the Germans would always be one step ahead. 'Hitler's secret weapon' had been a national joke ever since it had first been mentioned in 1939. Now here it was, and despite being rapidly nicknamed 'the doodlebug'—the Germans called it the V-1, from the German for Revenge Weapon No 1—it proved no joke at all. A new evacuation now began, which was different from the last; for former danger areas, like Manchester or Liverpool, could now receive evacuees.

It was a wretched summer, of rain and cloud, relieved by news from the battlefronts. The Russians were on the offensive everywhere, and sweeping all before them. In Normandy, after what had begun to seem stalemate, the Allies began to advance in late July. In mid August thousands of German troops were encircled at Falaise and the rest began a headlong retreat back towards the Reich. On 25 August Paris was liberated, followed on 3 September by Brussels.

The Germans produced another surprise, the V-2 rocket, which first descended on London on 8 September. It was the start of a new era in warfare. Yet the existence of the new weapon was not admitted by the authorities in Britain until 10 November, and most people outside the comparatively small area under fire—the borough of Ilford alone endured 35 V-2s, and the county of Essex 378—had no idea what their countrymen were suffering.

On land, too, the Germans still seemed far from beaten, though the first American units to reach German soil crossed the border near Aachen on 16 September. The following day the 1st British Airborne Division dropped on Arnhem, to seize the last of a series of bridges over which the land forces were to advance into Germany and, it was hoped, finish the war. The attempt failed, and the long front settled down into winter deadlock, broken in the grey dawn of 16 December by a huge, totally unexpected, German offensive in the Ardennes, which drove a deep wedge into the American lines. The year which had begun with high hopes in Britain ended in snow, mist and gloom.

On his native ground once more: the leader of the Free French, General Charles de Gaulle, set foot on French soil for the first time since the German invasion, when he visited Normandy in June. He had fled to London in 1940, to organise the Free French, and in his absence from France was sentenced to death by a military tribunal. In Normandy he visited General Montgomery (right) and British troops who had landed on D-Day.

Ike in charge: four-star American general Dwight D Eisenhower, the Allied Supreme Commander in Europe, seen here talking to an American soldier as preparations for the D-Day invasion built up in the early months of 1944. There were more than one million American service-men in Britain when this picture was taken.

THE ILLUSTRATED LONDON NEWS

1944

E · V · E · N · T · S

20 JULY In Germany, an attempt on Hitler's life narrowly failed

15 AUGUST Allied troops landed on the south coast of France

19 AUGUST Soviet forces crossed the German frontier in East Prussia

25 AUGUST Allied troops entered Paris to a tumultuous welcome

16 SEPTEMBER American armoured divisions invaded Germany

7 NOVEMBER President Roosevelt re-elected for his fourth term

jane's journal by PETT

Far from plain Jane: the cartoon character with her little German dog kept morale high and her clothes mostly off.

The assault on Fortress Europe: soldiers of the Middlesex Regiment on their landing beach on 6 June. 'At 6.33 a.m. on Tuesday, June 6, D-Day, long expected, arrived, the first notification coming from Berlin that Allied seaborne troops had landed between the estuary of the Orne and the Vire; that the entire coast between Le Havre and Cherbourg was involved in invasion operations and that paratroops had been landed 12 miles south-west of Le Havre ... Six heavy warships and twenty destroyers were reported off the mouth of the Seine.' (10 June 1944)

1945

EVERYONE BELIEVED this would be the year of victory, at least against Germany, but it began with the most miserable winter of the war. The weather, though bad, was not as severe as in 1939; but the nation was now war-weary and dispirited by recent disappointments. V-1 flying bombs and V-2 rockets were still arriving regularly from Germany. Coal was now so scarce that some 18-year-olds were sent down the mines when they were called up.

This year, fighting did not stop for the winter. On 3 January the Allies counter-attacked in the Ardennes, and by 23 January the last major stronghold gained by the Germans in the recent Battle of the Bulge had been retaken. In the East the Russians were on the move from the Baltic to the Danube. Warsaw had been captured in January, and Budapest was 'liberated' on 13 February, two days before Eisenhower's armies reached the Rhine. That week Churchill and Roosevelt, meeting at Yalta in the Crimea, conceded to Stalin what proved to be a virtually free hand in eastern Europe, in return for a promise of help against Japan.

On the night of 13 February Bomber Command delivered its most devastating attack ever against the German city of Dresden, which was crammed with refugees. A fire-storm worse than that at Hamburg 18 months before engulfed 11 square miles of property and inflicted an estimated 135,000 deaths.

On 7 March the US forces seized a bridgehead on the far side of the Rhine and on 23 March British troops stormed across in massive strength to occupy the Ruhr. For British civilians the 'fighting war' ended on 27 March with the landing, in Kent, of the last V-2. Two days later the final V-1, the last of nearly 6,000 to reach land, dived harmlessly to earth in the same county.

On 12 April the *ILN* reported that the world was stunned by the death of President Roosevelt:

> *The sudden death of President Roosevelt ... was received everywhere with profound sorrow and sympathy for the American people thus robbed of their great leader, and with scarcely less concern by the British nation ... He is doubtless destined to live in history as one of the greatest of United States Presidents.* (21 April)

On 15 April the British Second Army reached the concentration camp at Belsen, near Bremen; US troops entered Buchenwald and Dachau a little later. The coverage given to these horrors hardened hearts against the enemy.

For the British public the war really ended, as it had begun, a few days early, when the 'dim-out' (which had replaced the full black-out the previous September) was abolished on 24 April. The next day American and Russian troops joined hands at Torgau on the River Elbe, splitting Germany into two zones. On 28 April Mussolini was shot by his own disillusioned countrymen; and two days later Hitler shot himself as the Russians reached the heart of Berlin. On 2 May the German surrender in Italy was announced, but the release of the news for which the world waited was delayed to please the Russians. Only with Churchill's broadcast at 3pm on 8 May did the nation learn for certain that the German war was at an end. It was, at long, long last, time for the parties and bonfires of Victory in Europe Day—and the glorious realisation that the Allies had won.

Come ye back to Mandalay! Indian army machine-gunners looking out over the Burmese city of Mandalay (below), as battle raged in March for the strongpoint of Fort Dufferin. The Japanese were now being steadily driven back across Asia. Earlier in the year the drive to clear their supply route to Asia, the Burma Road, had begun. Their base at Mektila fell to the Allies in March and in May the capital city of Rangoon was retaken by British troops, who took numerous prisoners.

THE ILLUSTRATED LONDON NEWS

1945

E·V·E·N·T·S

23 MARCH The first Allied troops crossed the Rhine, at Remagen

26 MARCH Former British premier David Lloyd George died, aged 82

12 APRIL Death of President Roosevelt: succeeded by Harry S Truman

28 APRIL Mussolini and his mistress shot dead by Italian partisans

30 APRIL Hitler killed himself in his bunker in Berlin; Germany overrun

8 MAY The war in Europe officially ended as Germany signed a capitulation

The smashing of Dresden: the beautiful city famed as the 'German Florence' was ferociously bombed in February, with devastating effect (above). It is thought that 130,000 people were killed. 'Swarms of refugees were in the city at the time of the raid, sleeping in the streets, and it is believed that some six thousand bodies are still to be recovered.' (23 March 1945)

Benefits of the black-out: cartoonists took their humour where they could find it, but one long-term effect of the war was to accelerate the easing-up of the stricter sexual morality of the past.

Smiling through: John Sharpe of Leicester, one of 6,000 prisoners held by the Japanese in Changi Gaol, Singapore, under abominable conditions. The British recovered Singapore in September, as the Japanese forces laid down their arms everywhere in the Far East. It was then that the full extent of their cruelty to their prisoners was revealed. Once they were freed, starved and emaciated captives quickly regained their strength, but they had terrible tales of what they had endured.

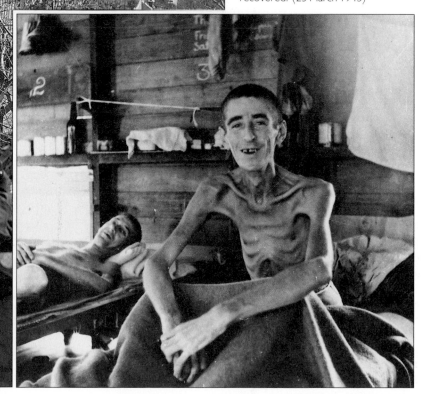

While the war in Europe had been hurrying towards its joyous conclusion, the 'Forgotten Army', as British troops in the Far East labelled themselves, had entered Rangoon and regained Burma. Malaya was still to be liberated and Churchill was also determined that British troops and ships should take part in the invasion of Japan. As the avenging Americans drew closer to Japan their navy regained mastery of the Pacific Ocean and their aircraft dominated the skies above it. On the night of 9 March, 280 B-29 super-fortresses inflicted a fire-storm on Tokyo equalling that suffered by Dresden a month earlier. Similar visits were soon made to nearly every major Japanese city, almost unchallenged.

But alarming signs existed of the ferocious resistance which any attempt to land on Japanese soil was likely to encounter. Suicide-bombers, known as *kamikaze*, had inflicted heavy losses on the US fleet. When, in June, the Americans captured the island of Okinawa, thousands of its defenders committed *hara-kiri*, ritual suicide, rather than surrender. In mid July, when President Harry Truman and Churchill met with Stalin at Potsdam, outside Berlin, they faced the grim prospect of one and a half million British and American dead if Japan was to be stormed that November as planned.

The leader of the British Labour Party, Clement Attlee, was with Churchill at Potsdam, for no one knew which of them would be Prime Minister at the time of the final offensive against Japan. Since 23 May Churchill had been head of a 'caretaker' government, holding office only until the outcome of the general election held on 5 July was known. The result, delayed until the Forces' votes could arrive from overseas, was announced on 26 July. It left Churchill's Conservatives and their supporters with a mere 213 seats, against 393 Labour MPs and 34 others. Since the last election 10 years before, there had been many signs of a massive move of British opinion towards the left, including the welcome the public had given the first blueprint for a post-war welfare state, expressed in the Beveridge Report of 1942. Even so, Clement Attlee's Labour Party had been elected far sooner than anyone had dared hope.

On Monday 6 August the war in the Far East was brought to its ultimate conclusion when a B-29 US Army Air Corps bomber dropped, for the first time ever, an atomic bomb on the Japanese city of Hiroshima, causing 80,000 deaths; on Thursday, 9 August another 40,000 died when a second bomb was dropped on Nagasaki. The *ILN* pointed out that:

> *The recent pictures of Hiroshima . . . provide an awful warning for civilisation; and the appalling and, it would appear, incalculable results of this most recent of science's achievements form a terrible commentary on modern war.* (15 September)

On 14 August the Japanese accepted the Allies' demands, and in Britain Wednesday 15 August was celebrated as Victory over Japan Day. The Second World War, which had caused at least 40 million deaths throughout the world, was over.

That autumn and winter the new British Labour government got to grips with the legacy of six years of fighting. The sudden ending of lend-lease, on 17 August, made Britain's economic situation worse than at any other time during the war. But as 'the boys' began to come home to 'civvy street', spirits were high. And, on 24 October, the United Nations Organisation came formally into existence, designed to prevent or counter future aggression. Perhaps, after all, in the future there might be peace.

Triumph in the West: Red Army soldiers raised a hammer-and-sickle Soviet flag on a pinnacle of the Reichstag, the parliament building in Berlin, as the shattered city fell (below). '. . . tremendous devastation by aerial and artillery bombardment . . . has been meted out to Berlin, the city to which Goering promised immunity. Since that vain boast Berlin has suffered innumerable air-raids from the Allies, and since April 20 the bombardment of the heavy guns of the Soviet artillery. In the course of the street fighting it has become the Russian practice to bring up field artillery to fire at close range at every building in which enemy resistance is shown . . . Russian soldiers in the centre of the city are looking vainly for architectural features described in tourist guide-books that German civilians have been giving away on the eastern approaches to the city.' (5 May 1945)

THE ILLUSTRATED LONDON NEWS

1945

E·V·E·N·T·S

5 JULY Voting in the British general election: Labour landslide

6 AUGUST An atomic bomb was dropped on the Japanese at Hiroshima

14 AUGUST President Truman announced the unconditional surrender of Japan

15 OCTOBER Pierre Laval, leader of Vichy France, shot by firing squad

20 NOVEMBER Opening of the trials of Nazi leaders in Nuremberg

Triumph in Trafalgar Square: two sailors and friends took to the fountains to celebrate VE Day. Outside Buckingham Palace '. . . by the time Big Ben sounded the three notes which heralded the Prime Minister's announcement of Victory, the throng numbered many thousands. After Mr. Churchill's announcement, the crowd roared for the King and Queen' (19 May 1945)

I'M COMING HOME STONY BROKE

Triumph at the polls: the new Labour Prime Minister, Clement Attlee, with his wife after the election result had been declared in July. 'Mr. Attlee's immediate comment was: "It will enable us to implement the policy of the Socialist Party." ' (4 August 1945). Now aged 62, Attlee had been the Labour Party's leader since 1935 and in Parliament since 1922. The government he led was to change the face of Britain. However, Britain was perilously close to being 'stony broke' (above).

For Better or Worse?

For I dipt into the future, far as human eye could see,
Saw the Vision of the world, and all the wonder that would be;
Saw the heavens fill with commerce, argosies of magic sails,
Pilots of the purple twilight, dropping down with costly bales;
Heard the heavens fill with shouting, and there rained a ghastly dew
From the nations' airy navies grappling in the central blue.

ALFRED, LORD TENNYSON

A BLINDING FLASH of white light seared the sky above the New Mexico desert at 5.30am on Monday 16 July 1945. Observers 10 miles away felt as if the door of a huge oven had been suddenly opened and saw the ominous, soon to be awesomely familiar mushroom cloud take shape as a giant fireball rolled up into the air with flashes of red, yellow and green. It was the test of the first atomic bomb, and Robert Oppenheimer, head of the Manhattan Project, remembered a line from a Hindu classic, the *Bhagavadgita*: 'Now I am become Death, the destroyer of worlds.'

Two months after the world's first atomic bomb was exploded, scientists gathered (above) at Alamogordo, New Mexico, to measure levels of radioactivity in seared sand particles.

The Japanese government spurned an Allied ultimatum demanding unconditional surrender and in August a B-29 bomber of the United States Army Air Corps, affectionately christened *Enola Gay* after the pilot's mother, took off from an island in the Pacific. On board was an object 10½ft long and 1½ft in diameter, weighing 4 tons and code-named *Little Boy*. On 6 August at 8.15 in the morning local time, *Little Boy* was unloaded over the city of Hiroshima.

The *Enola Gay*, 11 miles away at 30,000ft when the bomb went off, shuddered in the shock wave. The mushroom cloud welled up again, and where the city had been moments before, there was what looked like a huge pot of boiling black oil. On the ground, people within half a mile of the fireball were cooked and shrunk instantly into little black smoking packages. The blast obliterated 4 square miles and killed nearly 80,000 people, while almost 200,000 others died due to the effects of the fall-out over the next five years. A second bomb, dropped on Nagasaki three days later, killed another 40,000 people immediately, and it was then that the Japanese authorities surrendered.

How many Allied lives were saved compared with the lives that were taken by the bomb cannot be calculated, but *Little Boy* was a mere infantile plaything in comparison with the hydrogen bomb, which was tested in the 1950s. Nuclear weapons now proliferated—bombs, missiles, depth charges, land mines—and mankind possessed the capacity to destroy itself and perhaps all life on earth for the first time in its history.

Inventiveness is one of the characteristics which distinguishes man from other animals, and in the hundred years between 1890 and 1990 the pace of invention has gathered frenetic speed. Fundamentally, the inventions have been of two kinds: those which make it easier to kill people in larger numbers than before, and those which make life more comfortable for the people who have not been carried off by the first category.

Quite a few inventions, however, have turned out to have both murderous and peaceable uses. Atomic power is a case in point; its peaceful use was developed after 1945 with the construction of nuclear power stations—though there was (and is) considerable anxiety over the difficulty of disposing of nuclear waste safely, and over the risk of catastrophic accidents. The disasters at Three Mile Island in the USA in 1979 and at Chernobyl in the Soviet Union in 1986 have sent chills down many a spine.

A wartime development with beneficial peacetime uses was radar—an acronym for Radio Direction and Ranging. It was originally a product of military rivalry between the wars, and the German navy had its own radar system by 1933. In 1935 the British government asked Sir Robert Watson-Watt to invent a death-ray. Instead, he studied the steering methods of bats in order to devise a way of determining the position of

Two symbols of man's conquest of the air; (above), Mr Henry Farman winning the Deutsch–Archdeacon Prize at Issy, Paris, in January 1913, when he flew over a one-kilometre circular course in his heavier-than-air machine; and Little Boy (top), the 4-ton bomb that fell on Hiroshima on 6 August 1945.

an object by bouncing radio waves off it. A network of radar stations to detect approaching enemy bombers was constructed, and helped to win the Battle of Britain in 1940.

Later in the war, radar was used to detect submarines. It is now an accepted aid to air and sea navigation, and is also used in meteorology and astronomy. A by-product of radar is the microwave oven, first produced in the USA in the 1940s.

The pioneer of the jet engine was Frank Whittle, a young RAF officer who worked with government backing on the idea in the 1930s, but a German, Ernst Heinkel, built the first jet plane to fly, and it was the German Luftwaffe which had the only effective jets during the war. The main exploitation of the jet engine came after

1945, however, when it rapidly ousted the piston engine.

There are few more dramatic examples of twentieth-century technical advances than the story of flight. A few weird steam-driven contraptions contrived to fly for a second or two in the 1870s, 1880s and 1890s, but a new page of history was turned on 17 December 1903 at Kitty Hawk, North Carolina, when a rickety, kite-like object with a 40ft wingspan, appropriately named *Flyer*, stayed in the air for 59 seconds and covered about half a mile. It was piloted by Orville Wright, who had built it with his brother Wilbur.

The next stage belonged more to Europe than to the USA, as enthusiasts with names like Voisin, Blériot, Farman, Roe, Handley-Page and Sopwith were inspired to build flying machines. Wilbur Wright put on a series of exciting displays in front of huge crowds in France and Germany in 1908. On the last day of the year he made an astonishing flight of 77 miles, lasting two hours and 20 minutes, which broke all previous records and won him a substantial prize.

Progress was now extremely rapid. In February 1909 Britain's first aerodrome opened on the Isle of Sheppey in Kent. Then, on 25 July, Louis Blériot, who had sunk all his own and his wife's money in aviation, took off from France at 4.41am and landed near Dover 43 minutes later—the first man to fly across the Channel. In August, 23 planes took part in the first ever international air meeting, at which Blériot recorded the top speed of 48mph.

Casting their shadows before them, the years 1910 and 1911 witnessed, among other things, the first crossing of the Irish Sea by plane, the first flight over the Alps, the first air collision (in Austria), the first take-off and landing on water, the first official airmail flights and the first use of an airplane in war—for reconnaissance during the conflict between Italy and Turkey in 1911. In 1912 the Royal Flying Corps came into existence, the first British army plane fitted with a gun made an experimental flight, a French plane broke the 100mph speed barrier, and the first parachute jump was made from a plane.

Aircraft were used in the First World War for reconnaissance and for bombing—Paris was bombed in August 1914. Assisted by the invention of machine guns that would fire between the propellers, rival pilots engaged each other in dogfights and the great air aces of the day, like the German 'Red Baron' von Richthofen, won the admiration of their enemies as well as their own side. Von Richthofen was shot down and killed in April 1918, a few days before his 26th birthday.

The period between 1918 and 1939 was an age of flying circuses and stunts, Schneider Trophy races, regular airmail services and the first regular passenger services, as aircraft grew larger and more comfortable. In 1927 Charles Lindbergh made the first solo non-stop Atlantic crossing, in the *Spirit of St Louis*, in 33 hours 39 minutes, and Amy Johnson flew solo from England to Australia in a de Havilland Gipsy Moth in 1930.

The seaplane which won the Schneider Trophy in 1931 was the first to exceed 400mph.

The air was a far more important theatre of war in the Second World War than in the first, fought by aircraft with now almost legendary names: Hurricanes and Spitfires, Messerschmitts and Junkers, Lancasters and Flying Fortresses. Bouncing bombs and the first really efficient helicopters were among the war's more bizarre inventions, and the Germans developed 'flying bombs' and rockets. Bombing raids were now immeasurably more destructive. The Allied raid on Dresden in February 1945 took an estimated 135,000 lives.

The development of jet engines and rockets during the Second World War and immediately afterwards led to the breaking of the sound barrier in 1947 by an American rocket-propelled plane at a speed of nearly 700mph; the arrival of the commercial

Aviation has conquered space and time; through the space shuttle (right, top) and the sound-barrier breaking jump jet (below).

jumbo jet in 1969; the launching of the world's first supersonic airliners in the 1970s; and a huge expansion of air travel, which ceased to be the preserve of the rich. It also opened the way to the exploration of space, with its technology of gigantic rockets, spacecraft and satellites, crammed with complicated gadgetry. The Russian *Sputnik* went into orbit round the earth in 1957, the first weather satellite went up in 1960, and the USSR launched the first manned spacecraft and recovered it safely in 1961. In 1962 the American communications satellite *Telstar* sent the first television transmissions across the Atlantic.

On 21 July 1969 the American astronaut Neil Armstrong became the first human to stand on the moon ('a giant leap for mankind'). He was back on earth three days later. It was only 65 years since Orville Wright had left the ground for a fraction under a minute at Kitty Hawk. By the 1970s spacecraft had begun to probe far out among the stars, and in 1986 *Voyager 2* reached the planet Uranus, 783 million miles from earth.

In terms of both speed and safety the plane totally outstripped its older cousin, the car. Two German engineers, Gottlieb Daimler and Karl Benz, independently invented the modern petrol engine in 1885 and their first cars appeared in public the following year. Daimler also built the first motor cycle in 1885, while the diesel engine was invented by Rudolf Diesel in 1893.

Until 1896 the law in England required a 'horseless carriage' to be preceded on the highway by a man carrying a red flag, but as with aircraft, the development of the car was extremely swift. In 1899 a ride in a Daimler converted the future King Edward VII to motoring and conferred an aristocratic image, while in the same year the first British motorists were killed when a Daimler crashed in Harrow. In 1900 the earliest motorised ambulances were introduced in France. The Automobile Association was founded in 1905. In 1906 Grand Prix racing started and Henry Royce and

C S Rolls founded Rolls–Royce. In 1907 an Australian, S F Edge, drove a Napier car continuously for 24 hours at Brooklands at an average speed of 65mph. Henry Ford started to make the first Model Ts in 1908, and in 1913—a portent of things to come—his new factory in Detroit was equipped with a moving production line. Motor buses were replacing the horse-drawn variety in towns before the First World War.

Magic names still linger from the golden age of motoring before 1914; Panhard and Levassor, De Dion Bouton, Bugatti, Hispano-Suiza, Lanchester, Riley, Armstrong-Siddeley, Packard. The war inevitably took the petrol engine on to the battlefield with the invention of the tank. The first ungainly specimens seen in any numbers rumbled into the Battle of the Somme in 1916. In the desert T E Lawrence and his Arab irregulars charged the Turks using both Rolls–Royce armoured cars and camels.

The 1920s and 1930s saw motoring become accessible to the middle classes, with the introduction of small, reliable, cheap cars: in Britain, Austins and Morrises. Meanwhile, Rolls–Royces, Daimlers, Bentleys and their chauffeurs still conveyed the better-off. Sir Malcolm Campbell put the world land speed record up to 301mph in *Bluebird* in 1935. In the world of work, farming was being mechanised by tractors and other petrol-driven machines. Improvements in road technology were forced on by the increase in car traffic. The first motorways were built in Germany, Italy

Land speed records were smashed in the 1930s by Sir Malcolm Campbell in Bluebird.

and the USA in the 1920s. The first automatic traffic lights appeared in England in 1926, and the first cat's eyes appeared on British roads in the 1930s. A whole technology of petrol stations and pumps had to be invented, and car accessories and gadgets multiplied.

Tanks and armoured fighting vehicles had developed amazingly by 1939 and armoured units were the cavalry of the Second World War, while lorries provided unglamorous but essential transport. After

Model T Fords rolled off the world's first production line in Detroit (above). In 1955 the one-millionth Volkswagen Beetle was produced (right).

Concorde ushered in a new era of supersonic air travel in the 1970s

1945 car ownership became a mass phenomenon in Britain. Popular cars included the Morris Minor, the Volkswagen Beetle and the Mini (which soon lent its name to the mini-skirt). At the end of the 1980s, with 20 million vehicles on Britain's roads, one British household in five owned two cars.

By this time a technological revolution had occurred in the home, thanks to an army of labour-saving devices, entertainment equipment and assorted handy gadgets which would hardly have been believed in the 1890s. The intervening years had seen the invention and the main development of radio, television and record players, the telephone and the camera, instant and frozen foods, breakfast cereals, the refrigerator, the washer-dryer, and the computer.

No such transformation of domestic life had occurred in any previous century. The impetus, and the allied advertising and selling techniques, came mainly from the USA and many of the major household names were American: Singer, Hoover, Heinz, Gillette, Kellogg and Birds Eye.

Eating habits were revolutionised by processed and frozen foods, combined with the development of the refrigerator. The earliest refrigerators were invented for use in factories, hotels and shops. The first domestic one, worked by electricity, was produced in Chicago in 1913. Frigidaire began selling refrigerators in Britain in 1924. They were large and cumbrous and expensive, but as usual with new products, prices fell swiftly as demand increased.

Tinned food dates back to the early

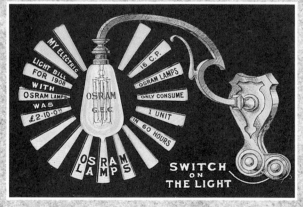

Hand in hand with domestic inventions came better advertising techniques (above and left), to tell the customer about new or improved products and sell them in adequate numbers.

H C Booth, the pioneer of the vacuum cleaner, made his first clumsy machines (below) for large-scale operations.

Liking a nice cup of tea in the morning became even more popular in the 1930s with the advent of machines like this one (right).

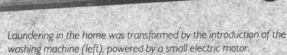

Laundering in the home was transformed by the introduction of the washing machine (left), powered by a small electric motor.

It took 18 minutes to boil a pint of water in an 1890s electric kettle, but in 1894 the City of London Electric Lighting Company advertised cooking by electricity as 'absolutely the best system of cooking'. It was already selling electric kettles, hotplates and irons. A catalogue of 1906 advertised electric curling tongs and an electric fire extinguisher. Electric cookers were still too expensive for most people in the 1920s, and their day did not really come until after 1945.

By 1989 there was a microwave oven in two British kitchens out of five, and a whole host of lesser gadgets had pushed or sidled their way in since 1890, when the Spong Company of London was selling mincers turned by a handle, with attachments for cutting meat, chopping vegetables and making sausages. Electric mincers and mixers appeared between the wars, followed in the 1970s by food processors. Le Magi-Mix was first exhibited in public in Paris in 1971 and the rival Cuisinart made its bow two years later. The non-stick pan was also developed in France in the 1950s.

Far back in the primitive 1890s the Automatic Water Boiler Company of Birmingham was selling a machine which woke you up in the morning with an alarm bell, lit its own spirit lamp, boiled a pint of water for shaving, made a pot of tea and rang a second bell to tell you everything was ready. The Goblin Teasmade began making early morning tea in the 1930s.

The hard, time-consuming work of cleaning the home was made easier and quicker with the development of vacuum cleaners. The earliest ones were for large-scale operations, and in 1902 a British pioneer, H C Booth, made an impression with his immensely powerful and noisy machine, which cleaned the Westminster Abbey carpets before the Coronation of Edward VII. Smaller models which could be used in the home soon appeared, but the breakthrough came in 1907 when William Henry Hoover, a middle-aged American harness-maker whose business was in trouble with the obsolescence of the horse, began to produce a portable vacuum cleaner with a dustbag attached to the handle. He made his fortune and his name became a generic term for vacuum cleaners.

Laundering was another slow, back-breaking labour in the old days, but the copper and the mangle were banished to museums by the washing machine. The early 1890s' models were giant objects of tremendous presence, standing 6ft (2 metres) high and weighing half a ton. They were turned by a handle. It was electricity which made the washing machine practical and increasingly popular in the 1920s and 1930s. They were still unusual in Britain in 1939, but half the households in the country owned one by 1963. Spin dryers became common in the 1960s, when the early automatic machines which did the whole job according to a programme began to arrive on the domestic scene.

With the washing machine, the sewing

The pioneer of frozen foods was the improbably named Clarence Birdseye, who went to Labrador as a fur trader and saw Eskimos thawing and eating fish and meat which had frozen in the icy Arctic air. Back home he experimented successfully, started his own company in 1924 and became a multi-millionaire with remarkable rapidity. Packs of frozen raw meat, fish and vegetables sold merrily in the 1930s, and in 1939 Birdseye put frozen cooked meals on the market, which only needed to be heated. The frozen fish finger made its début on the British table in 1955. Along with all this went the development of the refrigerator freezing compartment and the home freezer. By the late 1980s more than 50 per cent of households in Britain had a freezer.

The grandfather of the breakfast cereal was shredded wheat, invented in the USA in 1893 by Henry D Perky—suitably named in view of the atrocious perkiness of cereal commercials to come. Within a year or two the Kellogg Brothers had created the ubiquitous cornflake, which changed the breakfast habits of a hemisphere. John Harvey Kellogg, a Seventh Day Adventist, vegetarian and physician, ran a sanatorium in Battle Creek, Michigan, and he and his brother William devised cornflakes for their patients. One of the patients, C W Post, was so impressed that he founded a successful cereal firm himself.

Besides food itself, cooking equipment was transformed as gas and electric cookers supplanted open fires and ranges. Gas and electricity had been employed for lighting and heating before 1890—today's electric switches, fuses and wiring have changed very little since the 1880s, and the first single cord electric pull-switch was made in 1886—but it took time for them to move into people's homes. Mrs Beeton gave gas cooking her imprimatur in 1893. The early gas cookers were made of iron and still needed to be blackleaded and polished like coal ranges, but after 1918 sleekly enamelled gas stoves came in.

nineteenth century and was developed originally for sailors' and soldiers' rations. The archetypal tinned product of the twentieth century, baked beans in tomato sauce, was first manufactured in 1891 in the USA. H J Heinz began selling it in Britain in 1905. His company was already boasting about its '57 varieties' in 1896, and the first electric sign in New York City was put up in 1900 to advertise its products.

Edwards' Desiccated Soup, a dreary-sounding dried soup mix which could also be used to make gravy, was being advertised in Britain in 1907. Instant coffee had been invented in the USA in 1901, but did not really make any impression until the 1930s.

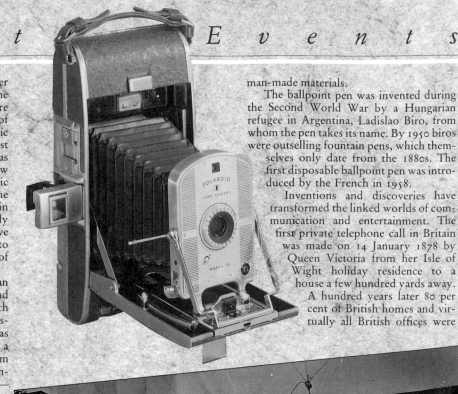

machine, the floor polisher and many other items, the key technical advance was the electric motor. The first viable ones were made in the 1870s and 1880s. The uses of electricity ranged bizarrely from the electric chair to the electric toothbrush. The first convict to die in the electric chair was executed at Auburn State Prison, New York, on 6 August 1890. The electric blanket was popularised in the USA in the 1930s. An electric hearing aid was devised in the USA in 1901, but it was uncomfortably large and clumsy: small ones did not arrive until the 1930s and really small ones had to wait until the 1950s, after the invention of the transistor.

The electric razor was invented by an American named Jacob Schick in 1928 and was an advance on the safety razor, which had been developed in the 1890s by a salesman named King Camp Gillette, who was fed-up with nicking himself messily with a cutthroat. The electric torch also dates from the 1890s, as do the first collapsible toothpaste tubes, while the electric toothbrush—that triumph of twentieth-century civilisation—was first manufactured in 1961.

More important were early electric sewing machines, developed between the wars. The sewing machine itself goes much further back and there was a fierce sewing machine 'war' between rival American manufacturers in the 1850s. The dominating figure at that time was Isaac Singer, a formidable womanising tycoon who was a pioneer of modern advertising and marketing methods, including door-to-door selling and selling on credit. Singer himself died in 1875, but his soul went marching on. The first Singer sewing machine entirely powered by electricity came out in 1921, and present-day machines are controlled by micro-processors.

Aspirin, the solution to the twentieth century's headaches, was manufactured by the Bayer Company in the USA in 1899 and was soon readily available at the chemist's. Alexander Fleming accidentally stumbled on penicillin in 1928, but it was not until after 1945 that the pharmaceutical industry went into overdrive with the bulk production of insulin, penicillin and streptomycin, vitamins and antihistamines, and other drugs and products which have changed modern medicine.

The zip-fastener, the twentieth century's answer to the button, was invented by an American engineer in 1893 and improved by another engineer 20 years later, but was not at first considered respectable. It was not adopted for women's fashions until the 1930s, and long after 1945 in Britain men's trousers were still equipped with fly buttons. Clothes were increasingly likely to be made of synthetic fibres, which were first developed in the 1890s with the manufacture of artificial silk from wood pulp: it was called rayon or viscose. Nylon was invented in the USA in 1930 by Wallace Carothers, and subsequent innovations included acrylic fibres, terylene and PVC. Today's textile industry relies heavily on

man-made materials.

The ballpoint pen was invented during the Second World War by a Hungarian refugee in Argentina, Ladislao Biro, from whom the pen takes its name. By 1950 biros were outselling fountain pens, which themselves only date from the 1880s. The first disposable ballpoint pen was introduced by the French in 1958.

Inventions and discoveries have transformed the linked worlds of communication and entertainment. The first private telephone call in Britain was made on 14 January 1878 by Queen Victoria from her Isle of Wight holiday residence to a house a few hundred yards away. A hundred years later 80 per cent of British homes and virtually all British offices were

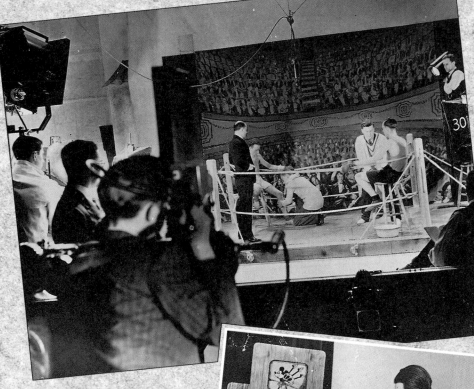

An early Polaroid camera (top). After its pioneering days in the nineteenth century photography blossomed into an art form and a major aid to science, industry and entertainment.

Advances in cameras and photography led on to films and television. A boxing match at the Crystal Palace (above) was transmitted by Baird Television Ltd in 1935, and in the same year the company demonstrated a cathode-ray television receiver for the home (right). The BBC started regular television broadcasts the following year.

copiously equipped with telephones and the ends of the earth could be dialled direct.

Marconi transmitted his first wireless messages in the 1890s and the first transatlantic radio signal flew from Cornwall to Newfoundland in 1901. The invention came of age 21 years later, when the BBC began radio broadcasting in 1922.

There were numerous nineteenth-century pioneers of the camera, and by the 1890s the first moving pictures and primitive cinemas had arrived. The Polaroid 'instant' camera was invented in 1947. Holography, or three-dimensional photography, also developed after the war. Its applications turned out to range from making visual voyages inside the human body to devices for reading bar-codes at supermarket check-outs.

The main developments in television came in the 1920s, and the BBC started regular television broadcasts in 1936. Video recorders appeared in the late 1970s. By the end of the 1980s there were few British households without a television set and about half owned a video recorder.

The home, like the office, was now in the grip of 'information technology', initially created by the invention of the transistor in the USA at the Bell Telephone Laboratories in 1947. The world's first electronic computer had been constructed at the University of Pennsylvania two years before: it could perform 5,000 additions per second. As it weighed 30 tons, it was hardly practical for home or pocket, but transistors made it possible to manufacture computers which were much smaller and faster.

The face that launched a thousand chips—silicon chips—belonged to Intel, a Californian firm which in 1971 produced the first microprocessor. This was a circuit with thousands of tiny transistors and other components mounted on a single silicon chip, which carried out computer-like operations but was much smaller, lighter and cheaper than earlier systems. The microprocessor has become essential to the control systems of a host of products and activities, from motor cars and weapons technology to word processors and electronic games; from robots and traffic control systems, to handling bank accounts and public library records.

As the 1980s came to an end, yet another technological revolution was approaching with the introduction of new superconducting ceramics materials, with names like yttrium and lutetium. Judging by the massive advances of the last century, anything seems possible in the next hundred years.

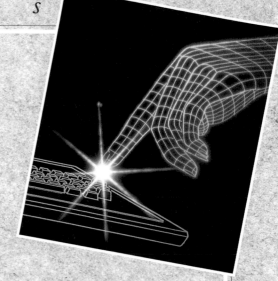

The computer-drawn illustration (above) shows a hand reaching out to a keyboard.

Computer technology, with silicon chips in a 'logic array' integrated circuit (below).

Laser technology (above), used here to remove a cancerous tumour from a patient's eye.
Solar power is another recent development. In 1987 a solar-powered car race was held in Australia (below), and was won by a Ford.

VICTORY DAY on 8 June this year was organised as a celebration of the end of the entire war, and was declared a national holiday in Britain. In London 20,000 men and women of the Armed Forces and the wartime civilian Services—everyone from the Life Guards to the Home Guard—marched in the biggest parade in the country's history. But the celebration could not mask the grimness of the country's situation.

Britain was broke. The nation's debts had risen from £500,000,000 at the beginning of the Second World War to £3,500,000,000 by the end of it, and virtually all British overseas investments had been liquidated. Britons found it hard to understand how a major world power, victorious in war, could be bankrupt and forced to go cap in hand to the Americans for an onerous loan.

The country now faced a period of pinched and grey austerity which in some ways was harder to bear than the war years, because there was no longer a foreign enemy to fight. There was much talk from public figures of tightening belts and putting shoulders to the wheel. Rationing not only continued, but got worse. In February the ration of butter, margarine and cooking-fat was cut from 8oz (226g) a week to 7oz (200g). Bread was rationed, for the first time ever, in July. The Ministry of Food helpfully circulated a recipe for squirrel pie. There were angry mutterings about black marketeering. Meanwhile, although the fighting was over, conscription still remained in force.

Depression hung over the international scene, too, with the intransigence of the Soviet Union and its satellites in Eastern Europe. Winston Churchill used a phrase which entered the language when he spoke in the USA in May: 'A shadow has fallen upon the scenes so lately lighted by the Allied victory . . . From Stettin on the Baltic to Trieste on the Adriatic, an iron curtain has descended across the Continent.'

Pinpoints of light appeared here and there in the encircling gloom. The inaugural session of the General Assembly of the United Nations took place in London in January, which gave people the feeling that, despite all, Britain still counted for something in the world. A long-lost visitor from overseas returned in the shape of the banana. The accustomed sporting rituals made a welcome reappearance, too: the first Grand National since the war, and the first Derby, won by Airborne.

Attention was also distracted from home troubles by the Nuremberg Trials of Nazi leaders as war criminals. The *ILN* reminded its readers of the appalling horrors of the concentration camps and the gas ovens, and took stern satisfaction in reporting the judgement of the court:

> *One by one, the members of the Tribunal, representing the Four Great Powers, took up the reading of the document . . . from morning until early evening, the voice of judgement inexorably summed up the case against the accused. When the court adjourned at nearly seven o'clock, the summing-up was complete.*
> (12 October)

Hermann Goering and 11 others were condemned to be hanged, three were given life imprisonment (one was Rudolf Hess), and three received shorter terms. Goering cheated the hangman by taking cyanide.

Judgement at Nuremberg: the scene in 'the greatest trial in history' as leading Nazis were indicted for war crimes. Goering, the most important of the accused, can be seen next to Hess in the second row back, at the left. He surprised everyone by putting his defence eloquently and with an impressive grasp of detail. He 'concluded his examination-in-chief . . . with words which he attributed to Mr. Churchill: "In a struggle for life and death there is no legality." His address lasted in all . . . for 12 hours. All along he attempted to prove that the Soviet preparations were responsible for the war. He maintained that the Hague Conventions . . . were outmoded by modern warfare.' (23 March 1946)

1946

E·V·E·N·T·S

3 JANUARY William Joyce ('Lord Haw Haw')
hanged for treason in UK
30 JANUARY The inaugural session of the UN
General Assembly opened in London
5 APRIL Lovely Cottage won the first post-war
Grand National
22 JULY Jewish dissidents blew up the King
David Hotel in Jerusalem
19 DECEMBER Hostilities broke out against the
French in Indochina

Making ends meet:
clothes rationing was still
in force, the coupon
book went to the shops
with you and rationing
actually grew worse after
the war, as a result of
Britain's parlous
economic state. Bread
was now rationed.

The 1946
Clothing Quiz

3d

ISSUED BY THE BOARD OF TRADE

HIS MAJESTY'S STATIONERY OFFICE
CROWN COPYRIGHT RESERVED

Brighter than the sun: an atomic bomb was
exploded on 30 June by the Americans at Bikini
Atoll, whose inhabitants had been removed
elsewhere. '. . . the world's first peacetime atom
bomb, whose construction had cost an estimated
£8,000,000, was dropped on a target fleet of
warships anchored in the lagoon of Bikini Atoll, in
the Pacific. The first visible evidence of its
disintegration was a great blinding orange flash,
reported to have been ten times brighter than the
sun, which was followed by a second explosion,
three times as big . . . Orange and yellow flames,
smoke and steam gushed skyward to a height of
60,000 ft in an awesome pillar which slowly
changed from a living rose-red to a dead grey-
white. The atoll had disappeared behind a veil of
billowing smoke, but after five minutes the base of
the pillar began to lift—to reveal some surprising
results, among them the fact that the "bull's-eye"
battleship *Nevada* was still afloat and that palm-
trees were still standing on the atoll.' (6 July 1946)

1947

I N THE EARLY MONTHS of the year Britain ground almost to a halt. A winter of arctic harshness brought 14ft (4½ metre) snowdrifts, and icebergs off the Norfolk coast. The sea froze at Margate, and in London temperatures went down to 16 degrees F (−9 degrees C).

The weather drove the ailing fuel and power industry to its knees. Unofficial strikes and persistent absenteeism hampered the coal mines, the dilapidated railways could not deliver supplies of coal quickly enough, and the power stations began to run out. In February the Prime Minister, Clement Attlee, went on the radio to announce 'an emergency of the utmost gravity' and appealed to everyone to economise. Not that there was much choice. Factories had closed down for lack of power. At home, people groped their way about by candle-light, and went to bed for warmth.

Ironically, Britain's coal mines had just been nationalised, and on 1 January a notice had gone up at their gates: 'This colliery is now managed by the National Coal Board on behalf of the people.'

The weather eased off eventually, but in June the milk allowance was reduced to 2½ pints (just over 1 litre) a week and newspapers were temporarily cut back to their wartime size of four pages. Later in the summer the meat ration was cut, holidays abroad were banned and so was motoring for pleasure.

On the other hand, the 'New Look' in women's fashions blew in like a springtime breeze from Paris, banishing the dreary, boxed-in 'utility' look with its square shoulders in favour of a figure-of-eight shape and romantically swirling skirts. The rag trade fell on the new style with glee and women loved it. So did men.

The public also found relief from austerity in following the romance of the 21-year-old Princess Elizabeth with her naval cousin, Lieutenant Philip Mountbatten (a nephew of Lord Louis Mountbatten, who was away presiding over the birth pangs of India and Pakistan). Crowds stood in the rain outside Buckingham Palace and cheered when the engagement of the royal couple was announced in July. The wedding on 20 November was the most glamorous royal occasion since before the war. Arrayed in a gorgeous ivory dress and tulle veil designed by Norman Hartnell, the bride drove to the ceremony with her father, King George VI, in the Irish State Coach, attended by the Life Guards and the Blues. Hundreds of thousands lined the route and the BBC covered the occasion in 42 different languages.

The media naturally plunged into an orgy of sentimentality, from which the *ILN* was not immune: 'The obvious happiness of the Royal Bride and Bridegroom,' it pronounced, bursting with loyalty and honorific capitals, 'meant more to the people of Britain than all the heart-stirring pageantry that attended the Royal wedding.'

In his sermon in Westminster Abbey, the Archbishop of York had sounded a similar note:

> *'Notwithstanding the splendour and national signifi-cance of the service in this Abbey, it is in all essentials exactly the same as it would be for any cottager who might be married this afternoon in some small country church in a remote village in the dales. The same vows are taken, the same prayers offered, the same blessings given.'* (29 November)

Farewell to the Raj: Lord Louis Mountbatten was sent to India in March as Viceroy, to bring British rule there rapidly to an end. He is seen here with Lady Mountbatten and Mr Jinnah, the Indian Muslim leader who became Governor-General of Pakistan. 'On August 15, British India ended; and in accordance with the grant of independence the two new Dominions of India and Pakistan came into being. At Delhi and Karachi respectively, the new flags were raised at the new capitals . . .' (23 August 1947)

The giant-killer: the ending of British rule in India was due largely to Mahatma Gandhi, whose long campaign for independence finally succeeded. '. . . to the many Britons who have been so closely associated with the history of the great sub-continent, probably the most poignant flag ceremony of the day will always remain the lowering . . . of the Union flag which has flown, night and day, over the ruins of Lucknow Residency since that city's recapture in 1858.' (23 August 1947)

THE ILLUSTRATED
LONDON NEWS

1947

E · V · E · N · T · S

25 JANUARY Al Capone, American gangster, died aged 48
5 JUNE General George Marshall proposed plan for European recovery
24 AUGUST Opening of first Edinburgh Festival under director Rudolf Bing
13 NOVEMBER Hugh Dalton resigned as Chancellor over a budget leak
20 NOVEMBER HRH Princess Elizabeth married Lieutenant Philip Mountbatten

Bilious: their health was about all most Britons could take on holiday in 1947.

Royal couple: Princess Elizabeth and the Duke of Edinburgh. 'The family tradition established by Queen Victoria and Prince Albert in the last century, and transmitted to our own changed and revolutionary age by Queen Mary and the present Queen, has stood the test of time and tempests. The marriage of Princess Elizabeth is an assurance that it will continue to endure.' (29 November 1947)

O<small>N</small> 30 JANUARY, Mahatma Gandhi was assassinated by a Hindu fanatic in New Delhi. The *ILN* sympathetically described the last journey of the 'great soul' (the literal meaning of Mahatma) to the burning ghat where his body was cremated. So huge was the sorrowing crowd that the flower-decked bier took five hours to travel five miles:

> *Though the massed crowds wept unrestrainedly as the cortège passed, the only cry to be heard was that of Mahatma Gandhi—ji Ki Jai (Victory to Mahatma Gandhi), for India does not forget that Gandhi achieved his life ambition, the termination of British rule in India.* (17 February)

The Berlin airlift began when the Soviet Union stepped up the Cold War and blockaded Berlin, cutting off all access to it by land. American and British planes flew food and supplies into the beleaguered city: something of a change for the Berliners, who four years before had been on the receiving end of Allied bombs, not flour and coal. RAF Dakotas were arriving at Gatow every four minutes in June. The Foreign Minister, Ernest Bevin, told the House of Commons: 'There has been an attempt to see how long our nerves would last, but there is no snapping yet.' He was loudly cheered by all parties. Britain was on the world stage again.

The Soviet bluff was called. When the airlift ended in September 1949, more than $2\frac{1}{4}$ million tons of supplies had been flown in over a period of 15 months. Meanwhile, the new state of Israel had been proclaimed in May.

The National Health Service (NHS) came into operation in July. The midwife who brought it to birth was Aneurin Bevan, the Health Minister, who was to resign from the Labour government three years hence when Hugh Gaitskell's budget put charges on spectacles and false teeth. For the moment, however, his enemy was the British Medical Association (BMA), the doctors' professional organisation, which detested the NHS scheme. A BMA poll in February had shown that 90 per cent of doctors were against it. By April the figure was down to 65 per cent, and when finally confronted with joining or trying to earn a living outside the state system, only 1,500 of the country's 20,000 doctors stayed out.

In its first year the NHS cared for $47\frac{1}{2}$ million patients and provided $5\frac{1}{4}$ million pairs of spectacles, 7,000 artificial eyes and 5,000 wigs, while its doctors wrote 187 million prescriptions. It was the most important of the Labour government's innovations, and the one which has had the deepest effects on lives and attitudes in Britain ever since. By 1950, 19 people out of 20 were using the NHS.

Eyebrows were raised with the publication of the bestselling Kinsey Report on *Sexual Behaviour in the Human Male*. Professor Kinsey, a zoologist by training, was head of the Institute for Sex Research at Indiana University. In the USA the *New Yorker* thought the report contained more dynamite than any scientific work since Darwin's *Origin of Species*, and the levels of sexual activity it revealed shocked conventional opinion in Britain.

The ancient custom by which the Home Secretary was present at royal births was dropped on King George VI's instructions when Princess Elizabeth's first child was born at Buckingham Palace on 14 November. A bouncing boy, he was christened Charles Philip Arthur George.

Last journey of a murdered saint: Gandhi was shot dead by a Hindu fanatic in New Delhi. 'India mourns Mahatma Gandhi, greatest and most beloved of her leaders with, to quote *The Times* correspondent, "An intensity of emotional abandon which the West cannot parallel or even imagine." Over 1,000,000 Indians from Delhi and the surrounding country paid their last tribute to their murdered saint on January 31, when his body, with the head exposed, was borne on a flower-decked bier along the five-mile route from Birla House (where he was assassinated on January 30) to the burning ghat on the banks of the sacred River Jumna . . . The scenes at the cremation were poignant. When the procession . . . reached the burning ghat—a brick platform on which piles of logs were heaped—the crowds rushed the barriers . . .' (7 February 1948)

First outing for a prince: a smiling Princess Elizabeth, with the infant Prince Charles. 'The baby Prince was photographed after his christening at Buckingham Palace . . . at 3.30 p.m. in the White and Gold Music Room.' (25 December 1948)

1948

E·V·E·N·T·S

30 JANUARY Mahatma Gandhi was assassinated in New Delhi
14 MAY Proclamation of Israel as an independent Jewish state
5 JULY The National Health Service came into operation
12 AUGUST Morris Minor cars started coming off the production line
23 AUGUST The World Council of Churches was formally constituted
31 DECEMBER Sir Malcolm Campbell, speed champion, died aged 63

Spirit of the games: the first Olympic Games since 1936 were held in Britain in the summer. Star athletes included the Czech Emil Zatopek, Fanny Blankers-Koen from Holland and the 17-year-old American, Bob Mathias.

There's a silver lining: on 26 April King George VI and Queen Elizabeth celebrated their silver wedding anniversary. Their 25 years of married life had brought them through both their unexpected accession and the Second World War.

1949

THE RUSSIANS lifted their blockade of Berlin in May—though the airlift was to go on for several months more—and a huge crowd of West Berliners gathered in front of the town hall to celebrate. The *ILN* told its readers that the ending of the 322-day blockade:

> . . . was received with heartfelt relief by the citizens of the beleaguered city. Their joy was combined with appreciation for the manner in which the air-lift has kept them supplied with the means of existence during this trying period. The R.A.F. announced that on May 12, when the blockade ended, 90,063 British and American aircraft landings had been made . . . this represents an average landing rate of one aircraft every 5 mins. 4 secs., and the delivering of $1\frac{1}{3}$ tons of freight per minute. (21 May)

The blockade had spurred the USA, Britain, France and other western countries to create a counterbalance to Soviet military might in Europe by founding what became the North Atlantic Treaty Organisation (NATO). The principal architect of the treaty on the European side was Ernest Bevin, and its effect was to commit the USA to the defence of western Europe.

On the other side of the world on 1 October, another enormous crowd assembled in the Square of the Gate of Heavenly Peace in Peking to hear the People's Republic of China formally inaugurated in a proclamation by its first Chairman, Mao Tse-tung, which declared victory in 'the war of the people's liberation' against the 'reactionary rule' of the Nationalists. Civil war between Communists and Nationalists had been going on in China ever since the Japanese had surrendered in 1945. The Communists were now in control of 400 million Chinese, while the Nationalist government had installed itself on the island of Formosa, or Taiwan.

The British government quickly recognised the Communist regime to protect its commercial interests. They needed protecting, as Britain's post-war malaise had deepened into a balance-of-payments crisis. Imports were cut in June and July, and in a shock move in September the pound was devalued by 30 per cent.

The British film industry, which was now largely in the hands of the flour-milling magnate J Arthur Rank, was also in crisis. A murderous entertainment tax, competition from Hollywood, and the commercial failure of too many British films proved disastrous. Studios closed, staff were laid off, and audiences were falling. It was a pity, for British film studios had been turning out some of the best films they had ever made, with Laurence Olivier's *Hamlet* and *The Red Shoes* taking Oscars in Hollywood in March. The quintessential British film made in this year was *The Third Man*, directed by Carol Reed, with a script by Graham Greene.

The writing was on the wall, not only for the old 78rpm gramophone records, now about to be replaced by LPs, but also for the old guard in the art world, personified by Sir Alfred Munnings, whose speech at the Royal Academy dinner denouncing modern art and Picasso was noisily heckled. The old guard at Wimbledon disapproved of Gussie Moran's provocative lace-trimmed panties, while Simone de Beauvoir's *The Second Sex* would later be hailed as a feminist classic.

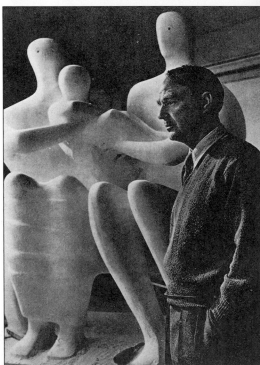

Truth in stone: an exhibition of Henry Moore's work was touring Europe. 'Many people, while sensitive to the power and importance of his work, find it difficult to understand . . . "Truth to material" is one of his articles of faith, and it is through this appreciation of the essential character of stone that he has developed his half-woman, half-landscape idiom.' (12 November 1949)

The ransomed of the Lord shall return and come to Zion: Chaim Weizmann, the President of the new state of Israel, which had been proclaimed in 1948, at the first meeting of the Constituent Assembly in Jerusalem. 'Behind the platform hung a portrait of Theodor Herzl, creator of modern Zionism, flanked by two large blue-and-white shields of David; and proceedings opened with the singing of the Jewish national anthem, *Ha'tiqva'*. (26 February 1949). Dr Weizmann was a scientist of international repute and distinction. The new state, which had opened its gates to Jewish immigrants from anywhere in the world, had been involved in violent conflict with Arab countries from its inception.

THE ILLUSTRATED LONDON NEWS

1949

E·V·E·N·T·S

1 MARCH Joe Louis, aged 34, retired as World Heavyweight Champion
2 MARCH A US air force plane made the first non-stop flight round the globe
15 MARCH Rationing of clothes ended in Britain after eight years
4 APRIL The North Atlantic Treaty, creating NATO, was signed by 12 nations
8 SEPTEMBER Richard Strauss, German composer, died aged 85

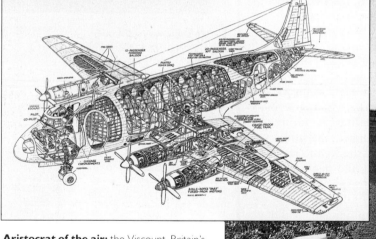

Aristocrat of the air: the Viscount, Britain's new turboprop airliner.' . . . it is the forerunner of the noiseless air travel of the future.' (1 January 1949)

Saviour from the sky: Germans cheering one of the last airlift flights coming in to land at Tempelhof Airport in Berlin. 'The ending of the 322-days blockade of Berlin . . . [which was] lifted just after midnight on Thursday, May 12 (local time), 1949, was received with heartfelt relief by the citizens of the beleaguered city. Their joy was combined with appreciation for the manner in which the airlift has kept them supplied with the means of existence during this trying period.' (21 May 1949)

1950

THE COLD WAR suddenly turned hot when North Korean troops and tanks invaded South Korea across the 38th parallel in June. The Soviet Union's temporary absence from the United Nations Security Council enabled the Council to condemn the aggression and call on United Nations members to aid the South Koreans. President Truman promptly sent in American forces. It was the first occasion on which the USA intervened by force to check Communist expansion. Britain sent troops to Korea in August, and the Chinese intervened in November. The *ILN* reported the 'sudden and unprovoked aggression' of Communist North Korea against the South, adding that 'the sequence of events is somewhat confused'. It was to keep its readers regularly up-to-date with the latest happenings:

> *While the U.S. Marines and the Royal Marine Commandos were making their magnificent fighting withdrawal from the Changjin (Chosin) reservoir area in north-east Korea . . . the operations on the western (or Eighth Army) front were on a much larger scale, but of a much less dramatic nature.* (23 December)

The war was to claim 5 million lives before it petered out.

A different variety of Communist initiative was punished when Klaus Fuchs was sent to prison for betraying British atomic secrets to the Russians. A German-born physicist with a British passport, he had worked on the atom bomb in the USA and then returned to England and the Atomic Energy Research Establishment at Harwell.

The novelist George Orwell (whose real name was Eric Blair) died of tuberculosis in a London hospital on 21 January, aged only 46. He had found it difficult to get his anti-Communist fable *Animal Farm* published in 1945, when the Soviet Union was still regarded as a heroic ally against Hitler. By 1949, when Orwell published his nightmare depiction of a totalitarian future, *Nineteen Eighty-Four*, the Cold War had changed the atmosphere. A convinced Socialist, Orwell fought for the Republicans in the Spanish Civil War, was badly wounded and acquired a loathing of Communist aims and tactics, which inspired his two best-known and most influential books.

Across the Atlantic, suspicion of Communism could become hysterical. After a state department official named Alger Hiss had been convicted of, in effect, passing US government secret documents to a Communist agent, Senator Joseph McCarthy of Wisconsin rose to speak at a women's luncheon in West Virginia. 'I have in my hand,' he announced, 'a list of 205 that were known to the Secretary of State as being members of the Communist Party and who are nevertheless still working and shaping the policies of the State Department.' The previously obscure McCarthy was to become a figure to reckon with.

In Britain the Labour government went to the polls in February, and after a cliff-hanging election was returned to office, but with its majority considerably reduced. Commentators suggested that the British public was content with the Socialism it had been given, but wanted no more.

The year ended with Scottish Nationalists making off with the Stone of Scone—on which the Kings of Scots had been crowned for centuries—having removed it from under the coronation chair in Westminster Abbey.

End of the road: the novelist and essayist George Orwell (below), author of *The Road to Wigan Pier*, *Animal Farm* and *Nineteen Eighty-Four*, died on 21 January. He was only 46. An Old Etonian and a former down-and-out in the slums of Paris and London, he was a strong Socialist, but his experiences in the Spanish Civil War inspired in him a passionate hatred of totalitarian Communism.

On their way: US infantry boarding a troop ship in Japan for the war in Korea, in July. The first British troops to reinforce the Americans arrived in South Korea in August. 'For some time before the full-scale attack was launched on June 25, Communist guerrilla bands had been attempting to infiltrate through the South Korean defensive line along the 38th Parallel—the frontier between the two Korean States. When the invasion was first reported, it was thought that it was merely another foray by a small force which could be handled by the strong points established along the border. However, the gun emplacements and machine-gun posts crumbled before the onslaught of armour and artillery and the drive on Seoul could not be halted.' (8 July 1950). Cyril Falls wrote that the USA, 'having issued a pledge to uphold the South Korean Republic . . . did well to fight'. (5 August 1950)

Man and superman: one of the last photographs of George Bernard Shaw, (above), playwright, critic and wit, who died on 2 November, aged 94. He was an ardent Socialist and an apologist for the Soviet system. He won the Nobel Prize for Literature in 1925.

THE ILLUSTRATED LONDON NEWS

1950

E·V·E·N·T·S

10 FEBRUARY Mark Spitz, American swimmer, born in Modesto, California

19 MARCH Edgar Rice Burroughs, creator of Tarzan, died aged 74

26 MAY Petrol rationing came to an end in Britain after 10 years

7 JUNE The BBC broadcast the first episode of *The Archers*

25 JUNE The Korean War began, when North Korea invaded the South

15 AUGUST Princess Anne, Princess Elizabeth's second child, born

Where eagles dare: 1950 was a vintage year in the development of children's comics. It witnessed the first issue of *Eagle*, in reaction against the 'horror comics' of the time. Among its features were the adventures of Dan Dare, 'pilot of the future'. This year also saw the launch of the Schulz comic strip *Peanuts*, which became a favourite with grown-ups as well.

1951

'I SEE THIS FESTIVAL as a symbol of Britain's abiding courage and vitality. With the spirit of our ancestors renewed in us we can, under God's providence, restore and expand the prosperity of which they laid the foundations. We can draw inspiration from their staunch example, and confidence from the modern achievements of our own industry. We have not proved unworthy of our past and we can do better in the years ahead.'

With this headmasterly mixture of pride in the past and slightly desperate exhortation for the future—entirely typical of its period—King George VI formally opened the Festival of Britain on 3 May 1951. Inspired by the Great Exhibition of 1851, the Festival was intended to be a tonic to the nation, a pat on the back after the years of war and austerity, and an advertisement for British technology and British design.

Events were held all over the country, but the main focus was on London, where 27 bomb-blasted acres near Waterloo were turned into the South Bank Exhibition. There the slender Skylon soared up 300ft (nearly 100 metres)—symbolising Britain, people said unkindly, because it had no visible means of support. There the Dome of Discovery told the story of British scientific and technological advance. Near by, the Land of Britain Pavilion concentrated on the country's physical geography, the Countryside Pavilion spotlighted British farming, the Power and Production Pavilion contained craft workshops and a model coal mine, while the Lion and the Unicorn Pavilion revealed aspects of the British national character.

The Royal Festival Hall was the only permanent building, though the National Theatre's foundation stone was laid in July. On the lighter side, there were the Festival Pleasure Gardens and Fun Fair in Battersea Park.

By the time the South Bank Exhibition closed, $8\frac{1}{2}$ million visitors had been to it. The *ILN* quoted the Archbishop of Canterbury's words at the closing ceremony:

> '*At such a time, when the international scene is one of strain and stress and we are hard-pressed at home to pay our way and meet our obligations, such a demonstration of vitality, enterprise and resilience declares that this old country is still in spirit young.*'
> (6 October)

A better index to the spirit of the young, perhaps, was the success of J D Salinger's *The Catcher in the Rye*, with its hero's attempt to escape from the adult world. The novel's rejection of adult values gave it a special cachet for the educated young in the 1950s; it was a portent of the approaching youth culture and 'generation gap'.

Pride in ancient institutions took a knock in Britain this year when two diplomats named Burgess and Maclean disappeared from view in the general direction of Moscow. Public school, Cambridge and a career in the Foreign Office were evidently no guarantee of loyalty to King and country.

Britain was struck by another balance-of-payments crisis this year, and the general election in October put the Conservatives into power with a majority of 17, although Labour achieved the biggest vote in its history, before or since: nearly 14 million, and 49 per cent of the votes cast. At the age of 77, Winston Churchill was back in 10 Downing Street.

Phoenix from the ashes: the South Bank site in London illuminated at night for the Festival of Britain. 'The South Bank of the Thames, so long a derelict area, is now transformed. Clad in the proud livery of Festival beauty, and, in spite of all prophecies to the contrary, ready in time for the Royal opening on May 3, it presents a scene of remarkable architectural beauty in the modern manner . . . The Skylon and the old Shot Tower point upward with modern aspiration and with solid nineteenth-century confidence respectively.' (12 May 1951). The Shot Tower was demolished after the Festival.

THE ILLUSTRATED
LONDON NEWS

1951

E·V·E·N·T·S

19 APRIL Miss Sweden won the first 'Miss
World' contest in London
29 APRIL Ludwig Wittgenstein, Viennese
philosopher, died aged 62
3 MAY King George VI declared the Festival of
Britain open in London
10 JULY Randolf Turpin beat Sugar Ray
Robinson for world middleweight title
25 OCTOBER Election day: Winston Churchill
returned to power

The last prize: Winston Churchill (left) with a cheering crowd after casting his vote in the general election. In his last major campaign speech he said that he was still in public life because he believed he might be able to contribute to 'bringing nearer that lasting peace settlement which the masses of people . . . in every land fervently desired. "I pray, indeed," he said, "that I may have this opportunity. It is the last prize I seek to win." ' (3 November 1951)

Some corner of a foreign field: as United Nations forces advanced in Korea, British soldiers found the grave of one of the 'glorious Gloucesters'. Many graves were found on the hillside on the Imjin River front, where the first battalion of the Gloucestershire Regiment made its heroic last stand.

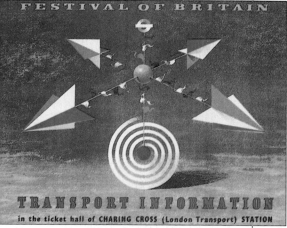

FESTIVAL OF BRITAIN

TRANSPORT INFORMATION
in the ticket hall of CHARING CROSS (London Transport) STATION

Festival frolics: a cheerful Festival of Britain poster. Entertainments on the lighter side in London included the Festival Pleasure Gardens and Fun Fair in Battersea Park and a mock-up of Mr Sherlock Holmes's sitting room at the mythical address, 22b Baker Street.

KING GEORGE VI spent what would prove to be the last day of his life shooting enjoyably at Sandringham. He died in his sleep early the next morning, on 6 February. He had endured a major operation for lung cancer the previous September and at the end of January, looking worn and ill, he saw Princess Elizabeth and the Duke of Edinburgh off at London Airport on their way to East Africa and a tour of Ceylon, Australia and New Zealand. Six days later, he was dead.

The news was telephoned through to the Edinburghs in Africa. Their tour was immediately called off and the 25-year-old Queen flew back to London from Entebbe Airport in Uganda, a slender figure, pale-faced in black.

The obituaries, if the King could have read them, would have left him in no doubt of the esteem and affection in which he had been held. He had been admired for his kindliness and the determination with which he had conquered his congenital shyness and dreadful stammer when he had unexpectedly become King on the abdication of his brother, Edward VIII, in 1936.

In its own warm tribute, the *ILN* said of King George and Queen Elizabeth:

> *Their simplicity, shining friendliness, modesty and manifest interest in every activity of life, their tact and warm-hearted understanding of all sorts and conditions of men, made every journey they undertook together a triumph. They radiated good will and kindliness, and it was so obviously a sincere good will and kindliness . . .* (16 February)

King George was buried in St George's Chapel, Windsor, on 15 February. The rest of the year seemed comparatively quiet. The economy began to improve. Tea came off the ration. Gene Kelly did his dance in *Singin' in the Rain*, Gary Cooper did what a man had to do in *High Noon*, and the wide screen came to cinemas in a vain attempt to keep audiences away from television. Dylan Thomas, at the end of his thirties and almost at the end of his life, brought out his *Collected Poems*. A play by Agatha Christie opened in London with Richard Attenborough in the lead: it was called *The Mousetrap*. A 28-year-old soprano named Maria Callas took Covent Garden by storm in Bellini's *Norma*.

Two young men named Christopher Craig and Derek Bentley, aged 16 and 19 respectively, were convicted of murdering a policeman in the course of an armed robbery. Craig did the killing, not Bentley, but it was Bentley who was to hang, because Craig was too young. The case caused an outcry and was a step on the way to the abolition of the death penalty.

The French were fighting the Viet Minh in Indochina, and British troops were sent to Kenya to combat the Mau Mau terrorists who were killing white settlers. In the USA in November, General Dwight D Eisenhower, formerly Allied Supreme Commander in Europe, swept Governor Adlai E Stevenson off the board in the presidential election: the new Vice President was Richard M Nixon.

At the end of the month the USA exploded a hydrogen bomb in the Pacific. Vastly more powerful than the atom bombs dropped on Japan in 1945, it blew an island to smithereens. The Soviet Union would claim to have its own hydrogen bomb within a year: the balance of terror held sway.

Off the rails: a 1927 tramcar in its final week of service in London, in July. Rattling their way along on their rails, under a grid of overhead wires, from which the pole all too frequently came adrift, electric trams were clumsy vehicles which inspired unreasoning affection. Whether getting rid of them was a good idea is still in some doubt.

Balance of terror: the USA exploded the first hydrogen bomb in November, at Eniwetok Atoll in the Marshall Islands in the Pacific. These new weapons, for which atomic bombs were used as detonators, were hundreds of times more powerful and destructive than atom bombs. The Soviet Union had tested its first atom bomb in 1949 and Britain set off its first in October 1952. In 1953 the USSR would claim to have its own hydrogen bomb and in 1960 the French would join the nuclear club by exploding three atomic bombs in the Sahara. Peace between the great powers depended on a balance of deterrence.

THE ILLUSTRATED LONDON NEWS

1952

E·V·E·N·T·S

6 FEBRUARY George VI died in his sleep at Sandringham, aged 56

21 MARCH Dr Kwame Nkrumah elected Prime Minister of the Gold Coast

26 JULY King Farouk of Egypt abdicated after a military coup

20 OCTOBER British troops sent to Kenya following 40 Mau Mau murders

4 NOVEMBER Dwight D Eisenhower elected President of the USA

24 NOVEMBER Agatha Christie's play *The Mousetrap* opened in London

The King is dead, long live the Queen: the news placards told their own story (left). 'The virtues with which we shall always associate King George's name were those that most become a man in time of trial: patience, calm, faith, courage, devotion to duty, unfailing dignity, endurance. Few men in supreme place have had more need to show these noble virtues or have done so with such unbroken consistency. They are the qualities for which we, living to-day, will always remember the late King with gratitude.' (16 February 1952). In April the new Queen, in mourning black, inspected the Grenadier Guards at Windsor Castle (above). It was her 26th birthday, and the last occasion on which she would inspect the regiment as its Colonel.

Elizabeth II
1953-1992

1953

JOURNALISTS AND BROADCASTERS have a special tone of voice, full of pomp and circumstance, which they reach for on State occasions, and the *ILN*, marking the Coronation of Queen Elizabeth II on 2 June this year, was no exception:

> *At 10.26 a.m. the curtain rose on the first act of the moving ceremony in which our young Queen carried out her act of dedication, and took formal possession of her sovereignty over the United Kingdom and Northern Ireland and of her other Realms and Territories, by her hallowing and crowning at Westminster Abbey.* (6 June)

It was a dull, wet day, but the weather did nothing to dampen the enthusiasm of the 2 million people who came to watch. Royal pageantry, tradition and finery, it was felt, were things at which Britain excelled. The House of Windsor had done its bit during the war and now was the opportunity for a massive gesture of support and affection for the new Queen.

It is estimated that another 20 million watched on television, many having purchased a set especially for the occasion. The promise of live pictures of a centuries-old ceremony had plunged Britain into a new era of mass communication. In future, royalty would become familiar faces in the nation's living rooms, but perhaps the sense of occasion would never be quite the same again.

With brilliant theatrical timing, the day of the Coronation also brought news of the success of the British Everest Expedition: Edmund Hillary, a New Zealander, and Sherpa Tensing had conquered the world's highest mountain. The *ILN* later described how the members of the expedition rode through the streets of Kathmandu in an open landau drawn by four horses with postilions in red and gold. The magazine also published a photograph of the 'corrugated iron hut' in which Tensing lived, and revealed that a Calcutta newspaper had started a fund to build him a home of his own.

The subsequent arrival of the expedition team in London was 'a dramatic and joyous occasion':

> *Each man was clapped as he came down the gangway of the BOAC aircraft which had brought the party from Zürich, where they had received a great reception from Swiss Alpinists. Colonel John Hunt, leader of the expedition, came out first, and waved an ice-axe bearing a small Union Flag...Tensing was accompanied by his wife and daughters who smiled happily with, perhaps, a touch of bewilderment at the scene.* (11 July)

The year began on a far from splendid note. At the end of January a car ferry sank in the Irish Sea, after high seas burst its doors open, and more than a hundred people drowned. Storms also lashed England's east coast and freak floods swamped Canvey Island, leaving many dead and thousands homeless.

Cries for the abolition of the death penalty intensified when John Christie confessed to multiple murders at 10 Rillington Place, including those for which Timothy Evans had previously been hanged. Parliament, however, rejected a bill to abolish hanging for a trial period of five years and, two weeks later, on 15 July, Christie, too, was executed.

Happy and glorious: 'As the golden State Coach—a fantasy of eighteenth-century baroque symbolism of royalty—drove out of the great gates of Buckingham Palace carrying her Majesty and her consort, H.R.H. the Duke of Edinburgh, they were greeted by a storm of cheers from the massed crowds of people...' (6 June 1953)

Long to reign over us: East-Enders in Morpeth Street celebrated the occasion with a cheerful, patriotic party. '... it would not be easy to find another case of such trust and confidence between Sovereign and people as so manifestly exist at the present time.' (6 June 1953)

God Save our Queen: the makers of every kind of publication and souvenir had a field-day as the Queen was crowned, amid much talk of a new Elizabethan Age about to dawn. The ceremony itself had been seen by the largest audience ever to witness a coronation, as it was shown on television.

THE ILLUSTRATED
LONDON NEWS

1953

E·V·E·N·T·S

31 JANUARY Gales and floods caused havoc
along Britain's east coast
5 MARCH Death of Joseph Stalin, Soviet leader
for more than 29 years
25 APRIL Crick and Watson proposed double
helix structure of DNA
29 MAY Edmund Hillary and Sherpa Tensing
reached the summit of Everest
2 JUNE Coronation of Queen Elizabeth II in
Westminster Abbey
6 JUNE Sir Gordon Richards won the Derby
for the first time in his career

Send her victorious: the Coronation in
the Abbey. 'In these days when men are
starved of splendour, the sense of
pageantry and grandeur in the occasion
becomes overwhelming; the individual is
lost in the sense of corporate magnificence
and of popular delight . . .' (6 June 1953)

Drink to me only: a commemorative
mug. The Coronation, Arthur Bryant
thought, was 'a prayer that the spirit of love
and sacrifice . . . may be vouchsafed to
Queen and people alike'. (6 June 1953)

While debates continued to take place on the morality of depriving criminals of their life, scientists were probing the nature of life itself. In Cambridge, Francis Crick and James Watson proposed that the key to heredity lay in the double helix structure of the deoxyribonucleic acid (DNA) molecule. In the Nevada desert, the route towards the destruction of life on a global scale was becoming clearer as the USA exploded newer and bigger atomic weapons.

In Britain, not all was gloom, however. Sweet rationing had come to an end at long last, income tax had been cut, and house-building was approaching record levels. Fans of the Goons practised funny voices in public, as a third series of the anarchic radio programme was broadcast. *The Goon Show* set standards for a whole new generation of radio and TV comics, but in the cinema a cosy, whimsical British humour prevailed in films such as *Genevieve* and *The Titfield Thunderbolt*.

Churchill, who had been elected Prime Minister again in 1951, caused grave concern when he collapsed at 10 Downing Street in June after a severe stroke. Not all cabinet ministers were informed of the illness immediately, and the full truth was concealed from the press, although it was soon clear to everyone that he was now partially paralysed. On a happier note, Churchill was awarded the Nobel Prize for Literature in December for his many historical works.

Meanwhile, in the world of sport, it was a varied year. England regained the Ashes in August for the first time since the controversial 'bodyline' tour of 1933, gaining an eight-wicket victory after four drawn Test matches. Sir Gordon Richards won his first Derby in June, riding the 5–1 favourite, Pinza, winning four lengths ahead of the Queen's colt, Aureole. In football, Blackpool beat Bolton 4–3 in the FA Cup final at Wembley, widely regarded as one of the most exciting matches ever. Later in the year, Hungary became the first overseas national team to defeat England 6–3 at Wembley, astonishing spectators with their impressive technique.

Joseph Stalin, described by the *ILN* as 'virtual dictator of Russia for 29 years', died in March. His passing, readers were told, 'leaves a vacuum, with effects of world-wide significance'. (There was, indeed, a vacuum, filled after considerable internal wrangling by Nikita Khrushchev. Khrushchev became First Secretary of the Soviet Communist Party on 12 September, the day on which Senator John F Kennedy married Jacqueline Bouvier.) The *ILN* described how, during the Second World War, Stalin had come into 'close contact with the Western Powers, whose aid he did not hesitate to accept . . . With peace came the subjugation of many peoples to the Communist yoke, the Cold War and the Korean War'.

This same war in Korea, which had now lasted three years and claimed more than 2 million lives, reached a grudging armistice on 27 July. The *ILN* told how:

> . . . *the Korean truce documents were signed by the local chief delegates at Panmunjom in an atmosphere of unparalleled chill and unfriendliness . . . Inside the building everybody was rigidly segregated as though an iron curtain divided the room . . . General Mark Clark, the UN Commander-in-Chief, said: 'We have stopped the shooting . . . therefore I am thankful. It is, however, only a step towards what must yet be done . . . I cannot find it in me to exult in this hour'.*
> (8 August)

Boxed-in: television broadcasting was originally monopolised by the BBC as a continuation of its role in radio, but in 1953 the government announced its approval of commercial television as a rival. In the mean time, the advance of technology had brought the washing machine into many a home, accompanied by a ferocious and highly expensive struggle between rival manufacturers of washing powder as to whose product really washed whiter.

THE ILLUSTRATED LONDON NEWS

1953

E · V · E · N · T · S

25 JUNE John Reginald Christie was sentenced
to death for four murders
27 JULY The Korean War ended with an
armistice signed at Panmunjom
12 SEPTEMBER Senator John F Kennedy
married Jacqueline Bouvier
9 NOVEMBER Welsh poet Dylan Thomas died
in a New York hotel, aged 39
10 DECEMBER Winston Churchill awarded the
Nobel Prize for Literature

Freedom's gate: a private of the
'Glorious Gloucesters' being welcomed as a
released prisoner of-war, following the
signing of a truce in Korea 'by . . . delegates
at Panmunjom in an atmosphere of
unparalleled chill and unfriendliness'.
(8 August 1953)

On top of the world: Sherpa Tensing
(left) standing triumphantly on the
summit of Mount Everest. 'June 2, 1953,
found Britain literally on top of the
world, for it was on Coronation
morning that the British public learnt
that Everest had finally been
conquered.' (6 June 1953)

LIBRARY 24 MAR 1993 HARTLEPOOL C.F.E.

1954

BOOK-BURNING is an activity which usually has sinister connotations, but there were few protests when, despite government warnings that they might be needed again, ration books were thrown to the flames in July this year. Although restrictions on a few commodities, such as newsprint, continued, domestic shopping was no longer subject to official control. Eating on a grand scale became possible again. Experts have since declared that the rationed diet was a healthy one—later, people ate the wrong things, put on weight and tried, by means of various diets, to impose their own restrictions on themselves.

To some extent, perhaps, smoking had become a substitute for eating, but the warning note was beginning to be sounded. During this year it was announced that the links between cancer and smoking must be regarded as established.

People argue over the precise origins of rock 'n' roll just as they argue about the beginnings of jazz. This was the year which saw the start of rock 'n' roll, but it is difficult to make claims for any one record or performer. Elvis Presley recorded his first single, but Bill Haley's *Rock Around the Clock*, often regarded as the anthem of the movement, was not an instant hit, only achieving success when it was used in the film *The Blackboard Jungle* a year later. Rock 'n' roll was, of course, pure American—the East Germans are said to have considered it part of a western plot to undermine Communism. For the rest of the decade British popular culture found much to admire across the Atlantic. Even American-style evangelism found favour when Billy Graham led a crusade in London and gave religion the hard sell.

This was the year of publication of Kingsley Amis' *Lucky Jim* and William Golding's *Lord of the Flies*. Dylan Thomas' *Under Milk Wood* was performed on the radio, a medium which still attracted huge audiences, including an estimated 10 million for *The Archers*.

Also this year, the *ILN* recorded how:

> *R.G. Bannister, in a match between the Amateur Athletic Association and Oxford University. . .on May 6, ran a mile in 3 mins. 59.4 secs., and so became the first man in the history of athletics to run a mile in under four minutes. (15 May)*

On 22 May the *ILN* devoted several pages to the six-month Commonwealth tour which had just been completed by the Queen and the Duke of Edinburgh, and invited Cyril Falls, a Professor of War History at Oxford and one of its regular contributors, to reflect on the tour's significance in a column entitled *Window on the World*:

> *For the Queen to place herself in close contact with the greatest possible number of [the Commonwealth's] people was a formidable undertaking. The venture was well planned, and the results exceeded expectation . . . everywhere wave on wave of enthusiasm, loyalty and affection flowed from the vast crowds . . . These are feelings of very high significance. Let us admit that the fire of enthusiasm lit by the Queen cannot go on burning unless it is fed. The fact remains that she has lit a great fire. The fault will be not hers, but ours, if it should be allowed to burn itself out. (22 May)*

Smiles all round: Roger Bannister (centre), the first man to run a mile in under four minutes, thanking his pacemakers, Chris Chataway (right) and Chris Brasher (left). 'Bannister's time of 3 min. 59.4 sec. has been accepted as an English native record by the Amateur Athletic Association and also approved by the British Amateur Athletic Association as a British All-Comers and British National record . . . Bannister . . . is a medical student at St Mary's Paddington . . .' (15 May 1954)

Sweetest day of their lives: two children celebrating the end of sweet rationing at a London confectioner's in February. Originally introduced in Britain in 1942, and briefly ended in 1949, sweet rationing had stood at 6oz (174g) per person per week since 1951. Food rationing, which had been in force in Britain for 14 years, finally came to an end in July.

1954

E · V · E · N · T · S

6 MAY Roger Bannister ran the first mile in under four minutes

8 MAY The Viet Minh defeated the French at Dien Bien Phu after 55-day siege

17 MAY The US Supreme Court declared school racial segregation illegal

3 JULY Food rationing, in force in Britain since 1940, finally ended

15 OCTOBER William Golding's novel *Lord of the Flies* published

3 NOVEMBER French painter Henri Matisse, leader of the Fauves, died aged 84

Death of a legend: the last photograph taken of the great French painter Henri Matisse, (left), on 4 October. He died the following month at the age of 84. A leader of the Fauves in the early years of the century, he later advanced to a simpler and more austere style, and was generally regarded as one of the outstanding figures of the modern art movement.

Sweet tooth: along with the end of sweet rationing came a blaze of enticing posters for tasty desserts and ice creams.

Waves of welcome: the Queen and the Duke of Edinburgh driving past thousands of children at Bathurst in Australia, on their first, epoch-making tour of Commonwealth countries. The Queen was 'the first British ruling Sovereign to set foot on Australian soil', and the tour was a great success. (13 February 1954)

SPORT

◆◆

Money, Politics
AND
Professionals

When the One Great Scorer comes to write against your name—
He writes—not that you won or lost—but how you played the game.

GRANTLAND RICE

A LARGER CROWD than usual gathered at Oxford University's athletics ground in Iffley Road on the afternoon of 6 May 1954 to see a match between the university and the Amateur Athletic Association. Word had gone round that something special was on the cards.

In the 1890s, times of 4 minutes 17 seconds had been recorded for running a mile. The great Finnish runner Paavo Nurmi, winner of more Olympic athletic medals than anyone in history, had run a mile in 4 minutes 10.4 seconds (4.10.4) in 1923. Ten years later the New Zealander, Jack Lovelock, clocked 4.07.6. Britain's skinny, bespectacled Sidney Wooderson brought the world record down to 4.06.4 in 1937, and Gundar Haegg to 4.01.3 in 1945.

So near and yet so far. Nine more years had gone by and still the magic mile in four minutes, the Everest of middle-distance running, had not been achieved. It was at last to be conquered, that afternoon in 1954, by a 25-year-old medical student and former Oxford blue, Roger Bannister, abetted by Chris Chataway and Chris Brasher. With first Brasher and then Chataway setting a scorching pace, the first three laps were run in less than a second over three minutes. Chataway was in front at that stage, with the tall Bannister looming behind him.

Urged on by the excited crowd, Bannister swooped past Chataway. 'I felt that the moment of a lifetime had come,' he wrote afterwards. 'There was no pain, only a great unity of movement and aim.' He tore round the last bend and up to the finishing tape, where he almost collapsed. The stop watches were consulted, while the spectators waited anxiously. The voice of the announcer came over the loudspeakers. 'Time, three minutes . . .' The rest was drowned in a huge roar from the crowd, but the exact time was 3.59.4. The barrier had been broken by three-fifths of a second.

Only six weeks later, the great Australian miler John Landy broke the barrier of 4 minutes again at Turku in Finland, setting a new record of 3.58.0. In August, Bannister and Landy met in what was justly labelled 'the mile of the century' at the British Empire Games in Vancouver. It was a spectacularly thrilling race. At the halfway mark Landy was well ahead of Bannister and the other finalists. Gradually Bannister managed to close the gap and on the final lap he was just behind. Landy sprinted, but Bannister held on, hurled himself past the Australian coming off the last bend and pounded to the finish, to win by 5 yards in 3.58.8.

The first four-minute mile is an example of the improvement in standards of performance which has occurred in every sport in the hundred years since 1890. There must, one day, come a limit— for example, in 1924 Nurmi set a world record for 5,000 metres at 14.28.2. In 1959 Vladimir Kuts of

the Soviet Union brought this record down by almost a minute, to 13.35.0, and in 1987 Said Aouita of Morocco reduced the record by another half-minute, when he ran the 5,000 metres in 12.58.39.

Performances improved as sport became more organised, more international, more professional and altogether more serious than it had been in the mid nineteenth century. This was fundamentally due to the growth of spectator sport, which came with increasing urbanisation and improved communications. Growing numbers of town-dwellers had more leisure than before, but could not enjoy outdoor pastimes as easily as earlier generations. They now tended to watch games, rather than play them. Then the onward march of the mass media— newspapers followed by radio followed by television—brought games anywhere in the world into the spectator's home. Audiences for major sporting events in the 1980s would be counted in millions. There was money to be made out of mass-spectator sports and the fierce nationalistic pride involved in them. The generous amateur attitudes of an earlier age could not survive. Winning the game became far more important than how you played it.

Britain had a dominant role in nineteenth-century sport, first in putting games on an organised footing and then exporting them to the rest of the world. It was in England that amateur athletics were first organised; the first national athletics

championships in any country were the English championships, staged in 1866 by the Amateur Athletic Club, which had been newly founded to organise competitions between 'gentlemen amateurs'.

In 1880 the Amateur Athletic Association was founded, and became the governing body of British athletics. International meets between English and American universities began in the 1890s. In 1912 the International Amateur Athletic Federation was formed, with 17 countries as members. By the end of the 1980s its membership was nearer 200 countries.

The main focus of modern international athletics has been the Olympic Games, which were revived in 1896 at Athens on the initiative of Baron Pierre de Coubertin, an idealistic Frenchman who wanted to bring the youth of the world together in friendly rivalry, to improve standards of physical excellence and contribute to world understanding. He founded the International Olympic Committee, which has run the games ever since.

The 1896 Olympic Games attracted fewer than 500 competitors, from most European countries, the USA and Australia. The British held mainly aloof, but the Americans sent an unofficial team of 13, which won nine events. The marathon,

Roger Bannister closing the gap on John Landy in the last lap of the 'the mile of the century' at the British Empire Games in Vancouver.

Roger Bannister becomes the first person to run a mile in less than 4 minutes (left).

appropriately, was won by a Greek named Spyridon Louis (in a time almost 50 minutes slower than that of the 1984 winner).

'The most important thing in the Olympic Games is not to win, but to take part,' de Coubertin said, 'just as the most important thing in life is not the triumph, but the struggle.' What has grown out of this admirable sentiment is the extraordinary mixture of sport, skill and courage, showmanship and commercialism, politics, patriotism and jingoism, which regularly grips the interest and imagination of more people, more widely spread over the world, than any other sporting occasion. Besides the track and field events, the programme for the 1896 Olympic Games covered swimming, gymnastics, fencing, shooting, tennis, cycling, weightlifting and wrestling. Other sports brought beneath the Olympic

umbrella later included boxing, hockey, football, yachting, rowing, canoeing and equestrian events. Winter sports were held separately from 1924 onwards. The competitors are now numbered in more thousands than there were hundreds in 1896. Today the games cost a fortune to stage, and can make, or lose, a fortune for the city which hosts them.

The founding Olympic ideal was firmly amateur; this was essential if taking part in the games was to be more important than winning them. At Stockholm in 1912 an American Indian named James Thorpe won both the pentathlon and the decathlon, but was declared a professional because years before he had pocketed a small payment for playing in minor league baseball. But the games themselves spurred ambition, made competition keener, drove performance standards up, and so made it increasingly difficult for the true amateur to take part. Struggling to remain true to the founding ideal, the Olympic authorities, like many other sports bodies, went through a stage of closing their eyes to the sham amateur until they were finally forced to recognise professionals. By the 1980s the world's top athletes were highly paid, and professional tennis players took part in the 1988 Olympic Games in Seoul. There were still no money prizes for Olympic events, however.

By this time another consequence of rampant professionalism had raised its head. At Los Angeles in 1984, for the first

At the Olympic Games in Berlin in 1936 the great American black athlete Jesse Owens (left) won the long jump as well as both the 100 metres and 200 metres. The 1988 Olympic Games in Seoul were sadly an advertisement for drug abuse. The 100 metre winner, Ben Johnson (below), was disqualified after a positive drugs test.

time, the winner of a track medal was disqualified after a positive drug test. At Seoul in 1988 there was a worldwide sensation when the 100 metres winner, Ben Johnson, was disqualified for the same reason.

The Olympic Games were originally intended to be not only amateur, but also non-political—again a vain hope: especially as events were contested between national teams, with much raising of national flags and playing of national anthems, while the world's media chauvinistically counted each country's haul of medals. The Berlin Games of 1936 were exploited by the Nazi government as a propaganda boost for the Third Reich. At Munich in 1972 a squad of 'Black September' Palestinian terrorists walked into the Olympic village in track suits, got into the Israeli team's headquarters, killed two of the team and took nine others hostage, demanding the release of Arab prisoners in Israeli jails. The games came juddering to a halt until helicopters took the terrorists and their captives to an air base 25 miles away. There an attack on the Palestinians went awry and all the hostages were killed.

Before the Munich Games, many African countries had threatened a boycott if a team from Rhodesia was allowed to compete. The International Olympic Committee gave way and kept the Rhodesians out. In 1976 the Montreal Games were boycotted by most of the African nations. The USA and West Germany boycotted the Moscow Olympic Games in 1980, and the USSR, East Germany and most of the Communist bloc in Europe retaliated by not attending the Los Angeles Games of 1984.

Another twentieth-century development which affected athletics and many other sports was the proliferation of events. The British exported their favourite games to their colonies, and sport became a route by which Commonwealth countries and their citizens could make a mark on the world and gain money and status. The first British Empire Games were held in Canada in 1930 and were successful enough to be repeated in London four years later. They are now the Commonwealth Games, held every four years, and have become another magnet for political manoeuvring. Besides the usual events, they include badminton and bowls. European Championships have been held every four years since the 1930s, and World Championships started in 1983. Sporting events make money, which is an incentive to hold as many as possible.

The game which the British exported most successfully of all to the Empire was cricket. The Royal Navy played a part here; sailors and traders had taken cricket to India and the West Indies early in the eighteenth century. The first match recorded in Australia was played in Sydney in 1803, and the game had probably been introduced to New Zealand and South Africa by that time. The first Test match between England and Australia took place at Melbourne in 1877, and Australia won.

The England XI of 1890 was captained

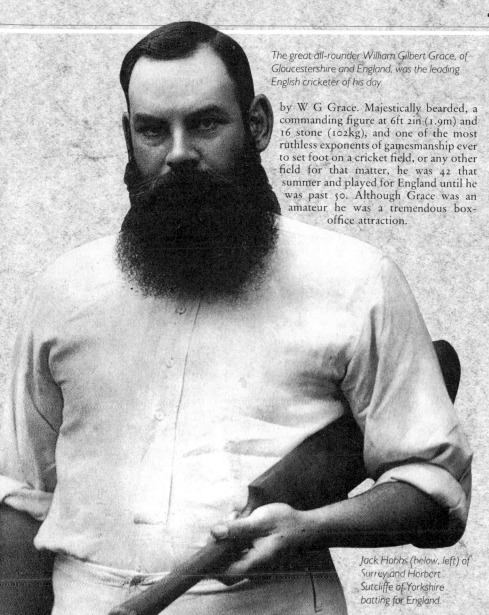

The great all-rounder William Gilbert Grace, of Gloucestershire and England, was the leading English cricketer of his day.

by W G Grace. Majestically bearded, a commanding figure at 6ft 2in (1.9m) and 16 stone (102kg), and one of the most ruthless exponents of gamesmanship ever to set foot on a cricket field, or any other field for that matter, he was 42 that summer and played for England until he was past 50. Although Grace was an amateur he was a tremendous box-office attraction.

However, a clear distinction was still drawn in cricket between amateurs, who were gentlemen, and the professionals, who were not. England and county sides were always captained by amateurs and one of the major occasions of each season at Lord's was the Gentlemen v Players match, which lasted until 1962. After the Second World War the distinction proved unworkable and Len Hutton, an archetypal Yorkshire professional, was the first non-amateur to captain England.

The golden age of cricket in England was the Edwardian period, when bat resounded firmly on ball for summer after gorgeous summer in the age of MacLaren, F S Jackson, Hobbs, Ranjitsinhji, Woolley, Trumper and Gilbert Jessup, perhaps the most ferocious hitter the game has ever seen. A Cambridge blue who went on to play for Gloucestershire, Jessup scored 286 in 175 minutes against Sussex in 1903. Against Yorkshire at Bradford he scored two centuries and hit eight balls clear out of the ground. At the Oval in 1902 against the Australians he went in with England at 48 for 5 and made 104 in 75 minutes, and he notched up his 53 centuries in first-class cricket at an average rate of 83 runs per hour.

The figure who sums up the whole era is C B Fry, who left Oxford with a first and a triple blue, played for England at both cricket and soccer, set a world record for the long jump and casually excelled at rugby, golf, tennis and rowing as well. He was offered the throne of Albania, but he could not afford to accept.

After 1918 the writing was on the wall for the gentleman amateur (or 'Corinthian'), as sport began to grow more serious, and meaner in spirit. A dramatic example was the notorious 'bodyline' bowling tour of Australia in the winter of 1933

Jack Hobbs (below, left) of Surrey and Herbert Sutcliffe of Yorkshire batting for England.

The British exported their favourite summer game to their colonies, where it was taken up with considerable enthusiasm. Some of the most brilliant exponents of cricket have come from overseas, including three of the game's most successful and thrilling batsmen, Don Bradman of Australia (left) and Garfield Sobers (right) and Vivian Richards (below) of the West Indies. All three captained their country's sides and Bradman and Sobers were both knighted for their contributions to the game.

by an England side captained by Douglas Jardine. Armed with a battery of fast bowlers, Jardine employed them in very fast short-pitched bowling directed straight at the batsman's body. The strategy was aimed especially at Don Bradman, the Australians' star batsman and the most effective runmaker in the game's history. Bodyline restricted him to an average of only 50 or so an innings (his Test average in 1930 had been 139), but it was fiercely unsporting, caused bitter ill-feeling in Australia and proved to be a grim portent of what was to come after 1945, when fast bowling became so intimidating and dangerous that batsmen were driven to wearing helmets. What Hobbs or Fry would have said hardly bears thinking of.

Don Bradman led the Australian team in England in 1948 on his last tour. They scored 721 against Essex, without appearing to hurry much, and won four Tests out of five. In his last appearance at Lord's Bradman made 150, and a moment of drama came with what was known would be his last Test innings of all, at the Oval. The great man was thunderously cheered all the way to the wicket, where he took guard and was clean-bowled second ball for a duck. Upon which the crowd cheered him all the way back to the pavilion again. A mere four runs that day would have given him a career Test average of precisely 100 per innings. He was knighted in 1949.

The West Indies, India and New Zealand had all achieved Test rank by the early 1930s. Pakistan joined the club in 1952 and Sri Lanka in 1982. The West Indies won a Test series in England for the first time in 1950 and went on to reign as the world's most powerful side, with Gary Sobers and Vivian Richards its most glittering stars. Sir Garfield Sobers was knighted by Queen Elizabeth II in Barbados before 50,000 delighted spectators in 1975.

Cricket's flagging finances had been revived by the introduction of one-day, limited overs matches in England in the 1960s. The crowds came back to the almost deserted country grounds and the counties were able to hire top players from overseas to boost their takings still more. Sobers played for Nottinghamshire, the South African virtuoso Barry Richards opened Hampshire's batting, and the South African all-rounder Mike Procter galvanised Gloucestershire. The first one-day international was played in 1971 and cricket has had a four-yearly World Cup since 1975.

Since then there has been such a proliferation of international matches, one-day and five-day, as to constitute something uncomfortably close to a glut. The Packer affair in 1977, when the Australian television magnate Kerry Packer hired his own teams of top-flight cricketers to play international matches as a counter-attraction to the official ones, helped to make cricket more of a branch of the entertainment business and less of a sport. Meanwhile the game was torn by strong feelings and threatened splits over the issue of contacts with South Africa.

Association football, or soccer, never really caught on in Britain's colonies, and the game has no South African problem, but plenty of others. Soccer had its heyday in Britain between 1900 and 1939 as the game of the industrial working class, but it was rationalised and organised in the last quarter of the nineteenth century by public schoolboys, when the amateur, Corinthian spirit was still strong. The Football Association was founded in London in 1863 to draw up an agreed set of rules. The first FA Cup Final was played in 1872, when Wanderers beat the Royal Engineers: both were amateur sides. The first international, between England and Scotland, was played in 1872 and was a 0–0 draw.

As late as 1894 and 1895, the brilliant amateur side called the Corinthians provided the entire England team for two successive matches against Wales. But the tide had turned away from amateurs and such clubs as Old Etonians and Old Carthusians, and towards the professional clubs in the industrial Midlands and North. The oldest football club still in existence is Sheffield United, whose history stretches back into the shadowy 1850s. Aston Villa and Bolton Wanderers, Blackburn Rovers, Everton, West Bromwich Albion and Manchester United were all products of the 1870s. In 1884 Preston North End openly admitted paying its players and in 1888 helped to found the Football League, which was set up to organise a sensible fixture programme for the leading professional clubs. Derby County and Wolverhampton Wanderers were founder members, but the wonderfully named Sheffield Wednesday and Nottingham Forest were rejected. Arsenal was the first London club admitted, in 1913.

Though not a success in the Empire, soccer was one of England's most popular exports to the rest of the world, to Europe and South America by 1890, later to Asia and Africa. The game's international gov-

erning body, the Federation of International Football Associations (FIFA), was set up in 1904 with seven members: France, Spain, Sweden, Denmark, Holland, Belgium and Switzerland. The Football Association cold-shouldered it until 1946, but by 1930 the game had such a following worldwide that FIFA was able to organise the first World Cup, in Uruguay. Brazil, with the magnificent Pele, won the World Cup in 1958, 1962 (although on this occasion Pele was unable to play due to a muscle injury), and 1970. England won in 1966, beating West Germany 4–2 in the final at Wembley in a match of high drama, with the West Ham forward Geoff Hurst scoring two goals in extra time. Alf Ramsey, the taciturn England manager, was rewarded with a knighthood.

As in every other sport, with money to be made, competitions proliferated. The Union of European Football Associations (UEFA) Cup began in 1955, the European Cup for club sides a year later, the European Championship in 1960, the European Cup Winners' Cup in 1961. In Britain the Football League Cup was introduced in 1961 and others even more dubious followed, but something was badly wrong with football in Britain. Foreigners seemed to play the game more skil-

One of Association Football's supremely gifted artists, Pele of Brazil, was revered all over the world and played for New York Cosmos in the twilight of his career in the 1970s.

The Sheffield United team which won the FA Cup in 1899 (below). Stanley Matthews, one of the most exciting soccer players in history, turning out for Blackpool in 1951 (right).

fully and sparklingly than the British could. While cricket attendances rose, football gates declined. Soccer became burdened with hooliganism and violence, culminating on 29 May 1985 at a game between Liverpool and Juventus in Brussels. English supporters went viciously on the rampage and 41 people were killed. A worldwide audience saw it all on television, the image of the British football fan as a drunken brute was vividly confirmed, and English clubs were promptly banned from Europe.

Other games, too, were affected by violence and loutishness, notably cricket, but Britain still had mighty achievements to take pride in, away from the mass-spectator sports, in areas of endeavour where the amateur spirit still survived. Pre-eminent among these was the conquest of Everest.

The peaks of the Swiss Alps had been mastered by British climbers with local guides in the nineteenth century. By 1900 mountaineering had become a more international pursuit and climbers went on to scale peaks in the Andes, the Rocky Mountains and the awesome Himalayas. Expedition after expedition left Britain to tackle Everest, at 29,028ft (8,848m) the world's highest mountain. Why? 'Because it is there,' said George Mallory, who in 1922 in atrocious weather reached 26,800ft (8,169m), the highest point on the mountain yet achieved. In 1924 Mallory and a companion were seen above 28,000ft (8,534m) —within 1,000ft (305m) of the top—when a swirling snowstorm blotted them from view. They were never seen again.

In 1953 an expedition under Colonel John Hunt arrived in Nepal and on 29 May a 34-year-old New Zealand beekeeper named Edmund Hillary and a 39-year-old Sherpa porter named Tensing stood on the summit of the great mountain at last. They planted the flags of Great Britain, Nepal, India and the United Nations, and Tensing left an offering of sweets and biscuits. After 15 minutes they started back down again. Excitement was intense when the news reached London, and Hillary and Hunt were both knighted.

Similar pride was taken in another triumph over the elements and human frailty in the 1960s, when Sir Francis Chichester sailed alone round the world. Sir Francis was 65 years old when he brought *Gipsy Moth IV* into Plymouth harbour in May 1967 after a voyage of almost a year's duration, and crowds cheered him all the way to a civic banquet at the Guildhall. Earlier in the decade he had won the first two single-handed transatlantic yacht races, in 1960 and 1962.

In the 1970s another hero emerged, a racehorse with star quality named Red Rum, which for five years in succession left other horses behind in the Grand National. In two of those years he went on to win, in two he came second; no horse had ever won the desperately taxing steeplechase more than twice, but in 1977, when Red Rum was 12 years old and carrying the top weight, he soared triumphantly over the final fence and won by 25 lengths, amid a tempest of applause. Many of the crowd were in tears. When Red Rum went back to his stable, the entire town of Southport turned out to welcome him home with two bands. He eventually retired from racing to make celebrity appearances and to open supermarkets, and in 1986 his 21st birthday was celebrated with a starry party in an enormous marquee.

Two more sports which had been pioneered in Britain were tennis and golf. Lawn tennis was invented by a cavalry officer named Wingfield, who patented it in 1874 under the strange name of Sphairistike. It was taken up by the All England Croquet Club at Wimbledon, swiftly ousted croquet in popularity and spread rapidly to the dominions and the USA. It began as an entirely amateur game and Wimbledon kept the amateur banner flying until 1968, when the trend of the times could be resisted no longer and the Wimbledon championships were opened to professionals. The men's and women's singles titles were won by Rod Laver of Australia and Billie-Jean King of the USA.

Golf had been dominated by professionals for far longer. Its origins are lost in the mists of time, but there are records of the game in Scotland in the fifteenth cen-

tury. The august Royal and Ancient Golf Club of St Andrews, which became the game's governing body in Britain and the Commonwealth, dates back to 1754. In the nineteenth century golf spread abroad: to India by the 1820s, Australia and New Zealand by the 1870s, South Africa by the 1880s. The game was put on an organised

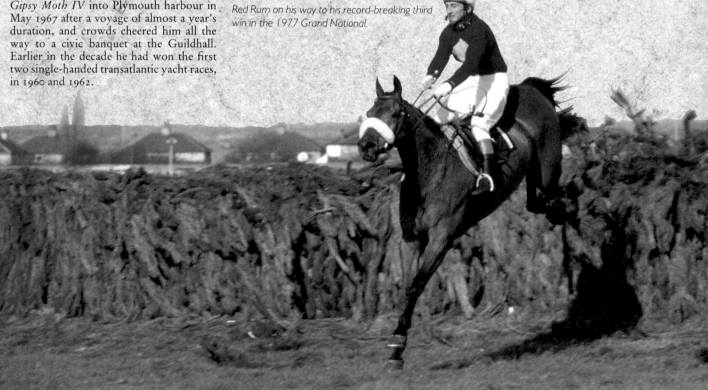

Red Rum on his way to his record-breaking third win in the 1977 Grand National.

Tennis ace John McEnroe losing both his temper and his racket at Wimbledon in 1981.

six times between 1896 and 1914. He gave way to a swashbuckling American, Walter Hagen, significantly the first golfer to employ a manager. Hagen won the US Open in 1914 and 1919, and four British Opens between 1922 and 1929. The astonishing amateur Bobby Jones retired at the age of 28 after winning the 'grand slam' (or 'impregnable quadrilateral') in 1930—all four British and American open and amateur titles. Henry Cotton was the leading British player of the 1930s, while Ben Hogan, an American who began as a caddie, ruled the roost in the 1940s and 1950s. His mantle fell on the broad shoulders of Jack Nicklaus, who won the US amateur title in 1959 when he was 19, and is widely regarded as the finest player ever to have touched a club.

Golf has kept itself comparatively free of the violence which has invaded so much sport. So has snooker, a late example of the British genius for games. Invented by British army officers in India in the nineteenth century, it did not become a popular spectator sport until the 1970s, when it was taken up by television. Joe Davis, who had beaten all comers in the 1930s and 1940s, won £6 10 shillings (£6·50) prize money when he carried off the first World Professional Snooker Championship in 1927. In the 1970s and 1980s the prize money ran into thousands of pounds and the number of events multiplied, but one of the things which attracted spectators was the civilised courtesy with which snooker was conducted. In the ordered ritual of the table, the undisputed rulings of

Jack Nicklaus, who is widely regarded as the greatest golfer of all time, was the successor to a long line of famous American players, including Walter Hagen, Bobby Jones, Ben Hogan and Arnold Palmer.

the referee, the uncomplaining acceptance of ill luck, the generosity to opponents, there seemed to survive the lamented Corinthian spirit of the nineteenth century.

Steve Davis, the player who dominated professional snooker in the 1980s.

Henry Cotton in play at Sandwich in 1934.

basis in the USA in the 1880s, and before the First World War there were even golf clubs in Bangkok, Shanghai and Tokyo.

At this time the world of golf was dominated by the British triumvirate of Harry Vardon, John Henry Taylor and James Braid. Vardon won the British Open

1955

WHEN WINSTON CHURCHILL stepped down as Prime Minister in April this year, the *ILN* paid tribute to his 50 years of political leadership. Earl Winterton, himself an MP from 1904 to 1951, contributed his views of Churchill in the magazine. He wrote that:

> *He not only inspired the nation and made a great contribution to victory by his speeches in Parliament during the Second World War, but he enhanced the status and reputation of the House itself.* (16 April)

Churchill's retirement from politics naturally provoked recollection of the dark days and finest hours of the Second World War. On the cinema screen, *The Dam Busters* had a similar effect. Wartime nostalgia continues today; some say that it started in the 1950s because the events of the past were so much easier to contemplate than a future under the shadow of the H-bomb. The philosopher Bertrand Russell, and a distinguished list of Nobel Prize winners agreed. In July they signed a declaration that 'nuclear weapons threaten the continued existence of mankind'.

The general election in May saw the installation of Sir Anthony Eden as the new Conservative Prime Minister, with a majority in the House of Commons of 58. The *ILN* revealed, in introducing Sir Anthony to its readers, that he was not only a distinguished statesman and former Foreign Secretary, but very much favoured by the Establishment and also married to a niece of Sir Winston Churchill—the business had not entirely passed out of the family. At the end of the year, the *ILN* bade farewell to Clement Attlee, who resigned as leader of the Labour Party at the age of 72. His successor, Hugh Gaitskell, spoke of Attlee's skill and wisdom, devotion and dignity.

In Cyprus, the situation was explosive. Members of Ethnikē Organōsis Kypriōn Agōniston (EOKA), the secret organisation fighting for union with Greece, used bombs and grenades to make their point. The *ILN* reported on 10 December that, after the declaration of a state of emergency on 26 November, outbreaks of terrorism, temporarily at least, diminished. 'Consequent with the state of emergency, British forces in Cyprus were placed on a wartime footing on November 28.'

At home, the death penalty was again under debate. MPs voted to retain it and Ruth Ellis went to the gallows, thereby becoming the last woman to be hanged in Great Britain. James Dean became one of those who live fast and die young when he crashed his sports car, but his legend lived on in films. Another fatality was Grace Archer, mercilessly murdered by scriptwriters of *The Archers* in an attempt to gain publicity for the BBC on the evening which saw the first broadcast by ITV. Both the first night of ITV and the death of Grace Archer did rather better in attracting audiences than Samuel Beckett's *Waiting for Godot*. Its sparsity of dialogue and lack of standard dramatic reference points left many bewildered.

A more popular choice of entertainment could be found in the work of Ian Fleming. The James Bond stories were beginning to appear: *Casino Royale* in 1953 and then *Moonraker* in 1955.

Throughout the 1950s men and women arrived in Britain from the Caribbean, in search of a new life. Offered menial jobs and dismayed by the frequent refusal of accommodation to 'coloureds', many found Britain a bleak and inhospitable place.

Magic casements to fairyland: visitors to the huge new fantasy amusement park which opened in July in the southern outskirts of Los Angeles might be greeted by a life-size Mickey Mouse, Goofy or Donald Duck. Disneyland cost $17,000,000 to build and included jungle and underwater rides, a haunted house, a moon trip, Sleeping Beauty's Palace and a host of vividly presented attractions, employing all the latest technology.

Speedy death: James Dean was only 24 when he died in a road accident in September. Seen here in *Giant*, he first appeared in the film of John Steinbeck's *East of Eden*. It was his role in *Rebel Without a Cause* which made him a cult figure who seemed to embody the moods, feelings and problems of a whole generation of restless teenagers. He loved fast cars and was killed when he crashed his Porsche.

Speedy triumph: Donald Campbell, 34-year-old son of Sir Malcolm Campbell, streaked across Ullswater in the Lake District at 202mph in July, to set a new world water speed record. Speed would kill him in the end, however. He died 12 years later, when the latest version of *Bluebird* crashed at high speed on the calm surface of Coniston Water.

1955

E·V·E·N·T·S

6 APRIL Sir Anthony Eden became Prime Minister after resignation of Churchill
13 JULY Ruth Ellis became the last woman to be hanged in Britain
22 SEPTEMBER Commercial television went on the air in Britain
30 SEPTEMBER A general strike took place in Cyprus against British rule
30 OCTOBER Princess Margaret decided not to marry Group Captain Townsend
26 NOVEMBER Declaration of a state of emergency in Cyprus

Femme fatale: Ruth Ellis, aged 28, was hanged at Holloway Prison in London in July, for the murder of her lover, David Blakely who had been having an affair with another woman. She said that she wanted to die, as it was the only way she could be with him. She was the last woman to go to the gallows in Great Britain.

1956

RACIAL TENSION was far greater in the southern states of the USA than in Britain. During this year, the *ILN* reported 'ugly scenes in Tennessee and Texas' and printed even uglier pictures, including one showing an effigy of a murdered Negro strung up outside the home of a black family which had moved into a previously 'all-white' part of Fort Worth. The trouble developed when the Supreme Court ruled against racial segregation in schools. Attempts to enforce the policy resulted in 'a number of unfortunate incidents':

> *Most serious were the riots in Clinton, Tennessee, where twelve Negro pupils had been assigned to the high school. The trouble here started with the arrival of an agitator from Washington, who was promptly sentenced to a year's imprisonment for violating an injunction against anti-Negro manifestations.* (15 September)

The southern race riots were just one aspect of a very turbulent year. Further violence in Cyprus resulted in the despatch of British Army reinforcements. Under an earlier agreement, British troops continued to be withdrawn from the Suez area. The last men left in June, but only a few months later, following Israeli attacks on Egyptian positions in Sinai, British forces were back, taking part in what Sir Anthony Eden described not as a war, but as an armed conflict with Egypt, resulting from Colonel Nasser's nationalization of the Suez Canal and a steady deterioration in Anglo-Egyptian relations over the previous few years. The *ILN* featured the first days of the Suez Canal under the new Egyptian regime, picturing trainee Russian pilots and describing how:

> *On September 14 about 500 European employees of the Suez Canal Company left their jobs, including about 100 pilots. Although Egyptian sources claimed that they had 70 qualified pilots . . . only two or three of these can be senior men and between 15 and 20 must be newcomers . . . The testing-time was expected to begin with the misty days of October . . . In the meanwhile a number of larger ships were being re-routed round the Cape.* (29 September)

The Suez episode came to be regarded as a fiasco, an undignified display of bullying involving the British, the French and the Israelis. At the time opinion was sharply divided. The *ILN* reported that:

> *On November 5 British and French parachute troops made landings in the Port Said area of Egypt at dawn, and afterwards there were landings by. . .airborne troops. This part of the Anglo-French action, described by Sir Anthony Eden as a police move to restore peace after Israel invaded the Sinai Peninsula, followed several days of bombing of military targets by Allied aircraft, which in turn followed the Egyptian rejection of the Allied twelve-hour ultimatum. . .Fighting ceased with the Allied cease-fire at midnight the following day, November 6.* (17 November)

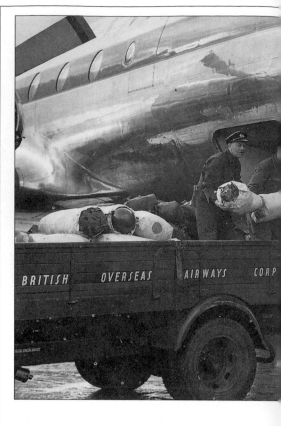

Armour of repression: Soviet tanks (below), rumbling through the streets of Budapest. 'In Parliament Square on October 25, 100 men, women and children, in a passive unarmed crowd, were mown down by sudden fire from Russian tanks . . . Some Russian troops are said to have shown reluctance in their task of repression, but others were wilfully brutal.' (3 November 1956)

Pack up your troubles: kit being loaded as soldiers flew to reinforce troops in the Canal Zone. Speaking to the nation on TV and radio in August, the Prime Minister had 'stressed the vital importance of the Suez Canal, which he described as "the greatest international waterway in the world." He emphasised that if Colonel Nasser's seizure of the Canal were to succeed, "each one of us would be at the mercy of one man for the supplies on which we live".' (18 August 1956)

THE ILLUSTRATED LONDON NEWS

1956

E · V · E · N · T · S

11 JANUARY Rising tension between Greeks and Turks in Cyprus; British troops sent

15 MARCH Lerner and Loewe's *My Fair Lady* had its première in New York

23 MARCH Pakistan was declared an Islamic Republic

19 APRIL American actress Grace Kelly married Prince Rainier of Monaco

23 OCTOBER The Hungarian uprising began with countrywide demonstrations

1 NOVEMBER The first premium bonds went on sale in Britain

The Pepsi culture: American styles and products played an increasingly dominant role on the British scene in the 1950s. Square-dancing was sufficiently 'in' to be used to promote sweets, while Coca Cola and its rival, Pepsi Cola, struggled for supremacy.

Starry-eyed: beautiful film star Grace Kelly married Prince Rainier of Monaco, a little French Riviera principality best known for the Monte Carlo gaming tables. Hundreds of guests were present at the fairytale ceremony in the Roman Catholic cathedral in Monaco-Ville to watch the blonde actress united with her prince, a descendant of the Grimaldis, who ruled Monaco in the Middle Ages.

For analysis, the *ILN* turned to its regular commentator, Cyril Falls. He failed to understand British opponents of Sir Anthony Eden, who, he claimed:

> *... foam with indignation when their own country, flouted and mocked, threatened with economic catastrophe, takes military precautions against a military dictator who has announced the wholly illegal seizure of international property.* (6 October)

Many feared that the crisis would escalate and nuclear weapons would be involved. Cyril Falls disagreed. 'The plea that such precautions endanger the peace of the world is contrary to all evidence. It serves simply as bedsocks for cold feet.' Nasser was portrayed by him as a sort of mini-Hitler:

> *Unless Britain and France are forced into a really unworthy surrender—and, happily, there are no signs that they are likely to be—it does not look as though Colonel Nasser's stature will continue to swell in the Middle East. The bigger he gets, the less pleasing he is to regard. How ludicrous it would be to give in to this petty dictator.* (6 October)

This was all good rousing stuff, of course, and intended to rally support, but in the end it was Nasser who retained prominence, and Eden who resigned. With the United Nations deploring Britain's action and the USA bringing powerful pressure to bear on the British economy, the episode seemed to confirm Britain's diminishing influence in world affairs.

While the Suez crisis was being thrashed out, Hungary became another scene of turmoil. The *ILN* remarked that:

> *All recent reports from Budapest emphasize the tremendous amount of damage inflicted on the city by the Russian tanks and guns ... It is estimated that at least 500 Russian tanks were in Budapest during the battle. The determined resistance of the freedom fighters resulted in the destruction of a very considerable number of these.* (24 November)

Although many died in the uprising, others escaped and arrived in Britain as penniless refugees. They found themselves in a land where 'self-service' shops were beginning to appear and premium bonds had just been introduced. These, according to the Archbishop of Canterbury, Dr Geoffrey Fisher, debased the nation's spiritual currency. Non-spiritual currency was also having a difficult time. The bank rate rose to the then alarmingly high rate of $5\frac{1}{2}$ per cent—its highest since 1931, and the credit squeeze was to become a fact of life for many months. The Clean Air Act was passed, intended to remove for ever the thick smogs which had blighted London in former years. The House of Commons voted for the abolition of the death penalty, but the Lords disagreed and an opinion poll found that 49 per cent of the population was still in favour of hanging.

In Monaco what many saw as a fairytale wedding took place in April between the American actress Grace Kelly and Prince Rainier. Something less than a fairytale marriage was portrayed by the dramatist John Osborne, when *Look Back in Anger* was staged at the Royal Court Theatre in London. The concept of the 'angry young man' was born.

A step along the road: British paratroopers moving on after the capture of a Canal Zone airfield. British casualties were minimal, but the damage done to Anglo American relations was potentially a good deal more serious. 'Among those who resent most deeply the action of the United States in the Suez affair, and still more her official attitude, are many who are her warmest friends and admirers.' (8 December 1956)

Assault on Port Said: after Egypt refused to accept the British and French ultimatum, Allied air forces attacked targets in Egypt. 'The first attacks were aimed at air-fields. Later on, other military targets were also attacked, including Egyptian radio stations . . . it was announced that a very high proportion of the Egyptian airforce had been put out of action, many of the aircraft destroyed being Russian-built MIG-15 fighters.' (10 November 1956)

1956

E · V · E · N · T · S

13 JUNE The last British troops left the Suez Canal Zone

26 JULY President Nasser announced nationalization of the Suez Canal

29 OCTOBER Israeli armed forces invaded Egypt via the Sinai Peninsula

31 OCTOBER Allied planes bombed targets in the Canal Zone

5 NOVEMBER British and French forces landed in Egypt

6 NOVEMBER A United Nations ceasefire came into effect in the Canal Zone

Heading for a war: British paratroopers in a plane taking off from Cyprus for the first landings in the Canal Zone on 5 November. Meanwhile, the crisis had provoked mixed feelings in Britain. ' "Law, not war" was the slogan of the national campaign against government policy in Egypt launched on November 4 by the National Council of Labour's mass meeting in Trafalgar Square.' (10 November 1956)

1957

PERHAPS BECAUSE OF DISAPPOINTMENT with what Britain had to offer in the post-war era, increasing numbers of people began thinking about a new life abroad. Harold Macmillan, who became Conservative Prime Minister following Eden's resignation in January this year, made a speech in July declaring that 'most of our people have never had it so good'. Unimpressed, some 2,000 people a week were said to be emigrating to Commonwealth countries. Those seeking a less permanent change of scene were beginning to be attracted by the offer of package holidays to resorts such as Benidorm in Spain.

In the spring, the *ILN* reported what it saw as 'a historic step towards the unification of Europe'. This was the signing of the Common Market Treaty at the Palazzo dei Conservatori in Rome. Representatives from Germany, Italy, France, Belgium, Holland and Luxembourg attended. Britain remained aloof for the time being, but feared the effects on trade which might be felt as a result of the new European alliance.

For popular entertainment, Britain continued to follow in the steps of the USA rather than Europe. American styles and fashions were widespread. Home-grown 'skiffle' music did enjoy some success, but nothing could compare with the huge audiences greeting Bill Haley and the Comets when they visited London. This was also the year in which Laurence Olivier portrayed Archie Rice in John Osborne's *The Entertainer*—an ageing stand-up comic whose successes and audiences belonged to the past. Humour was slicker, faster, less typically 'British' now, but in the USA something as British as the monarchy could still muster crowds that a rock 'n' roll group would envy. The *ILN* described the Queen's day in New York as 'the unforgettable climax' of her visit to the USA.

American confidence suffered a set-back when it was announced that the Russians had launched the first man-made satellite, *Sputnik I*. Few can have guessed at the revolution in telecommunications which would become possible as satellite technology advanced. At the time the military implications caused concern. The *ILN* said that the launch, on 4 October, 'came as a complete surprise to the rest of the world, and . . . completely overshadowed American plans for launching satellites', although these had been made known to the public in 1955. The magazine went on:

> *Considerable anxiety has been aired in the United States, because the Soviet achievement shows that Russian scientists have established a clear lead in rocket research and therefore in the field of intercontinental missiles as well.* (12 October)

The same year saw the detonation of a British H-bomb, at Christmas Island. A serious fire at the Windscale nuclear plant (now renamed Sellafield) in Cumbria led to contamination of local milk and a ban on sales, but the full details of the near-catastrophe were considered too alarming to be released at the time.

No one saw any reason to conceal details of the third worst railway disaster in the United Kingdom, which occurred in thick fog near Lewisham on 4 December. The *ILN* recorded that 'trains were running late, owing to the fog, and were crowded with Christmas shoppers and rush-hour passengers'. The crash killed 88 people and seriously injured more than a hundred.

Disaster in the fog: men working to clear the debris after two trains had collided in fog near Lewisham, under a fly-over bridge. 'The fly-over bridge, weighing hundreds of tons, collapsed on to coaches of the 4.56 from Cannon Street when part of the train crashed into the viaduct supports.' (14 December 1957)

Royal handshake: President Eisenhower, the Queen and Mrs Eisenhower at the White House during the visit of the Queen and the Duke of Edinburgh to Washington. 'Huge crowds lined the whole route and gave the Royal visitors a rousing welcome.' (26 October 1957)

The Common Market: the European Economic Community was formally established with the signing of the Treaty of Rome in March by six countries: France, West Germany, Italy, Belgium, the Netherlands and Luxemburg. The aim was economic union, with political union as an eventual possibility.

THE ILLUSTRATED LONDON NEWS

1957

E·V·E·N·T·S

10 JANUARY Anthony Eden resigned; Harold Macmillan new Prime Minister
25 MARCH Treaty of Rome signed, setting up the Common Market
30 AUGUST Malaya attained independence; 170 years of British rule there ended
4 OCTOBER The Soviet Union launched *Sputnik I*, the world's first space satellite
4 DECEMBER 88 died in the Lewisham train disaster

Women everywhere are delighted with the new *G.E.C.* Superspeed iron

NOW! MORE POWER, MORE ZIP!

...YET WITH GENEROUS M.P.G.

SUNBEAM RAPIER

A product of
ROOTES MOTORS LTD

Buoyant market: in the era of 'You've never had it so good' there was plenty of money in many people's pockets, which advertisers did their level best to siphon off. Cars like the Sunbeam Rapier were now increasingly within the reach of the working population, while women's lives were heavily dominated by doing the washing and ironing—or so the advertisers appeared to believe.

1958

NINETEEN FIFTY-EIGHT heralded an age of faster communications across greater distances. Subscriber trunk direct (STD) telephone dialling began to be introduced and Britain's first stretch of motorway opened in December. This was the eight-mile Preston Bypass (an early section of the M6). The public had to wait another year for the first stretch of the M1 to be completed. In April the *ILN* pictured the Minister of Transport, Harold Watkinson, laying a bronze seal in the parapet of one of the bridges of what was then termed 'the London–Yorkshire Motorway'. No maximum speed limit had yet been imposed on roads outside built-up areas, but in towns motorists were beginning to face the consequences of increasing car ownership. This year, roads began to be adorned with yellow no-waiting lines and parking meters were introduced on a trial basis in Mayfair. Meanwhile, on the world Grand Prix circuit, Britain was excelling in speed and skill. In October Mike Hawthorn became the first UK World Champion in Formula One motor racing. He retired, only to die in a crash on the Guildford Bypass three months later. It was the name of the runner-up, Stirling Moss, which was to become famous in years to come.

The invention of a new method of transport, the hovercraft, was announced this year, and travel across the Atlantic first became available by scheduled jet. An air disaster at Munich in February claimed the lives of many of the Manchester United football team—the Busby Babes—and for weeks their manager, Matt Busby, fought for his life.

Although the first signs of the awful consequences of the Thalidomide drug were already being recognised in Germany, international reaction proved tragically slow. On a wider scale, recognition of the terrible effects of nuclear warfare prompted the formation of a popular movement to oppose the manufacture of nuclear weapons—the Campaign for Nuclear Disarmament (CND). The first of many Easter marches from London to the Atomic Weapons Research Establishment at Aldermaston took place this year. Some 12,000 people were said to have attended the first rally at Aldermaston, and several hundred marched the full 50 miles from London. Although there were veteran pacifists among them, the popular image of the marchers was of youth on the move, eager to alert the world to the dangers of gambling with human life. Critics held that the campaigners were all ardent Communists, but this was far from the case. A contemporary film included interviews with well-spoken, and otherwise conventional mothers, some of whom had brought children with them. The same year saw the USA, the USSR and the United Kingdom meeting in Geneva to discuss the possibility of a nuclear test ban, but progress was slow.

Britain was continuing to shake itself free of some of the constraints of the past. The Lord Chamberlain, who still exerted the power of censorship over theatrical productions, ended the total ban which had existed on the portrayal of homosexuality in plays. Parliament witnessed the installation of the first Life Peers, including 14 women, while the annual presentation of Débutantes to the Queen and Prince Philip at Buckingham Palace was discontinued. The last 'Debs' made their curtsies to the Queen on 18 March.

Despite the sense of change which was in the air, or possibly because of it, John Betjeman's gently nostalgic *Collected Poems* appealed to a huge readership when they were published this year.

Tragedy in the snow: the bodies of victims at Munich Airport after an airliner had crashed on take-off. The casualties included members of the Manchester United football team, known as the Busby Babes after their manager, Matt Busby. He was seriously injured.

Last in line: Débutantes and their parents queueing outside Buckingham Palace as they waited to make their curtsies to the Queen. This was the last year in which Débutantes were presented at court.

THE ILLUSTRATED LONDON NEWS

1958

E·V·E·N·T·S

6 FEBRUARY Members of Manchester United
football team killed in an air crash
18 MARCH Last Débutantes presented to the
Queen at Buckingham Palace
1 JUNE Political crisis in France over
Nationalist rebellion in Algeria
28 OCTOBER Cardinal Roncalli elected Pope
with the title John XXIII
5 DECEMBER Britain's first stretch of
motorway, the Preston Bypass, opened
21 DECEMBER General de Gaulle elected first
President of Fifth French Republic

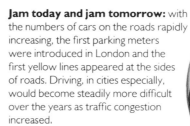

Jam today and jam tomorrow: with
the numbers of cars on the roads rapidly
increasing, the first parking meters
were introduced in London and the
first yellow lines appeared at the sides
of roads. Driving, in cities especially,
would become steadily more difficult
over the years as traffic congestion
increased.

First in step: the
London to
Aldermaston
marchers on their
way through
Berkshire. Their
philosophy was 'that
those who detest
war—which includes
nearly every man and
woman in these
islands—can best
avoid it by divesting
themselves of the
means of fighting it.'
(29 March 1958)

The 1960s, perhaps more than any other decade this century, have assumed their own very distinct character. Nostalgia and myth are still playing a part in embellishing the portrait, but few would deny that the era of Kennedy, the Beatles, the mini skirt and 'Swinging' London, of flower power and student protests, proved particularly memorable. It was a time which saw the world on the brink of nuclear war over Cuba and which marked the beginning of the lengthy period of 'conventional' warfare waged by the USA and the Viet Cong in Vietnam. Northern Ireland became synonymous with murder and violence, and terrorism became a topic of international concern. The 1960s had their dark side; yet pop music and fashion were all-important, and having fun was virtually obligatory.

In May 1960 Princess Margaret married Anthony Armstrong-Jones, and the *ILN* published a selection of wedding photographs. The wedding was 'romantic', the day a 'great and happy' one. In the same year the USA embarked on a love affair of its own: John F Kennedy was considered an unlikely candidate for the Presidency—he was young and he was Catholic—but he won the Democratic nomination and the election to the White House, defeating Richard Nixon, though not by an overwhelming majority. The White House rapidly came to be regarded as a glamorous and fashionable place.

In Britain strict, straight-laced morality was going out of fashion and a more permissive era beckoned. In November the Crown prosecuted Penguin Books, and brought about the notorious *Lady Chatterley's Lover* trial at the Old Bailey. The book was obscene, according to the prosecution, and Counsel asked members of the jury, in all seriousness, whether this was a book which they would want their wife or their servant to read. Having demonstrated the extent to which it was out of touch with the times, the prosecution failed and the book, written in the 1920s, became an immediate best-seller.

The outcome of the Lady Chatterley trial suggested that people were now free to read what they chose without interference from a moralising government. Further freedom from restraint was also on the way: this year saw relaxation of the restrictions on betting and the announcement of the end of National Service.

In February, Prime Minister Harold Macmillan spoke of a 'wind of change', referring specifically to the situation in Africa. The South African Parliament disliked his comment that, 'whether we like it or not, this growth of national consciousness is a political fact', and the *ILN* reported how opposition to the 'wind of change' in South Africa was resulting in violence:

On March 21 a crowd of thousands of Africans, urged by the militant Pan-African Congress to demonstrate against the carrying of identity cards, moved against the police station at Sharpeville and besieged seventy-five white police, who opened fire on them, killing seventy and wounding over 100 more. (9 April)

The United Nations deplored the action and called for the policy of apartheid to be abandoned.

Political unrest was mounting in East Germany, too, where food shortages and bleak prospects were driving more and more people to the West.

Fashion-conscious doll: young girls throughout the country had become aware of the Barbie Doll, whose developed physique was quite unlike that of the usual toddler variety, and which could be dressed up in the latest fashions.

Bride in royal splendour: 'In their glass coach Princess Margaret and Mr Anthony Armstrong-Jones drove from Westminster Abbey to Buckingham Palace after an impressive and moving wedding service conducted by the Archbishop of Canterbury [6 May]. With cries of "Good Luck" and "God bless you" greeting them on all sides, the smiling couple happily waved from the coach as they moved away from the Abbey . . . The marriage . . . is at once a symbol of the great changes in our Royal family . . .' (14 May 1960)

Ecstatic welcome: crowds in Los Angeles greeted John F Kennedy with a deluge of paper streamers and confetti. He 'is not only the first Roman Catholic President but also the youngest man ever to hold the post.' (19 November 1960)

THE ILLUSTRATED LONDON NEWS
1960
E · V · E · N · T · S

3 FEBRUARY Harold Macmillan made his 'wind of change' speech
21 MARCH 70 blacks shot and killed in Sharpeville, South Africa
2 APRIL The USA launched first weather satellite, *Tiros I*, into space
30 JUNE The Congo became independent after 80 years of Belgian rule
4 NOVEMBER Senator John F Kennedy won the US presidential election
31 DECEMBER Last day for call-up to national service in UK

Against the book: South Africans demonstrating against passbooks were fired on by police at Sharpeville on 21 March, and 70 were killed. The event 'heralded a new wave of bitter feeling in many parts of the world . . .' (9 April 1960)

The second death: a Dallas newspaper photographer took this picture at the city jail as Lee Harvey Oswald, accused of the murder of President Kennedy, was confronted by a nightclub owner, Jack Ruby, who fired a bullet into Oswald's stomach. Oswald died a few hours later.

Pedestrian precinct: the trend towards traffic-free shopping areas received a boost in the early 1960s when newly paved Carnaby Street, off Regent Street in London, was opened to the public. The rubberised pavement material was an innovation, too, and because of Carnaby Street's cultural links with the Beatles it became a major attraction for tourists.

The USA was about to be shattered by
catastrophe, described by the *ILN*:

*A crushing disaster, not only for the Uni
for the world at large, has spread disma
pity far and wide. None of us can measur
weight of the loss, but we surely all reali
be enormous, domestically as well as in f
President Kennedy, driving with his
Governor of Texas, Mr John Connall
of a long procession of cars, was s*
(30 November)

In a year of momentous events, this
everyone was to recall for decades afterwar
nedy era the White House had been compar
the fairy tale was over and the ending had
The *ILN* did its best to explain Kennedy's r

*... rulers, prime ministers and senior
countries have met Kennedy over affa
moment, and ... while only a few
classified as close friends, all have be
delighted by a youthful gaiety and f
remarkable even at his age, a strong
and, generally speaking, a broad-m
has on occasion led to unexpected con
world has lost a man ... of the most
... (30 November)*

The matter, of course, did not r
Oswald was arrested and accused of the
shot dead two days later by Jack Ruby
Marilyn Monroe (in which some have seer
the assassination in Dallas became a subj
there were rumours of Mafia involvemer
following the Cuban missile crisis.
Lyndon B Johnson was sworn in
and the end of the year brought a change
Harold Macmillan, whose government h
Profumo affair, resigned as Prime Minis
tive Party Conference. The Earl of Ho
successor, but not without controversy
and becoming known as Sir Alec Dou
cabinet in the knowledge that some lead
among them, had refused to serve un
election looming and mounting econor
pects were beginning to look less than

It was ostensibly because of the
the BBC curtailed broadcasts of *That*
The satire programme had achieved c
political influence was deemed to b
refusal to acknowledge the public's a
mind was at odds with the message of
proposed the establishment of new uni
of higher education to the thousands v
to realise their academic potential. T
selection procedure had begun to
experimental comprehensive schools
immediately after the war were beg
serious alternative to grammar and se

THE ESTABLISHMENT of a
April, was in keeping v
ments in education. BBC
output than the two existing
culture, science and the arts.
The Beatles visited the US
response which was now enact
med up in the word 'Beatlemania
provided fashionable sound, th
synonymous with the fashionable
was able to declare that Paris, pre
fashionable, was behind the ti
multiplying boutiques, was whe
In the general election it w
ment was also out of date. After
Labour Party finally came to
majority. Nevertheless, dramat
nationalization schemes and publ
high on the new government's
Afterthoughts in the *ILN*, Kings

*... Mr Wilson will find if he
plan designed to put a stop
provide houses at rents whic
he will meet with an overwh
... the Tory Party will hesi
of defeating even the bolde
housing reform. (24 Octobe*

A problem which was to re
for many years to come was that
June Ian Smith threatened unilate
in response to Britain's insistence
majority. At the same time the
effective moves towards civil right
to eliminate the last vestiges of i
crusading and non-violent work
Martin Luther King was awarded t
In South Africa there were no
Meanwhile, the *ILN* reported th
previously received a limited jail se
detained for life. 'The judge decide
but protests against "these savag
throughout the world.'
While the USA improved its
embarked on a foreign policy in
despair and demoralisation. A Nor
destroyer in August provoked an A
naval bases; withdrawal from this
impossible for the USA for years.
This was the year that saw the
the Soviet Union—he was forced
Leonid Brezhnev—and the death
become India's first Prime Minist
Affairs. Lyndon Johnson, who had
following Kennedy's assassination,
and, in Jerusalem, the Palestine Lib
was established.

Diversifying Pleasures

*Nature is a revelation of God;
Art a revelation of man.*

HENRY WADSWORTH LONGFELLOW

The Beatles, with Frankie Howerd. Beatlemania reached a worldwide peak in 1964 and 1965.

AT 1.35 ON THE AFTERNOON of 8
February 1964 a plane arrived at Kennedy Airport, New York, and
unloaded four amiable, cheeky young men
with mop-like haircuts and Liverpool
accents. Their names were John, Paul,
George and Ringo, and they were greeted
with ecstatic screams by a crowd of 10,000
which had turned out to welcome them.
Another excited crowd blocked the traffic
round their hotel. When they appeared on
prime-time television on the *Ed Sullivan
Show*, the programme clocked up a record
audience of 73 million people, and it was
reported that while it was on, not a single
major crime had been committed anywhere
in the USA by a teenager.
Beatlemania became a worldwide
phenomenon in 1964. John, Paul, George
and Ringo flew in and flew out of airports,
trying to keep their boyish smiles in place
while thousands of hysterical fans shrieked
at them. Their cars and hotel rooms were
mobbed. Pillowcases they had rested their

heads on were sneaked away and cut up into
small pieces and sold to avid buyers.
It went on for three years. As the
Beatles' biographer Hunter Davies des-
cribes it: 'There was perpetual screaming
and yeh-yeh-yehing from hysterical teenagers of every class and colour, few of whom
could hear what was going on for the noise
they were making. They became emotion-
ally, mentally, or sexually excited. They
foamed at the mouth, burst into tears,
hurled themselves like lemmings in the
direction of the Beatles, or just simply
fainted.'
The Beatles' first record had been
released in 1962: *Love Me Do*. The public
did, and the group's hits in 1963 included
Please Please Me, *I Want to Hold Your
Hand* and *She Loves You*, the advance
orders for which had reached 500,000 when
the record went on sale. Everywhere the
Beatles went, crowds and screams were sure
to go. Newspapers and magazines trotted
out psychologists to explain the

phenomenon to the puzzled older generation. The Beatles topped the bill on TV's
Sunday Night at the London Palladium and
in November they starred in the Royal
Command Variety Performance, which
reached an audience of 26 million on television. Their only real rivals were the Rol-
ling Stones, who came from a higher social
class and were much more anarchic, wild
and anti-establishment.
Beatlemania died away again after 1966.
By the end of the decade the group had
broken up, and although there were
frequent rumours that the Beatles might
join forces again, it never happened. Paul
McCartney flourished as a singer and composer in his own right, while John Lennon
turned into a kind of world peace mystic
and was eventually shot and killed outside
his home in New York City in 1980. He was
only 40, but he already seemed a figure from
a time long past.
Longer ago still, in the 1890s, a mob of
young girls screaming over a pop group

THE ILLUSTRATED
LONDON

196

E · V · E ·

19 JANUARY Mrs Indira Ga...
Minister of...
8 APRIL Leonid Brezhnev...
Secretary of the So...
30 JULY England defeated...
football to win W...
13 AUGUST Mao Tse-tu...
'cultural revolutio...
21 OCTOBER 116 children k...
collapsed in Aber...
9 NOVEMBER Art treasures...
worst storms in...

Their cup runneth ove...
England's captain, holds alo...
Rimet trophy after his side...
Germany 4–2, winning the...
game had run into extra tim...
scored twice ...' (6 August...

pop c...
became...
were E...
impuls...
date w...
the Cl...
jived i...
would...
fashio...
ally re...
would...
like A...
amplifi...
able sp...
British...
Roy I...
moved...
jects in...
painted...
tin la...
reprodu...

The...
mania,...
rical ce...
the 197...
in the...
the Sex...
were m...
than ev...
1960s...
Nurey...
1978 s...
saluted...
tor H...
great a...
above I...
1970s...
reactio...
and of...

Ci...
total ac...
75 mil...
activity...
the lat...
Britain...
them...
owned...
numbe...
said 'th...
hours a...
their o...
hundre...
less, b...
able t...
Shakes...
ever be...

highbrow poetry and novels were made dauntingly difficult. Two influential examples came out in 1922: T S Eliot's poem *The Waste Land* and James Joyce's novel *Ulysses*, which was based on a complicated scheme of symbolism but was banned in Britain and America for some years. Joyce would go on to explore language in the 1930s in *Finnegans Wake*, which flouted previously accepted literary conventions and made unprecedented demands on its readers.

Popular music, meanwhile, came increasingly from across the Atlantic. The Original Dixieland Jass Band toured Britain successfully in 1919. A craze for dancing swelled the profits of dance halls like the Palais de Danse in Hammersmith. American dances with such silly names as 'bunny hug' and 'turkey trot' made the waltz seem hopelessly sedate. The pulsing rhythm of the Charleston swept Britain like a fever in 1925 and soon the quickstep and the slow foxtrot would hold sway. Popular songs came from George Gershwin (*The Man I Love, Swanee, Fascinatin' Rhythm, Oh*

An ironic work (top) by Paul Nash. We Are Making a New World (1918). Faces from the movies (above): Charlie Chaplin with the blind flower-girl in City Lights (1931), and stars Johnny Weissmuller and Maureen O'Sullivan in Tarzan and His Mate (1934).

Lady Be Good) and Jerome Kern (*Smoke Gets in Your Eyes*), whose musical *Show Boat* gave Paul Robeson a hit with *Ol' Man River* and brought a story with a serious plot to the musical stage. Gershwin treated the jazz idiom seriously, in *Rhapsody in Blue* in 1924 and the opera *Porgy and Bess* in 1935. The era of big band swing began, with Paul Whiteman and his orchestra in the van: it was Whiteman who commissioned *Rhapsody in Blue*. On the British side of the water, bands led by Henry Hall and Jack Payne were broadcasting regularly in the 1930s.

There was nothing in the least transatlantic, however, about Agatha Christie's

Belgian detecti...
waxed moustac...
who made his...
Mysterious Affa...
there about t...
women crime w...
tations in the...
Sayers, Marge...
Marsh. On th...
Lord Peter Wi...
and Albert Ca...
both enjoyed r...
crust connectio...

Another po...
was to last we...
immortal tales...
ter, of the Earl...
tainous prize...
began appear...
Waugh's first...
out in 1928, J...
panions in 192...
Rock in 193...

would have been unthinkable. The youth culture was as yet unknown, the concept of the teenager unthought of. The popular entertainment of the day was for grown-ups—the music hall. Here working-class audiences laughed, sighed and sang with the great variety artists of the time: Dan Leno, champion clog-dancer, comic and pantomime dame *extraordinaire*; Vesta Tilley in top hat and tails; the young Harry Lauder with a touch of the bonnie, purple heather; Albert Chevalier, the coster laureate, who could bring a tear to the eye with *My Old Dutch*.

From 1890 to 1914 the Queen of the halls was undoubtedly Marie Lloyd; *I Do Like To Be Beside The Seaside, Oh My Porter, One Of The Ruins That Cromwell Knocked About A Bit*. Warm, vulgar, distinctly suggestive, she had, T S Eliot said solemnly, 'a capacity for expressing the soul of the people'. Worn with fame and gin, she died in 1922; Chevalier died in 1923, and by then the halls were losing their battle against cinema and radio.

The music hall was created by the demand for popular entertainment in the rapidly growing towns and cities of Victorian Britain. By a quirk of the law, patrons could not drink or smoke in a legitimate theatre, but music halls escaped the ban. In the 1890s, however, their proprietors were busy moving them up in the world socially and away from their public house atmosphere. Drink was no longer sold in the auditorium, rows of seats replaced tables and benches, and the artists' material was cleaned up a bit. This was not enough to

Stars of music hall and stage before the First World War included Marie Lloyd (above left), the great Russian ballerina Anna Pavlova (above right), famous for her performance of 'the dying swan', and Vesta Tilley (right), a male impersonator.

appease the strait-laced middle-class campaigners who regarded the halls as sinks of impurity, but it was enough to gain them social acceptance. The seal of approval was put on music halls in 1912, when King George V attended the first ever Royal Command Performance, Harry Lauder sang *Roamin' in the Gloamin'*, George Robey and Little Tich graced the stage.

Rivals to the music hall were musical comedy and revue. The great days of Gilbert and Sullivan at the Savoy Theatre had gone with the 1880s, but the chorus girls flashed their smiles enticingly at the Gaiety Theatre, and in 1912 a jazzy American show, *Hullo Ragtime* by Irving Berlin, took London by storm, with *Alexander's Ragtime Band* a hit song. Meanwhile, the first blurred and jumpy motion pictures were drawing audiences to the first crude cinemas. In 1895, when a French audience was shown a film of a train arriving at a station, some of them were so frightened that they ran away in panic.

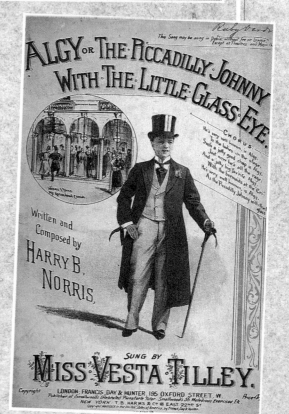

ALGY OR THE PICCADILLY JOHNNY WITH THE LITTLE GLASS EYE.

Written and Composed by
HARRY B. NORRIS.

SUNG BY
MISS VESTA TILLEY.

Further up market, it was the wit that was flashing in the years from 1892 to 1895, in a succession of comedies by Oscar Wilde, which included *Lady Windermere's Fan, A Woman of No Importance* and *The Importance of Being Earnest.* Wit of a subversive character could also be enjoyed in the early plays of George Bernard Shaw. The great tragediennes Duse and Bernhardt could still be seen on the London stage in 1895, and Sir Henry Irving was still in command at the Lyceum.

The curtain was falling, however, on the literary giants of the High Victorian age, as their successors strode on to the boards or hovered in the wings. Lord Tennyson, the greatest of them all, was 80 when the year 1890 dawned, and had less than two years to live. The past decade had removed Browning, Carlyle and Trollope, and the years leading up to the First World War would put paid to Robert Louis Stevenson and William Morris, Lewis Carroll and John Ruskin.

As 1890 began, Thomas Hardy was 49, his novels behind him but with reams of magnificent poetry still to flow. Rudyard Kipling was 24 and on his way to *Barrack Room Ballads, The Jungle Book, Kim* and the Nobel Prize. A E Housman was 30, and would publish *A Shropshire Lad* in 1896. In their twenties were Arnold Bennett, W B Yeats, H G Wells, John Galsworthy and J M Barrie, who would put the ageless *Peter Pan* on the stage in 1904. G K Chesterton, John Buchan, P G Wodehouse, James Joyce and Virginia Woolf were still at school. Still in the cradle were T S Eliot and Rupert Brooke. A 30-year-old doctor named Arthur Conan Doyle was about to quit his practice in Southsea and take to writing full time: he had invented a great detective named Sherlock Holmes, whose adventures

George Bernard Shaw in 1946.

Sir Edward Elgar, pictured about 1905.

would soon be all the rage in the *Strand Magazine.*

As time ran on towards 1914, Edward Elgar, one of the greatest English composers, gradually began to achieve recognition: with the *Enigma Variations* of 1899 and *The Dream of Gerontius*, despite its disastrous first performance at the Birmingham Festival in 1900. Alfred Gilbert's statue of Eros took its stand in Piccadilly Circus. Charles Rennie Mackin-

tosh began building the Glasgow School of Art and meanwhile another pioneer of Art Nouveau, the young Aubrey Beardsley, was drawing self-consciously wicked illustrations for *The Yellow Book* and Wilde's lushly decadent *Salome.*

Wilde died, ruined and an outcast, in 1900. Beatrix Potter's *The Tale of Peter Rabbit*, with its charming illustrations, came out two years later. Sir Percy Blakeney made his languid bow as the hero of *The Scarlet Pimpernel* ('They seek him here, they seek him there . . .'), while Conan Doyle, who had killed off Sherlock Holmes at the Reichenbach Falls, had to bring him back again by popular demand. Rat sang the praises of messing about in boats, and Toad felt the call of the open road in Kenneth Grahame's *The Wind in the Willows.*

In an art world accustomed to the Impressionists, Pablo Picasso's *Les Demoiselles d'Avignon* was received with general bafflement. Vaughan Williams wrote his *Sea Symphony*, Marcel Proust published *Swann's Way* and D H Lawrence *Sons and Lovers*, while the Paris audience jeered and hooted the first performance of Stravinsky's *The Rite of Spring*. With war-clouds gathering over Europe in 1914, there was time for three auspicious debuts: of a tenor named Gigli in Italy, of a pert flower-seller named Eliza in Shaw's *Pygmalion*, and of a character called Tarzan of the Apes in a story by Edgar Rice Burroughs.

Meanwhile, moving pictures had been coming along, from *The Great Train Robbery*, which lasted for all of eight minutes in 1903, by way of Mack Sennett's slapstick 'Keystone Kops' shorts, to D W Griffith's *Birth of a Nation* with a cast of thousands (literally, there were 10,000 extras), in 1915. The first studio in a sleepy, sun-baked place called Hollywood opened in 1913 on Sunset Boulevard. The star system was emerging by this time, and in 1915 Mary Pickford was

the most hig
Charlie Cha

Also eme
Thomas Alv
1877 by rec
into the we
production
in the 189c
record in 19
able, wind-
long before
would be a
classical an
ances by
became ava
dreamed o

During
like *Chu C*
Mountains
the minds
rors of th
should die
on his wa
buried in
Greek isla
and Edwa
Robert
survived.
suite *The*
recorded
of the W

While
music wi
cedented
serious n
son's rea
regions c
and Stra
direction
atonal o
in Berlin

The
literatur
ing and
naturali
towards
more p

1966

BRITISH PRIDE reasserted itself on the football field in July, when England won the World Cup at Wembley. The *ILN*, perhaps a little unaccustomed to detailed discussion of footballing techniques, described Alf Ramsey, the team's manager, as 'a dour, taciturn introvert—very unlike other football personalities'. England's defence had been 'rock-hard throughout the competition, but the forward line lacked penetration'. However, 'they were well-drilled and self-confident'. Victory was not entirely the result of skill, apparently. The *ILN* considered that 'the West Germans were the better footballers, but the teams were evenly matched: for what the English lacked in skill they more than made up in spirit'.

British spirit was taxed almost beyond endurance in October, when the village of Aberfan was engulfed in coal slurry. 'The disaster is particularly harrowing because of the large loss of life among children—the Minister of State for Wales has said "a whole generation of our children has been wiped out".' Grim reports in the *ILN* conveyed something of the horror:

> Throughout the long weekend, most of the time in heavy rain which threatened to bring down another avalanche of death, rescuers toiled on. Sandbags were used to try to contain the slurry, and a human chain worked day and night to get the excavated material out of the way. (29 October)

Days later there came news of devastating floods in Italy—described by the *ILN*'s reporter as the worst for 700 years. The streets of Florence 'were transformed into raging torrents. . . overturning cars, ripping up pavements, crushing in doors, and demolishing old buildings'. Hundreds died and, in addition to coming to terms with the loss of life and property, the Italian government had the problem of coping with countless seriously damaged works of art. Restoration, undertaken with much foreign assistance, was to be a long and expensive business.

In Britain, the Labour government, which called another general election and was returned to power with a viable majority, made cuts in foreign currency allowances and imposed a pay and wages freeze, but people wanted to travel abroad, and they did so, assisted by cheap flights and package deals offered by Freddie Laker. Rising inflation was a deterrent against saving, and the arrival of the Barclaycard—Britain's first credit card—made spending seem that much easier.

Debate continued to rage about whether the abolition of the death penalty had resulted in a more casual attitude to murder. In May, Ian Brady and Myra Hindley were sentenced to life imprisonment for the 'Moors murders' following what the *ILN* described as 'the most sensational murder trial of the century'. There were suggestions that others might try to impose the penalty which the government now refused to authorise; in the dock the defendants were protected by a bullet-proof screen.

Public outrage at the likely consequences of nuclear attack was something which the BBC did not wish to contemplate. A film, *The War Game*, was deemed unsuitable for broadcasting because of the terror it might induce, although CND protesters argued that the consequences of nuclear war should be made public and that a showing of the film would lessen the likelihood of a real nuclear attack.

1967

THE TELEVISION FILM *Cathy Come H*
Britain without any attempts at restra
and was repeated in January this y
homeless mother provoked an outcry. Home
national scandal, and the charity, Shelter,
attempt to ease the problem.

Television also broadcast powerful ima
when the oil tanker *Torrey Canyon* broke up
in March. Few, at that time, were alert to ecol
general threat posed to the environment b
world was barely recognised. The *Torrey*
demanded an end to complacency. The *ILN* d
arguing over whether it was better to try to d
which covered 100 square miles of the sea, or
use of huge quantities of detergents failed
reaching the shore. Eventually, the tanker
criticism of the government's handling of
vociferous.

In May, when Francis Chichester arrive
his solo voyage by yacht around the world,
how he had coped with a minor hazard posed b
boats; there was no mention of the hazard
Chichester's reception was remarkable and th
tinued when he arrived at Greenwich to b
Queen, with Sir Francis Drake's sword.

In September the Queen took a leadin
nautical ceremony when she christened 'her pr

**The Moors murc
and his girlfriend M
jailed in May for mu
children. The feelin
aroused by the def
that a bullet-proof s
around the dock fo
were sentenced to**

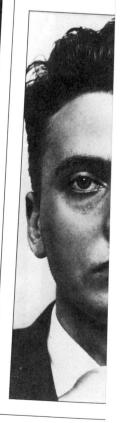

> The launching of a mighty liner is an inh
> matic, emotional occasion and there was n
> ing in this respect on September 20 when
> launched the Q4 at Clydebank and name
> Elizabeth II. For a full minute after the
> button was pressed, the new queen of the se
> not to move—as if regally pondering her co
> and considering the name she is expected t
> honour. Then the liner, her personality im
> the cheering thousands, moved swiftly an
> down to the water. . . (30 September)

Amid all the exuberant prose, one note of h
allowed to creep in. It was revealed that none o
John Brown's shipyard expected to be involve
project ever again.

Air travel had already signalled an end to m
liners, and in December *Concorde* was displaye
Toulouse. Despite this example of Anglo-Frenc
Britain's attempts to join the Common Marke
impress de Gaulle, but, in the year of *Sergeant*
Whiter Shade of Pale, membership of the EEC wa
generate great excitement in Britain. The law w
permit easier abortions and, if the law did not perm
tion with drugs, for many that was all the more r
Desmond Morris's book *The Naked Ape* did some
man's aggressive instincts, but there was little ho
was a bad and dangerous world. The hippies
Woburn for a festival of flower people knew that,
dropping out.

THE ILLUSTRATED
LONDON NEWS

1967

E·V·E·N·T·S

26 FEBRUARY US launched major attack on Viet Cong bases in Vietnam

28 MAY Francis Chichester completed his solo yacht voyage round the world

10 JUNE Israel victorious in six-day war against Egypt, Syria and Jordan

14 JULY Bill passed in the Commons to legalise abortion in UK

3 DECEMBER First heart transplant performed in South Africa by Christiaan Barnard

11 DECEMBER Prototype of world's first supersonic airliner, *Concorde*, revealed

Raining death and destruction: US helicopter gunships strafing the Vietnam countryside in a war that was becoming increasingly unpopular both at home and abroad. 'On October 21–22 protests against the Vietnam war were staged in nine European capitals, Japan, Australia and the US.' (28 October 1967)

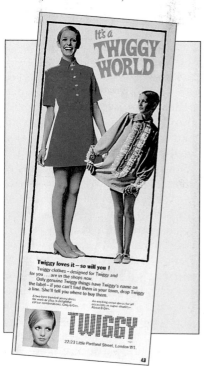

It's a
TWIGGY WORLD

Twiggy loves it – so will you !
Twiggy clothes – designed for Twiggy and for you ... are in the shops now. Only genuine Twiggy things have Twiggy's name on the label – if you can't find them in your town, drop Twiggy a line. She'll tell you where to buy them.

A two-tone banded jersey dress, for work or play is delightful for all occasions, in super shades— colour combinations. Only 6 Gn.   About 8 Gn.

TWIGGY
22.23 Little Portland Street, London W.1.

Opening an era of oil pollution: the *Torrey Canyon* aground on the Seven Stones reef off the coast of Cornwall in late March. About 13,000 tons of oil contaminated an 80-mile stretch of coast, destroying marine life and fouling the shoreline.

Thin girls, too, can be fashionable: the female figure now no longer had to conform to male notions of what was aesthetically pleasing. Twiggy's meagre dimensions hit the headlines and had a measurable impact on the output of the rag trade.

1968

TWO PROMINENT FIGURES of the 1960s did not live to see the end of the decade. In March Yuri Gagarin, the much-fêted pioneer spaceman, died in a plane crash. There has since been speculation as to whether his death was truly accidental or whether he was proving such a popular figure that someone wished him out of the way. News of the assassination of Martin Luther King was received by many with a disbelief similar to that which accompanied the shooting of Kennedy. King died in Memphis on 4 April at the age of 39, and the killing of the man who had advocated non-violence at all costs provoked turmoil across the USA. A curfew was imposed in Washington, thousands of troops were moved in to deal with rioting and looting, and, according to the *ILN*, 'similar incidents spread throughout the country, from Maryland to Mississippi'. Ian Lyon, in an article entitled *Who Could Succeed Martin Luther King?* which appeared on the front page of the *ILN* on 13 April, reckoned that 'the mantle of Dr King now rests on the shoulders of one man, President Lyndon Johnson. It will not be comfortable.'

At the time, Lyon had hopes that the American President would be able to withdraw the USA from its involvement in Vietnam, and concentrate on achieving social justice at home. In fact, the war continued to rage, attracting international protests. President Johnson announced that he would not be standing for another term and, at the end of the year, Richard Nixon was elected as the new Republican leader of the USA. Robert Kennedy's bid for the White House had come to a violent end in June, when he was shot by Sirhan Sirhan, a Palestinian Arab claiming to act for his country.

In addition to anti-Vietnam war protests, this year is also remembered for student riots in France. The *ILN* described it as: 'War in the streets: fighting on a scale not seen since the Liberation took place ... It sprang from the closing of the "Red University"—the faculty of letters at Nanterre.' Students from Nanterre joined others at the Sorbonne and barricaded themselves in, and they were evicted by police with hoses and tear gas. Youths were demanding reform of the education system and seeking student control of universities. Left-wing and Communist workers joined the protests and France suffered crippling strikes, but all attempts to bring down de Gaulle's government failed.

In Czechoslovakia, the increasingly liberal regime of Alexander Dubček and the reforms of the Prague Spring had the *ILN* fearing for the consequences as early as March: 'The danger is that, like Imre Nagy in 1956, Dubček may be driven to go too far, and, in so doing, force the Soviet Union to intervene.' Intervention came on the night of 20 August with the arrival of Russian troops and tanks, and a return to restrictions and censorship.

Enoch Powell claimed in April that Britain, too, was under threat of invasion. New legislation in Kenya was forcing many Asians out of the country, and those with British passports and their dependants were likely to take up residence in Britain. Powell was censured by fellow MPs for his predictions of 'rivers foaming with blood', and the Queen, in her Christmas message to the nation, asked for racial tolerance. The year had begun on the patriotic note of the 'I'm backing Britain' campaign, intended to boost the ailing economy and restore pride in British goods and services. By the end of the year it seemed that many identified racism with patriotism, and organisations such as the National Front had adopted the Union Jack as part of their insignia.

Dream and nightmare: Martin Luther King, who was shot dead in Memphis, Tennessee, on 4 April. 'For 13 years Dr King campaigned for Negro rights facing all the time not only the possibility of physical destruction ... but increasingly in later years the critics of his consistently held ideal of non-violence ... Dr King's funeral was at Atlanta, Georgia, on April 9. Tens of thousands surrounded the small Baptist church in which the memorial service was held and later followed the mule-drawn carriage to the cemetery after marching through the Negro slums.' (20 April 1968)

Home on wheels: refugees in Saigon (above), the South Vietnamese capital, with their motorcycle and belongings against a background of devastated buildings. This year saw the beginning of the end of the war in Vietnam. The US reduced its operations and 'talks about talks' commenced between the Viet Cong and the Americans in Paris.

Students in arms: police and students in Paris (right). '... there is one aspect of "student protest" which deserves serious consideration. It is the claim that modern industrial society and government are ignoring and repressing the creative and libertarian impulses of man.' (29 June 1968)

THE ILLUSTRATED LONDON NEWS

1968

E·V·E·N·T·S

4 APRIL Martin Luther King shot and killed in Memphis, Tennessee

5 JUNE Robert Kennedy assassinated by Sirhan Sirhan in Los Angeles

20 AUGUST Soviet and Warsaw Pact troops invaded Czechoslovakia

5 NOVEMBER Richard Nixon won US presidential election

27 DECEMBER Three US astronauts orbited the moon in *Apollo 8*

The eyes have it: Max Factor were busy promoting their cosmetics in the style of the 'Swinging Sixties' with psychedelic effects and expressions like 'groovy' and 'fabsville'. Teenagers enjoyed purchasing power beyond the dreams of earlier generations and the 'youth culture' roared ahead, accompanied by the mini skirt and the drug scene, flower power and pop music.

LIBRARY
24 MAR 1993
HARTLEPOOL C.F.E.

1969

THE AMERICAN FLAG was inevitably among the equipment which the crew of *Apollo* 11 took with them when they landed on the moon in July. The USA had lagged behind in the early stages of what later came to be called the space race, but it was the American *Apollo* programme which achieved the first, and still, 20 years later, only manned moon voyages. The Soviet Union, possibly deciding that there were more fruitful aspects of space research to pursue, seemed to have withdrawn from the race to the moon, but this did nothing to dull the Americans' sense of achievement. In many ways, it was not the lifeless moon which fired the imagination, but the pictures of the earth which were obtained from that vantage point.

With travel to the moon becoming possible, it was not unreasonable to expect an improvement in transport on earth as well. *Concorde* held out the hope of vastly reduced journey times and flight faster than the speed of sound. The first half-hour test flight took place in France in March, but the *ILN* noted:

> *Substantial hurdles still lie ahead ... The yardsticks of performance and finance will be applied ever more keenly. Already many anxieties have been laid to rest. Now the job is to prove to businessmen that* Concorde *is viable as well as flyable.* (8 March)

Concorde overcame the hurdles but remained an expensive and exclusive vehicle. It was the Boeing 747, which took to the air for the first time in February, which became the standard mode of travel for long-haul flights.

Monty Python's Flying Circus, first broadcast in October, had, of course, nothing to do with flying, nor with circuses, but everything to do with humour. Those inclined to analyse such things saw it as a visual successor to the humour of *The Goon Show*. There were plenty who considered John Lennon and Yoko Ono's attempt to bring about world peace through lying in bed for a week in March as another singularly funny event, and there was little sign that the gesture had its desired effect.

This year also marked the deployment of British troops in Northern Ireland, following bitter sectarian fighting there, and a whole new chapter of death, destruction and mutilation. Ian Lyon, in a piece in the *ILN* on *Battles in Ulster*, wrote:

> *To many at Westminster, it seems incredible that Britain should suddenly be haunted by the ghosts of the Irish troubles ... That British troops on UK soil should patrol streets and hope to stop civil war is a horror beyond normal duty ... When Miss Bernadette Devlin entered the Commons she brought grim warnings of impending disturbances. But London ... never really bothered with ... her remarks. It was thought simply splendid that someone so petite should go to the Commons at 21. It was really rather super that Modern Youth should have its say, though not many actually considered what she was saying.* (23 August)

In Vietnam the war raged on. In the Middle East, Yasser Arafat became head of the PLO. As the decade ended there was much talk of making love and not war, but events seemed to be heading in the opposite direction.

Welsh occasion: Prince Charles was formally invested as Prince of Wales by the Queen at Carnarvon Castle. 'In a simple but moving speech, he gave his pledge to associate himself in word and deed with the life of the Welsh people...' (5 July 1969)

Ulster wreckage: a British Bren-gunner, weary amidst debris in riot-torn Belfast. 'As Belfast held its breath in an uneasy peace guarded by British troops, citizens, Roman Catholic and Protestant alike, counted the cost.' (30 August 1969)

THE ILLUSTRATED
LONDON NEWS.

1969

E·V·E·N·T·S

3 FEBRUARY Palestine National Congress
appointed Yasser Arafat to head PLO
17 MARCH Golda Meir became Israel's first
woman premier
8 JUNE General Franco closed the land border
between Spain and Gibraltar
1 JULY Formal investiture of the Prince of
Wales at Carnarvon Castle
21 JULY Neil Armstrong became the first man
on the moon
1 SEPTEMBER King Idris of Libya deposed by
rebels led by Mu'ammar Gaddafi

Maiden flight: 'By the end of next
year, sailors, basking whales and . . .
Eskimos will have had an
opportunity of getting used to the
sonic booms . . .' (8 February 1969)

Vast leap for mankind: an
American astronaut on the moon.
'This epic belongs to the whole of
mankind—not just the Americans.'
(26 July 1969)

1970

T HE YEAR OPENED with the lowering of the age of majority from 21 to 18, with effect from 1 January. It was a triumph for the youth culture, but any impression that the 1970s would be a decade of youthful optimism and fresh vigour was misleading. The country was on the verge of a period of general pessimism, apathy and uneasy introspection.

The Vietnam War was dragging on, psychologically doing more damage to the USA than it was to the Viet Cong, as protests and demonstrations continued. B-52 bombers pounded the Ho Chi Minh Trail, along which North Vietnamese reinforcements and supplies were moving into Laos. Further south, Cambodia was also threatened, and at the end of April the Americans launched an attack on the Viet Cong forces there. In May an anti-war demonstration at Kent State University in Ohio turned to tragedy when the National Guard opened fire on the crowd and four students were shot dead.

There was no peace in Northern Ireland either, with riots in Londonderry and Armagh at Easter and numerous outbreaks of violence. In August British soldiers in Belfast used rubber bullets for the first time to quell a demonstration. Writing in the *ILN* the following month, Ulster MP Gerry Fitt complained:

> *The average Englishman, when forced face-to-face with his government's continuing 'Irish problem', almost automatically tends to embrace that trite, convenient, conscience-saving formula: 'The Irish—fighting among themselves again. Will they never settle their age-old religious squabbles?'* (5 September)

Harold Wilson called a general election in May, confident of a third consecutive Labour victory, and every indication appeared that he was right. On the eve of the election in June, a poll put Labour ahead by eight per cent and the bookmakers showed Labour as the clear favourite. But on the day there was the lowest turnout since the 1930s—72 per cent. Too many Labour voters stayed at home and Edward Heath led the Conservatives to victory with an overall majority of 30. Mrs Margaret Thatcher, a figure not well known to most electors at this time, moved into greater prominence when she was appointed Secretary of State for Education and Science.

The new decade brought with it signs of the times and of the future. International terrorism's prospects had brightened when Colonel Gaddafi came to power in Libya in September 1969. He now became both Prime Minister and Minister of Defence there. The link between pop music and the drug culture was underlined by the deaths of two rock stars from drug overdoses—Jimi Hendrix and Janis Joplin, both aged 27. That the 1960s were really over was clear from the fact that the Beatles were now suing each other.

The first jumbo jet arrived at Heathrow in January, inaugurating a new age of mass air travel. A South African cricket tour of England had to be called off because anti-apartheid protesters threatened to disrupt it. To the dismay of lovers of the Authorised Version, the New English Bible sold like hot cakes. One person at least thought there was something good about Britain—Natalia Makarova danced *Giselle* at the Royal Festival Hall with the Kirov Ballet to ecstatic reviews, and took the opportunity to defect to the West.

Showing the red card: forward into prosperity in China with the 'Thoughts' of Chairman Mao, on a 1970 poster. The 'great leap forward' of the 1950s had attempted to bring about a dramatic improvement in Chinese industrial productivity.

Solo dance: Soviet ballerina Natalia Makarova, in London with the Kirov Ballet, telephoned the police to say she wished to stay in Britain. Rudolf Nureyev, her previous partner, had defected nine years before.

1971

IN FEBRUARY Britain lived through a second D-Day—Decimal Day. The new decimal coins tolled the passing bell for the familiar shilling, florin and half-crown.

D-Day itself was a Monday and Lord Fiske, the Chairman of the Decimal Currency Board, sallied out decimal shopping. The *ILN* reported doubtfully:

> *At the end of the first day he said he was 'delighted' with the 'smooth and efficient changeover'. However, business on the first day was less brisk than usual— some housewives seemed reluctant to brave the new currency—and Lord Fiske is keeping his fingers crossed until the busy weekend shopping period.* (February)

To the accompaniment of much pleasurable grumbling the new currency was quickly accepted.

Decimalisation was part of Britain moving closer to Europe. Edward Heath saw Europe as Britain's only hope of a return to greatness, and negotiations for joining the EEC went on for months, while the political parties were sharply divided over the issue. A substantial minority of Conservative MPs opposed entry; a sizeable number of Labour members were in favour, but the Labour Party Conference in October came down heavily against entry.

In the House of Commons on 28 October entry was approved in principle by a majority of 112 votes, but one MP in five had voted against his party's line in the greatest display of independence in 30 years. The media were mainly in favour, but poll after poll found the British public fundamentally uncaring. Certainly there was no great enthusiasm for going in.

Inflation and unemployment figures were rising. Angus Maude, discussing *The Pace of Economic Recovery* in the *ILN*, warned. 'If the unemployment figures hit the one million mark, it will be a political event of very great significance . . . we might witness for the first time . . . genuine technological unemployment.' Meanwhile, the government's relations with trade unions were also deteriorating because of its attempt to diminish union power and curb unofficial strikes and industrial action. Tribunals and a National Industrial Relations Court were to be introduced to administer the law. The TUC mounted a formidable campaign, with a 140,000-strong demonstration in London chanting 'kill the bill' and a series of one-day strikes, but the Industrial Relations Act came into force in August. The next month, ominously, the miners demanded a 47 per cent pay rise.

Things went from bad to worse in Northern Ireland as well. A British soldier was killed during fighting in February: he would be the first of many. From August, on the advice of the new Ulster premier, Brian Faulkner, suspected IRA terrorists were interned without trial. Murders and bombings then proliferated, and growing violence stiffened Protestant resistance to making concessions to the Roman Catholics.

In mainland Britain, meanwhile, bombs were set off by a group calling itself the Angry Brigade, which turned out to be a few middle-class students protesting against capitalism, advertising, and the acquisitive society. They were packed off to prison— the judge said they had 'a warped understanding of sociology'— but their activities reinforced many people's feeling that violence for violence's sake was spreading like a cancer.

Going decimal: D-Day this year saw a successful invasion of Britain's shores from the Continent, instead of the other way round. Children were taught about the new decimal coins in school and the general public was indoctrinated for six weeks in an intensive campaign on television and radio, and in the newspapers.

On the way to a win:
a wave from Mr Heath at
a polling station near his
London home in June, as
the Conservatives went
into an election in which
they were given little
chance by opinion polls.
'The results of the
general election were a
slap in the face for the
opinion polls. It will be
years before they fully
recover their credibility
in Britain . . . From the
moment the first results
began to flow in the
soothsayers faced a
disaster.' (27 June 1970)

1970

E · V · E · N · T · S

1 JANUARY Age of majority lowered from 21 to
18 in Britain
12 JANUARY Civil war in Nigeria ended, with
defeat of Biafran rebels
19 JUNE Edward Heath became Prime Minister
in surprise election victory
5 OCTOBER Anwar Sadat nominated to succeed
Nasser as Egyptian President
9 NOVEMBER Charles de Gaulle, former French
President, died aged 79

Casting stones: protests broke out in
Londonderry when Bernadette Devlin's
appeal against a six-month sentence for
incitement to riot was turned down: she
was the independent MP for mid-Ulster.
Stones were hurled at troops.

1971

E·V·E·N·T·S

2 JANUARY 66 killed at football match at Ibrox Park, Glasgow

25 JANUARY General Idi Amin became President of Uganda

29 MARCH Murderer Charles Manson sentenced to death in Los Angeles

24 APRIL In Washington DC, 200,000 demonstrated against Vietnam War

5 NOVEMBER Princess Anne voted Sportswoman of the Year

17 DECEMBER Two-week war between India and Pakistan ended

Cloudless morning: setting aside all the troubles with the trade unions and with Ireland, the Prime Minister, Edward Heath, triumphantly led the British team to a victory in the Admiral's Cup yacht races, which had first been held in 1957. The three winning British boats were *Cervantes IV*, *Prospect of Whitby* and the Prime Minister's own *Morning Cloud*.

Aftermath of a football horror: at a local derby match in Glasgow between Rangers and Celtic at the Rangers' Ibrox Park ground, 66 people were crushed to death when crowd barriers collapsed in a surge of excited fans from the back of the stands.

Soaring to success: eventing gained considerably in popularity during the 1960s, and in 1971 Princess Anne was named Sportswoman of the Year for her prowess as a rider and her contribution to the sport. Earlier in the year she had won the Burghley Three-Day Event on her horse Doublet.

BRITAIN WAS SOON TO JOIN THE EEC. At the signing ceremony on 22 January a protester threw a bottle of ink at the Prime Minister. Worse than ink was spilled eight days later, on 'Bloody Sunday' in Londonderry, when British paratroopers, attacked by rioters, opened fire and killed 13 people. The IRA vowed to kill as many British soldiers as it could, and went on to take the lives of five women, a gardener and a Roman Catholic priest, with a bomb at the Parachute Brigade's headquarters in Aldershot. In March, to Protestant protests, the Heath government imposed direct rule of Northern Ireland from London.

Industrial strife was bitter, too. The miners went on strike in January. The government had made no preparations, coal stocks at power stations were low and in February more than 1½ million people were laid off or working reduced hours. At home everyone suffered through hours of black-outs. A hastily appointed court of inquiry, the Wilberforce Commission, recommended a 20 per cent pay increase, which the miners accepted. The government was humiliated and there was more trouble to come, with the railway unions and the dockers.

A new tactic in the strike had been the use of 'flying pickets'—strikers who went to depots and power stations to stop coal supplies moving. One detachment of Yorkshire pickets was led by an area official named Arthur Scargill, who boasted to all who would listen of the potential power of the working class.

Unemployment had risen above the million mark in January. To take advantage of joining Europe, Mr Heath and his Chancellor of the Exchequer, Anthony Barber, decided to cut taxes, boost demand and aim for dramatic growth in the economy. Unfortunately, this policy was to prove highly inflationary.

In September talks began between the government, the TUC and the Confederation of British Industry (CBI) to secure an agreed policy on the economy, wages and industrial relations. The discussions broke down in November, but the TUC leaders enjoyed a satisfying sense of their own importance. The government now announced a 90-day freeze on pay, dividends and most prices, to be followed by statutory controls.

An administration which had meant to give Britain's economy free rein had ended up putting it in leading strings. Ruefully justifying this reversal, the *ILN*'s political correspondent Angus Maude thought that 'there was great political pressure on the government to make at least a show of *governing*. The public is now solidly behind Mr Heath.'

Future patterns were glimpsed when five of Oxford's all-male colleges announced plans to accept women students. Memories of the past were stirred by the death in May of the Duke of Windsor, the former King Edward VIII. Thousands filed past his coffin in St George's Chapel, Windsor.

Meanwhile, on an international level, the onward march of terrorism continued with a massacre at Tel Aviv airport, when three Japanese Red Army men opened fire at random. In September, members of the Israeli team at the Olympic Games in Munich were taken hostage by 'Black September' Palestinian terrorists and killed in a gun battle.

The Vietnam War seemed at last to be approaching its end. In June there was a mysterious burglary at the Watergate building in Washington; five men were arrested, accused of 'bugging' the headquarters of the opposition Democratic Party there. In November President Nixon was re-elected by a landslide.

Grace and terror: Olga Korbut was a star of the Munich Games, which were overshadowed by terrorism. 'The Olympic peace was broken early on September 5 when guerrillas . . . attacked the quarters of the Israeli athletes, and killed two and took nine hostages.' (October 1972)

Two queens and one who might have been: the Duchess of Windsor at the funeral of the Duke, who in the 1920s had 'embodied the hopes and aspirations of those who had survived the First World War. It was glad, confident morning in those days . . .' (July 1972)

Champion of champions: 22-year-old Mark Spitz, the brilliant American swimmer, won seven gold medals at the Olympic Games in Munich, the most ever won by any athlete in the history of the games. He is seen here after his triumph in the 100m butterfly.

1972

E·V·E·N·T·S

9 JANUARY The *Queen Elizabeth* caught fire and sank in Hong Kong

30 JANUARY 'Bloody Sunday' riot in Londonderry; 13 killed

28 MAY The Duke of Windsor, formerly King Edward VIII, died aged 77

11 AUGUST US combat troops withdrew from South Vietnam

7 NOVEMBER Richard Nixon re-elected US President by a landslide

30 DECEMBER President Nixon halted US air offensive against North Vietnam

Burning issue: Vietnamese children were horribly burned and disfigured by napalm dropped by American planes. President Nixon was working hard to bring American involvement in South Vietnam to an end at last, and his visit to China this year 'started "the long process of building a bridge" across 12,000 miles and 22 years of non-communication'. (April 1972)

Great Events

1973

THE BATTLE between the Heath government and the unions went on all year. In January the government unveiled the second phase of its wages and prices programme: pay rises were limited to a maximum of £1 a week plus four per cent. The unions marked May Day with a one-day national strike which called out 1½ million people, and in September, 20 unions were expelled from the TUC for complying with the government's Industrial Relations Act.

In October, Egypt and Syria suddenly attacked Israel on Yom Kippur, the solemn Jewish day of repentance and fasting. The Israelis counter-attacked with such effect that they had crossed the Suez Canal and established outposts within 60 miles of Cairo by the time a ceasefire was agreed at the United Nations. In protest against US support for Israel, the Arab oil-producing countries announced huge price rises, which by the end of the year virtually quadrupled the cost of oil.

In Britain, trouble loomed again with the National Union of Mineworkers (NUM), which turned down a 13 per cent pay rise and banned all overtime. As coal supplies at power stations dropped, the government declared an emergency. In December Mr Heath announced a three-day week for industry, and a crisis budget chopped £1,200,000,000 off public spending. Under the headline BACK TO HARD TIMES, the *ILN* remarked that if the British character really showed its best in adversity, we could expect an opportunity to prove it again this winter.

Meanwhile, trouble continued in Northern Ireland and the IRA carried out a bombing campaign on the British mainland. The government was negotiating with the Ulster political parties to set up a power-sharing executive in the province. There was also a cod war, fought between British and Icelandic gunboats over fishing rights in northern waters.

A ceasefire in Vietnam, agreed in January, brought the war to an end for the USA, which had lost about 50,000 men in action. President Nixon said that the USA had achieved its objectives; the North Vietnamese said that right had defeated wrong. Neither side said that South Vietnam now lay open to a Communist takeover, though that was what would happen.

The USA was to suffer further psychological damage as the Watergate investigation came closer and closer to the White House and the President himself. At the end of April four of Nixon's principal aides resigned, implicated in the cover-up. On Watergate, the *ILN* suggested that:

> *If he is to overcome his latest and greatest crisis, which everyone must hope he will, for a lame President sets the world on a limp, Mr Nixon ... must open the doors of the White House so that power becomes more of a two-way process.* (June)

In July President Nixon refused to hand over tapes of his conversations, however, and by the time some were surrendered in October, there was serious talk of impeachment.

April had seen the death at 91 of Pablo Picasso, widely regarded as the greatest artist of the century. Two British politicians produced phrases which would stick in people's minds: Mr Heath spoke of 'the unpleasant and unacceptable face of capitalism' and Mr Healey, the Shadow Chancellor of the Exchequer, of 'taxing the rich until the pips squeak'.

Looking under stones: the US Senate investigation of the Watergate affair, in session. 'It is hard to believe now that confidence can be effectively restored in the Government while Mr Nixon remains at its head, in spite of his vigorous counter-attack in his television address to the nation on August 15.' (September 1973). Hearings began in May under the chairmanship of Senator Ervin of North Carolina, and the proceedings were televised.

Turning the tables: General Moshe Dayan, with his piratical black eye-patch, visiting the Israeli troops on the west bank of the Suez Canal, which they crossed in October. 'The United Nations Security Council's meetings were ineffectual ... The threat to world peace is evident. The resolution needed to end the conflict that threatens it has yet to be displayed.' (November 1973)

1973

E·V·E·N·T·S

23 JANUARY Ceasefire declared in Vietnam
after Paris peace talks
1 APRIL Value Added Tax (VAT) came into
effect in Britain
17 MAY Televised hearings into the Watergate
affair began in the USA
26 OCTOBER A UN-backed ceasefire ended war
between Israel, Egypt and Syria
14 NOVEMBER Wedding of HRH Princess
Anne to Captain Mark Phillips
28 DECEMBER Solzhenitsyn's *The Gulag
Archipelago* published in Paris

Death of a genius: Pablo Picasso,
regarded by many people as the
greatest creative figure in modern
art, died this year, aged 91. Born in
Spain, he had settled in Paris as a
young painter and spent the rest of
his life in France.

Princess Anne's wedding: 'Even
amid the heraldic trumpets, the
dress uniforms, the royal velvet and
the Gothic splendours of
Westminster Abbey, the familiar
and unambiguous words retained
their dignity and force. Princess
Anne had asked that the wedding
be kept as simple as possible . . .'
(December 1973)

1974

THE MOST SENSATIONAL event of the year was President Nixon's resignation in August. Faced with a collapse of support in Congress and the prospect of impeachment, he stepped down—the first holder of his office ever to do so. He was succeeded by Vice-President Gerald Ford. In a pen-picture in the *ILN*, Louis Heren dismissed Lyndon Johnson's jibe that Mr Ford was inept:

> *Ford is shrewd enough, but I doubt that he has ever had an original thought . . . He is typical of a certain type of Middle Westerner, as simple as their qualities are praiseworthy; hard-working, patriotic and God-fearing.* (August)

Britain had a new administration, too. In January, with the three-day week in force, the government and the unions were still at loggerheads. Mr Heath nearly called a general election, but delayed, which some Conservative critics thought was a crucial mistake. On 4 February a ballot of the miners produced an 81 per cent vote to strike. Three days later the election was called, for 28 February.

In the event, there was no decisive outcome. The Conservatives had slightly more votes than Labour, but ended with four fewer seats. The Liberal vote rose to almost 20 per cent. After a vain attempt to cobble together a coalition with the Liberals, Edward Heath left 10 Downing Street and Harold Wilson strode in. The miners' strike was swiftly settled with a 22 per cent pay rise on basic rates, the country returned to the normal five-day week and the Industrial Relations Act was abolished. Inflation was galloping out of control, however, at 16 per cent in June and 20 per cent by the end of the year. Under the 'Social Contract', the new government relied on the unions to keep pay demands within reasonable bounds in return for policies to their liking.

A second election was held in October. Another unpopularity contest, it gave Labour an overall parliamentary majority of only three, a healthy lead over the Conservatives nevertheless. North of the border the Scottish Nationalists won 11 seats.

The IRA's bombing campaign reached a peak of ugliness in the autumn, when bombs exploded in crowded pubs in Guildford and Birmingham, killing and maiming many soldiers and civilians.

Although the Heath government had fallen, its local government reorganisation went into effect on April Fool's Day. County boundaries were altered and four English counties—Cumberland, Westmorland, Rutland and Huntingdon—disappeared into others. Numerous historic Welsh and Scottish counties went with them. The three Yorkshire Ridings vanished as well, and inhabitants of the old East Riding found themselves living in Humberside. There was even an attempt to re-christen Shropshire as Salop, but it foundered on general derision.

Muhammad Ali came back into his own in November, defeating George Foreman for the heavyweight championship and so regaining the title which had been stripped from him. At the end of the year a disappearance and a reappearance excited interest. Lord Lucan vanished from view after the murder of the Lucan family nanny, while a former Labour minister named John Stonehouse, who had departed from Miami, Florida, leaving his clothes on the beach, was arrested in Australia.

Prime Minister again: Mr Harold Wilson won two elections in 1974, both with slender majorities, following power cuts, the three-day week and the parlous state of the economy. 'The Labour Government is pledged to make a mixed economy work, and to do so its priority must now be to rescue British industry.' (October 1974). Events later proved it was unable to do so.

The man who disappeared: the seventh Earl of Lucan, known to his gambling associates as 'Lucky', went missing towards the end of the year after the violent death of his family's nanny and the wounding of his wife. Despite reports that he was later sighted in various parts of Britain, South Africa and Australia, police never found the man of whom his wife had shrieked: 'He's murdered my nanny!'

THE ILLUSTRATED
LONDON NEWS

1974

E·V·E·N·T·S

11 JANUARY World's first surviving sextuplets born in South Africa

14 FEBRUARY Author Alexander Solzhenitsyn expelled from USSR

4 MARCH Edward Heath resigned as British Prime Minister

24 MAY Duke Ellington, American band leader, died aged 75

8 AUGUST President Nixon resigned as a result of the Watergate scandal

12 SEPTEMBER Emperor Haile Selassie of Ethiopia deposed

Goodbye, Watergate: Richard Nixon, the only President to leave office under threat of impeachment, boarding the White House helicopter. '… his ill-judged attempt to put the office and those who worked for it above the law will inevitably colour the final historical assessment of his Administration.' (September 1974)

Swearing not to lie: Gerald Ford was sworn in at the White House on 9 August. His main task 'was to steady the nation after the trauma of Watergate and the unprecedented resignation of a President.' (September 1974). Nixon's admission that he had obstructed the course of justice led his supporters to promise impeachment if he did not go willingly.

1975

IN FEBRUARY, Margaret Thatcher ran against Edward Heath for the leadership of the Conservative Party. On the first ballot of Conservative MPs she received 130 votes against 119 for Heath. He resigned in dignified disgust and a second ballot confirmed the 49-year-old Mrs Thatcher as the first woman ever to lead a major political party in Britain.

Mrs Thatcher's task, according to the *ILN*:

> *... will be to persuade the country that the party she leads is ready to take over the government. For this Conservative policies will have to be re-fashioned and then clearly defined and explained, for they will have to attract a substantial number of those who twice voted against the Conservative Party last year. To regain office the party will need to broaden, not narrow, its base, for it is still in the middle ground that elections are won.* (March)

The new leader, however, believed that the middle ground of politics had moved too far to the left. She intended to move the party, and eventually the country, decisively to the right: though many doubted whether a woman could win a general election.

Mrs Thatcher's success reflected a trend towards greater equality between the sexes. Equal pay for equal work was still a distant goal in practice, but in the mid-1970s women's wages were moving up towards 75 per cent of men's. The position of women before the law had improved and more women were entering the professions. Though there were still few women in Parliament, the number of women trade unionists was rising. So was the number of abortions.

At the end of the year the Wilson government's Sex Discrimination Act came into force, mainly with the aim of making it illegal to discriminate against women in employment, education, and in job advertisements. A new Equal Opportunities Commission was set up to police the act.

In the spring, Cambodia fell to the Communist Khmer Rouge, led by Pol Pot, and by the summer, stories of appalling atrocities had begun to seep out of the country. South Vietnam could no longer hold out either. North Vietnamese tanks rumbled into Saigon almost unopposed, amid scenes of panic as people fought to get on the last planes out. Saigon was renamed Ho Chi Minh City. Boatloads of desperate South Vietnamese refugees struggled to reach Asian ports.

Not much notice was taken in Britain, which was preoccupied with its own troubles. In June two-thirds of the votes cast in a referendum on the EEC were for staying in, but inflation had now reached 25 per cent and the pressure for high pay increases was inevitably intense. Meanwhile, the productivity of the British industrial worker was only between one-half and one-third of his equivalent in Japan and West Germany, and there was fierce criticism of the incompetence of British management. In July the government limited wage increases to £6 a week on incomes up to £8,500 a year. No rises were allowed on incomes above that figure, and price controls were continued.

One small gleam of light was cast by the arrival onshore in June of Britain's first oil from the North Sea, welcomed by Energy Minister Tony Benn. Otherwise it was a gloomy year, which notched up a record total of bankruptcies.

Before the fall: refugees in a tented camp near Saigon, shortly before the city fell to the Viet Cong. 'The North Vietnamese onslaught on South Vietnam began with the capture of Phuoc Bibh on January 6 ... President Thieu decided he could no longer hold the Central Highlands and on March 15 ordered his troops to withdraw to the coast. This, and other retreats, created panic ... and a mass movement of refugees ... down the coastal plain to Saigon.' (May 1975)

The place of skulls: mass grave at Phnom Penh (above). 'Communications with Cambodia were cut off when Phnom Penh, the capital, surrendered on April 17. First reports, three weeks later, revealed that widespread changes had been implemented.' (June 1975). These included mass killings.

THE ILLUSTRATED LONDON NEWS

1975

E·V·E·N·T·S

11 FEBRUARY Margaret Thatcher elected leader
of Conservative Party in Britain
17 APRIL Cambodia's capital, Phnom Penh, fell
to Communist Khmer Rouge rebels
31 APRIL Saigon fell to Communist North
Vietnamese forces
5 JUNE The British voted to join the EEC in a
national referendum
21 JUNE The West Indies beat Australia at
Lords for cricket's first world cup
20 NOVEMBER General Franco, dictator of
Spain for 35 years, died aged 82

Lives and property: 'The troops occupying
Saigon met with little resistance. [The
Communists] reassured the people that their lives
and property would be protected.' (June 1975)

THE COMMENTATORS were astounded and even indignant in March, when Harold Wilson suddenly announced his resignation as Prime Minister. He was only 60. Was he ducking some fresh economic horror coming round the corner? Mr Wilson said that he had intended to retire at this point all along, and went with an Order of the Garter and a controversial resignation honours list. He was replaced by James Callaghan, who beat Michael Foot in the final ballot of Labour MPs. The Liberals had to find a new leader, too. Jeremy Thorpe resigned in May, with the media enjoying a field day over allegations of homosexuality and murderous intrigue. David Steel replaced him.

In China, Chairman Mao died, while the USA celebrated the 200th anniversary of the Declaration of Independence and elected Jimmy Carter as President. Recognising that the new President with the 'flashing smile' was something of an unknown quantity, the *ILN* noted that:

> *. . . stimulus rather than reassurance is what the American voter seems to have been looking for, and it is this which Mr Carter will be expected to provide when he takes office.* (December)

The end of the cod war in the chill waters off Iceland prefaced the hottest summer in Britain for 250 years, emptying reservoirs and inflicting water rationing. Lester Piggott won the Derby for a record seventh time, and Bjorn Borg won his first men's singles title at Wimbledon.

To considerable media alarm, 'punks' appeared on the streets—young people with spiky and weirdly coloured hairdos, bedecked with chains, tattoos, swastikas and assorted fascist and sado-masochistic gear. The Sex Pistols were the leading punk music group and their record, *Anarchy in the UK*, was released in November. The following month there was a row when they used four-letter words on television.

Meanwhile, Ulster grew no safer. In August, after three children had been killed by a car which ran out of control when its terrorist driver was shot, the children's aunt, Mairead Corrigan, led demonstrations for peace which thousands of Protestants and Roman Catholics attended. The Women's Peace Movement won the Nobel Prize, but there was no peace.

The British economy lurched on in a critical state of combined stagnation and inflation. The pound fell to below $2 for the first time ever in March, by June it was below $1.75 and in September the Chancellor of the Exchequer, Denis Healey, had to beg a £2½ billion loan from the International Monetary Fund. Unemployment levels, which were even worse in Scotland and Wales than in England, were reinforcing nationalist demands for self-government, and in December Callaghan's cabinet put forward proposals for separate Scottish and Welsh assemblies.

Britain's black population now numbered about 2 million, about 40 per cent of whom had been born here. Tensions were increasing, and on August Bank Holiday in London, hundreds of people were hurt in violence at the Notting Hill Carnival. In November the Race Relations Act attempted to outlaw racial discrimination and created a new offence of inciting to racial hatred in a public place or at a public meeting, in speech or in writing. A Race Relations Board (replaced by the Commission for Racial Equality the following year) was set up to enforce it.

Punk and junk: punks became an object of concern to the media and interest to the tourist—young people with safety pins stuck through stray bits of their anatomy, weird and wonderful hairstyles and fascist and sado-masochistic trappings. Home-made magazines with titles like *Chainsaw* and *Sniffin' Glue* celebrated the music of the leading punk rock groups.

The end of a long march: Chairman Mao Tse-tung (above) died on 9 September at the age of 82. It remained to be seen who would follow him, as he had left no designated successor. 'No one, at least for many years, is likely to be able to put himself in the commanding position, both in terms of the exercise of power and of popular veneration, that Mao enjoyed . . .' (October 1976)

THE ILLUSTRATED LONDON NEWS

1976

E·V·E·N·T·S

31 JANUARY *Concorde* went into service from
London and Paris
16 MARCH Harold Wilson announced his
resignation as Prime Minister
10 MAY Jeremy Thorpe resigned as leader of the
British Liberal Party
3 JULY Israeli commandos rescued hostages at
Entebbe Airport, Uganda
9 SEPTEMBER Mao Tse-tung, leader of
Communist China, died
2 NOVEMBER Jimmy Carter elected to US
Presidency

Dried out: the hottest summer since the eighteenth
century in Britain brought drought. 'An advertising
campaign launched by the Government with the slogan
"Save Water to Save Jobs" appeared in national
newspapers.' (October 1976). Mr Dennis Howell was
appointed as minister with special responsibility.

Smiling through: Jimmy Carter celebrating his
election to the US Presidency. ' "Our policies," he
said in a speech, "should be as open and honest
and decent and compassionate as the American
people themselves." ' (December 1976)

1977

T HE 25TH ANNIVERSARY of Elizabeth II's accession to the throne was celebrated on 6 February this year. The *ILN* marked the occasion by reproducing a photograph of her as a young woman of 25, all in black, arriving at London Airport after the death of her father, King George VI, in 1952. The *ILN* also published the following appraisal:

> *The accession of a young Queen was greeted with enthusiasm as the dawn of a new Elizabethan Age, but though Britain may be said to be a more comfortable place today than it was in 1952 there has been a lowering of national confidence rather than a resurgence of national spirit during these 25 years, prompted no doubt by the sharp decline in the country's position as a political influence and economic force in the world.*

Even so, it went on:

> *Although . . . many national institutions are blamed for the change and associated with the decline, there is one that is not, and that is the monarchy. The Queen has adjusted the style of the monarchy in many small but significant ways to keep it in tune with the rapid changes that have taken place in British society during her reign, and the measure of her achievement is that the position of the monarchy, anachronistic though it may seem to republicans and revolutionaries, is as secure and popular in Britain today as it was 25 years ago.* (February)

This conclusion was borne out when the Queen was warmly fêted and applauded everywhere she went—and she travelled more than 50,000 miles, at home and abroad—during this Silver Jubilee year. More than 100,000 letters of praise and thanks flooded in to Buckingham Palace. Republicans and revolutionaries were ignored as people cheerfully celebrated with street parties—4,000 of them in London alone—ringing of church bells, parades, races and regattas, concerts and carnivals.

On 4 May, receiving loyal addresses from her faithful Lords and Commons, the Queen pointedly reminded them that she had been crowned Queen of the United Kingdom and had no intention of forgetting it. The rebuke to Scottish and Welsh nationalism made no difference to her welcome in those parts of the realm. On 6 June Her Majesty lit a giant bonfire in Windsor Great Park and across the country a hundred beacons flamed into the night. The next day, with Prince Philip and other royals, she rode in a procession of coaches to a thanksgiving service in St Paul's Cathedral. Traditional Welsh, Scottish and English melodies were sung, and afterwards the royal couple walked to a banquet in the Guildhall, chatting to the crowds as they went.

Only in Northern Ireland did the Jubilee go sour. In her speech there the Queen said: 'People everywhere recognise that violence is senseless and wrong and that they do not want it. Their clear message is that it must stop. And that is my prayer too.' Many Roman Catholics stayed away from the festivities, and some Protestants complained because the Queen wore a green dress. The hatreds were too deep to be bridged.

Showing the flag: and showing the products as well (above), as advertisers promoted the celebration of the Queen's 25 years on the throne. The Silver Jubilee was seen as 'an opportunity to offer the Queen our thanks for her service to the nation . . . The strength of her dedication to her unique and unenviable task has won the admiration of all her subjects, which is the message we hope to convey in this year of jubilee.' (February 1977)

On the house: a colourfully bedecked house in a street in Fulham, London. Houses were draped in flags and bunting, and poodles were dyed red, white and blue, as people joined in the Jubilee festivities, which brought a welcome suspension of class hostilities and a sense of national unity and good humour.

1977

E·V·E·N·T·S

20 JANUARY Jimmy Carter inaugurated as President of the USA
6 FEBRUARY 25th anniversary of Elizabeth II's accession celebrated
27 MARCH Collision of two jumbo jets in the Canary Islands; 574 dead
2 APRIL Red Rum won the Grand National for the third time
21 APRIL Prime Minister Bhutto declared martial law in Pakistan

Giving thanks: 'About a million people crowded the streets of London on Jubilee Day, June 7, to greet the Queen as she drove from Buckingham Palace to St Paul's Cathedral for the Service of Thanksgiving, and many more … watched the proceedings on television.' (July 1977)

When the All England Croquet Club decided in 1877 to hold a lawn tennis championship to pay for the repairs to their roller, they can have had little idea of what they were really starting. The £10 profit encouraged them to repeat the event . . . and the Wimbledon Championship attracted ever-increasing attention. (June)

The *ILN* was saluting Wimbledon's centenary, with nostalgic pictures of the great players of the golden days of the past—Suzanne Lenglen, Borotra, Perry and Tilden. On the courts in the summer of 1977, Bjorn Borg scored his second triumph in the men's singles, but there was special delight when the women's singles title was won by the leading British player, Virginia Wade. Britain still desperately needed moments of greatness.

Greatness departed for rock enthusiasts worldwide when Elvis Presley died in August at *Graceland*, his palatial mansion in Memphis, Tennessee, which was promptly besieged by hundreds of thousands of mourners. Only 42, he had been the uncrowned 'king' of rock for 20 years, and in a career which earned him something like $1 billion, he transformed western popular culture. Lurid tales circulated of his last years as a recluse, hiding from the outside world, paranoid, obese and drug-ridden among his entourage and his fleet of Cadillacs. His most ardent fans could not believe that he was really dead, and people visited his shrine like pilgrims to a medieval saint.

In Britain, more prosaically, the Callaghan government was now in a minority in the Commons because of Labour by-election losses. From March Labour was sustained by the 'Lib–Lab Pact', by which the Liberals kept Labour in office as long as it did nothing they disliked, which in effect meant as long as it did nothing. The result was a period of comparative tranquillity. The rate of inflation was falling, but unemployment rose to 1½ million by the autumn.

The peace was broken by the clatter of skateboards—the craze of the year—and by the Grunwick dispute. The factory was picketed, peacefully at first, to persuade the employer to let his workers belong to a union. In June the number of pickets swelled dramatically, with students and left-wing militants joining the crowd outside the gates. The number of policemen increased correspondingly and the media were attracted to the scene like wasps to jam. There were angry confrontations and clashes, shown on television, which seriously damaged the reputations of trade unions and the Left in general, and were grist to the mill of the Conservatives, who warned of the spread of 'red fascism'.

The National Front was enjoying a temporary rise in support, fuelled by resentment of immigrants. It polled better than the Liberals in some by-elections, with support from some electors who normally voted Labour. There was more violence in August, in Lewisham, when 56 policemen were hurt in protests over a National Front march. Smoke bombs and stones were hurled at them. At the beginning of the year, there had been other protests when anti-hunting saboteurs desecrated the grave of John Peel in the Lake District.

All the more welcome were intimations that peace and love might triumph after all, in the film *Close Encounters of the Third Kind* by the young Hollywood director Steven Spielberg. Another successful science fiction film, *Star Wars*, brought audiences back to the cinemas to enjoy a classic struggle between good and evil, while John Travolta in *Saturday Night Fever* carried on the legacy of the departed Elvis.

The king is dead: sorrowing fans of Elvis Presley gathered in huge numbers outside *Graceland*, the palatial mansion of the 'king' of rock and roll, in Memphis, Tennessee. He had been found dead in one of the bathrooms on August 16. Police said that some 20,000 people managed to get inside the house, hoping for a final sight of their hero. The mansion would later be turned into a kind of cult shrine to the entertainer.

Death in the Canaries: horror struck the airport at Tenerife in the Canary Islands on 27 March, when a KLM and a Pan Am airliner collided on the runway, causing the most severe death toll in the whole history of aviation: 574 were killed. Their numbers included all the passengers on the KLM plane. Many casualties were horribly burned.

THE ILLUSTRATED LONDON NEWS

1977

E·V·E·N·T·S

16 JUNE Leonid Brezhnev appointed President
of the USSR

1 JULY British player Virginia Wade won
the women's singles at Wimbledon

5 JULY General Zia ousted Bhutto, becoming
Pakistan's military ruler

11 AUGUST Geoffrey Boycott scored 100th
century of his career at Headingley

16 AUGUST Rock 'n' roll king Elvis Presley died
at Memphis, aged 42

19 NOVEMBER President Sadat of Egypt went to
Israel for peace talks

Long live the king: Elvis Presley at the
microphone, with which he made a fortune
and transformed popular culture in the West.
Born in Missouri in 1935, and known as 'Elvis
the Pelvis' because of the suggestive way he
shook his hips, he first made a big hit in 1956
with *Heartbreak Hotel*. Other hits included
Hound Dog, Jailhouse Rock, Love Me Tender and
Blue Suede Shoes. He starred in numerous films
and many television programmes, but his last
years were overshadowed by drugs.

A centenary winner:
Bjorn Borg, Sweden's ace
tennis star, was
presented with a special
medal by the Duke and
Duchess of Kent to mark
Wimbledon's centenary
year. Borg went on to
win the men's singles title
for the second time.
There was special delight
when the women's
singles were won by a
British player, Virginia
Wade. She defeated the
Dutch star, Betty Stove,
in a tense final, in which
Miss Wade lost the first
set. The first ever
Wimbledon
championships were
played in 1877.

1978

T HE WORLD'S FIRST TEST-TUBE BABY arrived this year, on 26 July by Caesarean section at the district general hospital in Oldham. Her name was Louise Brown and she proved an appealing demonstration of the progress of science.

Inflation sank below 10 per cent, the pound rose back above the $2 mark, North Sea oil was flowing in and the balance of payments was tilting the right way, but the Callaghan government was in trouble. The Liberals ended the 'Lib–Lab Pact' and the TUC refused to go on backing wage restraints and demanded a return to free collective bargaining. Some left-wing members of the Labour Party disliked the government's incomes policy just as much as the unions did. Left-wing activists in the constituencies wanted greater control of the party in Parliament and mandatory re-selection of Labour MPs was only just voted down at the party conference, by a disputed vote cast by one union.

Mrs Thatcher and the Conservatives, meanwhile, were finding support from a web of opinions and emotions now widespread across party political boundaries. There was resentment of arbitrary trade union power, alarm at rising levels of violent crime, dislike of comprehensive education and the allegedly falling standards in schools, disapproval of left-wing intolerance and militancy, suspicion of immigrants and of welfare 'scroungers', concern about sex and violence in the media: all mingling in a broad general disapproval of lowered standards and the prevailing disrespect for authority.

Pope Paul VI died in August. The occupant of St Peter's chair since 1963, he had struggled with the trends of the times and the attack on tradition, as the *ILN* pointed out:

> *Many of his decisions were controversial, such as his encyclical* Humanae Vitae, *which reiterated firmly the Church's prohibition of artificial birth control . . . Pope Paul was firm on maintaining the integrity of the Roman Catholic faith and doctrine and unyielding on matters of authority, even in the cause of ecumenism. Yet he ended the use of Latin as the sole language in the Mass and cut down on much of the ceremony of the Vatican.* (August)

The next Pope, John Paul I, died after only a month, and in October the Cardinals' choice fell on a Polish prelate, Karol Wojtyla, Archbishop of Cracow, the first non-Italian to become Pope for four centuries. John Paul II was to prove a redoubtable and charismatic figure.

At the end of November word came of horror in Guyana. More than 900 members of an American religious group had killed themselves there by drinking cyanide, on the orders of their leader, the Reverend Jim Jones, who was among the dead.

Revolution seemed to be on the march in Iran, where trouble flared up in the autumn with mass protests against the Shah, organised by fundamentalist Muslim leaders opposed to his policy of westernising and modernising. Buildings were set on fire and tanks rolled into the streets to quell riots in November. In Tehran the following month a huge peaceful protest march through the city was said to have been joined by 4½ million people. Many of the marchers carried placards embellished with pictures of the Ayatollah Khomeini, the veteran Muslim leader exiled in Paris, who was implacably hostile to the Shah.

Pope for a month: Pope John Paul I after his election in August. Sadly, he died of a heart attack after a reign which lasted only 33 days and in October was replaced by Cardinal Karol Wojtyla of Cracow, who took the name of John Paul II. 'As he is the first non-Italian Pope for over four centuries, is the first Pole to hold the office and comes from a Communist country, his election has been greeted as a bold experiment.' (November 1978)

Mass suicide: bodies of the victims littered the ground at the headquarters of the cult led by the Reverend Jim Jones. 'The prelude to the suicides was the shooting of Leo Ryan, a Democratic Congressman from San Francisco who had gone to Jonestown . . . to investigate allegations of abuses by Jones, including imprisonment and beating of his followers . . . the commune residents, on Jones's orders, administered poison to their children and then took it themselves.' (January 1979)

THE ILLUSTRATED LONDON NEWS

1978

E · V · E · N · T · S

18 MARCH Prime Minister Bhutto of Pakistan sentenced to hang for murder

3 APRIL The BBC began regular broadcasts from the House of Commons

26 JULY The world's first test-tube baby was born in Britain

6 AUGUST Pope Paul VI died in Rome, to be succeeded by John Paul I

16 OCTOBER Cardinal Wojtyla elected Pope as John Paul II

10 DECEMBER Millions marched in Iran demanding abdication of Shah

Champion for the third time: a huge crowd in the Superdome in New Orleans watched Muhammad Ali defeat Leon Spinks over 15 rounds in September, to win the world heavyweight championship for the third time—the first fighter ever to do so. He had lost the title to Spinks in Las Vegas the previous February.

Critical blow: Muhammad Ali slamming a right to the head of Leon Spinks during his victory over Spinks in New Orleans. Many good judges regarded Ali as the finest boxer ever to hold the heavyweight title, and he always called himself 'the Greatest'. An outgoing and engaging personality, he was born in Kentucky as Cassius Marcellus Clay and changed his name to Muhammad Ali when he became a Black Muslim. He first won the title against Sonny Liston in 1964.

1979

'NOW IS THE WINTER OF OUR DISCONTENT . . .' Discontented public sector unions did their utmost to make life miserable in Britain in the early months of the year, in protest against the Callaghan government's pay ceiling. Piles of rubbish sprawled uncollected in the streets, food and petrol supplies were disrupted by striking lorry drivers, and in Liverpool the dead lay unburied. Pickets at hospitals took it upon themselves to decide who should be treated. It was one of the most damaging episodes in the Labour Party's history, and the Conservatives rocketed in the opinion polls.

Abroad, meanwhile, the Shah of Iran's people danced joyfully in the streets as he fled into exile. Crowds shouted 'God is great' as the Ayatollah Khomeini returned from exile to establish an Islamic republic. In March, Egypt and Israel ended 30 years of hostility when they signed a peace treaty.

After all the fuss about devolution, a referendum in Wales overwhelmingly turned down a Welsh assembly. Only one-third of the Scots voted for a Scottish assembly. At the end of March the Callaghan government lost a vote of confidence, the first administration to be turned out of office by a House of Commons vote in 55 years. An election was called for early May.

The poll gave the Conservatives 339 seats to Labour's 268, and Mrs Thatcher became Britain's first female Prime Minister. Analysis of the results showed a substantial switch from Labour to Conservative by working-class voters, especially in the South. The election, the *ILN* commented:

> *. . .showed a considerable regional division between north and south, but it returned a government with an overall majority for the first time in nine years, and it gave Mrs Thatcher the biggest swing that any opposition leader has achieved since the war. The election was both a personal triumph and a convincing demonstration that voters were not prejudiced against her sex.* (June)

The Labour Party, meanwhile, was thrown into disarray, and a rancorous party conference carried a motion for mandatory re-selection of MPs.

Mrs Thatcher had lost a close friend and ally in March, when the Conservative MP Airey Neave, a known hard-liner on Northern Ireland, was murdered by an IRA bomb in the House of Commons car park. Then, in August, while fishing on a customary holiday in Ireland, the 79-year-old Earl Mountbatten was killed when his boat was ripped apart by another IRA bomb. So were his 14-year-old grandson and a 17-year-old local boy; others in the party were badly hurt.

In October, 80,000 people marched through London to protest against a parliamentary bill intended to restrict abortions. In Tehran in November followers of the Ayatollah broke into the US embassy and took many of the staff hostage. Warning was given that if the USA attacked Iran the hostages would be killed, and President Carter faced a problem that would haunt him.

In the same month in London it was revealed that the distinguished art historian, Sir Anthony Blunt, had spied for the Russians, and that the fact had been kept quiet for 15 years. Finally, at Christmas, Soviet troops invaded Afghanistan to prop up a Communist regime in Kabul.

Success, spiritual: Mother Teresa was awarded the Nobel Peace Prize. Of Albanian origin, she was born Agnes Gonxha Bejaxhui in 1910 in what is now Yugoslavia. She started to help the poor and the disabled in the slums of Calcutta in the 1940s and by 1979 she had opened 700 clinics and shelters in India for the disadvantaged.

Success, political: the election on 3 May brought to office a Conservative government with a clear majority. It also brought to power Britain's first lady Prime Minister.

THE ILLUSTRATED LONDON NEWS

1979

E · V · E · N · T · S

16 JANUARY Shah of Iran driven into exile by
supporters of Ayatollah Khomeini
1 FEBRUARY Ayatollah Khomeini returned to
Iran after 14-year exile
26 MARCH Egypt and Israel signed peace treaty
in Washington DC
3 MAY Mrs Thatcher became Britain's first
woman Prime Minister
27 AUGUST Earl Mountbatten murdered on his
boat in Eire by IRA bomb
4 NOVEMBER Nearly 100 US embassy staff
taken hostage in Iran

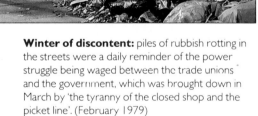

Winter of discontent: piles of rubbish rotting in
the streets were a daily reminder of the power
struggle being waged between the trade unions
and the government, which was brought down in
March by 'the tyranny of the closed shop and the
picket line'. (February 1979)

Expansion Soviet-style: the
Russian occupation of Afghanistan at
the end of December surprised the
world. Faced by widespread
condemnation and economic
sanctions, the Russians claimed they
had been invited in to support
President's Amin's tottering regime.
Fierce resistance from Muslim
guerrillas hinted that the take-over
might not be simple, and by 1980 it
was clear that more than 80,000
Russian troops were digging in for a
long campaign.

1980

WHEN THE YEAR OPENED, the world was still taking stock of the Russian invasion of Afghanistan. The build-up of Russian forces had continued and estimates put the total at 80,000 soldiers, but there was still hope that international pressure might compel Russia to withdraw. Conventional Communism was under attack on several fronts. In Poland a shipyard strike in Gdansk led to a confrontation between the government and the strikers, led by Lech Walesa, with the strikers gaining valuable concessions. Out of this was born the Solidarity movement, which quickly received full backing from the Catholic Church. The world watched and waited for the Russians to move into Poland, and when they failed to do so, hope grew that some form of liberalization might actually be tolerated.

A peaceful process of change was under way in Rhodesia. Robert Mugabe and Joshua Nkomo returned after years of exile, and Mugabe's Zimbabwe African National Union won the subsequent election. In April the Union Jack was lowered in Britain's last remaining African colony, and an unexpectedly moderate Mugabe took over as the first premier of Zimbabwe.

Elsewhere the forces of change were far from peaceful. President Carter's decision to send in the US Delta Force to try to rescue the embassy hostages in Iran backfired disastrously, when Operation Eagle Claw became a chaotic débâcle in the desert; Carter took full responsibility for the abortive raid. Later in the year, Iraq launched an attack on Iran's oil bases, the start of a Gulf war that sent shivers through the western world.

In the USA the Republicans picked former actor Ronald Reagan as their presidential candidate. The swing to the right this implied was confirmed in November when Reagan comprehensively beat Carter in an election dominated by America's need to restore its self-confidence. According to the *ILN*:

> *There was a strong note of nostalgia for old glories in Mr Reagan's campaign—for days when the nation's power was virtually undisputed, when energy was cheap and the living much easier. Those days have gone, and possibly the greatest dangers that Mr Reagan will eventually face are those of public disappointment and disillusion.* (December)

There was also an election in India, won by Mrs Gandhi, but the celebrations were cut short by the death of her eldest son, Sanjay, in a plane crash.

In Britain, unemployment figures climbed steadily throughout the year, reaching 2 million by August, the highest figure since 1936; with inflation still in excess of 20 per cent, Mrs Thatcher made her 'lady's not for turning' speech. The TUC called a nationwide day of action on 14 May. The militant tendency's plans to take over the Labour Party became widely known and Michael Foot replaced Callaghan as Labour leader. The government announced that controversial nuclear 'cruise' missiles were to be installed at Greenham Common and Molesworth, accompanied by public protests from CND and other anti-nuclear campaigners.

It was a bad year for deaths. John Lennon was shot outside his New York apartment, and representatives of 127 countries paid their last respects to President Tito. The Shah of Iran died in exile, shunned by the world.

Winning wave: Ronald Reagan's election as President of the USA in November was greeted with sneers by serried ranks of intellectual commentators. 'There is no record that Mr Reagan has ever read a book, apart from the Bible, and his mind is therefore free of the intellectual clutter that so often gets in the way of reaching simple, straightforward conclusions to all the multifarious problems of the 20th century.' (November 1980)

Waving banner: Mujahideen, or Afghan guerrilla fighters, with their Muslim standard. The Soviet invasion at Christmas time in 1979 was fiercely denounced by the Islamic countries and by the West. Opponents of the Communist regime in Kabul took up arms. There were riots in Kabul in February and numerous reports of Russian supply convoys being attacked. The Russians were soon to find themselves caught in a long and damaging struggle.

1980

E·V·E·N·T·S

4 MARCH Robert Mugabe became Prime Minister of Zimbabwe (Rhodesia)
25 APRIL US Delta Force failed to rescue US embassy hostages in Iran
5 MAY SAS men stormed the terrorist-occupied Iranian embassy in London
4 NOVEMBER Ex-actor Ronald Reagan won US presidential election
8 DECEMBER John Lennon shot and killed in New York

Rigour in Iran: the 80-year-old Ayatollah Khomeini, fundamentalist Muslim ruler of Iran. Fiercely hostile to the West and especially to the 'Great Satan', America, he impeded the efforts of the United Nations to arrange the release of the hostages who had been taken from the US embassy in Tehran late in 1979. President Carter's bid to rescue them failed miserably in April 1980.

Protest in Poland: striking Solidarity men in Gdansk. The Soviet Union held its hand and did not intervene in the dispute between the Polish Communist regime and the Solidarity movement. '. . . whatever happens to Poland in the future, the implications of what has happened so far will make an impact on the rest of eastern Europe. What Russia has permitted there, she is less likely to deny elsewhere.' (November 1980)

1981

O N 24 FEBRUARY the Prince of Wales' engagement to Lady
Diana Spencer was announced and Britain prepared to
celebrate the Royal Wedding on 29 July. This was a
splendid spectacle, watched live on television by 700 million
people round the world. The *ILN* noted that:

> *No last minute impediments were confessed, everyone
> arrived on time, the day was blessed with warmth and
> even some sunshine and the occasion was a memorable
> blend of punctilious pomp, traditional formality... and
> popular enthusiasm, with a new edge of conscientious
> but not too obtrusive security.* (August)

The wedding was the high point of an otherwise rather
difficult year. There were riots in many parts of Britain, with the
worst of the violence in Brixton and Liverpool. Lord Scarman's
inquiry into the Brixton riots was quickly launched, while
Michael Heseltine took charge in Liverpool, announcing bold
development plans for the city's derelict south dock area and a
£95,000,000 aid package for inner cities. The situation in Northern
Ireland worsened with the start of the IRA hunger strike
campaign, led by Bobby Sands; Sands' death provoked angry riots
in Belfast. In all, 10 IRA hunger strikers died before the campaign
was called off. In May Peter Sutcliffe was jailed for life, after being
found guilty of committing the Yorkshire Ripper murders.

Inflation had fallen to 15 per cent, but unemployment
continued to climb. The Labour Party drifted further to the left,
but still captured the Greater London Council (GLC) in local
elections, with Ken Livingstone emerging as the GLC's leader.
The 'Gang of Four' (Dr David Owen, Shirley Williams, Roy
Jenkins and William Rodgers) launched the Social Democratic
Party (SDP) in January, and several sitting Labour MPs joined this
new party. Following the SDP's alliance with the Liberals, the
Alliance celebrated its first election victory at Croydon
North-West.

Overseas, violent events continued to make headlines.
President Reagan was wounded in an attempt by a 25-year-old
disc jockey to assassinate him, and the Pope was shot and
wounded in Rome by a Turkish dissident. Both recovered, but in
Egypt army officers assassinated President Sadat and Vice-
President Mubarak succeeded him. Even the Queen was shot at in
the Mall, but luckily only with blanks. In Iran, now involved in a
full-scale war with Iraq, the US embassy hostages were released
after 444 days in captivity. Israel bombed an Iraqi nuclear reactor
in course of construction, and claimed she had a nuclear capability
and would use it against Arab aggression. Israel then bombed
Beirut, and broadened her attacks against the PLO. A further
threat to human life became evident with the first reports of a new,
and as yet unnamed, incurable disease among homosexual communities in Los Angeles, San Francisco and New York.

British sporting events now included the London marathon,
first won by an American, Dick Beardsley. Steve Davis became the
World Snooker Champion, John McEnroe ended Bjorn Borg's
domination of Wimbledon, Oxford's first girl cox steered the
team to victory in the Boat Race, and Bob Champion and Aldaniti
triumphed over illness and injury to win the Grand National.
England retained the Ashes, and Geoffrey Boycott took the
record for the most runs scored in Test matches.

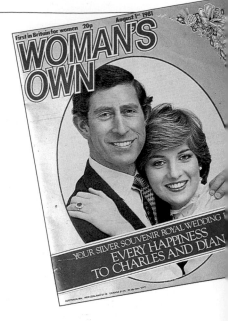

Royal magic: the romantic dreams of millions
of women, fired by the announcement of Lady
Diana Spencer's engagement to Prince Charles,
came to a head at the Royal Wedding in July.

Double victory: Bob Champion's gripping
story of his fight against cancer was published in
September, an event underlining the
miraculous way in which he had recovered to
win the Grand National earlier in the year on
Aldaniti, the horse which had also struggled to
overcome serious leg injuries.

Best-kept secret: the high point of the Royal
Wedding on 29 July was for many Lady Diana's
dress, '... made by Emmanuel of London, of
ivory pure silk taffeta and old lace ... with a
lace flounce round the neck ... there was a
sweeping train, 25 feet long, trimmed with
embroidered lace.' (August 1981)

Brixton violence: a police van burned on a rubble-strewn street '. . . during a weekend of rioting, mainly by black youths . . . which began after a stabbing incident.' (June 1981). Hundreds of injuries and widespread looting prompted a public inquiry, headed by Lord Scarman.

THE ILLUSTRATED
LONDON NEWS

1981

E · V · E · N · T · S

2 JANUARY Released US hostages flown from Iran to Algeria

25 JANUARY Social Democratic Party formed in the UK by the 'Gang of Four'

13 MAY Assassination attempt on the Pope in Rome

30 JUNE Blanks fired at the Queen during the Trooping of the Colour

29 JULY Prince Charles married Lady Diana Spencer in St Paul's Cathedral

1982

THROUGHOUT THE YEAR two countries remained firmly in the headlines. In Poland riots over rises in food prices marked the start of the year, and 3,500 people were arrested for violating martial law. At the end of March there was a brief respite and the curfew was lifted, martial law was relaxed and political prisoners were released, but further restrictions were quickly imposed against a background of increasing civil strife. Solidarity demonstrations were broken up by tear gas and water cannon, and in October Solidarity was outlawed as riot police and troops filled the streets. At the end of the year, Lech Walesa's unexpected release from prison reduced tension.

In the Middle East the Iran–Iraq war escalated, with Iran now on the offensive and threatening the oil port of Basra. However, the focus had now switched to the Lebanon following the Israeli invasion in late June. Beirut was bombarded as Israeli troops fought to drive the PLO out of the city, and soon the city was being destroyed by violent sectarian fighting. The president-elect of Lebanon, Gemayel, was killed by a car bomb and the Christian militia massacred Palestinian refugees in Beirut camps, causing outrage throughout the world. Even in Israel there were anti-government demonstrations. A multi-national peace-keeping force landed in a vain attempt at ending the strife in Beirut.

The USA announced it was sending assistance to the El Salvador government, while in neighbouring Nicaragua the Sandinista government declared a state of emergency, fearing intervention by the USA. In November the Soviet leader Leonid Brezhnev died and was succeeded by Yuri Andropov.

The Pope's visit to Britain in May helped to unite the nation, divided by social unrest and the Falklands War. In the words of the *ILN*:

> He came, he was seen and, as everywhere, he con-
> quered many hearts, and not only among Roman
> Catholics ... Britain was still at war with Argentina
> when he left for Rome that evening, but perhaps more
> at peace with itself as a result of his visit. (June)

The IRA bombed the Horse Guards and the band of the Royal Green Jackets in Regent's Park. The nation watched while the horse, Sefton, gradually recovered from injuries received during the bombing. In Ulster, violence reached a peak on 6 December when 16 died in a bomb attack on a pub disco. The Sinn Fein leaders invited to Britain by the GLC were banned from entering the country by the government.

At the start of the year Sir Freddie Laker's airline collapsed, leaving passengers stranded. Unemployment in Britain topped 3 million and the pound slid steadily downhill against the dollar. Ronald Reagan made history as the first US President to address a joint session of the British Parliament. On 21 June the Princess of Wales gave birth to her first son, Prince William. Europe's largest arts and conference centre was opened at the Barbican, and Henry VIII's flagship, the *Mary Rose*, was raised from the seabed. The inland telegram service ended, replaced by the telemessage, and the 20p coin went into circulation. Channel Four went on air, and the government gave the go-ahead to satellite television. In September the Greenham Common Peace Camp was established, and at the end of the year 20,000 women linked arms to encircle the base in a demonstration against cruise missiles.

Circle of protest: some of the 20,000 women demonstrators who linked arms to encircle the entire nine-mile perimeter of the American air base at Greenham Common in December. Women came from all over the country to protest at the proposed deployment of American nuclear cruise missiles in Berkshire; many were arrested.

Running for dear life: a woman of Abadan, Iran, with her daughter, fleeing for cover as their home was bombed by Iraqi aircraft in January. Fighting in the Iran–Iraq war intensified in March, and in May Iran claimed a notable victory with the recapture of the oil port of Khorramshahr from Iraq. The war ground bloodily on for the remainder of the year.

THE ILLUSTRATED LONDON NEWS

1982

E · V · E · N · T · S

3 MARCH The Barbican Arts Centre was opened by the Queen in London
28 MAY John Paul II arrived on first papal visit to Britain since 1531
20 JULY IRA bombs killed soldiers and horses in Hyde Park and Regent's Park
14 SEPTEMBER Princess Grace of Monaco was killed in a car crash
12 NOVEMBER Lech Walesa released from detention by Polish authorities
12 DECEMBER Mass protest against nuclear cruise missiles at Greenham Common

Born to be King: 'To general relief and rejoicing, the Princess of Wales safely gave birth to a son at 9.03pm on Monday, June 21 after a 16-hour confinement ... The Prince of Wales was present at the delivery ... The baby, Prince Charles said afterwards, was "fair and beautiful" ...' (August 1982)

Embattled leader: Lech Walesa of Solidarity. Tension between the movement and the Communist regime continued throughout the year. 'Riot police in Warsaw, Gdansk and other Polish cities on August 13 used water cannon, tear gas and batons on several thousand Solidarity protesters ... On the second anniversary of the foundation of Solidarity (August 31) there were confrontations between tens of thousands of demonstrators ... and the military in many Polish cities.' (October 1982). More than 4,000 were arrested.

For Britain, the key event of the year was the Falklands War, a conflict that no one expected, but whose rapid development from a local dispute into a major international war took the world by surprise.

In March a group of Argentine scrap merchants landed on South Georgia, an island 800 miles east of the Falklands, and raised the Argentinian flag. Then, on 2 April, without any warning, Argentine forces invaded the Falklands and captured the Governor. Britain broke off diplomatic relations with Argentina and an emergency debate at the United Nations carried a resolution supporting Britain and calling for Argentinian withdrawal. By 4 April the Falklands were under complete Argentinian control.

At great speed Britain prepared a task force and on 5 April a convoy of warships and commandeered transports, including the *Canberra*, led by the aircraft carriers *Hermes* and *Invincible*, set off on the 8,000-mile journey to the Falklands.

Despite considerable support for the war there was still a feeling that the conflict could be resolved by negotiation. The US Secretary of State, Alexander Haig, was involved in mediating in the crisis. Many people wondered whether the Falklands were worth fighting for, but as the *ILN* commented:

> *... there was more than* realpolitik *at stake. The Falkland Islands are a self-governing Crown Colony, and as such are under British protection. Their people, though few in number, have frequently indicated that they remain under British sovereignty by choice. They have been invaded and taken over by force of arms, and against their own wishes. They are entitled to protection, and to the freedom to choose their own destiny.* (May)

When Alexander Haig's mission finally failed, the USA gave full backing to Britain, and offered equipment and financial support.

On 25 April Royal Marine Commandos recaptured South Georgia and on 1 May RAF Vulcans bombed the runway at Port Stanley airfield. The next day the Argentine cruiser *General Belgrano* was sunk by the submarine *Conqueror* outside the exclusion zone. The large loss of life began to turn world opinion against Britain; and in Britain there was much debate about the future of the Falklands after the war.

The first blow for Britain came on 4 May, when HMS *Sheffield* was sunk by an Exocet missile and then, with the arrival of the task force, the war began in earnest. Events moved with great speed. On 21 and 22 May troops were landed in San Carlos Bay, despite the loss of the frigates *Ardent* and *Antelope*. British carrier-based Harriers soon began to take command of the air, but the threat posed by the Exocet was underlined by the sinking of HMS *Coventry* and the freighter *Atlantic Conveyor* on 25 May. On 29 May the Battle of Goose Green opened the road to Port Stanley and on 1 June the 5th Infantry Brigade was landed at San Carlos. The bombing of the landing craft *Sir Galahad* and *Sir Tristram* at Bluff Cove was a disastrous setback, but the advance continued and the Argentine forces surrendered on 14 June after heavy fighting around Port Stanley. Three days later General Galtieri was ousted as President of Argentina.

During July there was a formal end to hostilities, and Britain announced that all Argentine prisoners would be repatriated. On 26 July a Falklands Remembrance Service was held for the 255 British servicemen killed during the conflict.

Sinking at sea: the Argentine cruiser *General Belgrano* was sunk (left) by British torpedoes in May, outside the exclusion zone. 'From April 12 a 200-mile maritime exclusion zone was imposed by Britain around the Falkland Islands, with the warning that any Argentine warships . . . found within the zone would be liable to attack by British forces . . .' (May 1982)

Picture of the year: the Royal Navy frigate *Antelope* (below) was blown to pieces in San Carlos Bay in the Falkland Islands. The photograph won the 'News Picture of the Year' award. When the war ended in June, weary Royal Marines raised the flag (bottom).

THE ILLUSTRATED LONDON NEWS

1982

E · V · E · N · T · S

2 APRIL Argentine forces invaded the Falkland Islands

5 APRIL Ships of the British task force left Portsmouth for the Falkands

2 MAY The Argentine cruiser *General Belgrano* was sunk by British torpedoes

21–22 MAY British troops landed in San Carlos Bay

29 MAY British paratroopers defeated the Argentines at Goose Green

14 JUNE Argentine forces on the Falkland Islands surrendered

A kiss for Wales: while the Falklands War was raging, the Pope visited Britain. He is seen kissing the ground (above) on landing in Cardiff.

I N JUNE Britain went to the polls in an election that many hoped would change the shape of British politics. In the event the result was a Tory landslide, with Mrs Thatcher being returned to power with an overall majority of 144 seats. The Alliance gained 25 per cent of the vote and few seats, while Labour was devastated. In the aftermath Michael Foot was replaced by Neil Kinnock as Labour leader, and David Owen took over the SDP. While the result was a personal triumph for Mrs Thatcher, there was considerable concern about the inadequacies of the British electoral system:

> *Under almost any form of proportional representation the result of the election would have been not a Conservative landslide but a coalition government . . . Whether this would have been for the good of the country is certainly debatable . . . But it may also be questioned whether it is a properly democratic system that allows a party to more than treble its majority in Parliament when its total of votes has in fact marginally declined.* (July)

In Ireland the Derby winner Shergar was kidnapped and a £2,000,000 ransom demanded, and 134 prisoners escaped in a mass break-out from the Maze prison. In December the IRA detonated a car bomb outside Harrods. Breakfast television arrived in Britain, along with the compulsory use of seat belts in cars and the first wheel clamps.

Throughout the year, it was events overseas that took the limelight. In Beirut the Lebanese army took control but failed to stop the fighting. A car bomb destroyed the US embassy, and then suicide bombers attacked the headquarters of the US and French peace-keeping forces, killing 241 marines and 58 French paratroopers. The PLO, at the nadir of its fortunes, withdrew totally from Lebanon into Tunisia.

In March the Queen and Prince Philip were entertained by the Reagans in the USA and in the same month President Reagan launched the Strategic Defence Initiative (SDI or Star Wars). In May, Reagan announced US backing for the Contra rebels fighting the Sandinista government in Nicaragua. Later in the year, US troops invaded Grenada to stop a Marxist coup which had been launched with Cuban backing. The American action in the former British colony caused a brief chill in Anglo-American affairs.

In Poland, demonstrations continued to call for the restoration of Solidarity and in August martial law was lifted. The Pope's visit included a private meeting with Lech Walesa, and at the end of the year Walesa was awarded the Nobel Peace Prize. In Argentina democracy returned as President Alfonsin ended military rule.

In September the world was outraged when Russian fighters shot down a Korean Airlines 747, killing all 269 people on board. After days of denials the Russians grudgingly admitted responsibility, but never apologised or admitted that they had made a tragic error. The *ILN* wrote:

> *The fate of KAL 007 has tragically dramatized the inadequacies of international safeguards against potential disasters, and in a nuclear age such inadequacies are not tolerable.* (October)

Journey into space: *Challenger*, America's second space shuttle, on its adapted 747 transporter shortly after its successful maiden flight on 4 April. Later in the year, *Challenger* carried Sally Ride, the first American woman astronaut, into space.

Korean crisis: relatives of the victims of the Korean airliner downed by the Russians. '. . . the idea that nations have a right to shoot down anything that moves above their territory is unacceptable . . . the international community will have to get this message across to the Russian leaders.' (October 1983)

Tory landslide: Mrs Thatcher with her supporters after winning the June election. Labour lost heavily and the Alliance gained votes but not seats in an election that many had predicted would break the mould of British politics. 'My victory is greater than I had dared to hope,' claimed the Prime Minister, cheered by her overall majority of 144.

1983

E · V · E · N · T · S

7 FEBRUARY Iranian forces crossed the border in mass attack on Iraq

23 MARCH US President Reagan proposed new 'star wars' defence system for USA

2 OCTOBER Neil Kinnock elected leader of the British Labour Party

24 NOVEMBER Mother Teresa invested with the Order of Merit by the Queen

10 DECEMBER Alfonsin became first civilian President in Argentina for eight years

Polish progress: supporters of Solidarity, still an outlawed organisation, took to the streets in Poland again, encouraged by the lifting of martial law, the visit of the Pope, and the award of the Nobel Peace Prize to Lech Walesa, which was received on his behalf by his wife Danuta at a special ceremony in Oslo on 10 December.

INDIA DOMINATED THE NEWS, as religious strife spread through the sub-continent. There were violent confrontations between Hindus and Muslims, and the army stormed the Golden Temple at Amritsar in July to drive out armed Sikh extremists who had taken control of the Sikh shrine. The *ILN* reported the reaction:

> *The Indian Prime Minister, Mrs Indira Gandhi, was shot dead . . . in the grounds of her Delhi home by two Sikhs in her own security guard. Her son Rajiv was swiftly sworn in to succeed her . . . as Hindu mobs took revenge on the Sikh community by killing, burning and looting.* (November)

At the end of the year another disaster engulfed India as a cloud of poison gas leaked from the Union Carbide plant in Bhopal, killing and maiming thousands.

In Beirut, civil war tore the city to pieces following the withdrawal of international peace-keeping forces, while more than 900,000 took to the streets in the Philippines in popular demonstrations against the Marcos government. Corazon Aquino began to emerge as the popular choice to lead the country.

In Poland, more than 600 political prisoners were released, but the pro-Solidarity priest, Father Popieluszko, was kidnapped and murdered by the army. A crowd of 200,000 attended his funeral.

There was a change at the top in Russia, when Konstantin Chernenko took over following Yuri Andropov's death. In the USA, President Reagan was re-elected for a second term.

In Britain the main event of the year was the coal strike. A dispute in South Wales quickly escalated into a national strike, following proposals by the National Coal Board to close up to 20 'uneconomic' pits and the threat of 20,000 redundancies within a year. Confrontations between pickets and police came to a head at the Orgreave coke plant, where a pitched battle resulted in one death. Among those arrested was Arthur Scargill, the head of the NUM, who refused to condemn the violence. Later in the year the battle shifted to the courts where the strike was declared illegal and the assets of the NUM were seized. By December there was a steady drift back to work by disillusioned miners.

The IRA suffered a major blow with the discovery of a large arms shipment on a trawler, but struck back in October by bombing the Grand Hotel in Brighton during the Tory Party Conference. Four died in the blast; Mrs Thatcher and other ministers had narrow escapes. The *ILN*'s reaction was unequivocal:

> *One of the IRA's fundamental misconceptions of Britain is that it might be bombed into doing what it otherwise cannot be persuaded to do . . . there have recently been troubling signs in our own society that violence is regarded by some as an acceptable way of obtaining objectives that have not been achieved in the ballot box.* (November)

In November the world was shocked by the effects of famine in Ethiopia, and relief money poured in, largely thanks to Bob Geldof's Band Aid and the single, *Do They Know It's Christmas?*

Russia's Vietnam: the Afghan war drained Russian resources as the Mujahideen rebels maintained their campaign of attrition against a background of both tacit and active western support. Russia's absence from the Los Angeles Olympics kept the war in the news.

India's grief: Mrs Gandhi's body lay in state in her father's former home while her country mourned her death at the hands of two Sikhs in her own bodyguard. Her son Rajiv, India's new premier, lit her funeral pyre beside the holy Jumna river in Delhi.

Harry's début: the Princess of Wales showing off her second son, Prince Henry, born on 15 September.

1984

E · V · E · N · T · S

17 APRIL Policewoman Yvonne Fletcher shot outside Libyan embassy in London
9 JULY York Minster struck by lightning and badly damaged by fire
12 OCTOBER IRA bomb exploded at Tory Party Conference, Brighton; four killed
31 OCTOBER Assassination of Mrs Indira Gandhi, Indian Prime Minister
6 NOVEMBER Ronald Reagan won second term in US presidential election

Brighton bomb: the attack on the Grand Hotel in Brighton by the IRA during the Conservative Party Conference on 12 October caused public outrage. 'There will be total support for any move that promises to bring to an end this sort of violence.' (November 1984). Four people were killed and more than 30 others injured by the bomb. Mrs Thatcher narrowly escaped.

1985

THE YEAR STARTED IN BRITAIN with a debate over surrogate motherhood, with Kim Cotton's baby being released to its American 'parents' by order of the High Court. The NUM called off the coal strike after more than 50 per cent of miners had returned to work, but recriminations continued, resulting in the formation of the breakaway Union of Democratic Mineworkers. The pound slipped to an all-time low of $1.07, but the stock market boomed. In November the Anglo-Irish Agreement was signed, giving Eire a consultative role in the administration of Northern Ireland for the first time.

It was a disastrous year for football. A fire at Bradford City's ground killed more than 40 spectators, and then at the end of May, rampaging Liverpool fans caused the deaths of 41 Italian and Belgian supporters at the Heysel Stadium in Brussels. English clubs were banned from European competitions.

On the international front, an increasing threat worldwide was Acquired Immune Deficiency Syndrome (AIDS), which was reaching epidemic proportions in some areas. Beirut remained in the news; Terry Waite, the Archbishop of Canterbury's special envoy, negotiated the freedom of four British hostages there, while the civil war continued. The Shias took over the city and the Lebanese Cabinet fell. The conflict spread to a wider stage as the Israelis bombed PLO offices in Tunis. In June a TWA jet was hijacked and diverted to Beirut and its 39 American passengers were held hostage by Shia terrorists for 16 days until 700 Lebanese Shia prisoners were released from Israel. Less successful was the hijack of the Italian cruise ship *Achille Lauro* by a group of Palestinian pirates.

Violence was also the dominant theme in South Africa with a broad pattern of racial strife spreading through the townships. The ban on mixed marriages ended, but there was increasing pressure from the Commonwealth for international sanctions to be applied to South Africa. Meanwhile, in South Africa, a state of emergency was declared and strict press restrictions were imposed.

An earthquake destroyed much of Mexico City, and there was a major famine in Ethiopia. The *ILN* noted that:

> *The plight of 150 million starving people in Ethiopia and other African countries after two years of drought and consequent famine has at last reached the conscience of the world . . . As relief pours in, getting food to the centres is taking priority; but irrigation and agricultural equipment, designed to guard against future catastrophe, is being held up and may now arrive too late to assure the next harvest. Only the arrival of rains would give hope.* (November)

The Greenpeace ship *Rainbow Warrior* was sunk by a bomb in New Zealand this year; the French secret service eventually admitted responsibility. In the Philippines, President Marcos called a general election, and Corazon Aquino was nominated by the people to stand against him. Albania's Stalinist dictator Enver Hoxha died, having ruled since 1944, and in Russia Mikhail Gorbachev took over following Chernenko's death in March. At a summit conference in Geneva in November, Reagan and Gorbachev promised arms reductions and increased co-operation between their countries in future.

Change at the top: the funeral after only 15 months in office of Konstantin Chernenko, the former Soviet president, was held on 13 March in Moscow. Among the world leaders attending was Mrs Thatcher, who took advantage of the occasion to have talks with the new Russian leader, Mikhail Gorbachev. George Bush, the American Vice-President, invited him to a summit later in the year.

Football inferno: a fire that engulfed the stand at Bradford City's stadium provoked an inquiry into safety standards at other grounds. 'Many of the dead had been trapped at the back of the stand where the turnstiles had been locked . . . those who escaped did so by clambering out of the stand on to the pitch, which they would not have been able to do, had barriers been erected.' (June 1985)

THE ILLUSTRATED LONDON NEWS

1985

E·V·E·N·T·S

3 MARCH Year-long miners' strike ended in Britain

11 MARCH Mikhail Gorbachev became leader of the Soviet Union

11 MAY Bradford City soccer ground fire; more than 40 people dead

29 MAY Heysel Stadium disaster in Brussels; 41 football fans killed

15 NOVEMBER Anglo-Irish Agreement signed on Ulster

21 NOVEMBER End of Geneva arms reduction talks between USA and USSR

Hostage hero: following his mission that resulted in the release of four British hostages held captive in Libya, the British envoy Terry Waite flew back to Beirut in November to try to win freedom for other hostages.

Mexican misery: in a year that was marked by disasters and violence all over the world, much of Mexico City was devastated by a huge earthquake. Hundreds were killed when tower blocks collapsed like packs of cards, but there were many miracle rescues, including 58 new-born babies found alive after some days in the wreckage of their maternity hospital. Despite the hardship, Mexico went on to host the World Cup in 1986.

1986

THE YEAR STARTED WITH A SPECTACULAR DISASTER, when the US space shuttle *Challenger* exploded shortly after take-off. The *ILN* reported:

Viewed live by millions on television, the moment of tragedy was witnessed from Cape Canaveral by the family of Christa McAuliffe, a 37-year-old teacher who had captured the public imagination by being the first ordinary citizen chosen to fly in space. (January)

In April there was another, far more significant disaster. An explosion at the Russian nuclear reactor at Chernobyl in the Ukraine allowed radioactivity to drift over northern Europe, affecting milk, crops and livestock in many countries. The fall-out was expected to have serious long-term effects.

Internationally, it was not a good year for the USA. Tension in the Mediterranean came to a head with clashes between US and Libyan aircraft, and then the US air force bombed Libyan targets. Mrs Thatcher allowed some US F111 aircraft to fly from British bases, thereby invoking criticism throughout the world. US foreign policy was also in tatters over Iran, when it became known that profits made by the USA in selling arms to Iran had then been secretly used to help Contra rebels in Nicaragua. For a while the 'Irangate' scandal theatened Reagan's presidency, but in the end Admiral John Poindexter and Colonel Oliver North took the rap. At Reykjavik, a summit between Reagan and Gorbachev was stalled by Reagan's insistence on retaining the US Star Wars defence scheme.

Elsewhere, events provoked both pessimism and optimism. The Swedish Prime Minister Olaf Palme was assassinated, for no clear reason, and in the French election the extreme right under Jean Marie Le Pen made a stir. Corazon Aquino won the general election in the Philippines, ousting Ferdinand Marcos.

Meanwhile, 'Baby Doc' Duvalier was thrown out of power in Haiti, there were massive student demonstrations in China where changes at the top hinted at a halt in the process of liberalisation, and the Iran–Iraq war dragged on. The US Congress voted for sanctions against South Africa, and Esso and Barclays Bank withdrew their investments from that country.

In Britain, Leon Brittan and Michael Heseltine resigned over the Westland helicopter sale, and Jeffrey Archer resigned as Deputy Chairman of the Conservative Party. Mrs Thatcher and President Mitterrand signed the Channel Tunnel agreement, and the GLC and other metropolitan boroughs ceased to exist. A £20,000,000 campaign to tell the public about the risk of AIDS was also launched. The 'Big Bang' in the City was judged a qualified success, and the British Gas share sale was heavily oversubscribed. However, a government probe into the take-over of Distillers by Guinness suggested that all was not entirely well in the City.

All these events were overshadowed by the engagement of Prince Andrew to Sarah Ferguson, and their wedding. The *ILN*'s view was that:

The marriage of Prince Andrew and Sarah Ferguson on July 23 contrived to be both magnificent and very jolly. For the jolliness we had the character of the royal couple to thank, in particular the bride's . . . Here was a royal lady with whom people could identify. (August)

Shuttle disaster: millions watched in horror as the space shuttle *Challenger* exploded 72 seconds after lift-off from Cape Canaveral on 28 January, a dramatic accident caused by a ruptured rocket.

Doomed crew: the public death of the crew of the US *Challenger* shocked America. In this photograph taken shortly before lift-off, Christa McAuliffe is second from the left in the back row. As America mourned, 'President Reagan attended a brief public memorial at the Johnson Space Center, and pledged that America's space programme would continue.' (March 1986)

Fergie's triumph: it was a happy scene full of spectacle and splendour as Sarah Ferguson married the Duke of York in Westminster Abbey on 23 July. As the couple drove off on the start of their honeymoon in the Azores, they were showered with confetti and rose petals. 'A new chapter in the life of the royal family has most happily begun.' (August 1986)

1986

E·V·E·N·T·S

28 JANUARY US *Challenger* space shuttle blew up, killing its crew

25 FEBRUARY President Ferdinand Marcos and his wife fled the Philippines

15 APRIL US planes, some launched from British bases, bombed Libya

26 APRIL Chernobyl nuclear power station ablaze; radioactive fall-out emitted

23 JULY Prince Andrew married Sarah Ferguson

23 DECEMBER Dr Andrei Sakharov, leading Soviet dissident, freed in USSR

1987

IN JUNE, Britain elected Mrs Thatcher's government for a third term. After the failure of the SDP–Liberal Alliance, which ended up with only 22 seats, the Liberals and the SDP started the process of merging into the Social and Liberal Democrats (SLD). Dr David Owen retained his own breakaway Social Democrat Party (SDP). Princess Anne became the Princess Royal and the Church of England voted for the ordination of women.

However, the year will inevitably be remembered for all the things that went wrong. While trying to negotiate the freeing of western hostages, Terry Waite was himself taken hostage in Beirut. In March, the Townsend Thoresen ferry, *Herald of Free Enterprise*, suddenly capsized as it left Zeebrugge harbour with the loss of nearly 200 passengers. In August, Michael Ryan ran amok in Hungerford shooting 13 people dead before killing himself. In October southern Britain was devastated by a great storm, which uprooted millions of trees. In November, the IRA bombed the Remembrance Day parade at Enniskillen, Northern Ireland, and a few days later a fire at London's King's Cross underground station claimed 31 lives.

The *ILN* reported the arrival of the 'provocative' American rock star, Madonna, in Britain:

> *. . . amid much hype and hysteria, to give four sell-out concerts in Leeds and London, billed as the biggest extravaganza since the Beatles . . . The 29-year-old . . . will stop at nothing to get into the headlines and is certainly her own greatest admirer.* (September)

The Guinness affair dragged on as Guinness's former Chairman, Ernest Saunders, was first sacked and then charged, but the worst day for the City was 'Black Monday', 19 October, when an international stock market collapse wiped millions from share prices. In contrast, the art market took off, with the sale of Van Gogh's *Sunflowers* for £24,000,000 at Christie's, and *Irises* for £30,000,000 at Sotheby's.

In the USA the report on the 'Irangate' affair blamed President Reagan, but he nevertheless escaped serious censure. The American public admired Colonel Oliver North's patriotic stance, and the support given to him by his secretary, Fawn Hall. The USA was drawn further into the Iran–Iraq war—the Iraqis mistakenly attacked a US frigate, and US warships captured an Iranian minelayer and shelled Iranian oil platforms. In Beirut, the Palestinian refugee camp Chatila was starved by Shi'ite Amal militia until the Syrian army broke the siege.

In Fiji, a coup by General Rabuka and native Fijians in September, inspired by Indian dominance of Parliament, led ultimately to the declaration of a republic. This was not recognised by the Queen, and Fiji left the Commonwealth. Violence by Tamil separatists escalated in Sri Lanka, despite attempts by the Indian army to restore order.

The best news of the year came from Russia, with Gorbachev announcing a wide range of domestic reforms. The words *glasnost* (openness) and *perestroika* (restructuring) became increasingly familiar to the West as hundreds of Russian dissidents were freed. In December, at the Washington summit, Reagan and Gorbachev signed an agreement to dismantle their arsenals of medium- and short-range nuclear missiles, which was regarded as the first major step towards world peace.

Ferry disaster: bow doors left open capsized the *Herald of Free Enterprise* just outside Zeebrugge harbour on 6 March, and the wreck lay there until it was refloated at the end of April. The inquiry's report stated that the management of Townsend Thoresen was 'infected by a disease of sloppiness'.

Olympics under threat: South Korean protesters, angered by the exclusion of North Korea from the games, burnt the Olympic flag to try to undermine international confidence in the South Korean government's ability to host the 1988 Olympics in Seoul.

The Great Hurricane: the worst storm in over 250 years swept across southern England during the early hours of 16 October. Winds of 110mph were recorded. Hundreds of buildings were damaged, cars destroyed and about 15 million trees felled.

1987

E·V·E·N·T·S

6 MARCH Zeebrugge disaster: nearly 200 ferry passengers drowned
17 AUGUST Rudolf Hess, ex-Nazi leader, apparently killed himself in prison
19 AUGUST Gunman Michael Ryan killed 13 in Hungerford before shooting himself
16 OCTOBER Gale-force winds caused havoc in southern England
19 OCTOBER Black Monday; share values crashed on international stock markets
18 NOVEMBER Fire claimed 31 lives at King's Cross underground station

'Black Monday': on 19 October Wall Street led the world's stock markets into a massive downward spiral, wiping millions from share prices. By the end of the week the FT index in London had lost 22 per cent of its value, a collapse heightened by feelings of unease in the City following the Guinness scandal. As computers dictated decline, the crash developed its own momentum, and the drawback of the 'Big Bang' became painfully apparent.

1988

IN A YEAR OF MIXED FORTUNES, there was plenty to celebrate on the international front. In Russia the spirit of *glasnost* continued to flourish and the fourth, and last, summit conference between Gorbachev and President Reagan maintained the pattern of progress. In May Russian troops began to withdraw from Afghanistan in phases; this was to be completed by early 1989. In the Middle East tension mounted as neutral shipping came increasingly under attack from mines and Iranian gunboats. The USA's peace-keeping role was questioned when her planes bombed Iranian oil platforms and sank Iranian ships; matters came to a head when a US warship shot down an Iranian airbus, killing all 290 people on board. The US government quickly admitted its error and offered compensation to the victims' families. Unexpectedly, this disaster seemed to bring all sides involved in the conflict to their senses. Iran agreed to accept unconditionally United Nations Resolution 598, which called for an end to hostilities with Iraq, and although fighting continued for some weeks, the peace process was under way. A cease-fire came into effect on 20 August, and brought the eight-year Iran–Iraq conflict to an end. However, the full scale of Iraq's attacks on Kurdistan now became clear, with thousands of Kurdish refugees fleeing into Turkey.

American courts indicted Panama's military leader and *de facto* ruler, Noriega, on drugs charges but did not thereby bring about his downfall. The war on drugs also became a major theme at the Olympic Games in Seoul, when several athletes were banned from competing after they failed drugs tests.

In Chile, President Pinochet was defeated by a popular referendum, while in Pakistan President Zia's untimely death in a plane crash in August opened the way for a return to democracy, with free elections resulting in a win for Benazir Bhutto. In the US presidential election the Republican, George Bush, easily defeated the Democratic candidate, Michael Dukakis, and the US space shuttle started flying again.

The most unexpected event of the year was the agreement by the USA to enter into discussions with the PLO, following Yasser Arafat's speech to a specially convened United Nations assembly in Geneva. The tide of world opinion was finally turned against Israel and Zionism by the violence of Israeli soldiers in their attempts at controlling the uprising by Palestinians on the West Bank and in Gaza.

Events in Ireland took a turn for the worse. Accusations that Britain was operating a 'shoot-to-kill' policy against the IRA came to a head in March, when three IRA terrorists were shot down in Gibraltar, apparently with little or no warning. The IRA revenge took the form of bomb attacks on a van being used by soldiers attending a charity run, and on a coach full of soldiers, but the greatest outrage was caused by a mob killing two off-duty army corporals who drove in error into an IRA funeral in Belfast. The *ILN* commented:

> . . .captured on film, the brutal beating of these young men [has] vividly brought into people's homes the full hatred and horror of life in Northern Ireland . . . the IRA [has] vowed to continue its campaign of violence. (March)

Anglo-Irish relations were more strained by these events than at any time during the decade.

Rain of death: on 22 December a New York-bound Pan Am jumbo, blown apart by a terrorist bomb, fell as a fireball on to the little Scottish town of Lockerbie, bringing death and destruction on the ground and scattering bodies and wreckage over a wide area. It was the worst ever air crash in Britain.

Republican rout: former Vice-President George Bush steadily overtook Democrat Michael Dukakis in the race for the White House and finally gained a resounding victory at the polls. Despite his famous 'watch my lips' speech, Bush appeared to have no immediate answer to America's economic woes.

Afghan evacuation: after nearly ten years of painful, expensive and ultimately useless warfare, the Russians began to pull their weary troops out of Afghanistan in May. According to the Geneva agreement, the phased withdrawal was to be completed early in 1989, a target met on time.

Armenian disaster:
problems at home continued
to threaten Gorbachev's
reforms, not least the
earthquake that devastated
Soviet Armenia (below) in
December. Severe weather
hindered aid parties
struggling to free the dead
from the rubble.

THE ILLUSTRATED
LONDON NEWS

1988

E · V · E · N · T · S

3 MARCH Agreement reached on Soviet
withdrawal from Afghanistan
7 MARCH Three IRA terrorists shot and killed
by SAS in Gibraltar
6 JULY *Piper Alpha* oil rig in North Sea
exploded; 166 deaths
11 NOVEMBER George Bush defeated Michael
Dukakis in US presidential election
22 DECEMBER A Pan Am jet exploded over
Lockerbie, Scotland; more than 300 dead

Olympic triumph: 'Not even
harmful revelations of drug taking
could quench the spectacular
brilliance of the athletic
performances and the South
Koreans' mounting of the Games.'
(November 1988)

I N ITS FIRST ISSUE OF THE YEAR, the *ILN* looked back over 1988:

The great moment, which signalled the end of the Cold War and the dilution of eastern bloc socialism, was the peace accord between the superpowers. The world's attention, so long fixed on the possibility of nuclear confrontation between the USSR and USA, came to focus instead upon the increasing threat to the environment posed by man's energetic reproduction and consumption. Politicians of all colours found it expedient to publicise their Green credentials, even in Communist China. The year produced a number of disasters and outrages, but it will be remembered for what was the remarkable outbreak of peace in so many different areas of conflict. (January 1989)

The optimistic note was to prove justified, for this was the year which saw the destruction of the Iron Curtain and the final conclusion of the Cold War. In February the Soviet Union completed its withdrawal from Afghanistan, after an occupation that had lasted nine years. The last soldier to leave, General Boris Gromov, made the final part of the crossing on foot. In April it looked as if democracy might be coming to China as students demonstrated unchecked in Beijing (Peking), and in May a reconciliation between the USSR and China was cemented when Mr Gorbachev visited the Chinese capital, the first Soviet leader to do so for 30 years. Meanwhile, thousands of students and their supporters were denouncing the regime and demanding freedom of speech and freedom of the press, under the watchful eyes of international news cameras. In Tiananmen Square they unveiled a statue of the Goddess of Democracy and Freedom, modelled on the Statue of Liberty, but in the early days of June the government sent in the tanks. Troops opened fire on the demonstrators and thousands were killed in the repressive aftermath.

An era had ended in Japan in January, when the 82-year-old Emperor Hirohito died of cancer after a reign lasting 62 years. World leaders attending his funeral included the Duke of Edinburgh, which caused some unease in Britain, where memories of World War II horrors were far from extinct.

A shadow was cast by the ferocious hostility aroused in the Muslim world by Salman Rushdie's novel *The Satanic Verses*. The Ayatollah Khomeini, leader of Iran, passed a death sentence on Rushdie and exhorted faithful Muslims to assassinate him. A leading Iranian cleric put a price of $1 million on Rushdie's head and the author was forced to go into hiding.

A spate of disasters included the horrific deaths of Liverpool football supporters who were crushed in the crowd at the Hillsborough ground in Sheffield. Concern over the destruction of the environment, especially the 'greenhouse effect', continued to mount and governments slowly began to take action. March brought the worst oil spill disaster in American history, when a giant tanker ran aground in Alaska and 11 million gallons of oil smothered Prince William Sound in a glutinous black tide. In the same month, however, European environment ministers agreed to phase out CFCs (chlorofluorocarbons)—believed to damage the ozone layer—from all products by the end of the century.

In remembrance: Liverpool Football Club's Anfield ground (above) in April, showing tributes to 95 supporters who died when they were crushed during an FA Cup match against Nottingham Forest at the Hillsborough ground in Sheffield. The tragedy was a grim reminder of the dark side of mass-spectator sport in the twentieth century.

Broken giant: early in January a Boeing 737 crashed near Kegworth in Leicestershire (above) after engine failure, scattering debris over the M1 motorway. Together with the disaster at Lockerbie in Scotland in December 1988, which was caused by sabotage, the accidents were the latest in a whole series of twentieth-century aeronautical disasters. It seemed that man's triumphant conquest of the air had to be paid for by a harvest of tragedy: from the deaths of early pilots and experimenters to those of jet passengers by the hundred in the last three decades.

1989

· · ·
E · V · E · N · T · S

7 JANUARY Death of Emperor Hirohito of
Japan in Tokyo after a 62-year reign
20 JANUARY George Bush sworn in as 41st US
President, succeeding Ronald Reagan
15 FEBRUARY The USSR completed its
withdrawal of troops from Afghanistan
3 JUNE Ayatollah Khomeini, leader of Iran's
Islamic revolution, died aged 86
4 JUNE Massacre of students demanding
greater democracy in Peking
5 JUNE UN-backed World Environment Day
to raise international concern

· ◆ ·

Herald of change:
Mr Gorbachev at 10
Downing Street (left)
in April. The 'Iron
Curtain' that had
fallen over Europe in
the 1940s was, at last,
lifting.

Voice of the people: individuals attempted to
force the hand of governments this year. The man
(below) singlehandedly stopped a line of tanks in
Peking on 5 June, pleading for an end to the
shooting of thousands of student demonstrators
for democracy. He was pulled away by
bystanders, and the tanks rolled on.

In July the celebrations in France to mark the 200th anniversary of the French Revolution and the storming of the Bastille came to a head with a pageant and a supercolossal fireworks display. Britain, sweltering in summer heat, saw a food scare as numerous cases of salmonella poisoning were reported. The rapid progress of nuclear disarmament was highlighted when the last cruise missiles were removed from the Greenham Common air base in Berkshire, watched by some of the women protesters who had camped there for eight years.

On the Thames in London one August night, death overtook the pleasure-boat *Marchioness*, packed with revelling party guests, when she was rammed from astern and sunk by a hulking ocean-going dredger, the *Bowbelle*. It was 'like a tank running over a Mini,' an eyewitness said. At Deal in Kent an IRA bomb killed and injured bandsmen at the Royal Marines School of Music. In San Francisco hundreds were killed as a severe earthquake rocked the city. Buildings collapsed and a section of double-decker motorway fell and crushed cars travelling on the lower deck.

In eastern Europe the hardline regimes were crumpling, too, and in November a thrill of excitement shot round the world as the Berlin Wall, the concrete symbol of so many years of East–West conflict, came down at last. On 9 November, as the *ILN* reported:

> *For the first time since the Berlin Wall was built in 1961, East Berliners were able to pass freely through Checkpoint Charlie and other crossing-points to the West following the lifting of virtually all travel restrictions by the East German government. Jubilant crowds began streaming through the Wall within hours of the 6.55pm announcement.* (Winter 1989)

In the following weeks hundreds of thousands of people from East Berlin flocked into West Berlin to gaze at the shop windows like excited children and buy everything from cassettes to fluffy toys and, above all, bananas — bananas in truck loads — before returning home with their spoils.

Early in December President Bush and Mr Gorbachev, while taking further steps to reduce their nuclear weaponry, announced that the Cold War was officially over. Non-communist governments took over in East Germany and Czechoslovakia. In Romania anti-government riots broke out in the city of Timisoara when the authorities moved against a priest named Laszlo Tokes, who had been preaching against the regime. Troops opened fire and killed about 100 protesters, but a spirit of rebellion suddenly flared up all over the country and giant crowds assembled in Bucharest. Crucially, the army changed sides and supported the protesters and suddenly the regime cracked. The hated 71-year-old President Nicolae Ceausescu and his wife Elena, trying to flee abroad, were caught, court-martialled and shot amid immense jubilation.

In Panama, American troops took control of Panama City and ousted the dictator, General Manuel Noriega, suspected of involvement in massive drug-running operations. The general and his henchmen took refuge in the Vatican embassy. They ate their Christmas dinner blasted by rock music, launched from loudspeakers by US forces.

Sky on fire: the sky over Paris exploded in a blazing torrent of fireworks as France celebrated the 200th anniversary of the fall of the Bastille and the beginning of the French Revolution. A pageant portrayed the revolution as a key event in the establishment of democracy and human rights, though among the bangs of the rockets dissenting noises off could be heard from Mrs Thatcher.

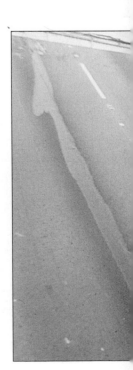

Horror by land: crowds were strewn about like toys thrown down by a child in a temper after part of San Francisco's Bay Bridge collapsed in an earthquake. The city had been waiting nervously for California's notorious San Andreas fault to come back for a second bite of the cherry, ever since the famous disaster of 1906 which had destroyed almost the entire city. The new shock, which checked in at 6.9 on the Richter scale, caused heavy damage and loss of life.

Horror by water: salvage workers examining the wreck of the Thames pleasure boat *Marchioness*, after she had been raised from the depths. She had been sunk and rammed by the dredger *Bowbelle*, a monster of close to 1,900 tons compared with the river boat's mere 80 tons. The *Marchioness* had been hired for a party and had just negotiated Blackfriars Bridge near 2 o'clock in the morning with young guests dancing cheerfully on board, when the dredger loomed up behind, 'like something from a horror movie' as one of them said.

THE ILLUSTRATED LONDON NEWS

1989

E·V·E·N·T·S

11 JULY Laurence Olivier, widely regarded as the supreme stage actor of his day, died aged 82

22 SEPTEMBER Death of Irving Berlin, American song-writer, aged 101

19 OCTOBER An earthquake struck the San Francisco Bay area, causing severe damage

9 NOVEMBER East German border points were opened, followed by demolition of the Berlin Wall

20 DECEMBER US troops took action in Panama to oust General Noriega

25 DECEMBER Execution of President Ceausescu of Romania and his wife by firing squad

Change of heart: a Berlin border guard, looking pensive. East Germany's frontier guards, detested for their arrogant ways, had to alter course. They suddenly became friendly and helpful when border controls relaxed and the Berlin Wall was broken.

An Empire Falls

There is a term in historical science and also in political vocabulary, 'revolution from above.' There have been quite a few such revolutions in history. But they should not be confused with coups d'état *and palace revolutions. What is meant is profound and essentially revolutionary changes implemented on the initiative of the authorities themselves but necessitated by objective changes in the situation and in social moods.*

MIKHAIL GORBACHEV

THE MOST DRAMATIC EVENT of the 1980s was the collapse of the Communist regimes of the Soviet Union and eastern Europe. People all over the world who had lived for 40 years in the shadow of the Cold War and in fear of a nuclear holocaust watched with incredulous relief as the Iron Curtain lifted. It happened with astonishing speed. Pitying amusement would have greeted anyone who, as New Year's Day dawned in 1985, had seriously predicted that the end of the decade would see the fall of the Soviet empire, with the satellite states freed and the USSR itself disintegrating, the Berlin Wall torn down and the nuclear arms race abandoned. But it all happened.

The principal individual figure in these remarkable developments was Mikhail Gorbachev, who became General Secretary of the Communist Party of the Soviet Union in March 1985. Born in 1931 to a peasant family in the Stavropol area of southern Russia, he took a law degree at Moscow State University, where he met his attractive wife Raisa, who was to become almost as admired a figure in the Western media as her husband.

Returning home to Stavropol to climb the local party ladder, Gorbachev came up against the inefficient and demoralised condition of the region's agriculture. He introduced a system of incentive bonuses for small productive groups of farmers. This innovation soon raised the wheat output by 30 per cent and more, but conservative party officials eyed it askance as a threat to the collective principle and the beginning of a return to private enterprise and private property. Moving to the centre of affairs in Moscow, Gorbachev became the youngest member of the ruling Politburo and in 1985, at 54, he was the candidate for General Secretary of those who saw the

Mikhail Gorbachev, pictured in 1988. His efforts to improve the Soviet system were to end in its destruction.

necessity for, or the inevitability of, drastic change.

Gorbachev addressed himself immediately to the desperate condition of the Soviet economy. The rate of economic growth had been falling since the 1950s. Planned targets were not being met and the USSR could no longer afford to keep up with the nuclear Joneses by continuing the arms race with the USA. It was necessary to end the Cold War, and by the beginning of 1986 Gorbachev was proposing doing away with all nuclear weapons by the year 2000.

By the end of 1986 Gorbachev had begun to say publicly that the Soviet

economy could only be cured by a thoroughgoing reconstruction and democratisation of the whole system, which would give ordinary people a direct stake in it. 'A house can be put in order,' he said, 'only by a person who feels that he owns the house.'

Under the banners of *perestroika*, 'restructuring', and *glasnost*, 'openness' (literally 'speaking aloud'), Gorbachev encouraged open debate, criticism of officials by their subordinates and the public, and greater freedom for the media and the churches. He even declared that voters at Soviet elections ought to have a choice of more than one candidate. Dissenters were pardoned, including the most notorious of all, the nuclear physicist Andrei Sakharov. He and his wife were released after six years of internal exile and allowed to return to Moscow.

Another sign of radically changing times was a new attitude to the past. Officially discredited figures who had been convicted in Stalin's show trials were posthumously rehabilitated. On the other hand, the late Leonid Brezhnev, the General Secretary who died in 1982, was now openly derided for awarding himself a chestful of World War II gallantry medals when he had taken good care to keep well away from any fighting. It was even publicly revealed that he had been virtually dead throughout his last six years in office.

Late in 1987 at a summit meeting in Washington, Gorbachev and President Reagan took a long step towards terminating the Cold War when they agreed to dismantle both superpowers' stocks of medium-range and short-range nuclear missiles. Meanwhile in Russia a new name had come to the fore—new to most people in the West, at least—when Boris Yeltsin, the head of the Communist Party in

The last of the Soviet Union's SS-23 missiles was destroyed (above) at the Saryozek base in Kazakhstan on 27 October 1989. The need to end the Cold War, which the Soviet Union could no longer afford, was one of the fundamental motives behind Mr Gorbachev's reform efforts. By the end of 1989 the Soviet Union and the United States were able to announce that the Cold War, which had preoccupied both countries since the close of World War II, was finally over and done with.

As the outside world breathed a huge sigh of collective relief, the Soviet Union's subject peoples saw an opportunity to break free from the grip of tyranny. Banner-carrying demonstrations, like this one in Vilnius, the capital of Lithuania (below right), demanded freedom and independence. Mr Gorbachev had tried to keep the Soviet Union together, but in the end the demand proved impossible to resist. The two other Baltic republics, Latvia and Estonia, followed the trail blazed by Lithuania, and the Soviet Empire started to break up.

Boris Yeltsin (right), seen here in 1989, was born in 1931 in Sverdlovsk. Joining the Communist Party, he became First Secretary of the Sverdlovsk region in 1976. He was moved to the centre of affairs in Moscow as a protegé of Mikhail Gorbachev, with whom he later fell out.

Moscow, was removed from office for criticising the slow pace of *perestroika*.

Gorbachev found himself under heavy fire from opposite directions. On one side were radicals like Yeltsin pressing for reform to go further and faster. On the other were conservative apparatchiks, army officers and KGB men thoroughly alarmed by changes which threatened the whole Soviet system and their own comfortable positions within it.

At the same time, as Gorbachev and his supporters raised the lid of the pressure cooker, fierce jets of nationalist, ethnic and religious steam began to erupt from it. There was trouble all through 1988 and the subsequent years in the south-west, where the Christian republic of Armenia lay cheek by jowl with the Muslim republic of Azerbaijan, with the Armenian enclave of Nagorny-Karabakh marooned inside Azerbaijan. Violent demonstrations, riots and strikes broke out over Nagorny-Karabakh, with Soviet troops repeatedly

and vainly sent in to restore peace and order.

Meanwhile nationalists in the Baltic republics of Lithuania. Latvia and Estonia, which had been swallowed up by Stalin in the 1940s, were starting to demand autonomy from Moscow. Further south, on the Black Sea, the same demand was coming from Georgia. The satellites were beginning to stir, too. In Prague a freedom demonstration in Wenceslas Square had to be broken up by police with tear gas, dogs and water cannon.

Signs of the times multiplied in 1988. In May President Reagan visited 'the evil empire', as he had called it, and went genially walkabout in Moscow's Red Square—an unbelievable spectacle only three or four years before. The following month the first-ever Miss Moscow was crowned. Uncrowned in October was the hatchet-faced Andrei Gromyko, an incarnation of the hidebound Soviet old guard. He ceased to be President of the Supreme Soviet and Gorbachev replaced him.

The Soviet Union could no longer afford the Cold War and it was now officially admitted that the Soviet system was in important respects a failure. From both points of view, it made no sense to go on imposing the system on the satellite countries by force. Even before Gorbachev had become General Secretary, the USSR had refrained from armed intervention against the Solidarity movement in Poland. Now the hardline regimes in East Germany, Hungary and Czechoslovakia were crumbling. Defiant crowds demonstrated in major cities. Communist parties began to reveal an unsuspected appetite for democracy, free elections, capitalism and free enterprise as they realised that the Soviet Union was no longer going to keep them in power by force.

In 1989 the pressure cooker boiled over. In Poland the first non-Communist leader in the Soviet bloc took office in August, when Tadeusz Mazowiecki became premier. He was a close associate of the Solidarity leader, Lech Walesa, and his cabinet was dominated by Solidarity ministers, outnumbering the Communists.

That summer brought 'the great escape', a huge wave of emigration from East Germany as thousands voted with their feet against Communism and poured over the frontiers into the neighbouring countries. Gigantic crowds assembled in East Berlin and Leipzig, demanding freedom. The regime began to topple. Erich Honecker, the grim hardline leader, resigned in October and ran away to Moscow to hide. Early in November a colossal protest march in East Berlin was reported to involve an army of a million people with banners. The government resigned and its successor abandoned any attempt to pen its citizens in. The Berlin Wall fell, torn down by bulldozers, with only two stretches left standing as reminders of the most potent symbol of Communist oppression.

Before the end of 1989 hardline rule had also ended in Hungary, Bulgaria and Czechoslovakia, where the playwright Vaclav Havel, who had been sentenced to prison for dissent in February, found himself President in December. Meeting in amiable if queasy goodwill on a ship in the heaving Mediterranean, Gorbachev and President Bush told the world that the Cold War was definitely over. Even the viciously tyrannical regime in Romania, apparently an impregnable bastion of hardline rigour, was suddenly overthrown when its own army turned against President Ceausescu, who was deposed and executed.

It was one thing to tear down a totalitarian system, allow rival political parties free rein and topple statues of hated tyrants, but quite another to build some-

Crowds cluster round the graffiti-daubed Berlin Wall (left), with the Brandenburg Gate in the background. East Berliners flooded into West Berlin in hundreds of thousands in the weeks after the Wall fell, wearing out their initial welcome from West Berliners.

Nicolae Ceausescu (above), President of Romania since 1974, headed one of the grimmest regimes in the Communist world. He joined the Romanian Communist Party at 15 and became its Secretary General in 1965, promoting his family to high and lucrative positions, while the country's economy declined. After his overthrow in 1989, red stars and other symbols of tyranny were torn down (left).

thing stable in its place. Gorbachev was an admirer of Lenin, who meant to hold fast to the spirit of the Revolution and preserve its achievements, while adopting the best ingredients from other systems, too. The new socialism, he had said in a speech in 1988, would be 'true and tangible human- ism in which man is really the measure of all things'. There would still be central planning, but individual business enter- prises would be encouraged and successful entrepreneurs rewarded. But to introduce capitalism into a country not only unac- customed to it, but indoctrinated to con- sider it immoral, proved no easy task.

In practice, as 1990 wore on, Gor- bachev was given wider and wider powers, but the Soviet Union started to fall apart. Lithuania proclaimed its independence in March and Latvia and Estonia were to fol- low. The Russian Federation, by far the largest of the 15 constituent republics of the USSR, stretching all the way from Moscow across Siberia to the Pacific, pro- claimed itself a sovereign state. The lead was followed by the Ukraine and by Kazakhstan, a Muslim republic which spread from the Caspian Sea to China.

October 3 was set as the date for the formal reunification of Germany, but how long the USSR could continue to exist was a serious question. The economic situation grew so bad that food was airlifted to Moscow from Germany in October, and the USA, anxious in case hardliners should regain control, sent emergency aid. Food was rotting in the fields because the dis- tribution system had foundered and there were interminable queues in the cities, while the Kremlin's economic reforms had sent the price of bread, meat and other products rocketing up.

In 1991 Yugoslavia tore itself apart in a

Flags, flowers and fanfares heralded a hoped-for new dawn as Boris Yeltsin was formally sworn in as President of the Russian Republic at a ceremony in the Kremlin on 10 July 1991. The largest and most important of the Soviet Union's constituent republics, it had proclaimed itself a sovereign state the year before.

vicious civil war. In April Georgia declared itself independent of the USSR. In June Boris Yeltsin was elected President of the Russian Federation. Tough, burly, hard- drinking, outspoken, Yeltsin was often compared by outsiders to Danton in the French Revolution. It was Yeltsin who led the resistance to an attempted coup in August, a desperate bid by conservatives to regain control and turn the clock back. Gorbachev was held under house arrest in the Crimea, where he had gone for a holiday, but in Moscow and other cities the barricades went up against troops and tanks sent in by the plotters. Much of the army and the KGB refused to back the coup, which ignominiously collapsed.

After this the break-up of the Soviet Union was swift, as many of the republics declared themselves independent. There was much complicated manoeuvering before December, when the leaders of Rus- sia, the Ukraine and Byelorussia declared that the USSR no longer existed and announced the formation of a looser grouping, the Commonwealth of Independent States. Kazakhstan and most of the other republics joined the new feder- ation, leaving Georgia and the three Baltic states outside. On Christmas Day Mikhail Gorbachev went on television to announce his resignation. The future was full of uncertainy, but one of history's most powerful empires had fallen.

A startling sign of the new attitude in the Soviet Union was the opening of a McDonald's fast food restaurant in Moscow.

1990

DAWNING IN OPTIMISM, the year went downhill as the economic and political problems confronting the Soviet Union and eastern Europe were revealed in all their severity.

In Panama the beleaguered General Noriega left his noisy sanctuary in the Vatican embassy, surrendered and was flown to Miami to await trial. Though the prison doors closed on him, they opened in South Africa, where President de Klerk lifted the government's ban on the African National Congress (ANC) and two other anti-apartheid organisations. He invited black leaders to 'walk through the open door' to negotiations with the government and followed up by releasing the 71-year-old Nelson Mandela, leader of the ANC and the world's most celebrated political prisoner, who had been in jail since 1962. Mr Mandela announced that the ANC was suspending its 'armed struggle' after 29 years, but violence between ANC supporters and the Zulu-dominated Inkatha Freedom Party was to cost many lives.

Meanwhile, an estimated 160 million bottles of Perrier had been withdrawn from the shelves after minute traces of possibly carcinogenic benzine had been discovered in the world's best-known mineral water. In Britain a health scare developed over 'mad cow disease' (bovine spongiform encephalopathy). Sales of beef dipped sharply and France, West Germany and Italy put a ban on British beef.

Alarm was expressed on another front about the new poll tax. Protests in English cities culminated in scenes of mayhem in London at the end of March, as the *ILN* reported:

> *In central London a mass rally against the poll tax erupted into some of the worst street violence ever seen in the city when a minority of extremists began fighting with police. Serious rioting, which police claimed was confined to about 3,000 people, spread along St Martin's Lane and Charing Cross Road and continued until 8pm. There were instances of arson and widespread looting; 330 police and 86 civilians were injured and there were 341 arrests. (Summer 1990)*

In Liberia President Samuel Doe was overthrown and savagely killed. Relations between the Iraqi government and the West deteriorated rapidly with the execution in Baghdad, for alleged spying, of a journalist named Farzad Bazoft, who worked for the London *Observer* newspaper. Within a few days the British and Americans announced the discovery of a plot to export nuclear detonators to Iraq. In April British customs officers pounced on a consignment of steel pipes bound for Iraq which they suspected were designed to form the 130ft barrel of a gigantic nuclear 'supergun'.

In May Van Gogh's *Portrait of Dr Gachet* was knocked down to a Japanese business tycoon for a cool £49.5 million, the highest price ever paid for a painting. In Washington a less open-handed President Bush confessed that his best-remembered pledge—'Read my lips, no new taxes'—was inoperative. Taxes were to rise after all, to reduce the colossal US budget deficit. Corn circles were posing puzzling questions as the English harvest ripened. Were they made by beings from outer space or wind patterns or ingenious hoaxers? No one knew.

Stop the plague: AIDS demonstrators protesting in San Francisco. The threat of a new epidemic of plague-like proportions could seem an ironic consequence of the new 'progressive' morality. The early victims were almost all homosexuals and drug users, but it was constantly proclaimed that heterosexuals, too, were at risk.

Solitary end: the fabulously beautiful Greta Garbo, who died in April, had been a recluse since retiring from films in 1941 after her last movie, *Two-Faced Woman*, flopped. 'I want to be alone,' she had said in *Grand Hotel*.

Stop the tax: a protester confronts police in riot gear during a demonstration in London against the poll tax, which turned violent when the march reached Trafalgar Square. More than 400 people were injured, shop windows were smashed all along Regent Street, cars were set on fire and sporadic fighting went on until midnight. The poll tax would eventually be withdrawn.

1990

E · V · E · N · T · S

3 JANUARY General Noriega surrendered to US forces in Panama City

11 FEBRUARY Nelson Mandela, leader of the African National Congress, was released from prison in South Africa

15 MARCH British journalist Farzad Bazoft was hanged as a spy in Iraq

15 APRIL Death of Greta Garbo, Swedish-born film star, after many years as a recluse, aged 84

8 JULY West Germany won the World Cup football final, defeating Argentina 1–0.

Welcome release: Nelson Mandela, his wife Winnie and clenched-fist salutes in South Africa. A successful lawyer in his youth, Mr Mandela led the African National Congress campaign against apartheid for 20 years, until sentenced to life imprisonment in 1964.

At the beginning of August Iraqi tanks rumbled across the border into Kuwait. Most of the Kuwaiti ruling family decamped to Saudi Arabia, leaving their subjects to be cruelly ill-used by the triumphant Iraqis. The United Nations Security Council, displaying more determination and cohesion than for many years, passed Resolution 661, imposing economic sanctions on Iraq including an embargo on oil. The USSR and China both voted for the resolution, which only Cuba and Yemen declined to support.

The Iraqi strongman, Saddam Hussein, defied the United Nations and took the occasion to end his 10-year war with Iran. While attempts to resolve the situation came to nothing, a powerful force of troops, armour, planes and warships began to assemble in Saudi Arabia and the Persian Gulf. The crisis crystallised Western fears that a new enemy was appearing in the shape of belligerent Islam.

In Pakistan Benazir Bhutto was accused by the president of undermining the country's constitution, and her government was sent packing in what she called 'a constitutional *coup d'état*'. Fireworks cascaded down the night sky in Berlin in October as East Germany ceased to exist and the two Germanys were formally reunited. Federal Chancellor Helmut Kohl said, 'Germany is our fatherland, the united Europe our future.' The prospect of a united Europe was less welcome to Mrs Thatcher, however, who later in the month found herself in a minority of one as the other EC leaders agreed to move towards a common monetary policy and a single European currency.

Mrs Mary Robinson became the first-ever woman President of Ireland, but Britain's leader was in serious trouble as her longest-serving colleague, Sir Geoffrey Howe, resigned from the Government over her attitude to Europe. What was rapidly coming nearer was not just a common European market but something like a United States of Europe. Michael Heseltine, an ex-Cabinet minister, now challenged Mrs Thatcher for the party leadership. The first round of voting proved inconclusive and the Iron Lady regretfully resigned, after 11 years in office. The *ILN* gave, on the whole, a favourable verdict:

> *The record of the Thatcher years has been pretty good. Her ambition, as she said when she first took office in 1979, was to change attitudes and transform the state of the nation—to change Britain from a dependent to a self-reliant society.*
>
> *In many ways she succeeded. Socialism has been eliminated. Trade union power has been broken. A market economy has been encouraged, many top-heavy state enterprises sold off and privatised, the creation of wealth rewarded, the owning of property and shares greatly increased. Overseas her firmness contributed to the collapse of communism and the ending of the Cold War. (Winter 1990)*

The leadership election ended in a victory for the Chancellor of the Exchequer, John Major. At 47, the son of a circus trapeze artist, he came from humble beginnings and had left school at 16. It seemed another sign of the times when Britain technically ceased to be an island. This happened on 1 December, when English and French workers on the Channel Tunnel broke through and joined hands in celebration. By this time the UN Security Council had passed Resolution 678, which authorised the use of force to expel the Iraqis from Kuwait.

In power: Saddam Hussein and his entourage in Baghdad. Born in 1937, Saddam took a major role in the revolution in Iraq in 1968, which overthrew the government and set up the socialist Revolutionary Council.

Out of power: Benazir Bhutto arrives home after she and her government were ejected from office by the President of Pakistan. She had become Prime Minister in 1988. Her father Zulfikar Bhutto, founder of the Pakistan People's Party and Prime Minister in the 1970s, was executed in 1979.

THE ILLUSTRATED LONDON NEWS

1990

❖

E · V · E · N · T · S

2 AUGUST Iraqi invasion of Kuwait
8 AUGUST Benazir Bhutto was dismissed as
Prime Minister of Pakistan
3 OCTOBER Formal reunification of East and
West Germany
22 NOVEMBER Resignation of Mrs Margaret
Thatcher as Prime Minister of Britain; she was
succeeded by John Major
29 NOVEMBER The Security Council of the
United Nations authorised the use of force
against Iraq

❖❖

Out of office: Britain's first woman Prime Minister, Mrs Thatcher, leaves 10 Downing Street with her husband Denis for the last time.

Hands beneath the sea:
Frenchman Philippe Cozette and
Briton Robert Graham Fagg exchange
flags deep beneath the English
Channel as the two tunnel-boring
parties meet, to end Britain's 9,500
years of isolation. The French and
British Transport Ministers and the
chairmen of the two tunnel companies
shared the celebrations. Digging the
new Channel Tunnel began in 1986,
though there was considerable
misgiving about it on the British side.

1991

By early 1991 the allied force in Saudi Arabia had swelled to a total strength of some 700,000, of whom more than 60 per cent were American. Final attempts to persuade President Saddam Hussein to withdraw from Kuwait failed, and the allies launched Operation Desert Storm with an air bombardment of appalling ferocity. Allied planes and Tomahawk cruise missiles blasted Iraqi missile sites, air bases, industrial installations, power stations and bridges. Baghdad and other cities were battered and Iraqi troops took a fearful hammering from the most sophisticated weaponry in the history of warfare.

Iraq fired Scud missiles at targets in Israel and Saudi Arabia, to little effect, and the Israelis refused to respond to the provocation. American and British warships put paid to the Iraqi navy and much of Saddam's air force took refuge in Iran.

The air assault went on for more than five weeks until the burly allied commander, General Norman Schwarzkopf of the US Army, unleashed his ground forces in a manoeuvre which took his armour round the Iraqi right flank. For four days the allied troops stormed forward, inflicting huge casualties and taking prisoners in droves, while suffering minimal losses themselves, until President Bush ordered a ceasefire. This was a humane decision in the short term, but in the long run it left Saddam still in power in Iraq.

Saddam savagely repressed insurrections against him in Basra and other southern Iraqi cities and by the Kurds in the north. By the end of March millions of Kurds had fled to the mountains on the borders with Turkey and Iran, where the embarrassed West made efforts to help them. In Kuwait the formidable tasks had to be tackled of putting out hundreds of oil well fires which the vengeful Iraqis had started, and of cleaning up a huge oil spill in the Gulf.

While all this was happening, the Soviet army had intervened in Lithuania and Latvia to discourage independence moves, but in vain. Yugoslavia was disintegrating. The *ILN* described an audacious IRA attack in London:

> *Two members of an IRA hit squad launched a mortar attack on 10 Downing Street while a meeting of the War Cabinet was in progress. The mortars were fired from a van parked in Whitehall, one of the bombs exploding in the garden behind the Prime Minister's house, blowing in some windows. The other two landed in another garden nearby. No one was seriously hurt, and ministers resumed their meeting after moving to the basement.* (Spring 1991)

British Rail solemnly blamed 'the wrong kind of snow' for delaying the trains. In South Africa President de Klerk pressed on with the dismantling of apartheid and the doors were opening to welcome South Africa back into international sport, but bloody violence between black factions continued. In May in southern India a woman approached Prime Minister Rajiv Gandhi with a bouquet of flowers and blew him and herself to pieces with a concealed bomb. In the same month the savage Communist regime in Ethiopia was overthrown by force. On 12 June the city of Leningrad decided to resume its pre-Revolutionary name of St Petersburg, and on the same day the charismatic Boris Yeltsin was elected President of Russia.

Pillar of fire: an abandoned Iraqi tank is silhouetted against the fiercely burning Burgan oilfield. The land war began only after Iraq had been subjected to a devastating assault from the air, and after President Saddam Hussein had rejected the final ultimatum to withdraw his forces from occupied Kuwait. The land attack, brilliantly directed by General Norman Schwarzkopf of the US Army (inset), deceived and outmanoeuvred the Iraqi crack Republican Guard with an encircling movement round its right flank. American, British and French armour played the main part. The Iraqi Army hastily withdrew from Kuwait, leaving the oil wells in flames behind them. With Kuwait free, President Bush ordered a halt to combat operations.

Pillar of smoke: a Patriot anti-missile missile hurls itself avengingly into the sky. The Gulf War was fought with the most up-to-date technology.

THE ILLUSTRATED
LONDON NEWS

1991

E · V · E · N · T · S

16 JANUARY Operation Desert Storm launched against Iraq

7 FEBRUARY IRA mortar bombs were fired at 10 Downing Street in London, from Whitehall

21 FEBRUARY Death of Margot Fonteyn, British prima ballerina assoluta, in Panama, aged 71

24 FEBRUARY Allied invasion of Iraq began; President Bush called a ceasefire on 27 February

21 MAY Assassination of Rajiv Gandhi, Prime Minister of India

25 JUNE Slovenia and Croatia declared themselves independent

Funeral fire: Rajiv Gandhi's wife Sonia, son Rahul and daughter Brivanka in mourning white at the funeral of the assassinated Indian premier. He was cremated in New Delhi in the presence of many world leaders. Mrs Gandhi was pressed to succeed her murdered husband, but declined, and the Gandhi dynasty's days of power seemed to be over.

The black shadow of civil war lengthened over Yugoslavia, as the six-republic federation splintered. Ancient hatreds between Orthodox Serbs and Roman Catholic Croats, and bitter memories of World War II atrocities were revived. A substantial Muslim population was another element in an unstable equation.

In June the republics of Slovenia and Croatia declared themselves independent. Meanwhile a Serbian enclave inside Croatia had declared its own independence and set off the bloodiest fighting between Serbs and Croats since the 1940s. The hardline president of Serbia, Slobodan Milosevic, was suspected of planning to create a 'Greater Serbia' which would bite off parts of Croatia and Bosnia. The Yugoslav national army, ominously, was dominated by Serb officers.

In July Milosevic warned all Serbs to be ready to fight. In August the Yugoslav army and air force, supported by Serb irregulars, besieged the city of Vukovar in eastern Croatia. The European Community intervened and a peace conference met at the Hague. Ceasefires were announced with great frequency and broken with matching promptitude.

Elsewhere, Western hostages were being released by Iran-backed terrorist groups in the Middle East. The Arab-owned, fraud-riddled Bank of Commerce and Credit International was closed down by the Bank of England and international banking authorities, and thousands of depositors discovered that their money had vanished into thin air. Mr Major issued the 'Citizen's Charter', proposing to make the public services more responsive to the public. Albanian refugees were flooding across the Adriatic to Italy, where they were not wanted, sharpening fears that the West was threatened with a tidal wave of immigrants from eastern Europe and the Third World.

There was intense alarm in August over the coup in the Soviet Union which took Mr Gorbachev prisoner, and equally intense relief when it failed. Lithuania, Latvia and Estonia were installed as independent members of the United Nations.

The media went into a frenzy when Elizabeth Taylor was married for the eighth time, in California, and again when allegations of sexual harassment were levelled against Clarence Thomas, a black judge nominated to the US Supreme Court, and yet again when William Kennedy Smith, a Kennedy family connection, was tried and acquitted of rape in Florida. The Nobel Peace Prize was awarded to Aung San Suu Kyi, the heroic 46-year-old leader of resistance to the brutal regime in Burma.

The European Community imposed sanctions on Serbia, with little apparent effect, as the beautiful medieval walled town of Dubrovnik on the Adriatic endured all the horrors of siege. More ceasefires were agreed and promptly broken.

There was a sensation in November, when Robert Maxwell, the pugnacious, Czech-born publishing tycoon, fell or jumped from his glamorous yacht *Lady Ghislaine* in Canary Islands waters. He was buried on the Mount of Olives in Jerusalem amid general plaudits, which soon proved embarrassing, as it became clear that he had committed massive frauds. Later that month the British media saluted the release of Terry Waite, the Archbishop of Canterbury's emissary, who had been held hostage in Beirut since 1987. As the year moved towards its close, Britain signed the Maastricht Treaty, which looked toward closer union in Europe, while the USSR finally ceased to exist. It was replaced by a looser federation, the CIS (Commonwealth of Independent States). Russia took over the Soviet Union's seat at the UN and an era came to an end on Christmas Day when Mr Gorbachev resigned.

Out of captivity: Terry Waite had his feet firmly planted on British soil when he arrived at the RAF base at Lyneham after being released from his chains in Beirut. He had been held hostage for almost five years after going to Beirut as an envoy of the Archbishop of Canterbury.

Under siege: the main street of the old city of Dubrovnik, known for its beauty and antiquity as 'the pearl of the Adriatic', during a fierce attack in November as the siege continued. Cut off by a naval blockade, the city was fiercely pounded by artillery, tank and mortar fire.

Out of money: outside 10 Downing Street in London where alarmed depositors of the Bank of Credit and Commerce International handed in a letter asking that those of the Bank's operations which were still solvent should be allowed to carry on. The request failed. The Bank had been closed down because of extensive and persistent frauds.

THE ILLUSTRATED LONDON NEWS

1991

E·V·E·N·T·S

19 AUGUST President Gorbachev was held prisoner in a short-lived coup by conservatives in the Soviet Union

5 NOVEMBER Death of Robert Maxwell, publisher, at sea, aged 68

18 NOVEMBER Terry Waite was released by Palestinian terrorists in Beirut

23 NOVEMBER The siege of Vukovar in Croatia ended, as the city surrendered

21 DECEMBER Formal establishment of the Commonwealth of Independent States (CIS), which replaced the USSR

25 DECEMBER Resignation of President Gorbachev

Out of patience: as the scale of financier and publisher Robert Maxwell's frauds was revealed, Britain's *Daily Mirror* newspaper turned on its former proprietor. It appeared that he had stolen millions of pounds from pension funds of the Mirror Group and other companies which he controlled. The Serious Fraud Office was investigating.

1992

THE YEAR OPENED WITH FIGHTING IN GEORGIA, where a military junta seized power by force. The other countries of the former Soviet Union were struggling to sort out who was to control the Black Sea fleet. The Algerian elections were called off to forestall the victory of the fundamentalist Islamic Salvation Party, which threatened to introduce an 'Islamic state'. In the USA, the world heavyweight boxing champion, Mike Tyson was sent to prison for raping a beauty queen. A legal case in Ireland caused an uproar when a court ruled that a 14-year-old girl, pregnant as the result of a rape, could not travel to England for an abortion. After protests and much heart-searching, the Supreme Court reversed the decision.

Heartening news came from South Africa when a whites-only referendum gave the thumbs-up to progress towards a multi-racial parliament. 'Today,' said President de Klerk, 'we have closed the book on apartheid.' The account books were being opened, however, in Britain, where the late Robert Maxwell proved to have stolen his employees' pension money, and some members of Lloyds of London insurance syndicates faced ruin to meet unprecedented losses.

In April Euro Disney opened the doors of fantasyland outside Paris, and in Britain the Conservatives won a fourth successive general election in defiance of election polls which had forecast a Labour victory. Neil Kinnock was succeeded as Labour leader by John Smith. The recession continued unabated.

The Germans were finding reunification alarmingly expensive, and when a Danish referendum rejected the Maastricht Treaty, opinion against a federal Europe suddenly sharpened. There was serious rioting in Los Angeles when a jury contrived to acquit police officers of beating up a man named Rodney King after seeing a videotape of them doing it. The situation in Yugoslavia went from bad to worse, and the repulsive euphemism 'ethnic cleansing', meaning the ruthless expulsion of people from their homes, infiltrated the British media. Bosnia-Herzegovina declared its independence and was engulfed in civil war. Sarajevo was besieged and savagely bombarded, to the accompaniment of yet more meaningless ceasefires.

The *ILN* was disapppointed by the much-vaunted Earth Summit in Rio de Janeiro in June:

> *The conference failed to make any significant progress on one of the most contentious issues, the destruction of tropical rain forests. This subject divided north and south nations more visibly than any other, but in the end the Third World countries could not be persuaded to accept binding measures to protect the world's forests, which are currently disappearing at the rate of more than 15 million hectares a year. All the summit could come up with was a series of principles offering some guidelines on good forestry management.* (Summer 1992)

A billionaire Texan businessman, Ross Perot, threw his hat into the ring as an independent candidate in the coming American presidential election, but took the hat back again. Governor Clinton of Arkansas clinched the Democratic nomination, while President Bush stood low in the polls, but as the summer passed the zenith it looked like anyone's race.

Break for bread: citizens of Sarajevo struggle to buy bread during a pause in the bombardment. Efforts by the European Community and the United Nations to put an end to the savage fighting in the former Yugoslavia failed as warlords and guerillas on the ground took no notice of ceasefires agreed by politicians. Meanwhile thousands of people were being driven from their homes in the process called 'ethnic cleansing' as old scores were paid off, and both Serbs and Croats bit off as much territory as they could. In Europe and the United States there was mounting pressure for armed intervention to end the worst conflict seen in Europe since World War II ended in 1945.

Break for burning: flames engulfed buildings in downtown Los Angeles during days of rioting and looting. The disturbances erupted after a jury had acquitted Los Angeles police officers of the savage beating of a black motorist named Rodney King after stopping him for traffic violations. A video of the officers attacking Mr King had been shown all over the country on television. The riots were finally quelled by detachments of the US Army and the National Guard.

THE ILLUSTRATED LONDON NEWS

1992

E · V · E · N · T · S

14 JANUARY A hastily created High Committee of State took control of Algeria

17 MARCH Progress towards ending apartheid was approved by a whites-only referendum in South Africa

9 APRIL A general election in Britain gave the Conservative Party its fourth victory in a row

29 APRIL Rioting broke out in Los Angeles and continued for several days

2 JUNE A referendum in Denmark narrowly disapproved the Maastricht Treaty

10 JULY General Manuel Noriega, former dictator of Panama, was sentenced by a Miami court to 40 years' imprisonment for drug dealing and racketeering

Break for celebration: John Major and his wife Norma wave cheerfully from the window of Conservative Party Central Office after news that, for the first time since the early years of the 19th century, the Conservatives had won their fourth general election victory in a row. With 42 per cent of the votes cast, they won 336 seats, 39 fewer than in 1987.

In hot pursuit: at the Olympic Games in Barcelona Chris Boardman won a gold medal for Britain on a special new kind of bicycle, and in an aerodynamic hat. The Games attracted entries from a record number of 172 countries.

Index

Page numbers in bold italics refer to captions

Acknowledgements

The publishers would like to thank the many individuals who have helped in the preparation of this book. Special thanks are due to *The Illustrated London News* Picture Library, and to the photographers and libraries listed below.

Photographs have been credited by page number, from top to bottom and from left to right. Pictures across the spine have been credited to the page on which the majority of the picture appears.

Abbreviations have been made as follows:

AA	Automobile Association	IWM	Imperial War Museum	NOV	Novosti Press
ALL	Allsport UK Ltd	KOB	Kobal Collection	NPG	National Portrait
AP	Associated Press	LTM	London Transport		Gallery
AUC	Auckland		Museum	POP	Popperfoto
BAM	British Airways Museum	MAG	Magnum Photos Ltd	PPL	Picture Point Ltd
CAM	Camera Press	MAN	The Mansell Collection	REX	Rex Features Ltd
CHA	Charmet	MAR	Marlborough Picture	RH	R. Hunt
CI	Courtauld Institute		Library	RS	R. Sheridan
COL	Coloursport	MCC	Marylebone Cricket	S & G	S & G Press
EH	English Heritage		Club	SM	Science Museum
HILL	Hillelson	ME	Mary Evans Picture	SPL	Science Photo Library
HUL	Hulton Picture Co.		Library	TME	T M English
ILN	Illustrated London	MRT	Mary Rose Trust	TOP	Topham Picture Library
	News	OPIE	Robert Opie collection	VOL	Volkswagen Press

PAGE 8 ILN: *10* ILN: *14* HUL: *15* MCC/MAN/ILN: *16* POP: *17* HUL/MAN/MAN/MAN: *18* ILN: *19* ILN/ILN/HUL: *20* ILN: *21* POP/ME/HILL: *22* ILN/ME: *23* ILN/OPIE/OPIE/HUL: *24* TOP: *25* TOP/ POP/POP/PPL: *26* HILL: *27* TOP/POP/PPL: *28* TOP: *29* TOP/POP/OPIE/TOP: *30* HUL: *31* POP/ILN: *32* POP: *33* ILN/OPIE/OPIE/ME: *36* ILN: *37* OPIE/ME/HUL: *38* OPIE: *39* ILN: *40* ILN: *41* ILN/ILN/POP: *42* HILL: *43* ILN/AA/TOP: *44* PPL: *45* HUL/POP/HUL: *46* HUL: *47* POP/TOP: *48* CAM: *49* POP: *50* KOB/ POP: *51* TOP/POP/TOP: *53* POP/OPIE/ILN/ILN: *54* POP/ILN: *55* ME: *58* OPIE: *59* ILN: *61* TOP/POP/ ILN: *62* POP/ILN: *63* ME/TOP: *64* HILL/OPIE: *5* HUL/POP: *66* POP/PPL: *67* POP/TOP/POP/RH: *68* HUL/ILN: *69* HUL/POP: *70* ILN: *71* POP/ME/ILN: *72* ME: *73* NPG/ILN: *74* POP/RH: *75* ILN: *76* TOP: *77* ILN/ILN/NOV: *78* POP/OPIE: *79* POP/NOV/ILN: *80* PPL: *81* ILN/TOP: *82* ILN: *83* ME/POP: *84* POP/ ILN: *85* POP/ILN/OPIE/ILN: *86* ILN: *87* ILN/ILN/TOP: *88* ILN: *89* ILN/OPIE: *90* ILN: *91* POP/PPL/ILN: *92* ILN: *93* ILN/TOP: *94* OPIE/POP/POP: *95* ILN: *96* POP: *97* ILN: *98* ILN: *99* ILN: *100* ILN: *101* ILN/ ILN/ILN/POP: *102* HUL: *103* RS: *104* TOP/EH: *105* RS: *106* RS: *107* RS/RS/MRT: *108* ILN: *109* ILN/ILN/ ILN/ILN/OPIE: *110* ILN/TOP: *111* POP/OPIE/ILN: *112* ILN: *113* ILN/ILN/OPIE/POP: *114* HILL: *115* ILN/OPIE/ILN: *116* POP: *117* TOP: *118* ILN: *119* ILN/OPIE/ILN/ILN: *120* POP: *121* ILN/POP/OPIE: *122* POP/ILN *123* ILN/LTM/ILN: *124* ILN/POP: *125* TOP/OPIE/POP: *126* ILN/POP: *127* HILL/OPIE/ TOP: *128* POP: *129* ILN/OPIE/ILN: *130* TOP: *131* TOP/OPIE/HILL: *132* TOP: *133* ILN/POP/POP: *134* IWM: *135* ILN/OPIE/HILL: *136* POP: *137* TOP/ILN/ILN: *138* ME/POP: *139* HILL/ILN: *142* ILN: *143* ILN/OPIE/ILN: *144* POP/POP: *145* ILN/OPIE/CHA: *146* POP: *147* POP/OPIE: *148* ILN: *149* POP/ HILL/CHA/TOP: *150* CAM: *151* CAM/OPIE/TOP: *152* TOP: *153* OPIE/POP/RH/CAM: *154* CAM: *155* ILN/IWM/ILN: *156* CAM/NOV: *157* ILN/OPIE: *158* ILN: *159* NOV/ILN/ILN/ILN: *160* ILN/POP: *161* CAM/OPIE/TOP: *162* NOV/AUC: *163* ILN/ILN/CHA: *164* POP: *165* CAM/ILN/OPIE/ILN: *166* TOP: *167* TOP/CAM/OPIE/ILN: *168* CAM: *169* POP/CAM/OPIE: *170* POP: *171* POP/OPIE/MAR: *172* NOV: *173* CAM/OPIE/POP: *174* POP: *175* POP/ILN: *176* SPL/TME/POP: *177* TOP/ME/VOL/HILL: *178* OPIE/ OPIE/SM: *179* SM: *180* SM/HUL: *181* SPL: *183* POP/OPIE/POP: *184* ILN/POP: *185* POP/OPIE: *186* ILN: *187* POP/BAM/ILN: *188* ILN *189* POP/ILN: *190* POP: *191* TOP/OPIE/TOP: *192* POP: *193* TOP/AP/LTM: *194* LTM/POP: *195* ME/POP: *198* HUL: *199* TOP/TOP/OPIE/OPIE: *200* OPIE: *201* TOP: *202* POP: *203* POP/TOP/TOP/TOP/POP: *204* POP: *205* POP: *206* TOP/S & G: *207* TOP: *208* S & G/TOP/COL: *209* COL: *210* COL: *211* TOP/TOP/S & G/TOP: *212* TOP: *213* TOP: *214* REX: *215* POP/OPIE/OPIE: *216* TOP/POP: *217* TOP: *218* TOP: *219* POP/POP/OPIE/OPIE: *220* TOP: *221* TOP: *222* TOP: *223* POP/ MAG/OPIE: *224* OPIE: *225* TOP/POP/POP: *226* TOP: *227* POP: *228* TOP *229* POP/TOP: *230* POP/TOP: *213* POP/TOP: *232* TOP: *233* POP/TOP: *234* POP: *235* TOP *236* OPIE/TOP: *237* POP/TOP: *238* KOB: *239* TOP/POP/ME: *240* ILN/HUL: *241* CI/KOB/KOB: *242* KOB: *243* KOB/POP/KOB/KOB: *244* KOB: *245* OPIE/CAM/TOP/CAM: *246* POP: *247* TOP/POP: *248* POP: *249* MAG/POP/POP: *250* POP/TOP: *251* POP/TOP/OPIE: *252* POP: *253* POP/OPIE/POP: *254* TOP: *255* POP/TOP: *256* CHA/POP: *257* POP: *258* POP/TOP: *259* POP: *260* TOP: *261* TOP/REX: *262* MAG: *263* TOP/TOP/POP: *264* POP/TOP: *265* POP: *266* TOP: *267* REX: *268* REX: *269* TOP/TOP/POP: *270* OPIE: *271* POP/TOP: *272* POP/REX: *273* REX/POP: *274* TOP: *275* REX/POP: *276* TOP: *277* POP/TOP/REX: *278* REX: *279* REX: *280* OPIE/TOP: *281* TOP: *282* TOP/POP: *283* REX: *284* TOP: *285* TOP: *286* TOP/REX: *287* TOP/REX: *288* REX: *289* REX: *290* REX: *291* REX/REX/POP: *292* POP: *293* REX: *294* REX: *295* REX/POP/TOP: *296* TOP/REX: *297* TOP/TOP/REX: *298* TOP: *299* TOP/TOP/AP: *300* TOP: *301* TOP/MAG/TOP: *302* TOP: *303* TOP: *304* MAG/TOP/TOP: *305* TOP: *306* TOP: *307* TOP/MAG: *308* TOP: *309* TOP/REX: *310* TOP: *311* TOP: *312* TOP: *313* TOP: *314* TOP: *315* TOP/TOP/ALL (DAVID CANNON)